Y0-BQT-448

OHIO
NORTHERN
UNIVERSITY
LIBRARY

The New York University
List of Books in Education
Compiled and Edited by Barbara S. Marks
Head Librarian, School of Education

Citation Press, New York • 1968

Library of Congress Catalog Card Number: 68-27638

Cover design by June Martin

Copyright © 1968 by Scholastic Magazines, Inc.
Published by Citation Press, Educators Service
Division, Scholastic Magazines, Inc.
Editorial office: 50 West 44th Street, New York, N.Y. 10036

1st printing July 1968
Printed in the U.S.A.

016.37
M34n

Preface

Books are written or compiled for many reasons, which are often obscure. No one should ever wonder why *The New York University List of Books In Education* came into being—it is simply a very useful volume. It answers many questions: What is a good book on reading, or IQ tests, or administrative theory? What books should every education library have? What books do faculty members in schools of education need? What books should a graduate student know to be considered knowledgeable in his field?

Barbara S. Marks, Head Librarian for the New York University School of Education Library, has been asked these and similar questions for many years. She thought that a single comprehensive list of books was the answer so she marshalled the resources of the School of Education to produce this volume. The result is the most comprehensive, annotated bibliography of books available in education.

Professors, department chairmen, and division heads in the School of Education deserve high commendation for their work in nominating titles and writing annotations. But the highest commendation must be reserved for Barbara Marks who conceived the idea for the volume and then moved the idea to reality.

The reader will find that her labors have been worth the effort. At least one generation of students will find between these covers a lode of knowledge.

DANIEL E. GRIFFITHS, DEAN
School of Education
New York University

85264

Introduction

This bibliography came into being as the result of two long-expressed needs: student requests for recommended titles and public and college library requests for a comprehensive list that could be used for acquisitions.

The book has been compiled from lists of titles put together by the departments of the New York University School of Education. The guiding principle for selection in each subject area was that the books should be those with which a graduate student should be familiar to be expert. The titles are by no means, however, all on an advanced or graduate level.

Current availability was not a criterion. The list is restricted to books, some pamphlets, yearbooks, and a few monographic series. Journals, journal articles, dissertations, and USOE Cooperative Research Project Reports have been excluded.

Reflected in the bibliography are the twin goals of education—the extension of knowledge and the improvement of practice. As much as possible titles not directly related to teaching have been omitted. In such areas as the behavioral sciences, however, it is difficult to draw a line, especially as there appears to be a growing tendency in the field of education to draw from other disciplines. In fact, every department's list included excellent books that had to be left out because their relationship to teaching was either tenuous or nonexistent.

An invitation to contribute went to every department of the School of Education, which accounts for the inclusion of some subjects that are only indirectly related to education. Probably as the result of history and administrative accretion, the School has interests not necessarily or usually associated with teacher training, for example, rehabilitation.

The bibliography makes no claims for being either complete or free from prejudice and partiality. Another faculty might compile a different list; everyone has his favorite titles. Within the New York University School of Education and within its departments there is not necessarily agreement on which books are best and most significant.

The list reflects past efforts and present pursuits. Emphasis is on newer books. They will not all survive, but their inclusion is essential as an indication of what is happening.

A phenomenon that becomes apparent to the bibliographer in this field is that attention focuses on a subject for a time and then dwindles. Today's undergraduate has probably not heard the term "education for life adjustment," and yet there are books on this subject less than 20 years old. It is easy to trace such superficial shifts of interest, the fads and fashions of educators.

What is also apparent is that the entire field of education is undergoing profound change; yesterday's mood of assurance is dissipating and being replaced by one of doubt and self-questioning. Judging simply from the books now being published, there is a growing re-examination of such fundamentals as what is the child *learning?* This is surely a sign of health and strength.

ORGANIZATION AND ADDITIONAL SOURCES

The subject headings are direct and were derived from the content and emphasis of the books selected for inclusion. Usefulness has been the criterion for the choice of subject heading terminology and for the decisions where to place individual titles. This has resulted in some inconsistencies. A book on teaching English to disadvantaged children has been placed with other books on teaching the disadvantaged. However, religious education for the disadvantaged has been put with other titles on religious education, in the belief that it is users with the latter interest who will want such a book. The editor assumes full responsibility for all decisions relating to terminology and the classification of titles.

Cross references refer the user to related subjects and have been included in an effort to allow for differences of semantic opinion in the matter of subject terminology. They are used also to refer to books that include material on a subject but are not confined to it. In general the references are from the smaller to the larger, from BRAIN INJURED to EXCEPTIONAL CHILDREN but not the reverse. This has been done with the thought that users would tend to go directly to a specific topic.

Within subjects the arrangement is alphabetical by author. The only subdivisions are for grade levels of teaching, i.e., Elementary, Secondary, and College, and for the history of a particular subject. The latter appears at the end of a section. "History" includes overviews of a subject and pioneering works that once were influential but no longer have relevance.

When two people were responsible for a book, both names appear. When there were more than two, only the first, as designated on the title page, is listed. In cases where an association is both author and publisher, books are usually listed under title. Paging has been included since users are entitled to some indication of size. The abbreviation "biblio." refers to all references to other readings, whether footnotes, at chapter ends, or at the end of the book. It is the editor's belief that all related writing is potentially useful and that the form in which it appears is irrelevant.

A bibliography quickly becomes out of date. In addition to special interest journals, there are several excellent sources for new publications. *Choice*, a monthly publication of the Association of College and Research Libraries (Chicago, American Library Association), devotes a section to books in the field of education. All titles are critically annotated. The May issue of the *NEA Journal* includes, with brief annotations, the "Best Books of the Year." *Educational Horizons*, published by Pi Lambda Theta in Washington, has a lengthy list in its summer issue. The summer issue of *School and Society* (New York, Society for the Advancement of Education) has an annotated list of more than 250 books published in the preceding year. The *Saturday Review* (New York) reviews both briefly and at length books of general interest in its Education Supplement, which is published with the third issue of each month. Finally there is the annual *Subject Guide to Books in Print*, published by R. R. Bowker in New York.

Out-of-print books can often be located by dealers. Additional sources are such reprint houses as Kraus and AMS in New York and University Microfilms in Ann Arbor, Michigan. The latter has an extensive collection on microfilm and in photocopy and will often supply titles on request.

ACKNOWLEDGEMENTS

In addition to the members of the New York University faculty who have contributed to this bibliography, acknowledgement must be made to others who labored long and tediously, notably, H. T. Gregory, Helen Laurila, Robert E. Mundy, Ida P. Welch, Pauline R. Yeargans, and Alice H. Yucht. I am grateful also to the staff of the Education Library for their patience and assistance, and particularly thank Ruth Cardeli, Conrad Cummings, Jr., Ines Hochmann, Yoshiko Kato, and Eduardo Marceles.

Finally I must express my appreciation to the Office of Educational Research Services of the New York University School of Education and to its Director, Dr. Joseph J. Azzarelli, without whose financial assistance this project would not have been possible.

BARBARA S. MARKS
New York
February 1968

Contributors

NEW YORK UNIVERSITY SCHOOL OF EDUCATION

Elmer C. Baker
J. Darrell Barnard
Howard S. Conant
Walter A. Cutter
Irene F. Cypher
George G. Dawson
Dan W. Dodson
Alfred Ellison
Henrietta C. Fleck
Emilio Guerra

Walter Kob
Richard C. Lonsdale
John G. Miller
Henry J. Perkinson
Martha E. Rogers
I. David Satlow
Bette J. Soldwedel
Norma H. Thompson
William Van Til
Raymond A. Weiss

Ellis F. White

and the assistance of

Evelyn P. Adlerblum
Ethel J. Alpenfels
Louise Antz
Ezri Atzmon
Joseph Badi
Edith L. Ball
Martin L. Beck
Robert S. Berlin
Roger C. Boardman
John V. Brooks
Roscoe C. Brown, Jr.
Charles A. Bucher
Alvina T. Burrows
John M. Capozzola
Edward M. Carroll
Paul A. Cullinan
William F. Dalton
John Carr Duff
Louise S. Fernandez
Marjorie H. Friedberg
Constantine Georgiou
Luther W. Goodhart
Howard R. Goody
Robert L. Granger

Hulda G. Grobman
Marian V. Hamburg
Harry L. Hartley
Katherine E. Hill
Mozell C. Hill
Irving Hochberg
Fred N. Kerlinger
Judith E. Kranes
Vincent P. Lannie
Florence B. Lewis
Helen L. Lightner
Frank W. Lutz
Carol A. Millsom
Joseph G. Minskoff
Nancy Modiano
Elizabeth D. Munves
Roger P. Phelps
Charles F. Reasoner
Frederick A. Rodgers
David Rudavsky
Prabha Sahasrabudhe
Margaret D. Simko
Gilbert M. Trachtman
Stephen S. Willoughby

Abbreviations

AAAS	American Association for the Advancement of Science
AAJC	American Association of Junior Colleges
AASA	American Association of School Administrators
ACE	American Council on Education
ACEI	Association for Childhood Education International
AEA	Adult Education Association
AERA	American Educational Research Association
ALA	American Library Association
ASCD	Association for Supervision and Curriculum Development
CAL	Center for Applied Linguistics
CARE	Center for Applied Research in Education
CEEB	College Entrance Examination Board
CSLEA	Center for the Study of Liberal Education for Adults
DAVI	Department of Audiovisual Instruction
EFL	Educational Facilities Laboratory
FAE	Fund for the Advancement of Education
GPO	U.S. Government Printing Office
LC	Library of Congress
MENC	Music Educators National Conference
MIT	Massachusetts Institute of Technology
MLA	Modern Language Association
NAEA	National Art Education Association
NASSP	National Association of Secondary School Principals
NBEA	National Business Education Association
NCEA	National Catholic Education Association
NCSS	National Council for the Social Studies
NCTE	National Council of Teachers of English
NCTM	National Council of Teachers of Mathematics
NEA	National Education Association
NSSE	National Society for the Study of Education
NSTA	National Science Teachers Association
SRA	Science Research Associates
TC	Teachers College
UCEA	University Council for Educational Administration
UNESCO	United Nations Educational, Scientific and Cultural Organization
UP	University Press
USOE	United States Office of Education

Subject Headings

New York University
List of Books in Education

ACADEMIC FREEDOM

1 Baade, Hans W., and Everett, Robinson O., eds. *Academic Freedom: the Scholar's Place in Modern Society.* Dobbs Ferry, N.Y., Oceana, 1964. 241p. biblio.

Papers of a symposium concerned with the responsibilities of both institutions and students for establishing a climate in which freedom can flourish. Also covers legal aspects.

2 Commager, Henry S. *Freedom, Loyalty, Dissent.* New York, Oxford UP, 1954. 155p.

A collection of essays by an outspoken historian on the necessity of freedom in the American society: freedom of inquiry, of dissent, of association, and freedom in education, science, literature, and politics.

3 Gardner, David P. *The California Oath Controversy.* Berkeley, U of California P, 1967. 329p. biblio.

A sophisticated account of the struggle between the faculty and Regents that racked the University of California for three years. Focuses on the issue of academic freedom, a question still unresolved either in California or anywhere else.

4 Joughin, George L., ed. *Academic Freedom and Tenure: a Handbook of the American Association of University Professors.* Madison, U of Wisconsin P, 1967. 343p. biblio.

A compilation of current practices and doctrines, plus the answers to many questions, may be found in this guide, the result of 50 years of the Association's experience with these central concerns of the academic profession.

5 Lazarsfeld, Paul F., and Thielens, Wagner J. *The Academic Mind: Social Science Teachers in a Time of Crisis.* New York, Free Press, 1958. 460p.

The report of a national survey of social sciences teachers on questions of academic freedom and its pressures.

6 MacIver, Robert M. *Academic Freedom in Our Time.* New York, Columbia UP, 1955. 329p. biblio.

A companion book to Hofstadter and Metzger (#9). A thoughtful attempt to define academic freedom in ideal terms and to probe into its relationship to public opinion, government, student and teacher, and the social order.

7 Williamson, Edmund G., and Cowan, John L. *The American Student's Freedom of Expression: a Research Appraisal.* Minneapolis, U of Minnesota P, 1966. 193p.

An investigation of the present status of student academic and social freedom, based on data from more than 800 campuses of all kinds and provided by students, faculty members, and administrators. Reveals much diversity and the need for clarification on such issues as discussion, visiting speakers, organized protest, student publications, and student participation in policy-making.

History

8 Beale, Howard K. *A History of Freedom of Teaching in American Schools.* New York, Octagon, 1966. 343p. biblio.

A critical study by an historian of the varied forms (sectional, social, moral, and economic) in which repression has appeared over the years in different environments. Reprint of a 1941 book.

9 Hofstadter, Richard, and Metzger, Walter P. *The Development of Academic Freedom in the United States.* New York, Columbia UP, 1955. 254p. biblio.

Two classic essays shedding new light on intellectual freedom in its historical and current context.

10 Hyman, Harold M. *To Try Men's Souls: the Loyalty Test in American History.* Berkeley, U of California P, 1959. 414p. biblio.

The story of the various means that have been used to test loyalty from 16th century England to the United States in the 1950's, with descriptions of particular events and incidents along the way.

ACHIEVEMENT see **MOTIVATION AND ACHIEVEMENT**

ADMINISTRATION OF SCHOOLS

11 Callahan, Raymond E. *Education and the Cult of Efficiency.* Chicago, U of Chicago P, 1962. 273p.

The author traces the interplay of societal forces and the self-perceived professional role of school administration since the turn of the century.

12 Campbell, Roald F., and Gregg, Russell T., eds. *Administrative Behavior in Education.* New York, Harper, 1957. 547p.

The first team effort to apply organizational theory and an interdisciplinary approach to educational administration. Eighteen authors participated in the effort.

13 _____ and Lipham, James M., eds. *Adminstrative Theory as a Guide to Action.* Chicago, Midwest Administration Center, U of Chicago, 1960. 203p.

Papers presented at the second of two University of Chicago seminars on organizational theory during the late 1950's (See also #27).

14 _____ and others. *Intorduction to Educational Administration.* 3rd. rev. ed. Boston, Allyn and Bacon, 1966. 474p. biblio.

Content reflects an interdisciplinary approach and use of organizational theory. Contains an outstanding section on the personal qualifications of an administrator.

15 Carlson, Richard O. *Executive Succession and Organizational Change: Place-bound and Career-bound Superintendents of Schools.* Chicago, Midwest Administration Center, U of Chicago, 1962. 84p.

An analysis of the effect on educational change of the latent roles of the local and the cosmopolitan among school superintendents.

16 Coladarci, Arthur P., and Getzels, Jacob W. *The Use of Theory in Educational Administration* (School of Education, Educational Administration Mono. no. 5). Stanford, Stanford UP, 1955. 28p.

Probably the first publication relating organizational theory in its current sense to educational administration.

17 Culbertson, Jack A., and others. *Administrative Relationships: a Casebook.* Englewood Cliffs, N.J., Prentice-Hall, 1960. 517p.

Contains 17 cases in educational administration, plus chapters on the case method, communicating, building morale, administering change, and decision-making.

18 ———, and Hencley, Stephen P., eds. *Preparing Administrators: New Perspectives.* Columbus, Ohio, UCEA, 1962. 173p.

Report of a 1961 UCEA national conference setting forth some of the more progressive conceptualizations and plans for the preparation of school administrators.

19 Goodlad, John I. *Planning and Organizing for Teaching.* Washington, NEA, 1963. 190p. biblio.

Focuses on improving the organization of educational systems.

20 Graff, Orin B., and others. *Philosophic Theory and Practice in Educational Administration.* Belmont, Cal., Wadsworth, 1966. 314p. biblio.

Introduction to several divergent philosophies in educational administration. The influence of attitude and a priori values is revealed in a simple but effective manner.

21 Griffiths, Daniel E. *Administrative Theory.* New York, Appleton, 1959. 123p. biblio.

Defines and describes uses of theory of educational administration and reviews different attempts to theorize in both educational and non-educational fields.

22 ———, ed. *Behavioral Science and Educational Administration.* (NSSE 63rd Yearbook, Part II.) Chicago, U of Chicago P, 1964. 348p.

A combination of syntheses and original formulations of organizational theory. One of the best single treatments of organizational theory related to education.

23 ———, *Organizing Schools for Effective Education.* Danville, Ill., Interstate, 1962. 338p. biblio.

Develops a theory of organization, treats basic concepts and issues, and applies them to concrete school situations. Detailed and explicit treatment of many new ideas and concepts in the field of administration.

24   _____, *Research in Educational Administration: an Appraisal and a Plan.* New York, TC, Columbia, 1959. 59p.

Purpose is to stimulate interest in and discussion of research among professionals in educational administration. Designed to be a challenge and indicate future directions. Appraises the who, what, and how of research and proposes a reorienting of the who and the what, as well as improvement of the use of research.

25   _____, *The School Superintendent.* New York, CARE, 1966. 115p. biblio.

A descriptive study of the position of the school superintendent. The first part is historical; the second combines a status study with a projection of what the superintendency might become.

26   Gross, Neal, and others. *Explorations in Role Analysis: Studdies of the School Superintendency Role.* New York, Wiley, 1958. 379 p. biblio.

Role theory applied to and developed in connection with a study of superintendent-school board relationships in Massachusetts.

27   Halpin, Andrew W., ed. *Administrative Theory in Education.* Chicago, Midwest Administration Center, U of Chicago, 1958. 188p.

Papers presented at the first of the two University of Chicago seminars on organizational theory (see also #13), which was also the first of the Career Development Seminars of the UCEA.

28   _____, *Theory and Research in Administration.* New York, Macmillan, 1966. 352p. biblio.

A compilation of Halpin's research in organizational theory, including his use of the concepts of "consideration" and "initiating structure in interaction" and his research on organizational climate.

29   Jenson, Theodore J., and Clark, David L. *Educational Administration.* New York, CARE, 1964. 118p. biblio.

A panoramic view of the entire field of the administration of educational institutions, succinctly covering the legal organization of public education, with discussion of the sociological, cultural, economic, political, and size factors that influence this organization.

30   Lewis, Leonard J., and Loveridge, Arthur J. *The Management of Education: a Guide for Teachers to the Problems in New and Developing Systems.* New York, Praeger, 1965. 124p. biblio.

Brief and simple handling of the problems and challenges confronting the administrator. Its purpose is to foster better communication between faculty and administration as well as to provide teachers with the knowledge that will permit them to be transferred into administration.

31   Miller, Van. *The Public Administration of American School Systems,* rev. ed. New York, Macmillan, 1965. 608p. biblio.

Places the initial responsibility for the school system on the community. Discusses the discharge of that responsibility and the distinctive role of the school administrator in American education.

32   Moehlman, Arthur B. *School Administration: Its Development, Principles, and Function in the United States,* 2nd ed. Boston, Houghton Mifflin, 1951. 514p.

Encyclopedic, but no longer up to date factually or theoretically. This and the original 1940 edition represented the best thinking of the time and were the outstanding texts in general school administration.

33   Moore, Hollis A., Jr. *Studies in School Administration: a Report on the Cooperative Program in Educational Administration.* Washington, AASA, 1957. 202p.

A summary of the studies in the eight regional centers and elsewhere of the CPEA, which was sponsored by the W. K. Kellogg Foundation in the 1950's.

34   Morphet, Edgar L., and others. *Educational Organization and Administration: Concepts, Practices and Issues,* 2nd ed. Englewood Cliffs, N.J., Prentice-Hall, 1967. 569p. biblio.

Uses an interdisciplinary approach and is as comprehensive as the earlier Moehlman text.

35   Mort, Paul R., and Ross, Donald H. *Principles of School Administration,* 2nd ed. New York, McGraw-Hill, 1957. 451p.

A distillation of the authors' research and of their philosophy, which centers on humanitarianism, prudence, tempo and principles. Includes chapters on adaptability, flexibility, and stability.

36   Ross, Donald H., ed. *Administration for Adaptability: a Source Book Drawing Together the Results of More Than 150 Individual Studies Related to the Question of Why and How Schools Improve*, rev. ed. New York, Metropolitan School Study Council, TC, Columbia, 1958. 643p.

The best single summary of Paul Mort's 20-year program of research on the phenomenon he has called adaptability.

37   Sachs, Benjamin M. *Educational Administration: a Behavioral Approach*. Boston, Houghton Mifflin, 1966. 412p. biblio.

A humanist's view of the psychological bases of democratic leadership and of the relation of behavioral concepts to administration, with practical applications.

38   Sargent, Cyril G., and Belisle, Eugene L. *Educational Administration: Cases and Concepts*. Boston, Houghton Mifflin, 1955. 474p.

The first major book of cases in educational administration. Contains 35 cases plus chapters on the case method and on conceptualizing in educational administration.

39   Sears, Jesse B. *The Nature of the Administrative Process: with Special Reference to Public School Administration*. New York, McGraw-Hill, 1950. 623p. biblio.

A forerunner of the current emphasis on the application of social concepts and organizational theory to education.

40   Walton, John. *Administration and Policy Making in Education*. Baltimore, Johns Hopkins UP, 1959. 207p. biblio.

An attempt at a coherent and consistent framework to explain the wide range of administrative phenomena: the nature and function of administration, necessary operational conditions, and the relationship of administration to other activities.

41   Wilson, Robert E., ed. *Educational Administration*. Columbus, Ohio, Merrill, 1966. 853p. biblio.

Encyclopedic in scope and breadth, this offers excellent coverage as well as readability.

Elementary Schools

42   Elsbree, Willard S., and others. *Elementary School Administration and Supervision*, 3rd ed. New York, American, 1967. 520p. biblio.

A basic text providing a broad overview of the problems

faced by principals and supervisors, which develops guidelines for action. The revision focuses on new concepts, research, and operational developments.

43 Hemphill, John K., and others. *Administrative Performance and Personality: a Study of the Principal in a Simulated Elementary School.* New York, TC, Columbia, 1962. 432p.

A report of a comprehensive study of administrative behavior in education, based on the test performance of 232 elementary school principals from all over the United States.

44 Mickelson, Peter P., and Hansen, Kenneth H. *Elementary School Administration.* New York, McGraw-Hill, 1957. 335p.

Identifies the main problems of elementary education and describes the methods a principal may use to attack them successfully.

45 Misner, Paul J., and others. *Elementary School Administration.* Columbus, Ohio, Merrill, 1963. 422p. biblio.

Emphasizes that effective administration is dependent upon all staff, not just the principal. Describes some of the most promising practices currently used in various schools.

46 Otto, Henry J. *Elementary School Organization and Administration,* 4th ed. New York, Appleton, 1964. 409p.

A basic handbook, especially suitable for graduate courses in elementary school organization and administration.

47 Shuster, Albert H., and Wetzler, Wilson F. *Leadership in Elementary School Administration and Supervision.* Boston, Houghton Mifflin, 1958. 505p.

Research findings and new understandings in the fields of educational and personnel administration, industrial management and psychology are used in projecting the role of the elementary school principal.

Secondary Schools

48 Anderson, Lester W., and Van Dyke, Lauren A. *Secondary School Administration.* Boston, Houghton Mifflin, 1963. 593p.

An introductory text with a pragmatic approach.

49 Corbally, John E., Jr., and others. *Educational Administration: the Secondary School.* Boston, Allyn and Bacon, 1961. 385p.

Aims to clarify the task of the secondary school administrator, the problems he faces in performing this task, and the processes he uses in meeting problems. Drawn from research and writings in general administration as well as educational administration.

50 Douglass, Harl R. *Modern Administration of Secondary Schools: Organization and Administration of Junior and Senior High Schools,* 2nd ed. Boston, Ginn, 1963. 636p.

A comprehensive introduction to secondary school administration with a task-oriented and process-oriented approach.

51 French, Will, and others. *American High School Administration: Policy and Practice,* 3rd ed. New York, Holt, 1962. 590p. biblio.

Revised to reflect current changes and challenges in secondary education, and designed to encourage skilled and effective leadership.

52 McLeary, Lloyd E., and Hencley, Stephen P. *Secondary School Administration: Theoretical Bases of Professional Practice.* New York, Dodd, 1965. 339p. biblio.

A good balance between the theoretical and conceptual approach, drawing heavily from parent disciplines in the social and behavioral sciences, with ample technical help for the practitioner.

53 Williams, Stanley W. *Educational Administration in Secondary Schools.* New York, Holt, 1964. 529p. biblio.

An introductory text that broadly surveys secondary school administration processes and functions.

History of School Administration

54 Cubberly, Elwood P. *Public School Administration: a Statement of the Fundamental Principles Underlying the Organization and Administration of Public Administration.* Boston, Houghton Mifflin, 1916. 479p. biblio.

Provides historical perspective on the evolution of the theory of educational administration and of general textbooks in this field.

55 Knight, Edgar W. *Readings in Educational Administration.* New York, Holt, 1953. 534p.

Historical documents in the development of education and educational administration.

ADMINISTRATORS—TRAINING

56 Davies, Daniel R. *The Internship in Educational Administration.* New York, CARE, 1962. 117p. biblio.

An overview of the internship as preparatory training for administrators, with useful ideas for initiating and operating internship programs.

57 Hencley, Stephen P., ed. *The Internship in Administrative Preparation.* Columbus, Ohio, UCEA, 1963. 159p. biblio.

Report of a professional task force, which discusses roles and relationships, problems, issues, and learning experiences as well as "new horizons."

58 *Inservice Education for School Administration.* (AASA) Washington, NEA, 1963. 208p.

The report of a two-year study on in-service education that includes suggestions for developing programs.

59 *Professional Administrators for America's Schools* (AASA 38th Yearbook). Washington, NEA, 1960. 310p. biblio.

This final AASA yearbook gives an analysis of the then-current status, needs and proposals for the improvement of preparation programs, procedures for selecting administrators, and programs for continuing professional development.

60 Tope, Donald E., ed. *A Forward Look: the Preparation of School Administrators 1970.* Eugene, Bureau of Educational Research, U of Oregon, 1960, 177p.

Compilation of papers delivered at a 1960 conference on major developments in providing a more adequate preparation program for potential educational administrators.

ADOLESCENCE
see also CHILD DEVELOPMENT

61 Bandura, Albert, and Walters, Richard H. *Adolescent Aggression: a Study of the Influence of Child-Training Practices and Family Interrelationships.* New York, Ronald, 1959. 475p. biblio.

Based on interviews with 52 adolescent boys and their parents, the data present evidence relating to the development of anti-social, aggressive behavior. Discusses the socialization process and the behavior and attitudes of adolescent boys.

62 Bloch, Herbert A., and Niederhoffer, Arthur. *The Gang: a Study in Adolescent Behavior.* New York, Philosophical, 1958. 231p. biblio.

A detailed survey of adolescent behavior in a wide variety of primitive and modern cultures, based on research in sociology, psychology, and psychiatry. Attempts to apply these findings to youth in our culture.

63 Blos, Peter. *The Adolescent Personality: a Study of Individual Behavior.* New York, Appleton, 1941. 517p. biblio.

Sponsored by the Commission on Secondary School Curriculum, this study is an attempt to assist in developing an educational program based on adolescent needs and growth. Case histories presented increase understanding of adolescent behavior and development.

64 Blos, Peter. *On Adolescence: a Psychoanalytic Interpretation.* New York, Free Press, 1962. 269p. biblio.

A highly readable psychoanalytic theory of normal adolescent growth and development, profusely illustrated with case material.

65 Coleman, James S. *The Adolescent Society: the Social Life of the Teenager and Its Impact on Education.* New York, Free-Press, 1961. 368p. biblio.

An investigation of the values and behaviors of teen-agers in 10 large American high schools, which showed that the aspirations and actions of American adolescents were primarily determined by the "leading crowd" in the school society. Coleman says, "If secondary education is to be successful, it must successfully compete with cars, sports, and social activities for the adolescents' attention."

66 ———. *Adolescents and the Schools.* New York, Basic, 1965. 121p.

An examination of the adolescent, his subcultures, and his schooling in an effort to resolve two questions: what should adolescents learn to live in the world today, and how can formal education best help them learn?

67 Friedenberg, Edgar Z. *Coming of Age in America: Growth and Acquiescence.* New York, Random, 1965. 300p.

A compelling study of student values as they affect and are expressed in the choices young people make about school situations and their attitudes toward school.

68 Goodman, Paul. *Growing Up Absurd.* New York, Random, 1960. 296p.

A provocative, controversial, and lively book of social criticism and a serious effort to understand the relation between society and disaffected youth, concluding that the burden of proof rests with society.

69   Gottlieb, David, and others. *The Emergence of Youth Societies: a Cross-Cultural Approach.* New York, Free Press, 1966. 416p. biblio.

For specialists in the field of adolescent behavior, this includes a formulation of an explanatory model supported by cross-cultural data but is primarily a bibliography of research literature in the field of adolescence.

70   Havighurst, Robert J., and others. *Growing Up in River City.* New York, Wiley, 1962. 189p.

The results of a research study conducted between 1951 and 1960. An account of the growing up from ages 11-20 of a group of children in a Midwest city, in an effort to show, for predictive purposes, in what ways social background and personality characteristics determine growth and performance and to find out what environment produces competency.

71   Horrocks, John E. *The Psychology of Adolescence: Behavior and Development,* 2nd ed. Boston, Houghton Mifflin, 1962. 711p. biblio.

A carefully organized approach to the study of adolescence, which is a critical discussion of theory, synthesizing the best current thinking of psychologists and of those in such related disciplines as biology.

72   Hurlock, Elizabeth B. *Adolescent Development,* 3rd ed. New York, McGraw-Hill, 1967. 719p. biblio.

A well written, comprehensive text that portrays the adolescent in America today and attempts to show how he differs from his counterpart in other cultures.

73   Jersild, Arthur T. *The Psychology of Adolescence,* 2nd ed. New York, Macmillan, 1963. 468p. biblio.

A description of the objective and subjective aspects of the adolescent's growth and behavior and of the ways in which his development influences and is influenced by his ideas and attitudes about himself.

74   Mallery, David. *High School Students Speak Out.* New York, Harper, 1962. 171p.

Report of a committee study, sponsored by the Educational

Records Bureau of New York, of the impact of high school experiences on students.

75 Mead, Margaret. *Coming of Age in Samoa: a Psychological Study of Primitive Youth for Western Civilization.* New York, Morrow, 1928. 297p.

A classic attempt, based on the author's experience in Samoa, to answer the question: are the disturbances that vex adolescents in the United States due to the nature of adolescence or to our culture?

76 Muuss, Rolf E. *Theories of Adolescence.* New York, Random, 1962. 184p. biblio.

A systematic and comprehensive review of various theoretical positions on adolescent development. A multidisciplinary approach that covers biogenetic and psychoanalytic theories, as well as those of cultural anthropology and social psychology, and attempts to show the relationships among them.

77 Seidman, Jerome M., ed. *The Adolescent: a Book of Readings,* rev. ed. New York, Holt, 1960. 870p. biblio.

A selection of original contributions of specialists who have created or expanded the knowledge of the field, which covers new areas of investigation, improved methods of research, and new understandings.

78 Sherif, Muzafer, and Carolyn W. *Reference Groups: Exploration into Conformity and Deviation of Adolescents.* New York, Harper, 1964. 370p. biblio.

Discusses adolescents and their problems, group structures, and intergroup conflict and suggests action programs designed to cope with the social problems of this age group.

ADULT EDUCATION

79 Bergevin, Paul E. *A Philosophy for Adult Education.* Greenwich, Conn., Seabury, 1967. 176p.

An attempt to formulate a precise philosophy in a relatively new field of study and operation, which adapts what is known of learning to the needs of adults.

80 Brunner, Edmund de S., and others. *An Overview of Adult Education Research.* Chicago, AEA, 1959. 275p.

Valuable reference and a scholarly inventory of research

in non-vocational adult education. Concise, factual, and comprehensive.

81 Bryson, Lyman. *Reason and Discontent: the Task of Liberal Adult Education.* Pasadena, Cal., FAE, 1954. 48p.
   Three lectures on the importance, significance, and implications of liberal adult education.

82 Carey, James T. *Why Students Drop Out: a Study of Evening College Student Motivations.* Chicago, CSLEA, 1954. 54p.
   Of 800 former students approached, nearly half responded to a questionnaire and interviews. Most were satisfied with the educational offering and had dropped out for personal reasons.

83 Clark, Burton R. *Adult Education in Transition: a Study of Institutional Insecurity.* Berkeley, U of California, 1956. 202p. biblio.
   A sociological study of the educational administration of the adult school in California and its emergence as a distinct type of public school enterprise. The character of adult education has apparently been adaptive to local needs rather than affected by professionally set goals.

84 Dyer, John P. *Ivory Towers in the Market Place: the Evening College in American Education.* Indianapolis, Bobbs Merrill, 1956. 205p.
   A report on the university evening college, its nature, its practices, its problems, and a suggestion of what its role should be in our contemporary society.

85 Farmer, Martha L., ed. *Student Personnel Services for Adults in Higher Education.* Metuchen, N.J., Scarecrow, 1967. 211p. biblio.
   A dozen articles covering such topics as the history and development of evening colleges, administration, admissions, counseling, student activities, financial aid, personnel workers, the relation between the evening college and the business community, and leisure.

86 Feldman, Jacob J. *The Dissemination of Health Information: a Case Study in Adult Learning.* Chicago, Aldine, 1966. 274p.
   A monograph of the National Opinion Research Center, this is primarily concerned with how adults learn to take

better care of their health and is an interesting study of public attitudes and mass education.

87   Goldwin, Robert A., ed. *Toward the Liberally Educated Executive.* White Plains, N.Y., Fund for Adult Education, 1957. 111p.

The thesis that business executives, to function well, should have a comprehensive approach that the liberally educated mind can provide is discussed by authors of varying backgrounds.

88   Grattan, Clinton H. *In Quest of Knowledge: a Historical Perspective on Adult Education.* New York, Association, 1955. 337p.

Some space is devoted to Europe and Great Britain, but principally this covers American adult education in all its various aspects. Sponsored by the FAE, it includes current needs such as the gap between goals and realities.

89   Green, Ernest. *Adult Education: Why This Apathy?* London, Allen and Unwin, 1953. 145p.

Findings of a study to determine the reasons for apathy among former adult students. Findings and conclusions helpful, taking into consideration previous educational inadequacies and promoting broader offerings.

90   *Handbook of Adult Education in the United States,* rev. ed. Chicago, AEA, 1960. 624p.

The latest revision of a book first published in 1934. The basic reference work in the field, which includes 54 articles covering background, concerns, institutional programs and resources, methods, techniques, and program areas. Listings of organizations, associations, and agencies.

91   Havighurst, Robert J., and Orr, Betty. *Adult Education and Adult Needs: a Report.* Chicago, CSLEA, 1956. 66p.

A study conducted in Kansas City covering needs, motivation, and qualities of effective programs, with illustrative cases.

92   Hely, Arnold S. *New Trends in Adult Education, from Elsinore to Montreal.* Paris, UNESCO, 1962. 136p. biblio.

A comparison of the findings of the International Conference on Adult Education in Denmark in 1949 with the World Conference on Adult Education in Canada in 1960 reveals many changes in structure and status.

93 Houle, Cyril O. *The Inquiring Mind*. Madison, U of Wisconsin P, 1961. 87p.

Lectures based on the author's exploratory and pioneering research into the little understood motivations of the adult who continues to learn.

94 Johnstone, John W., and Rivera, Ramon J. *Volunteers for Learning: a Study of the Educational Pursuits of American Adults*. Chicago, Aldine, 1965. 624p. biblio.

A national survey with a social-psychological approach examined the needs, motives, and satisfactions of adults in a formal learning situation.

95 Kallen, Horace M. *Philosophical Issues in Adult Education*. Springfield, Ill., Thomas, 1962. 90p.

Four essays written at different times, for different occasions, present kaleidoscopic rearrangements of data, issues, and concepts regarding the principles and practices of adult education in the United States.

96 Kempfer, Homer. *Identifying Educational Needs of Adults* (USOE Circular no. 330). Washington, GPO, 1951. 64p.

An evaluation and description comparing 37 administrative practices used in inferior and superior programs.

97 Kidd, James R. *Financing Continuing Education*. New York, Scarecrow, 1962. 209p.

Consideration of some of the financial implications of continuing education in a society committed to the education of every citizen. Proposals deal mainly with the United States, with some relevant data from other parts of the world.

98 ———. *How Adults Learn*. New York, Association, 1959. 324p.

An examination of all factors reveals evidence of a life-long ability to learn.

99 ———. *The Implications of Continuous Learning*. Scarborough, Ontario, Gage, 1967. 122p.

An anecdotal discourse that attempts to confront a topic of importance in an era of increasing leisure.

100 Knowles, Malcolm S. *The Adult Education Movement in the United States*. New York, Holt, 1962. 335p. biblio.

Concerned with the nature, characteristics, dynamics, and direction of adult education. Traces the emergence of adult education institutions, the shaping of adult education as a coordinated field, and includes some predictions.

101 *Liberal Education for Adults.* White Plains, N.Y., Fund for Adult Education, 1956. 78p.

Five speeches given at the Community Leadership Institute in Estes Park, Colorado, in 1956, which describes the need for liberal education to preserve and strengthen a free society, for upgrading the character of adult education, and to remind teachers that they are leaders of self-directed adults as differentiated from teachers of children.

102 Lindeman, Eduard C. *The Meaning of Adult Education.* Montreal, Harvest, 1961. 143p.

A noted teacher describes the past and clarifies the present and future in this undefined area of education.

103 McMahon, Ernest E. *The Emerging Evening College: a Study of Faculty Organization and Academic Control in Ten Eastern University Evening Colleges.* New York, TC, Columbia, 1960. 163p. biblio.

Focuses on degree-granting programs for part-time students by means of case studies.

104 Mezirow, Jack D., and Berry, Dorothea, comps. *The Literature of Liberal Adult Education, 1945-1957.* New York, Scarecrow Press, 1960. 308p.

A useful annotated listing of books, parts of books, and journal articles, which covers philosophy, trends, research, and the roles of various sponsoring agencies.

105 Morton, John R. *University Extension in the United States.* U of Albama P, 1953. 144p.

A report of a survey sponsored by the National University Extension Association covering 76 universities. Origins and development, functions, administrative arrangements, facilities, staffing, finances, methods of instruction, and courses of study are among the topics.

106 *Notes and Essays on Education.* No. 1-   1952-   . Chicago, CSLEA.

Irregularly published monographs on all aspects of liberal adult education: philosophy, methods, and administration. Now numbering more than 50, a recent title, (1967) is *The Continuing Task: Reflections on Purpose in Higher Continuing Education.*

107 Olds, Edward B. *Financing Adult Education in America's Public Schools and Community Councils.* Washington, AEA, 1954. 124p.

A well documented research report listing findings and making recommendations. Appendix includes methods and sources used.

108 *Patterns of Liberal Education in the Evening College: a Case Study of 9 Institutions.* Chicago, CSLEA, 1952. 82p.

The study was made to determine problems and needs. Revealed was a need for closer relationships between day and evening groups and among faculty.

109 Peers, Robert. *Adult Education: a Comparative Study.* New York, Humanities, 1958. 365p. biblio.

A comprehensive account of the English adult education movement, past and present. Investigates adult learning and teaching methods and examines adult education in the United States, Germany, and the underdeveloped countries.

110 Peterson, Renee, and William. *University Adult Education: a Guide to Policy.* New York, Harper, 1960. 288p. biblio.

Combines a broad, factual survey of university adult education with a perceptive and critical analysis. Examines questions of university responsibility and policy as well as organizational and administrative problems.

111 Shannon, Theodore J., and Schoenfeld, Clarence A. *University Extension.* New York, CARE, 1965. 115p. biblio.

Comprehensive, authoritative, and vivacious in style and considering its brevity, thorough in its coverage.

112 Smith, Helen L. *Adult Education Activities in Public Libraries: a Report on the ALA Survey of Adult Education Activities in Public Libraries and State Library Extension Agencies in the United States.* Chicago, ALA, 1954. 128p.

Summarizes services and reasons for deficiencies in some services. Describes library programs for adults and includes recommendations.

113 Thatcher, John H., ed. *Public School Adult Education: a Guide for Administrators and Teachers,* rev. ed. Washington, National Association of Public School Adult Educators (NEA), 1963. 199p.

Deals with concepts and the elements of public school

adult education as well as with administrative responsibilities, problems, and practices.

114   Ulich, Mary E. *Patterns of Adult Education: a Comparative Study.* New York, Pageant, 1965. 205p.

Adult education in Denmark, Germany, England, and the United States are studied and compared to "detect the trends of the past in order to understand better the ways of the future."

115   UNESCO. *Adult Education: Current Trends and Practices.* New York, Columbia UP, 1949. 148p. biblio.

A collection of articles dealing with the most characteristic achievements of adult education in the mid-20th century. The detailed studies of work and experiments in progress as well as statements of problems make this still relevant.

116   Verner, Coolie, and Booth, Alan. *Adult Education.* New York, CARE, 1964. 113p. biblio.

Concise coverage of scope, need, functions, and institutions. Analyzes both learner and teacher. Considers kinds of learning, methods, and teaching techniques especially appropriate for adults as well as the administration and supervision of programs.

117   _____. *Adult Education Theory and Method: a Conceptual Scheme for the Identification and Classification of Processes.* Chicago, AEA, 1962. 34p.

Distinguishes between "dissemination of information," which may be a personal independent pursuit of knowledge, and "systematic diffusion of knowledge," which is defined as adult education. This precise definition serves as a basis for identifying methods and techniques. Discussion also of the degree to which adult education is related to institutional function.

ADULT EDUCATION—TEACHING AND TEACHING METHODS

118   Bergevin, Paul E., and others. *Adult Education Procedures: a Handbook of Tested Patterns for Effective Participation.* Greenwich, Conn., Seabury, 1963. 245p.

For those involved in developing learning experiences for adults. More than a dozen techniques examined in detail.

119 ———, and Morris, Dwight. *Group Processes for Adult Education*. Greenwich, Conn., Seabury, 1955. 86p. biblio.

In outline form presents the characteristics, advantages, and limitations of commonly used techniques and methods in adult education.

120 Cass, Angelica W. *Adult Elementary Education: Teaching Methods and Practices, Administration Principles and Procedures*. New York, Noble, 1956. 275p. biblio.

An experienced teacher and administrator offers a wealth of practical ideas and suggestions. A handbook of daily operations.

121 Essert, Paul L. *Creative Leadership of Adult Education*. Englewood Cliffs, N.J., Prentice-Hall, 1951. 333p.

Focuses on taking advantage of the experience the adult brings to his schooling and developing means to help adults educate themselves. Includes practical suggestions and recommendations.

122 Jensen, Gale E., and others, eds. *Adult Education: Outlines of an Emerging Field of University Study*. Washington, AEA, 1964. 334p. biblio.

Outlines requirements for graduate training programs for adult educators and, in general, is directed to those responsible for planning and conducting adult and continuing education programs.

123 Liveright, Alexander A. *Strategies of Leadership in Conducting Adult Education Programs*. New York, Harper, 1959. 140p.

Concerned with the voluntary association of adults in informal groups under lay leadership for the purpose of self-education. A handbook for the lay leader offering tools and insights for analyzing and improving his role.

124 Lowy, Louis. *Adult Education and Group Work*. New York, Whiteside and Morrow, 1955. 224p. biblio.

Covers work with young and older adults, parent education, and principles of group work applied in adult and adult liberal education.

125 Miller, Harry L. *Teaching and Learning in Adult Education*. New York, Macmillan, 1964. 340p. biblio.

Adult teaching and adult learning in relation to the adult's world, and an examination of the various kinds of teaching situations: small and large groups, residential, and self-instruction. A chapter on measuring the effectiveness of method.

126 Morgan, Barton, and others. *Methods in Adult Education.* Danville, Ill., Interstate, 1963. 189p. biblio.

A how-to manual of particular use to volunteer leaders responsible for organizing and directing conferences, workshops, and study groups.

127 Powell, John W. *Education for Maturity: an Empirical Essay on Adult Group Study.* New York, Hermitage, 1949. 242p.

Small group study with leadership is advanced as a means of promoting maturity as well as gaining enjoyment. Use of books and other media is covered.

128 Solomon, Daniel, and others. *Teaching Styles and Learning.* Chicago, CSLEA, 1963. 164p. biblio.

Applies some findings from an earlier study (*Exploration in Teaching Style,* 1961) in a more rigorous set of observations of actual teacher behavior in adult classrooms and finds a relationship between teaching style and student learning.

History of Adult Education

129 Grattan, Clinton H., ed. *American Ideas about Adult Education.* New York, TC, Columbia, 1959. 140p.

Documents illustrate characteristic thinking about adult education over a period of more than 200 years. Selections relate to actual undertakings and are those that had impact.

130 Harrison, John F. *Learning and Living, 1790-1960: a Study in the History of the English Adult Education Movement.* Toronto, U of Toronto P, 1961. 404p.

A social history of some aspects of popular thought and intellectual interests as expressed in that variety of institutions and learning situations known collectively as the adult education movement. The theme is the growth of democracy.

ALCOHOL EDUCATION

131 McCarthy, Raymond G., ed. *Alcohol Education for Classroom and Community: a Source book for Educators.* New York, McGraw-Hill, 1964. 408p.

A basic source book for secondary and college teachers, prepared by scientists in several disciplines. Comprehensive study of facts and attitudes; examines questions of social concern.

132 Monroe, Margaret E., and Stewart, Jean. *Alcohol Education for the Layman: a Bibliography.* New Brunswick, N.J., Rutgers UP, 1959. 166p.

Highly selective and valuable annotated listing of materials in all media.

ARITHMETIC see MATHEMATICS

ART EDUCATION

133 Arnheim, Rudolf. *Toward a Psychology of Art: Collected Essays.* Berkeley, U of California P, 1966. 369p. biblio.

A delightful collection of illuminating essays, ranging from discussions of experiments in the perception of shape, to observations on children's art, to broad deliberations on the nature of images and inspiration.

134 Barkan, Manuel. *A Foundation for Art Education.* New York, Ronald, 1955. 235p.

A philosophical discussion of the how and why of art education that identifies some basic teaching problems and relates them to significant concepts about human behavior.

135 Brittain, W. Lambert, ed. *Creativity and Art Education.* Washington, NAEA, 1964. 147p. biblio.

A symposium of important studies and research in art education and creativity. Bibliography is extensive.

136 Conant, Howard S. *Art Education.* New York, CARE, 1964. 116p. biblio.

A brief but comprehensive overview of the entire field of art education covering historical development and philosophy, teaching skills, and practices at all levels of schooling from nursery through graduate study. Concludes with comments on the outlook for the future.

137 ———, and Randall, Arne. *Art in Education.* Peoria, Ill., Bennett, 1959. 345p. biblio.

Creative development is examined. Detailed discussion of a good art program and the most effective methods of presenting such a program.

138 _____, ed. *Art Workshop Leaders' Planning Guide.* Worcester, Mass., Davis, 1958. 43p.

Report of a series of leadership seminars held at New York University. Useful for teachers working with adults on a workshop basis.

139 D'Amico, Victor. *Creative Teaching in Art,* rev. ed. Scranton, Pa., International, 1953. 257p.

A source book of creative art teaching based on the needs and interests of growing children at all school levels. Well illustrated explanations of teaching art creatively without resorting to laissez-faire or directed methods.

140 De Francesco, Italo L. *Art Education: Its Means and Ends.* New York, Harper, 1958. 652p.

Presents the case for art education as an essential feature of a superior educational program. A well-documented and well-organized treatment of art education, which includes discussions of adult education, supervision, and administration.

141 Eisner, Elliot W., and Ecker, David W. *Readings in Art Education.* Waltham, Mass., Blaisdell, 1966. 468p. biblio.

An excellent collection of essays on the major issues and questions in the field of art education with an emphasis on the need for research. Well-organized, with sections on history, theory of art, art and human development, art education and society, etc.

142 Feldman, Edmund B. *Art As Image and Idea.* Englewood Cliffs, N.J., Prentice-Hall, 1967. 528p.

An approach to art criticism that stresses the connection between art and modern life and analyzes art in terms of function, style, structure, and technique in relation to society.

143 Hastie, W. Reid, ed. *Art Education* (NSSE Yearbook, 64th, Part II). Chicago, U of Chicago P, 1965. 357p.

Concentrates on teaching and learning and attempts to relate research theory and practice and to identify future guidelines. Authors selected for their perceptiveness and experience.

144 Hausman, Jerome J., ed. *Report of the Commission on Art Education.* Washington, NAEA, 1965. 160p. biblio.

Chapters by each of the Commission members examine

some aspects of the role of art, the artist, and art education in today's society.

145 Hook, Sidney, ed. *Art and Philosophy: a Symposium.* New York, New York UP, 1966. 346p.

The report of the seventh New York University Institute of Philosophy Symposium dealing with how art is to be evaluated, how the meaning of art criticism is to be interpreted, and the relationship of art to reality. Food for thought for the perceptive art teacher.

146 Kaufman, Irving. *Art and Education in Contemporary Culture.* New York, Macmillan, 1966. 531 p.

Intended primarily to reorient present-day thinking about art education to stress a perceptual appreciation of art, its creative methods, and aesthetic forms. Enlightening discussion of the content of art education.

147 Kaupelis, Robert. *Learning to Draw: a Creative Approach to Expressive Drawing.* New York, Watson Guptill, 1966. 138p. biblio.

Combines artistic, aesthetic, and instructional considerations in a way significantly different from any other text. Illustrated with choice examples and perceptive analyses. An important survey of creative classroom techniques.

148 Landis, Mildred M. *Meaningful Art Education.* Peoria, Ill., Bennett, 1951. 185p. biblio.

Art as a creative activity in terms of growth and developmental learning.

149 Munro, Thomas. *Art Education: Its Philosophy and Psychology.* New York, Liberal Arts, 1956. 387p.

Essays constituting a comprehensive theory of art, aesthetics, and art education, firmly based on a humanistic philosophy that is uncompromisingly devoted to the overall task of making the arts a more important part of life.

150 Read, Herbert. *Education Through Art,* 3rd ed. New York, Pantheon, 1958. 328p. biblio.

Philosophy of education and the relationship of art to the whole educational structure. This latest edition of the well-known work first published in 1943 has been fully revised to include recent contributions to the subject. Generously illustrated with the art of children.

151 Smith, Ralph A., ed. *Aesthetics and Criticism in Art Education: Problems in Defining, Explaining and Evaluating Art.* Chicago, Rand McNally, 1966. 513p. biblio.

Relates aesthetic theory to an understanding of art education and instruction and coordinates traditional and modern analytical methods to clarify and solve the problems of defining, explaining, and evaluating art.

152 Whipple, Guy M., ed. *Art in American Life and Education* (NSSE 40th Yearbook). Bloomington, Ind., Public School Publ., 1941. 819p.

An extensive collection of articles related to many phases of art education: teacher training, the development of motion pictures, the dance, etc. A landmark in art education, being the first yearbook devoted to art to be prepared by a society interested in entire field of education.

153 Wickiser, Ralph L. *An Introduction to Art Education.* New York, World, 1957. 342p.

A scholarly combination of the theoretical and the practical. Relates art, psychology, sociology, and educational methodology to promote an awareness of the importance of art in education.

Elementary Schools

154 Bannon, Laura. *Mind Your Child's Art: a Guide for Parents and Teachers.* New York, Farrar, 1952. 62p.

Written by an experienced teacher. A simple and down-to-earth explanation of growth through creative art.

155 Benson, Kenneth R. *Creative Crafts for Children.* Englewood Cliffs, N.J., Prentice-Hall, 1958. 106p. biblio.

A manual of craft activities suitable for children of all ages. Contains 40 illustrated craft projects, with step-by-step procedures, arranged from the simple to the complex.

156 Bland, Jane C. *The Art of the Young Child: 3 to 5 Years.* New York, Simon and Schuster, 1957. 47p.

Based on teaching methods used in classes at the Museum of Modern Art. Discusses the proper understanding and appreciation of the work that accompanies the creative growth of young children and suggests means and materials by which adults can help.

157 Erdt, Margaret H. *Teaching Art in the Elementary School,* rev. ed. New York, Holt, 1962. 367p.

A practical guide for art teachers and elementary class-room teachers. Specific lesson plans are provided, yet stereo-typed procedures are avoided.

158 Gaitskell, Charles D., and Margaret R. *Art Education in the Kindergarten.* Peoria, Ill., Bennett, 1952. 40p.

Based on a two-year study of 9,000 children, age four to six, in Ontario kindergartens, this discusses what a young child produces in art, how he works, the guidance he needs, and how he progresses.

159 _____. *Children and Their Art: Methods for the Elementary School.* New York, Harper, 1958. 446 p. biblio.

Practice illuminates theory and theory guides practice in this practical text. Useful for the student and helpful to the teacher.

160 Greenberg, Pearl. *Children's Experiences in Art: Drawing and Painting.* New York, Reinhold, 1966. 132p.

An enthusiastic art teacher offers advice to elementary classroom teachers and art teachers on art as an integral part of the curriculum and as an invaluable help in general education. Useful ideas interspersed with children's comments and reproductions of their work.

161 Jefferson, Blanche. *Teaching Art to Children: the Values of Creative Expression,* 2nd ed. Boston, Allyn and Bacon, 1963. 286p. biblio.

A description of the various and differing methods of art education, emphasizing the values and implications of creative methods and processes and clarifying the role of the teacher in creative expression.

162 Kellogg, Rhoda. *Analyzing Children's Art.* Palo Alto, Cal., National, 1968. 211p. biblio.

An analysis of thousands of examples of children's art reveals the same stages of development throughout the world. The focus is on preschool children, but the investigation extends to the work of eight-year olds. The author finds that child art is a self-taught creativity.

163 _____, and O'Dell, Scott. *The Psychology of Children's Art.* Del Mar, Calif., CRM, 1967. (dist. by Random, N.Y.) 109p.

A developmental analysis of young children's art, profusely illustrated, which, like *Analyzing Children's Art*, finds that all children pass through the same stages. A highly recommended book cautioning that children's gifts develop best when they are left alone.

164 Lark-Horovitz, Betty, and others. *Understanding Children's Art for Better Teaching*. Columbus, Ohio, Merrill, 1967. 259p. biblio.

Reasonably comprehensive, covering teaching art in elementary school and the developmental stages of children's art. Illustrated with examples of children's work. Excellent summary of research included.

165 Lowenfeld, Viktor, and Brittain, W. Lambert. *Creative and Mental Growth*, 4th ed. New York, Macmillan, 1964. 412p. biblio.

Relates the child's general growth to his creative development and provides the basis for a deeper understanding of children's artistic expression. Analyzes the various stages of development in children's art from the age of two through adolescence.

166 McFee, June K. *Preparation for Art*. Belmont, Cal., Wadsworth, 1961. 338p. biblio.

Research in cultural anthropology and psychology are integrated with the practice of teaching in a discussion of art experiences for children. Stresses the individual child and his response.

167 Marshall, Sybil M. *An Experiment in Education*. New York, Cambridge UP, 1966. 222p.

A warm and perceptive personal account combining childhood memories and teaching art to children. Many examples of children's poetry and art work as well as actual lessons and children's reactions.

168 Packwood, Mary M. *Art Education in the Elementary School*. Washington, NAEA, 1967. 112p.

A guide for the elementary school art teacher with discussion of art today, art in the school, and the use of community resources. Practical suggestions for teaching included.

169 Peck, Ruth L., and Aniello, Robert S. *What Can I Do for an Art Lesson? a Practical Guide for the Elementary Class-*

room Teacher. Englewood Cliffs, N.J., Prentice-Hall, 1966. 224p.

A good how-to book, based on sound art education theory and realistic classroom experience. Emphasis in the 60 lessons presented is on the intrinsic value of the art experience without reference to or correlation with the rest of the curriculum.

170 Schultz, Harold A., and Shores, J. Harlan. *Art in the Elementary School: Practical Suggestions for the Classroom Teacher.* 2nd ed. Urbana, U of Illinois P, 1954. 102p.

A bulletin of the College of Education describing creative, appreciative, and social art activities from nursery school through grade six.

Secondary Schools

171 D'Amico, Victor, and others. *The Visual Arts in General Education.* New York, Appleton, 1940. 166p. biblio.

Sponsored by the Progressive Education Association's Commission on the Secondary School Curriculum, this concentrates on the adolescent and his experience in art and on the use of individual growth as an evaluative index rather than the art product. Includes methods of teaching.

172 Gaitskell, Charles D. *Art Education During Adolescence.* New York, Harcourt, 1954. 116p.

The development of a practical philosophy of art education, centered on the unique needs and interests of the adolescent. Based upon extensive research and experimentation.

173 Kainz, Louise C., and Riley, Olive L. *Exploring Art.* New York, Harcourt, 1948. 265p.

An important reference on the exploratory approach to art education at the secondary level.

174 Reed, Carl. *Early Adolescent Art Education.* Peoria, Ill., Bennett, 1957. 205p. biblio.

Stresses the importance of understanding the young adolescent in order to achieve a successful art program and the value of art in the junior high school curriculum. Describes a planned program adapted to the needs of this age group.

Colleges

175 Griswold, A. Whitney, and others. *The Fine Arts and the University.* New York, St. Martins, 1965. 89p. biblio.

A collection of five lectures given at New York University on the relationships and the benefits of the various arts to the academic and the university system.

176 Ritchie, Andrew C., and others. *The Visual Arts in Higher Education.* New York, College Art Association, 1966. 195p.

The report of a Ford Foundation-sponsored study on the teaching of art history, the practice of art, and the present state of the college or university museum. A reconsideration of methods, techniques, and goals, with statistical data emphasizing that departments of art history are not attracting or producing a sufficient number of well-trained graduates to meet the present teacher shortage in this field.

177 Ziegfeld, Ernest. *Art in the College Program of General Education.* New York, TC, Columbia, 1953. 239p. biblio.

A thorough examination of the implications of general education and of the arts as an aspect of living, as they relate to the college art program.

History of Art Education

178 Logan, Frederick M. *The Growth of Art in American Schools.* New York, Harper, 1955. 310p.

A succinct and lucid survey of movements, philosophies, and directions in art education from the early 1900's to mid-century.

179 Mathias, Margaret E. *The Beginnings of Art in the Public Schools.* New York, Scribner, 1924. 119p.

The use of fundamental materials with many definite problems outlined or suggested. Clear discussions of the craft and of the art values in the use of each material. A pioneering text when first published; now a classic.

ATHLETICS see PHYSICAL EDUCATION AND ATHLETICS
ATTITUDES AND PREJUDICE

180 Adorno, Theodore W., and others. *The Authoritarian Personality.* New York, Harper, 1950. 990p. biblio.

One of a series of studies dealing with prejudice. Using socio-psychological research findings, this demonstrates that there is a close correlation between a number of deep-rooted personality traits and overt prejudice.

181 Allport, Gordon W. *The Nature of Prejudice.* Cambridge, Mass., Addison Wesley, 1954. 537p. biblio.

An analysis of the dynamics of human prejudice with universal validity that deals with preferential thinking, group differences, socio-cultural factors, the acquisition of prejudice, and group tensions.

182   Bettelheim, Bruno, and Janowitz, Morris. *Dynamics of Prejudice: a Psychological and Sociological Study of Veterans.* New York, Harper, 1950. 227p.

A study of World War II veterans, their anxieties about adjustment, and the relation of their anxieties to intolerance. Shows that anxieties have deeper roots than immediate fears and are unrelated to the condition of war or peace.

183   Dean, John P., and Rosen, Alex. *A Manual of Intergroup Relations.* Chicago, U of Chicago P, 1955. 193p. biblio.

Based on a six-year study by the Cornell Social Science Research Center of intergroup relations in a number of communities, especially ongoing action programs. A how-to book for those interested in improving relations between majority and minority groups in organizations and in the community.

184   Goodman, Mary E. *Race Awareness in Young Children,* rev. ed. New York, Collier, 1964. 352p. biblio.

Using case studies, an anthropologist investigates the complex processes underlying the culturally predominant pattern of "white over brown" that persists in our society. Contains a summary of relevant research since 1950.

185   Lambert, Wallace E., and Klineberg, Otto. *Children's Views of Foreign People: a Cross-National Study.* New York, Appleton, 1967. 319p.

The report, by two prominent social psychologists, of a ten-year study of the formation of stereotypes in children's minds.

186   Rokeach, Milton. *The Open and Closed Mind: Investigations into the Nature of Belief Systems and Personality Systems.* New York, Basic, 1960. 447p. biblio.

A report of research on the nature of belief systems, covering authoritarianism, general intolerance, and the dynamics of disbelief systems—all such rigidities and prejudices being regarded as inhibitions of normal cognitive functions.

187   Segal, Bernard E., ed. *Racial and Ethnic Relations: Selected Readings.* New York, Crowell, 1966. 492p.

Forty high quality readings on a rather advanced level, as many of the contributors presuppose statistical knowledge. The focus is on fundamentals and on black-white relations. A problem-centered, interdisciplinary approach.

188   Sherif, Muzafer, and Hovland, Carl I. *Social Judgment: Assimilation and Contrast Effects in Communication and Attitude Change.* New Haven, Yale UP, 1961. 218p. biblio.

A brilliant exposition of the basic psychological processes underlying the expression of attitudes and their modifiability through communication, based on research studies by the authors and others.

189   Smith, Mahlon B., and others. *Opinions and Personality.* New York, Wiley, 1956. 294p. biblio.

Based on data drawn from a close study of the opinions of ten men, this examines the relationships between opinion and personality and attempts to develop a coherent framework for conceptualizing these relations.

190   Stember, Charles H. *Education and Attitude Change: the Effect of Schooling on Prejudice Against Minority Groups.* New York, Institute of Human Relations, 1961. 182p.

A study sponsored by the American Jewish Committee, which attempts to determine if formal schooling can improve attitudes toward religious, ethnic, and racial minorities. Concludes that education reduces overt discrimination but by no means eliminates it.

191   Thomas, R. Murray. *Social Differences in the Classroom: Social-Class, Ethnic, and Religious Problems.* New York, McKay, 1965. 195p. biblio.

An interesting and clearly written analysis of differences among students and of the teacher's role in helping students develop greater understanding of both local and international cultural differences.

192   Wright, Betty A. *Educating for Diversity.* New York, Day, 1965. 250p. biblio.

A much needed book that summarizes integration issues, reviews civil rights legislation, and then dwells at length and extremely effectively on prejudice, stereotyping, and ethnocentrism. Specific suggestions for reorienting attitudes and thinking are provided in abundance, along with lists of books and audiovisual aids.

AUDIOLOGY AND AUDIOMETRY see DEAF

AUDIOVISUAL AIDS
see also **TEACHING AIDS**
     TELEVISION IN EDUCATION
     TEXTBOOKS

193   *Audio-Visual Equipment Directory.* Fairfax, Va., National Audio-Visual Association. Published annually.

     The single, most complete source of information on virtually all AV products on the market. Basic information and specifications.

194   Brown, James W., and others. *A-V Instruction: Materials and Methods,* rev. ed. New York, McGraw-Hill, 1964. 592p. biblio.

     Basic text on the characteristics and utilization of all types of audiovisual instructional equipment and materials. A separately published manual gives well-illustrated instructions for creating materials and operating equipment.

195   ————, and Thornton, James W., Jr. *New Media in Higher Education* (DAVI). Washington, NEA, 1963. 182p. biblio.

     Reports and findings on 90 outstanding undertakings in over 40 colleges and universities. Offers a general rationale of the new media in education and poses critical questions on the relationship between audiovisual practices and the purposes of higher education.

196   Chandler, Anna C., and Cypher, Irene F. *Audio-Visual Techniques for the Enrichment of the Curriculum.* New York, Noble, 1948. 252p. biblio.

     Integrates instructional materials with actual classroom situations by giving examples of teaching units as well as hints on utilizing dioramas, graphic displays, radio, and TV.

197   Cross, A. J. Foy, and Cypher, Irene F. *Audio-Visual Education.* New York, Crowell, 1961. 415p. biblio.

     A basic text planned to be of practical help to the professional educator in schools, colleges and industry. Comprehensive coverage of audiovisual materials and equipment, television, teaching machines, instructional materials centers, and the role of audiovisual techniques in international education. Glossary and classified directory.

198 _____, and Cypher, Irene F., eds. *Planning Schools for the Use of Audio-Visual Materials.* (In 4 parts: No. 1, *Classrooms,* 3rd ed.; No. 2, *Auditoriums;* No. 3, *The AV Instructional Materials Center;* No. 4, *Audio-Visual Centers in Colleges and Universities* (DAVI) Washington, NEA, 1953-59.

Handbooks containing illustrated information on types of equipment and drawings of floor plans to assist in planning facilities. Provides building standards for use of modern instructional materials.

199 Dale, Edgar. *Audio-Visual Methods in Teaching,* rev. ed. New York, Dryden, 1954. 534p.

Believing that all teaching can be greatly improved by the intelligent use of audiovisual methods, the author provides teachers with a basic philosophy and with vitalized teaching techniques in almost every curriculum area.

200 DeKieffer, Robert E. *Audiovisual Instruction.* New York, CARE, 1965. 117p. biblio.

Audiovisual experiences and devices are categorized into non-projected, projected, and materials and equipment. Covers administration, school design, and research.

201 East, Marjorie, and Dale, Edgar. *Display for Learning: Making and Using Visual Materials.* New York, Dryden, 1952. 306p.

Shows specifically how to make visuals—pictures, graphs, chalk boards, charts, bulletin boards, posters, etc.—a more vital part of teaching.

202 Eboch, Sidney C. *Operating Audio-Visual Equipment.* San Francisco, Chandler, 1960. 73p.

A manual describing technical features and operating principles of classroom audiovisual equipment.

203 Ely, Donald P., ed. *The Changing Role of the Audiovisual Process in Education: a Definition and a Glossary of Related Terms.* (Audiovisual Communication Review, Supplement No. 6). Washington, NEA, 1963. 156p.

A special publication containing a clear statement of audiovisual rationale, which also established a professional lexicon.

204 Erickson, Carlton W. *Fundamentals of Teaching with Audiovisual Technology.* New York, Macmillan, 1965. 400p. biblio.

Audiovisual technology as a vital factor in the classroom. Describes and evaluates the major technological media, but primarily concerned with their relationship to productive learning. Stress is on creative use rather than on mechanics. Nine case studies.

205   *Film Evaluation Guide, 1946-64.* New York, Educational Film Library Association, 1965. 535p.

The essential facts about more than 4,500 carefully evaluated films, title: running time, color, price, release date, producer, and distributor. Also subject, synopsis, technical quality, objective criticism, and age level for which intended. Well indexed.

————— *1967 Supplement.*

Contains additional 1,100 titles.

206   Finn, James D., and others. *Studies in the Growth of Instructional Technology: Audio-Visual Instrumentation for Instruction in the Public Schools, 1930-1960, a Basis for Take-Off.* (DAVI) Washington, NEA, 1962. 108p. biblio.

An attempt to assess the growth of instructional technology in the American school system as measured by the growth of audiovisual equipment supply. (See #2718 for companion volume.)

207   Forsdale, Louis, ed. *8mm. Sound Film and Education.* New York, TC, Columbia, 1963. 166p. biblio.

Papers from a 1961 conference of authorities in the fields of industry, religion, education, and the military concerned with the status and the development possibilities of the 8mm film medium.

208   Freedman, Florence B., and Berg, Esther L. *The Classroom Teacher's Guide to Audio-Visual Material,* rev. ed. Philadelphia, Chilton, 1967. 279p. biblio.

Designed for the average classroom teacher who, not having had training in the use of audiovisual materials in the classroom, tends not to use the so-called newer media. Includes a guide to resources, lesson plans, and practical suggestions.

209   Henry, Nelson B., ed. *Audio-Visual Materials of Instruction* (NSSE 48th Yearbook, Part I). Chicago, U of Chicago P, 1949. 320p. biblio.

Many leaders in the audiovisual field cover the history of audiovisual education, school use, obstacles, function of teachers, and in-service teacher training. Basic principles still valid.

210   Kemp, Jerrold E., and others. *Planning and Producing Audiovisual Materials.* San Francisco, Chandler, 1963. 169p.

An excellent guide for those wishing to produce instructional materials. Clear diagrams and explicit directions.

211   Kinder, James S. *Audio-Visual Materials and Techniques.* 2nd ed. New York, American, 1959. 592p. biblio.

Philosophy, theory, and techniques described in detail. Covers classroom light control, closed circuit TV, graphic materials, and the influence of color in the classroom. Explanation of terms and listing of source materials.

212   *Library of Congress Catalog: Motion Pictures and Filmstrips.* 1953-   . Washington, Library of Congress.

A quarterly listing, with annual and quinquennial cumulations, of the works represented by Library of Congress cards. Constitutes a reference and research tool of all films of educational and instructive value that have been released in the United States and Canada.

213   *Library of Congress Catalog: Music and Phonorecords.* 1953- Washington, Library of Congress.

A semiannual listing of Library of Congress cards, with cumulative annual and quinquennial cumulations, which is a reference and research tool and includes phonorecords (both musical and non-musical), and libretti.

214   McCarty, Henry R. *The Cooperative Approach to Audio-Visual Programs.* (DAVI) Washington, NEA, 1959. 80p.

Reports on a survey of over 100 cooperative audiovisual education centers in the United States in terms of staff, budgets, and programs.

215   May, Mark A., and others. *Learning from Films.* New Haven, Yale UP, 1958. 357p.

Report of the Yale Motion Picture Research Project, initiated in 1946 for the experimental evaluation of some pilot teaching films. The study was expanded and the present volume includes studies of production, utilization, findings on knowledge gained from film, effects on subsequent learning, and techniques for evaluating films.

216   *National Tape Recording Catalog.* Washington, NEA, 1954-

Cumulative and published "from time to time." Contains

a descriptive listing of about 5,000 tapes selected on the basis of curricular relevance and production quality. Listed by subject and title.

217   *Newer Educational Media.* University Park, Pennsylvania State U, 1961. 104p. biblio.

Papers of the Regional Research Council's Conference on Newer Educational Media. Summarize research findings on the use of motion pictures and other pictorial media, television, and automated instruction. Implications for curriculum change, administrative organization, and teacher education are outlined.

218   Reid, Seerley, and Grubbs, Eloyse. *U.S. Government Films for Public Educational Use,* 1963 ed. (USOE Circular 742). Washington, GPO, 1964. 532p.

An attempt to provide an accurate and complete list, as of July 1, 1963, of all the government-owned motion pictures and filmstrips available for public use by purchase or loan. Information about each includes a summary as well as date, running time, source, etc. Title listing and subject index.

219   Rufsvold, Margaret I., and Guss, Carolyn. *Guides to Newer Educational Media,* 2nd ed. Chicago, ALA, 1967.

A comprehensive annotated guide to the catalogs, lists, professional organizations, and specialized periodicals that systematically provide information on films, filmstrips, kinescopes, phonodiscs, phonotapes, programed instruction materials, slides, transparencies, and videotapes. Covers guides from 1957 through April 1967.

220   Stewart, David D., ed. *Film Study in Higher Education.* Washington, ACE, 1966. 174p. biblio.

The report of a conference sponsored by Dartmouth College and the ACE on the inclusion of courses in film history, criticism, and appreciation in the college curriculum. The articles are direct, critical, and present opposing views. Bibliographies, listings of distributors, associations, film societies and libraries, and current course offerings make this especially valuable.

221   Wittich, Walter A., and Schuller, Charles F. *Audio-Visual Materials: Their Nature and Use.* 4th ed. New York, Harper, 1967. 500p.

A comprehensive and scholarly treatment of audiovisual

materials and their use. Discussion of methods, educational television, language laboratories, and programed learning. Emphasis is on creative teaching through the use of the various instructional aids.

222 _____, and Fowlkes, C. *Audio-Visual Paths to Learning*. New York, Harper, 1954. 534p. biblio.

A report on the investigation of several methods of integrating films with the curriculum. Establishes the value of adequate preparation and follow-up.

BEHAVIOR
see also PERSONALITY THEORY

223 Anastasi, Anne. *Differential Psychology: Individual and Group Differences in Behavior*, 3rd ed. New York, Macmillan, 1958.

Viewing differential psychology as one approach to understanding behavior, this attempts to coordinate various topics and report major problems in this approach. A well-known text that examines common pitfalls and sources of error in the interpretation of results.

224 _____, ed. *Individual Differences*. New York, Wiley, 1965. 298p.

A variety of judiciously chosen articles and excerpts in differential psychology, dating between 1869 and 1962, with illuminating comments by the editor.

225 Berelson, Bernard, and Steiner, Gary A. *Human Behavior: an Inventory of Scientific Findings*. New York, Harcourt, 1964. 712p. biblio.

An inventory of reports on ontogenic findings covering the present state of scientific knowledge about human behavior, what we know, what we think we know, and what we claim to know.

226 Berlyne, D. E. *Conflict, Arousal, and Curiosity*. New York, McGraw-Hill, 1960. 350p. biblio.

Relevant data from several specialities in the field of psychology, especially information theory, contribute to a theory of exploratory and epistemic behavior.

227 Bloom, Benjamin S. *Stability and Change in Human Characteristics*. New York, Wiley, 1964. 237p. biblio.

An especially noteworthy compilation and interpretation

of available longitudinal studies on factors related to human behavior. A must for all researchers in the field of education.

228   Combs, Arthur W., and Snygg, Donald. *Individual Behavior: a Perceptual Approach to Behavior*, 2nd ed. New York, Harper, 1959. 522p. biblio.

A theory first developed by the authors in an earlier (1949) edition of this book and here extended and developed. Seeks to understand the behavior of the individual from his own point of view, as opposed to the external frame of reference. Includes the application of this approach as treatment.

229   Goffman, Erving. *The Presentation of Self in Everyday Life*. New York, Doubleday, 1959. 255p.

A dramaturgical theory of individual and social behavior.

230   Hull, Clark L. *Principles of Behavior: an Introduction to Behavior Theory*. New York, Appleton, 1943. 422p. biblio.

231   _____. *A Behavior System: an Introduction to Behavior Theory Concerning the Individual Organism*. New Haven, Yale UP, 1952. 372p. biblio.

An influential pair of books that have provided a base for further research. The earlier title states primary behavior principles and is a Herculean effort to organize known facts about learning. The later book is an account of the application of Hull's postulates to the behavior and learning of mammals, with consideration of the implications for understanding human learning.

232   Meehl, Paul E. *Clinical vs. Statistical Prediction: a Theoretical Analysis and Review of the Evidence*. Minneapolis, U of Minnesota P, 1954. 149p. biblio.

An examination of the problem of predicting individual behavior, which discusses the rationality of inference from class membership, the special powers of the clinician, and empirical comparisons of clinical and actuarial prediction.

233   Miller, George A., and others. *Plans and the Structure of Behavior*. New York, Holt, 1960. 226p. biblio.

A theoretical essay proposing a cognitive approach to the analysis of behavior and concerned with discovering whether cybernetic ideas have any relevance to psychology.

234 Skinner, Burrhus F. *Science and Human Behavior.* New York, Macmillan, 1953. 461p.

A basic sytematic text for the author's school of behavioral science, which argues the possibility of a science of human behavior and its application to the control of the behavior of groups and social institutions and agencies.

235 Spence, Kenneth W. *Behavior Theory and Learning: Selected Papers.* Englewood Cliffs, N.J., Prentice-Hall, 1960. 403p. biblio.

Twenty-two papers, including a number of experimental articles, that have served as vehicles for elaborating the author's behavior theory approach, and some theoretical essays on the methodological basis of psychology, behavior theory, and discrimination learning.

236 Thomas, Alexander, and others. *Behavioral Individuality in Early Childhood.* New York, New York UP, 1963. 135p.

Based on a longitudinal study from birth of 136 children from middle- and upper-middle class homes.

237 _____. *Temperament and Behavior Disorders in Children.* New York, New York UP, 1968. 320p.

The earlier book deals with the theoretical groundwork; this deals with behavior problems that developed in 42 of the 136 children. Concerned with the factors that contribute to the disorders and with the new, shortened treatment method emphasizing parent guidance. Cases, methods of data collection, and analyses are described.

238 Tyler, Leona E. *The Psychology of Human Differences,* 3rd ed. New York, Appleton, 1965. 572p. biblio.

Current interest in social reforms makes this study of differences among individuals and groups particularly useful. Covers varieties of group differences, such as age, sex, race, intelligence, and social class, and the factors producing them. Final chapter analyzes new research methods based on behavior and development.

239 Woodworth, Robert S. *Dynamics of Behavior.* New York, Holt, 1958. 403p. biblio.

An enlightening, lucid study of the causes and effects of human activities and achievements in relation to motivation, perception, and learning.

BLIND

see also EXCEPTIONAL CHILDREN

240   Hathaway, Winifred. *The Education and Health of the Partially Seeing Child,* 4th ed. New York, Columbia UP, 1959. 201p. biblio.

Published originally in 1943 and one of the first texts in the field of teaching exceptional children, this revision offers a sound discussion of philosophy and methods for providing optimum educational opportunities for partially sighted children.

241   Jones, John W. *The Visually Handicapped Child at Home and School: Developments and Trends in Educational Programs for Blind and Partially Seeing Children* (USOE Bulletin (no. 39). Washington, GPO, 1963. 55p. biblio.

Summarizes recent developments in the field of educating visually handicapped children and describes the resources available to assist educators initiate and improve educational programs.

242   Lowenfeld, Berthold. *Our Blind Children: Growing and Learning with Them.* Springfield, Ill., Thomas, 1956. 224p.

A useful book in a field that has few, this is a practical guide to methods of teaching independence in the simple activities of daily life. A source of information for teachers and for those who guide parents in meeting the needs of blind children.

243   Norris, Miriam, and others. *Blindness in Children.* Chicago, U of Chicago P, 1957. 173p. biblio.

A study designed to establish developmental norms for young blind children that can serve as a basis for clinical evaluation and for social and educational recommendations. Particular reference to factors that promote or retard optimal growth.

244   Pelone, Anthony J. *Helping the Visually Handicapped Child in a Regular Class.* New York, TC, Columbia, 1957. 99p.

A comprehensive handbook for the regular classroom teacher faced with helping blind or partially sighted children.

BRAIN INJURED
see also EXCEPTIONAL CHILDREN
MENTALLY RETARDED

245 Bender, Lauretta. *Psychopathology of Children with Organic Brain Disorders.* Springfield, Ill., Thomas, 1956. 151p. biblio.

An examination of the responses and personality problems of children frustrated by organic disorders of the brain. Includes data used by Bellevue Hospital (New York City) researchers and clinicians for diagnosis and evaluation.

246 Birch, Herbert G., ed. *Brain Damage in Children: the Biological and Social Aspects.* Baltimore, Williams and Wilkins, 1964. 199p. biblio.

The outgrowth of a 1962 conference sponsored by the Association for the Aid of Crippled Children, which is a multidisciplinary assessment of the current state of knowledge and an attempt to delineate new lines of inquiry. Contains an extensive annotated bibliography, pages 133-199, which has also been published separately by the Woods School and Residential Treatment Center, Langhorne, Pa.

247 Cruickshank, William M. *The Brain-Injured Child in Home, School, and Community.* Syracuse, N.Y., Syracuse UP, 1967. 294p. biblio.

An overview of the issues germane to the adjustment of brain injured children, which offers insights into growth problems and their implications for home and school.

248 _____, ed. *The Teacher of Brain-Injured Children: a Discussion of the Bases for Competency.* Syracuse, N.Y., Syracuse UP, 1966. 334p. biblio.

Specialists from several disciplines discuss the qualifications, competencies, and training of teachers of children with learning disabilities. A clearly written, excellent resource that presents sometimes diverse opinions with authoritative editorial comment.

249 _____, and others. *A Teaching Method for Brain Injured and Hyperactive Children: a Demonstration-Pilot Study.* Syracuse, N.Y., Syracuse UP, 1961. 576p. biblio.

Provides extensive data on an educational program for these children in the hope of developing a method of teaching and a system of education adequate to meet their complex needs.

250 Gallagher, James J. *The Tutoring of Brain Injured Mentally Retarded Children: an Experimental Study.* Springfield, Ill., Thomas, 1960. 194p.

The report of a three-year experimental program involving 42 institutionalized children. Reveals that tutoring can offer modest gains that, however, dissipate when tutoring ceases.

251 Lashley, Karl S. *Brain Mechanisms and Intelligence: a Quantitative Study of Injuries to the Brain.* New York, Hafner, 1929. 186p. biblio.

A classic report on experiments with rats analyzing the neural mechanisms that play a part in learning. Interprets results in relation to earlier and then-current theories and deals with the influence of brain injuries on the capacity to learn and upon retentiveness.

252 Strauss, Alfred A. *Psychopathology and Education of the Brain Injured Child,* 2 vols. New York, Grune and Stratton, 1947 and 1955. biblio.

Volume I, written in collaboration with Laura E. Lehtinen, is a research-based classic delineating disturbances in brain injured retarded children and presenting some general educational principles and suggestions for modifying classroom procedures. Volume II, subtitled *Progress in Clinic and Therapy* and co-authored by Newell C. Kephart, is concerned with the brain injured child of normal IQ and presents some newer views on brain functioning.

253 Taylor, Edith M. *Psychological Appraisal of Children with Cerebral Defects.* Cambridge, Harvard UP, 1959. 499p.

A report of clinical experience with a number of children with different types of central nervous system damage at different ages and a subsequent follow-up on 244 children 3 to 12 years later. In 73 per cent of the cases, intelligence remained the same.

BUILDINGS—SCHOOLS

254 Caudill, William W. *Toward Better School Design.* New York, Dodge, 1954. 271p. biblio.

Presents no total solutions or plans but concentrates on the methodology to be applied to each planning situation. Includes case studies. Illustrated.

255   Educational Facilities Laboratories. *Profiles of Significant Schools.* New York, 1960-

A series of well-illustrated reports on representative examples of school buildings embodying unique and often experimental designs that adapt buildings to changing instructional methods.

256   Englehardt, Nickolaus L., and others. *Planning Secondary School Buildings.* New York, Reinhold, 1949. 252p. biblio.

Nearly 20 years later, this attempt to envisage the secondary school of the future remains a valuable guide. Detailed considerations of space requirements and of the various activities and programs of a school are based on sound experience.

257   _____, and others. *School Planning and Building Handbook.* New York, Dodge, 1956. 626p.

A handbook for administrators and architects based on the experience of school boards, superintendents, and architects. Practical coverage of all aspects of building, such as site selection, contracts, land use, public relations, standards, specifications, bidding, drawings, costs, financing, etc.

258   *Guide for Planning School Plants.* East Lansing Mich., National Council on Schoolhouse Construction, 1964. 156p.

The latest of a series designed to guide those working in the field of school plant planning and educational program activity. Stresses guiding principles and performance goals.

259   Leu, Donald J. *Planning Educational Facilities.* New York, CARE, 1965. 115p. biblio.

How to determine school building needs, how to plan, how to modernize, and how to finance. An informative discussion of the principles of educational facilities, plus fundamentals such as estimating enrollments and evaluating existing facilities.

260   MacConnell, James D. *Planning for School Buildings.* Englewood Cliffs, N.J., Prentice-Hall, 1957. 348p. biblio.

Covers planning problems and their solutions, personnel involved in planning, organizational patterns of programing, and economies in school building.

261   Perkins, Lawrence B., and Cocking, Walter D. *Schools.* New York, Reinhold, 1949. 264p. biblio.

The point of view of the architect, practical as well as

aesthetic. In fact, a plea for the best of contemporary architectural thinking in conjunction with the best of educational planning. "Form follows function." Well-chosen photographs and drawings illustrate the text.

262 Roth, Alfred. *The New Schoolhouse*, 4th ed. New York, Praeger, 1966. 304p. biblio.

An attractive attempt to persuade school building planners that quantitative needs and rising costs need not rule out quality. Describes and illustrates 36 new school buildings of all types in almost as many countries.

263 School Environments Research Project. *Research Reports*, 3 vols. Ann Arbor, Architectural Research Laboratory, U of Michigan, 1965.

An effort sponsored by EFL to determine how the total environment affects the learning process. Series I, II, and III: *Environmental Abstracts* includes some 600 abstracts of existing literature that describe the relationships linking environment with human behavior; *Environmental Evaluations* presents the project staff's papers summarizing and appraising the present state of knowledge regarding the affects of space, heat, light, sound, and the social environment in relation to the learning situation; *Environmental Analysis* presents a proposed method of investigating and processing of information needed in environmental design.

264 *Schools for America*. (AASA) Washington, D.C., NEA, 1967. 175p.

Superseding two previous publications of the AASA that stressed standards, this report emphasizes new information, insights, and guidelines. An illustrated, basic resource.

BUILDINGS—COLLEGES AND UNIVERSITIES

265 Dober, Richard P. *Campus Planning*. New York, Reinhold, 1963. 314p. biblio.

Describes trends in design and includes suggestions for coordinated campus planning of facilities and landscaping.

266 Educational Facilities Laboratories. *Bricks and Mortarboards: a Report on College Planning and Building*. New York, 1964. 168p.

A well-illustrated attempt to counteract expediency and to

encourage quality in the enormous building programs forced upon colleges today. Individual authors cover classrooms, laboratories, libraries, dormitories, the campus, and renovations.

267 Riker, Harold C., and Lopez, Frank G. *College Students Live Here: a Study of College Housing.* New York, EFL, 1961. 152p. biblio.

Illustrated with photographs and floor plans, this is a practical guide, concerned with architecture, the living and learning environment, master plans, financing, and the use of facilities.

BUSINESS EDUCATION
see also VOCATIONAL EDUCATION
VOCATIONAL GUIDANCE

268 Dame, John F., and Brinkman, Albert R. *Guidance in Business Education,* 3rd ed. Cincinnati, South-Western, 1961. 380p. biblio.

A working manual of guidance techniques to assist business educators in helping students make educational and occupational decisions.

269 Douglas, Lloyd V. *Business Education.* New York, CARE, 1963. 115p. biblio.

A broad approach to business education, which although concerned with teaching skills, is not confined to them. Covers the wide range of students and student abilities as well as the wide potential of this field.

270 _____, and others. *Teaching Business Subjects,* 2nd ed. Englewood Cliffs, N.J., Prentice-Hall, 1965. biblio.

A popular methods book updated to include discussions of electronic data processing, programed learning, and changes in professional organizations in this field. Covers skill and nonskill subjects; offers projects and case problems.

271 Dry, Samuel W., and Nellie E. *Teaching Gregg Shorthand and Transcription.* Portland, Me., Walch, 1962. 177p.

An illustrated manual describing tested techniques and offering numerous helpful suggestions and activities.

272 Grant, Earl S. *Successful Devices in Teaching Bookkeeping.* Portland, Me., Walch, 1962. 244p.

Devoted entirely to suggested teaching techniques and covering all phases of bookkeeping, with some attention to such related areas as business arithmetic, interest, and discount. Includes the use of teaching aids.

273 Hansen, Kenneth J., and Liles, Parker, eds. *Administration and Supervision in Business Education.* (NBEA) Washingington, NEA, 1965. 357p. biblio.

A compilation of 42 articles from *The National Business Education Quarterly* intended as a reference. Covers history, problems of administration, and supervision at state, city, and local levels as well as in institutions of higher education.

274 Hardaway, Mathilde. *Testing and Evaluation in Business Education,* 3rd ed. Cincinnati, South-Western, 1966. 487p. biblio.

An inclusive text covering basic principles and techniques, testing practices in business subjects, and the analysis of test scores.

275 Huffman, Harry, ed. *How to Teach Business Subjects, Especially Designed for Student Teachers.* Washington, National Association for Business Teacher Education, 1959. 175p.

Four selections dealing with orientation, supervision, evaluation, and instruction.

276 NBEA. *Yearbook.* 1st.- 1963- Washington, NEA.

A fairly new series focusing each year on a different area of teaching business. Recent titles: *Recent and Projected Developments Affecting Education* (1964), *New Media in Teaching the Business Subjects* (1965), and *Business Education Meets the Challenge of Change* (1966).

277 Nolan, Carroll A., and others. *Principles and Problems of Business Education,* 3rd ed. Cincinnati, South-Western, 1967. 681p. biblio.

A thorough coverage of the nature and purpose of business education at all levels, dealing with curriculum and curriculum criteria, testing and evaluation, and guidance and job placement. Appendix contains the Vocational Education Act of 1963.

278 Place, Irene, and Hicks, Charles B. *College Secretarial Procedures,* 2nd ed. New York, McGraw-Hill, 1958. 502p.

Intended for use in training top-level executive secretaries in post-high school courses. Covers personal relations as well as skills and responsibilities.

279   Russon, Allien, and Wanous, Samuel J. *Philosophy and Psychology of Teaching Typewriting: with Suggested Teaching Procedures.* Cincinnati, South-Western, 1960. 440p.

    Help for teachers in developing efficient, purposeful procedures for teaching typewriting more quickly and effectively. Explains the whys as well as the hows.

280   Satlow, I. David. *Teaching Business Subjects Effectively.* Valley Stream, N.Y., Teachers Practical Press, 1964. 63p.

    A helpful guide to teaching techniques that includes numerous aids and suggestions.

281   South-Western Publishing Company. *Monographs.* No. 1-1925- . Cincinnati.

    A series of monographs now numbering well past 100, each of which covers a particular aspect of the field of business education. Some recent titles: *Improving Research in Business Education, An Evaluation Plan for Business Education Programs in High Schools,* and *Motivation in Teaching General Business.*

282   Tonne, Herbert A., and others. *Methods of Teaching Business Subjects,* 3rd ed. New York, McGraw-Hill, 1965. 488p.

    Presents a unified concept of methodology dealing with all business subjects and providing a body of teaching materials for introductory methods courses in college.

283   _____. *Principles of Business Education,* 3rd ed. New York, McGraw-Hill, 1961. 538p. biblio.

    Attempts to correlate the treatment of principles, practice, and problems with the latest trends in education for business at the secondary and collegiate level.

284   White, Jane F., and Dewar, Thadys J. *Successful Devices in Teaching Clerical Practice.* Portland, Me., Walch, 1959. 223p.

    More than 300 tested ideas for teaching clerical typing, letter writing, simple record keeping, use of business machines, filing, and communication. Includes outlines of course.

285   _____.*Teaching Typewriting.* Portland, Me., Walch, 1964. 170p.

    A helpful guide containing numerous suggestions for the teacher.

CAMPING AND OUTDOOR EDUCATION
see also PLAY AND GAMES
RECREATION AND LEISURE

286 Freeburg, William H., and Taylor, Loren E. *Philosophy of Outdoor Education.* Minneapolis, Burgess, 1961. 445p.

Covers the basic concepts of educating in the outdoors and educating for outdoor living.

287 Gabrielson, M. Alexander, and Holtzer, Charles. *The Role of Outdoor Education.* New York, CARE, 1965. 117p. biblio.

Outdoor education in school, community playground, and summer camp is thoroughly covered, with advice on designing the program, financing, resources, equipment, leadership, and providing a diversified array of activities.

288 Goodrich, Lois. *Decentralized Camping: a Handbook.* New York, Association, 1959. 256p.

A guide to the concepts and methods for conducting decentralized camping programs.

289 Hammett, Catherine T., and Musselman, Virginia. *Camp Program Book.* New York, Association, 1959. 380p.

A comprehensive exploration of all aspects of camp programing.

290 _____, and Horrocks, Carol M. *Creative Crafts for Campers.* New York, Association, 1957. 431p.

Describes a variety of craft projects that may be developed at and are suitable for camps.

291 Mitchell, A. Viola, and Crawford, Ida B. *Camp Counseling: an Illustrated Book of Know-How for the Camp Worker,* 3rd ed. Philadelphia, Saunders, 1961. 412p. biblio.

A useful and practical resource, covering methods, materials, and the problems involved in camp counseling.

292 Smith, Julian W. *Outdoor Education.* Englewood Cliffs, N.J., Prentice-Hall, 1963. 322p.

Provides a guide for learning experiences in the outdoors and for teaching the skills required for living in the outdoors.

CATHOLIC EDUCATION
see also RELIGIOUS EDUCATION

293 Hofinger, Johannes. *The Art of Teaching Christian Doctrine: the Good News and Its Proclamation,* 2nd ed. Notre Dame, Ind., U of Notre Dame P, 1962. 290p. biblio.

An examination of the catechetical task in the light of contemporary developments in religious education. Covers the task, structure, and content of catechetics, and the qualifications for the catechetical apostolate.

294 Kolesnik, Walter B., and Power, Edward J., eds. *Catholic Education: a Book of Readings.* New York, McGraw-Hill, 1965. 512p.

A collection of 54 articles reflecting a Catholic point of view, divided into sections, each of which starts with a series of questions designed to stimulate thinking and discussion. Covers issues, problems, psychology, adolescents, education for values, teaching, and counseling.

295 Koob, C. Albert, ed. *What Is Happening to Catholic Education?* Washington, NCEA, 1966. 212p.

Based on speeches by both Catholic and public school educators presented at 1965 and 1966 summer workshops, this is a collection of essays that identify some critical areas, make many needful recommendations, and point the way to procedures that would improve Catholic education.

296 Link, Mark J., ed. *Faith and Commitment: Aim of Religious Education.* Chicago, Loyola UP, 1964. 309p. biblio.

Studies by 26 internationally known catechetical experts on the modern Biblical-liturgical approach to teaching religion.

297 _____, ed. *Teaching the Sacraments and Morality.* Chicago, Loyola UP, 1965. 214p. biblio.

A collection of 17 catechetical studies on theory, practice, and empirical research that convey the new mood in Catholic religious education with its Biblical-liturgical approach.

298 Sloyan, Gerard S., ed. *Modern Catechetics: Message and Method in Religious Formation.* New York, Macmillan, 1960. 381p. biblio.

Articles rooted in psychology and using the modern approach to catechesis set forth detailed methods of communicating the Christian message for use with all age groups, inside and outside the Catholic school.

History

299 Betts, George H. *The Curriculum of Religious Education.* New York, Abingdon, 1924. 535p.

A comprehensive coverage of the historical background, the theory, principles, and materials available in the early days of the church.

300 McCluskey, Neil G. *Catholic Education in America: a Documentary History.* New York, TC, Columbia, 1964. 205p.

A briefly sketched history of Catholic education from 1792 to 1950 accompanies letters and other documents of the clergy.

301 Sherrill, Lewis J. *The Rise of Christian Education.* New York, Macmillan, 1944. 349p. biblio.

A comprehensive history of Christian education from its earliest Hebrew origins through the medieval period. Various educational philosophies and techniques emerge as different periods are examined.

CATHOLIC SCHOOLS
see also CHURCH-SPONSORED SCHOOLS

CEREBRAL PALSY
see also BRAIN INJURED
EXCEPTIONAL CHILDREN

302 Cruickshank, William M., and Raus, George M., eds. *Cerebral Palsy: Its Individual and Community Problems,* 2nd rev. ed. Syracuse, N.Y., Syracuse UP, 1966, 704p. biblio.

A comprehensive overview of the problems of the cerebral palsied, whose rehabilitation requires the services of a large team of professionals. A synthesis of the medical, psychological, therapeutic, social work, educational, and rehabilitative points of view.

303 Geer, William C., and Wolfe, William G. *Education of the Cerebral Palsied in the South.* Atlanta, Southern Regional Education Board, 1960. 74p.

A report of an investigation of existing facilities and unmet needs in 15 Southern states, which has extensive universal implications in terms of the special problems of the cerebral palsied and the special training required by all, including the teacher, who wish to help them. Includes tables of potential help to those who might wish to conduct similar studies.

304 Illingworth, Ronald S., ed. *Recent Advances in Cerebral Palsy.* Boston, Little Brown, 1958. 380p. biblio.

A collection of essays providing comprehensive coverage of such problems as diagnosis, educational practices, therapy, and community services. Both British and American authors have contributed, and the British bibliographic references are an added asset.

CHILD DEVELOPMENT
see also LANGUAGE DEVELOPMENT IN CHILDREN
LEARNING THEORY

305 Baldwin, Alfred L. *Behavior and Development in Childhood.* New York, Holt, 1955. 619p.

A neo-Gestalt approach to child behavior and development, which describes behavior in specific situations and discusses change and the factors determining change.

306 ———. *Theories of Child Development.* New York, Wiley, 1967. 618p. biblio.

An explorative survey in depth of seven major theories of child development, with an emphasis on methodological and philosophical backgrounds and a critical evaluation of each. A noteworthy book for graduate or advanced courses.

307 Barker, Roger G., and others, eds. *Child Behavior and Development: a Course of Representative Studies.* New York, McGraw-Hill, 1943, 652p. biblio.

Reports of selected studies, some of which are classics otherwise hard to find, each describing fully a particular investigation and giving the processes as well as the products of research.

308 Breckinridge, Marian E., and Murphy, Margaret N. *Growth and Development of the Young Child,* 7th ed. Philadelphia, Saunders, 1963. 564p. biblio.

Covers birth to age five in a discussion of the interrelationships in a child's physical and psychological development and in his family life.

309   Carmichael, Leonard, ed. *Manual of Child Psychology*, 3rd ed. New York, Wiley, 1962. 1295p. biblio.

An excellent collection of research-based articles on important aspects of normal growth and development.

310   Erikson, Erik H. *Identity and the Life Cycle: Selected Papers*. New York, International Universities, 1959. 171p. biblio.

Three papers dealing with psycho-social development, focusing on the dynamics of the stages of the human life cycle as related to the social environment.

311   Freud, Anna. *Psychoanalysis for Teachers and Parents*. Boston, Beacon, 1960. 119p.

Four lectures, originally published in 1935, are devoted to a psychoanalytic reconstruction of childhood. Translated from the German.

312   Gesell, Arnold, and Ilg, Frances L. *Child Development: an Introduction to the Study of Human Growth*. New York, Harper, 1949. 475p. biblio.

A single volume edition that includes *Infant and Child in the Culture of Today* and *The Child from 5 to 10*, previously published separately. Based on Yale University's longitudinal studies, this is a report of the growth and development of the white middle-class American child. The handbook for parents until it was replaced by Dr. Spock.

313   _____, and Amatruda, C. S. *Developmental Diagnosis: Normal and Abnormal Child Development: Clinical Methods and Pediatric Applications*, 2nd ed. New York, Harper, 1947. 496p.

An excellent discussion of growth and development in the young child that, although oriented to pediatric clinical investigation, is a sound guide for the psychologist.

314   Hoffman, Martin L., and Lois W. *Review of Child Development Research*, 2 vols. New York, Russell Sage Foundation, 1964-66. biblio.

Planned as a continuing publication to disseminate the advances in scientific knowledge about children in such areas as pediatrics, social work, clinical psychology, nursery and elementary education, and child psychiatry.

315   Hurlock, Elizabeth B. *Child Development*, 4th ed. New York, McGraw-Hill, 1964. 776p. biblio.

Thorough coverage of all aspects of child development

with the addition, in this revision, of research findings in the area of child training, family relationships, emotional deprivation, social class differences, and social mobility.

316   _____. *Developmental Psychology*, 2nd ed. New York, McGraw-Hill, 1953. 556p. biblio.

A survey of the developmental changes of the total life span of the human being. Includes findings from older as well as recent studies.

317   Itard, Jean-Marc-Gaspard. *The Wild Boy of Aveyron.* New York, Appleton, 1962. 104p.

An absorbing account, translated from the French, of an early 19th century attempt to educate a 12 year old who had apparently never had any human contact. Of particular interest for its description of the development of the senses, the intellect, and the emotions.

318   Klein, Melanie. *The Psychoanalysis of Children.* New York, Grove, 1960. 393p. biblio.

A Freudian approach to child development and the treatment of psychopathology. A classic, first published in 1932 and translated from the German.

319   McCandless, Boyd R. *Children and Adolescents: Behavior and Development,* 2nd ed. New York, Holt, 1967. 671p. biblio.

With special emphasis on those aspects of child development that are pertinent to schooling, this new edition incorporates the latest research in the field. An excellent review of such topics as Piaget's theories, the middle-class teacher, the measurement of intelligence, and educational practices.

320   Martin, William E., and Stendler, Celia B., eds. *Readings in Child Development.* New York, Harcourt, 1954. 513p. biblio.

An excellent collection of readings on child growth and development that focus on the child's heritage, the society and culture into which he is born, and the influences of his life experiences.

321   Mead, Margaret, and Wolfenstein, Martha, eds. *Childhood in Contemporary Cultures.* Chicago, U of Chicago P, 1955. 473p. biblio.

The results of a study, part already published as the *Study of Culture at a Distance*, stressing the need to develop insight into child development and to use that insight in rearing children. Random sampling of other cultures.

322 Meyer, William J. *Developmental Psychology.* New York, CARE, 1964. 116p. biblio.

An eloquent and scholarly review of the important contemporary findings in child development with an assessment of their implications for the educative process.

323 Mussen, Paul H., and others. *Child Development and Personality,* 2nd ed. New York, Harper, 1963. 625p. biblio.

A revision of a basic, general text in child development. Reviews theory and research pertaining to all age levels through adolescence.

324 _____, ed. *Handbook of Research Methods in Child Development.* New York, Wiley, 1964. 1061p. biblio.

A compendium of articles concerned with methodology appropriate to research in the various areas of child development.

325 _____. *The Psychological Development of the Child.* Englewood Cliffs, N.J., Prentice Hall, 1963. 109p. biblio.

An introductory and succinct discussion with an emphasis on broad perspectives.

326 _____, and others, eds. *Readings in Child Development and Personality.* New York, Harper, 1965. 480p. biblio.

A collection of current research articles keyed to the themes of *Child Development and Personality* (#325) and designed to supplement it.

327 Olson, Willard C. *Child Development,* 2nd ed. Boston, Heath, 1959. 497p. biblio.

Most valuable for its presentation of an organismic age concept of the child. Emphasizes the reasons for self-selection in curriculum decisions.

328 Palermo, David S., and Lipsitt, Lewis P., eds. *Research Readings in Child Development.* New York, Holt, 1963. 572p.

A collection intended to exemplify various research approaches to the study of child behavior. Organized to a number of sections that deal with a variety of behavior phenomena, including discrimination, generalization, transposition, and motivation.

329 Piaget, Jean. *The Language and Thought of the Child,* 3rd rev. ed. New York, Humanities, 1959. 288p.

Published originally in French in 1926, this is an analysis of language that reveals the various stages of development and is based on research and studies of child logic and egocentric language.

330 Prescott, Daniel A. *The Child in the Educative Process.* New York, McGraw-Hill, 1957. 502p. biblio.

Establishes the thesis that learning, development, and adjustment are individual matters that take place in a group context and analyzes the knowledge and skills required by teachers to understand pupils as developing individuals.

331 *The Psychoanalytic Study of the Child.* Vol. 1-   1945- New York, International Universities.

An annual collection of original papers by psychoanalysts in the United States and England, centering on psychoanalytic hypotheses. The 1967 yearbook includes papers on problems of psychopathology and therapy as well as theoretical and clinical contributions.

332 Redl, Fritz, and Wattenberg, William W. *Mental Hygiene in Teaching,* 2nd ed. New York, Harcourt, 1959. 562p. biblio.

Fundamental principles of mental hygiene and their application in the classroom to help teachers guide young people.

333 Roach, Eugene G., and Kephart, Newell C. *The Purdue Perceptual-Motor Survey.* Columbus, Ohio, Merrill, 1966. 82p. biblio.

An exposition of techniques developed by the authors for surveying children's abilities and levels of development in perceptual-motor areas and the methods employable in evaluating development. A diagnostic follow-up of Kephart's theoretical position as presented in *The Slow Learner in the Classroom* (#2439) and of enormous potential.

334 Rosenblith, Judy F., and Allinsmith, W., eds. *The Causes of Behavior: Readings in Child Development and Educational Psychology,* 2nd ed. Boston, Allyn and Bacon, 1966. 608p.

A superior selection of a variety of approaches to understanding children. The final section deals with research and problems that have specific educational implications.

335   Sears, Robert R., and others. *Patterns of Child Rearing.* Evanston, Ill., Row Peterson, 1957. 549p. biblio.

    A report of how more than 350 American mothers bring up their preschool children, that, although not prescriptive, does relate practices to outcomes and methods to behavior and personality. Of particular interest are findings concerning effect of punishment on behavior.

336   Society for Research in Child Development. *Monographs.* v.1-   1935-   . Chicago, U of Chicago P.

    An important series of an interdisciplinary group composed of medical men, scientists, educators, and sociologists, which reflects the varied interests of society. There are now more than 100 monographs; they appear irregularly during each year and are primarily research studies. Recent titles: *Adult Status of Children with Contrasting Early Life Experiences,* (vol. 31, no. 3, series no. 105) by Harold M. Skeels, and *The Development of Conservation and Differentiation of Numbers,* (vol. 31, no. 6, series no. 108) by Herbert Zimiles.

337   Stendler, Celia B., ed. *Readings in Child Behavior and Development.* New York, Harcourt, 1964. 498p. biblio.

    A collection of recent and classic research studies covering various aspects of child and adolescent behavior.

338   Stevenson, Harold W., ed. *Child Psychology* (NSSE 62nd Yearbook, Part I). Chicago, U of Chicago P, 1963. 550p. biblio.

    A comprehensive picture of our present knowledge about the behavior and development of normal children and a synthesis of the findings of recent research in child psychology.

339   Stone, Lawrence J., and Church, Joseph. *Childhood and Adolescence: a Psychology of the Growing Person.* New York, Random, 1957. 456p. biblio.

    An excellent systematic, integrated, and interpretive description of child development. The facts are ordered and organized around the central concern of personality and subordinated to a concept about how people behave and develop.

340   Sullivan, Harry S. *The Interpersonal Theory of Psychiatry.* New York, Norton, 1953. 393p.

    Lectures by the influential and dynamic neo-Freudian

trace human development from infancy to adulthood and consider mental disorders in later life. Includes such familiar Sullivan characteristics as his use of an operational approach and field-theory concepts, his recognition of the analyst as a *participant* observer, and his use of concepts from cultural anthropology.

341 Thompson, George G. *Child Psychology: Growth Trends in Psychological Adjustment,* 2nd ed. Boston, Houghton Mifflin, 1962. 714p. biblio.

An integrated interpretation of research literature on child growth and behavior, summarizing relevant studies and covering the newborn infant, maturation, learning, psychological adjustment, and sensory and perceptual development.

342 Watson, Robert I. *Psychology of the Child,* 2nd ed. New York, Wiley, 1965. 635p. biblio.

A basic introductory text that deals with the principles of individual development in infancy and childhood and discusses behavior, social learning theory, psychoanalytic theory, and neo-Freudian interpretations.

343 Watts, A. F. *The Language and Mental Development of Children: an Essay in Educational Psychology.* London, Harrap, 1944. 354p. biblio.

By means of objective tests specifically designed for the purpose, explores the part played by language in the mental development of English children, revealing children's efforts to adapt themselves to the world by means of language.

344 Whiting, John W., and Child, Irvin L. *Child Training and Personality: a Cross-Cultural Study.* New Haven, Yale UP, 1953. 353p. biblio.

Based on a cross-cultural comparison of 75 societies, this draws on modern behavior theory, psychoanalysis, and cultural anthropology to investigate variations in child training practices, fixation, guilt, fear, and customs relating to illness.

345 Young, Leontine. *Life Among the Giants.* New York, McGraw-Hill, 1966. 193p.

For a greater understanding of children's feelings, needs, interests, hopes, dreams, and worries, this is an adult's journey back to childhood. Well-written and illuminating.

History

346   Aries, Philippe. *Centuries of Childhood.* New York, Knopf, 1962. 447p. biblio.

A unique facet of social history, translated from the French, which is a sociological, historical study of the place of children, family relationships, and changing attitudes toward children. Material drawn from primary sources. Although the focus is French, the picture is applicable generally to Western culture.

CHILDREN'S LITERATURE

347   Arbuthnot, May H., comp. *The Arbuthnot Anthology of Children's Literature,* rev. ed. Chicago, Scott Foresman, 1961. 418p.

A large selection of poetry, folk and fairy tales, modern realistic stories, and biography, organized according to well-defined categories. Included is a brief, illustrated history of children's literature. A fine sourcebook.

348   ————. *Children and Books,* 3rd ed. Chicago, Scott Foresman, 1964. 688p. biblio.

A broad survey of literature for children as related to their emotional and intellectual needs. Includes historical backgrounds and brief author biographies to increase understanding of their writings. Modern and traditional prose and poetry examined for their intrinsic values and sound suggestions offered on how to teach literature to convey those values.

349   *Best Books for Children: a Catalog of 4000 Titles.* New York, Bowker, 1959-

Revised annually, this is a selected, briefly annotated list of books chosen for excellence, for long-sustained popularity, and for timeliness. Arranged by grade levels and subjects.

350   *Books for Children: 1960-1965.* Chicago, ALA, 1966. 448p.

A classified, annotated list of the 3,068 titles recommended for library purchase in the Children's Books section of *The Booklist and Subscription Books Bulletin* from September 1960 to August 1965. Includes adult and young adult titles suitable for children. Grade levels are indicated. Updated by an annual supplement.

351 *Children's Catalog: a Catalog of 4214 Selected Books for Public and School Libraries,* 10th ed. New York, Wilson, 1967. 1015p.

Updated by annual supplements, this classified catalog has author, title, subject, and analytic indexes as well as a listing of books by grade levels. Includes a directory of publishers.

352 Crosby, Muriel, ed. *Reading Ladders for Human Relations,* 4th ed. Washington, ACE, 1963. 242p.

An excellent annotated list of over 1,000 books for young people developed around six human relations themes and arranged in order of maturity and difficulty.

353 Duff, Annis. *A Bequest of Wings: a Family's Pleasures with Books.* New York, Viking, 1944. 191p. biblio.

A description of a family's adventures in reading with important implications for educators. Excellent list of recommended books and records, unfortunately somewhat dated.

354 Eakin, Mary K., comp. *Good Books for Children: a Selection of Outstanding Children's Books Published 1950-65,* 3rd ed. Chicago, U of Chicago P, 1967. 407p.

Nearly 1,400 annotated titles, listed alphabetically by author. This revised edition excludes out-of-print books and adds 300 published from 1962 to 1965. Quality, appeal, and curriculum usage are among the criteria used in selection.

355 _____, comp. *Subject Index to Books for Intermediate Grades,* 3rd ed. Chicago, ALA, 1963. 308p.

356 _____, and Merritt, Eleanor, comps. *Subject Index to Books for Primary Grades,* 3rd ed. Chicago, ALA, 1967. 167p.

Of enormous use to the classroom teacher, especially those involved in individualized reading programs, as the books are not only arranged by subject but also have a grade level notation.

357 Fenner, Phyllis. *The Proof of the Pudding: What Children Read.* New York, Day, 1957. 246p.

An enthusiastic and discriminating contributor to the field of children's literature discusses some of the best liked books of all times, why a child likes them, and how old he is when he enjoys them. An introduction to popular authors and editions that includes some suggestions for reading aloud.

358 Fenwick, Sara I., ed. *A Critical Approach to Children's Literature*. Chicago, U of Chicago P, 1967. 129p.

A series of addresses delivered at the 31st Conference of the University of Chicago Graduate Library School by people from various related literary fields. Designed to widen the knowledge, sharpen the perceptions, and deepen the insights required to evaluate and interpret children's literature.

359 Georgiou, Constantine. *Children and Their Literature,* Englewood Cliffs, N.J., Prentice-Hall, 1968. 600p.

Focuses on the major divisions of universal literature and analyses and annotates carefully selected children's books within each division. Approached from a literary point of view, the text includes chapters on literary criticism, the history of writing for children, and criteria for evaluating children's books.

360 Haviland, Virginia, ed. *Children's Literature: a Guide to Reference Sources.* (LC) Washington, GPO, 1966. 341p.

An illustrated, annotated bibliography of books, articles and pamphlets, selected with reference to timeliness, excellence of presentation, or relevance to research. Divided into six major headings with a wide scope.

361 Hazard, Paul. *Books, Children, and Men,* 4th ed. Boston, Horn Book, 1960. 176p.

A French scholar pleads for more imaginative writing for children, more honesty, and less didacticism. A unique and refreshing book.

362 Huber, Miriam B., ed. *Story and Verse for Children,* 3rd ed. New York, Macmillan, 1965. 848p. biblio.

More than 500 carefully chosen selections from recognized classics and the best of contemporary children's books. Includes biographical sketches of authors and artists as well as critical and historical comments.

363 Huck, Charlotte S., and Young, Doris A. *Children's Literature in the Elementary School.* New York, Holt, 1961. 522p. biblio.

An attempt to integrate knowledge of child development, books, and the learning process. Discusses book selection in relation to growth patterns and provides a review of children's literature.

364 *Junior High School Catalog.* New York, Wilson, 1965. 768p.
A recent addition to the Wilson catalog family, this follows the familiar format: a classified listing of, in this case, 3,278 recommended titles, with author, subject, title, and analytic indexes. Annual supplements.

365 Larrick, Nancy. *A Teacher's Guide to Children's Books.* Columbus, Ohio, Merrill, 1960. 316p.
An effort to help teachers help children "find joy in good books," which reviews the interests of children and the books that meet their needs. Discusses ways to arouse interest and to relate books to personal and social growth. Includes annotated lists of books.

366 Meigs, Cornelia, and others. *A Critical History of Children's Literature: a Survey of Children's Books in English from Earliest Times to the Present.* New York, Macmillan, 1953. 624p. biblio.
An excellent history of juvenile literature that is a critical analysis of what has endured and why. Its only fault is a tendency to neglect or disparage books of questionable literary quality that children nevertheless have read and will continue to read with genuine pleasure.

367 Perkins, Ralph. *Book Selection Media: a Descriptive Guide to 170 Aids for Selecting Library Materials,* rev. ed. Champaign, Ill., NCTE, 1967. 168p.
An annotated list of good acquisition media for books for children, school and college libraries, and public libraries. Some editing faults but basically an excellent evaluative guide.

368 Pilgrim, Geneva H., and McAllister, Mariana K. *Books, Young People and Reading Guidance,* 2nd ed. New York, Harper, 1968. 235p.
The revisions simply update and improve an already excellent text whose primary purpose is to make enthusiastic readers of adolescents and help guide them toward maturity through reading. For all concerned with reading guidance.

369 Robinson, Evelyn R., ed. *Readings about Children's Literature.* New York, McKay, 1966. 431p. biblio.
Articles provide a comprehensive coverage of the subject.

370   *Senior High School Catalog*, 9th ed. New York, Wilson, 1967. 1044p.

This new edition of the *Standard Catalog for High School Libraries* picks up where the new *Junior High School Catalog* leaves off and is a classified listing of 4,231 titles for 10th through 12th grades. Includes adult titles for young people, author, title, and analytic indexes, and a directory of publishers. Five annual supplements are planned.

371   Smith, James S. *A Critical Approach to Children's Literature*. New York, McGraw-Hill, 1967. 442p. biblio.

A discussion of the differences and similarities between adult and children's literature that succeeds in avoiding the twin faults of indulgence and being patronizing.

372   Smith, Lillian H. *The Unreluctant Years: a Critical Approach to Children's Literature*. Chicago, ALA, 1953. 193p.

A consideration of books for children as literature and some of the standards by which they can be judged with discussion of various types of children's literature, such as the fairy tale, epics and sagas, picture books, historical fiction, and books of knowledge.

373   Spache, George D. *Good Reading for Poor Readers*, rev. ed. Scarsdale, N.Y., Garrard, 1966. 206p.

An invaluable source of assistance for teacher and librarian as the selections are those that have been used successfully with reluctant readers. Helpful prefatory comments and mostly annotated titles.

374   Strang, Ruth M., and others. *Gateways to Readable Books: an Annotated, Graded List of Books in Many Fields for Adolescents Who Find Reading Difficult*, 4th ed. New York, Wilson, 1966. 245p.

A comprehensive listing of more than 1,000 titles by subject, with helpful and useful additional material including bibliographies, lists of reading textbooks, books in series, adapted and simplified editions, magazines and newspapers, and simple dictionaries. Indexed for grade level of reading difficulty.

375   Voigt, Melvin J., and Treyz, Joseph H. *Books for College Libraries: a Selected List of Approximately 53,400 Titles Based on the Initial Selection Made for the University of California's New Campuses Program and Selected with the*

Assistance of College Teachers, Librarians, and Other Advisers. Chicago, ALA, 1967. 1056p.

Actually 53,410 titles are included in this mandatory source of recommended books. A monumental work that is an invaluable bibliographic tool.

History

376 Smith, Dora V. *Fifty Years of Children's Books, 1910-1960: Trends, Backgrounds, Influences.* Champaign, Ill., NCTE, 1963. 149p. biblio.

A review of developments in the creation of what has become a highly specialized body of literature described in relation to children's learning, education's function, and changing concepts and ideals.

CHURCH AND STATE
see also LAWS AND LEGISLATION

377 Brickman, William W., and Lehrer, Stanley, eds. *Religion, Government and Education.* New York, Society for the Advancement of Education, 1961. 292p.

Focuses on the issues involved in church-state school cooperation to encourage a more rational approach to solving a dilemma charged with emotionalism.

378 Butts, R. Freeman. *The American Tradition in Religion and Education.* Boston, Beacon, 1950. 230p. biblio.

Designed to provide historical perspective upon which to base a sound public policy. The widespread debate rampant in 1950 continues, and although some issues seem settled for the moment, the book is still pertinent.

379 Douglas, William O. *The Bible and the Schools.* Boston, Little Brown, 1966. 65p.

An examination of the historical, legal, and philosophical aspects of the separation of church and state and specifically related to the schools.

380 Duker, Sam. *The Public Schools and Religion: the Legal Context.* New York, Harper, 1966. 238p. biblio.

A discussion of well selected excerpts from 12 precedent-making decisions of the U.S. Supreme Court pertaining to religion and the public schools. Unresolved issues of interest to scholars and administrators are included in this accurate, objective, and well-written book.

381 Educational Policies Commission. *Public Education and the Future of America.* Washington, NEA, 1955. 98p.

A discussion of the development of American education with almost exclusive reference to the public school. By emphasizing the belief that a democratic society can best be achieved through the medium of a school system common to all, it added fuel to the church-state controversy.

382 Hook, Sidney. *Religion in a Free Society.* Lincoln, U of Nebraska P, 1967. 120p.

A philosopher who believes in speaking to non-philosophers lectures to the U.S. Supreme Court with taste, historical perspective and a sense of humor. Education, he argues, and not the conflicting decisions and ever-changing composition of the Court, should preserve state neutrality in religion.

383 Oaks, Dallin H., ed. *The Wall Between Church and State.* Chicago, U of Chicago P, 1963. 179p. biblio.

Articles on specific facets of state-church relationships, with critical analyses and evaluations of legal aspects.

History

384 Lannie, Vincent P. *Public Money and Parochial Education: Bishop Hughes, Governor Seward, and the New York School Controversy.* Cleveland, Case-Western Reserve UP, 1968. 375p. biblio.

A study of an unsuccessful attempt by Roman Catholics in the 1840's to obtain public funds for parochial schools.

385 Wilson, John F. *The Church and State in American History.* Boston, Heath, 1965. 224p. biblio.

Emphasizes the interrelationships of the political, legal, and religious phenomena and the interpretation to be placed upon these phenomena.

CHURCH-SPONSORED SCHOOLS

386 Friedlander, Anna F. *The Shared Time Strategy: Prospects and Trends in the Growing Partnership between Public and Church Schools,* St. Louis, Concordia, 1966. 87p. biblio.

Believing that shared time is the formula by which federal, state, and local governments can best aid parochial and other nonpublic school students without directly aiding those schools, the author raises some pertinent questions and provides basic information for decision-making.

387   Greeley, Andrew M., and Rossi, Peter H. *The Education of Catholic Americans.* Chicago, Aldine, 1966. 368p.

A report of research sponsored by the USOE and the Carnegie Foundation. Focuses on issues that concern both defenders and critics of Catholic schools. Both will find support for their views, as data have been examined as objectively as possible and strengths and weaknesses are indicated.

388   Hassenger, Robert, ed. *The Shape of Catholic Education.* Chicago, U of Chicago P, 1967. 378p.

A group of young Catholic intellectuals investigates major criticisms of American Catholic higher education. Studies range from the historical reason for the existence of Catholic schools to speculation about their future and deal with academic freedom and the attitudes of faculty and students.

389   Neuwien, Reginald A., ed. *Catholic Schools in Action: a Report.* Notre Dame, Ind., U of Notre Dame P, 1966. 328p.

A report of a study sponsored by the Carnegie Corporation. An objective view and a study in depth of the Catholic school, achieved through questionnaires (included in the Appendix) to which 92 per cent of the elementary schools and 84 per cent of the secondary schools responded. Coverage of goals, enrollment, staff, teacher preparation, religious instruction, and student and parent attitudes and opinions.

390   Pattillo, Manning M., Jr., and MacKenzie, Donald M. *Church-Sponsored Higher Education in the United States.* Washington, ACE, 1966. 309p.

This Report of the Danforth Commission is an assessment, with recommendations, of the position and purpose in American higher education of church-affiliated colleges and universities. Based on a study of 817 Christian and Jewish institutions, of which 50 were studied in depth.

391   Shuster, George N. *Catholic Education in a Changing World.* New York, Holt, 1968. 224p.

A companion commentary to Neuwien and, to a lesser extent, Greeley and Rossi. Examines the historical roots of American Catholic schools, their aims, quality of instruction, the status of religious vs. lay faculty, problems in higher education, and federal aid to church schools.

392 Stanford, Edward V. *A Guide to Catholic College Administration.* Westminster, Md., Newman, 1965. 231p.

A useful handbook giving full attention to the technical, nonacademic aspects of college administration and perhaps insufficient attention to leadership and planning. The clear discussion of administrative and community relationships within the Catholic college will provide non-Catholics unfamiliar with ecclesiastical terminology with insights into their intricacies.

393 Treacy, John P., and others. *The Pastor and the School.* Milwaukee, Bruce, 1966. 244p.

Several well-known Catholic educators contribute to a thorough study of the role of the pastor, who has canonical authority and responsibility for directing the parish school. Although focused on the pastor, this is an excellent handbook on the administration of parish schools.

394 Wicke, Myron F. *The Church-Related College.* New York, CARE, 1964. 116p. biblio.

An important, though dwindling, influence in American higher education is studied in relation to the secular institution. Marked differences are found between the two types of institutions as well as enormous diversity among church-related schools, which vary in control, objectives, programs, students, and faculties.

COLLECTIVE BARGAINING AND NEGOTIATIONS

395 Chamberlain, Neil W. *Collective Bargaining.* New York, McGraw-Hill, 1951. 534p.

The classic work. Covers the evolutionary aspects of the bargaining process and analytical and conceptual probing of the process as well as legal contributions, organizational aspects, the economic impact on society, and the politics of power relations.

396 Elam, Stanley M., and others, eds. *Readings on Collective Negotiations in Public Education.* Chicago, Rand McNally, 1967. 470p. biblio.

Forty-one carefully chosen articles from some prestigious

educational organizations with a wide range of viewpoint provide background on the development of collective negotiations as well as the specific bargaining process. Intended as a companion to #397.

397 Lieberman, Myron, and Moskow, Michael H. *Collective Negotiations for Teachers: an Approach to School Administration.* Chicago, Rand McNally, 1966. 745p. biblio.

A comprehensive handbook discussing history and current status. Presents positions of National Education Association and American Federation of Teachers but more closely reflects the latter's stand. Appendices of legislation, contracts, and documents.

398 Moskow, Michael H. *Teachers and Unions: the Applicability of Collective Bargaining to Public Education.* Philadelphia, Wharton School of Finance, U of Pennsylvania, 1966. 288p. biblio.

A clear and objective presentation of the facts and issues involved in the movement for collective determination of teacher wages and working conditions, a movement given impetus by the successful unionization of New York City teachers in 1961.

399 Stinnett, Timothy M., and others. *Professional Negotiations in Public Education.* New York, Macmillan, 1966. 309p. biblio.

A handbook covering history and status of negotiation and the role of the superintendent. Represents the position of the National Education Association. Includes sample legislation, contracts, and documents.

400 Walton, Richard E., and McKersie, Robert B., eds. *A Behavorial Theory of Labor Negotiations: an Analysis of a Social Interaction System.* New York, McGraw-Hill, 1965. 437p.

A theory applicable to general interactional systems, covering four aspects: distributive bargaining (competitive behavior), integrative bargaining (compromising and problem-solving behavior), attitudinal structuring (sentiment-building activities between the parties), and intra-organizational bargaining (maintenance behaviors).

History

401 Dulles, Foster R. *Labor in America: a History.* New York, Crowell, 1949. 402p. biblio.

A basic reader. Well-written, concise review of the American labor movement from Colonial times to the late 1940's.

COLLEGE ADMISSIONS

402 Bloom, Benjamin S., and Peters, F. R. *The Use of Academic Prediction Scales for Counseling and Selecting College Entrants.* New York, Free Press, 1961. 145p. biblio.

Deals with problem of academic standing. Variations in academic grades stem from at least three sources: errors in teacher judgments, differences among students in achievement and motivation, and difference in standards from teacher to teacher and school to school. Conclusions drawn regarding testing methodology and educational research.

403 Fuess, Claude M. *The College Board: Its First Fifty Years.* New York, Columbia UP, 1950. 222p.

A description of the founding, growth, development, and activities of the College Entrance Examination Board.

404 *They Went to College Early.* New York, FAE, 1957. 117p.

A report that concludes that early college admission of particularly able students can be advantageous. Based on the Program for Early Admission to College.

405 Thresher, B. Alden. *College Admissions and the Public Interest.* New York, CEEB, 1966. 93p. biblio.

An examination of the broad, social implications of the college admissions process as it affects the student, the college, and, in relation to talent supply and demand, society as a whole.

COLLEGE STUDENTS

406 Barry, Ruth E., and others. *Case Studies in College Student-Staff Relationships.* New York, TC, Columbia, 1956. 117p. biblio.

Twenty-two case studies presented with questions for discussion.

407 Brookover, Wilbur B. *The College Student.* New York CARE, 1965. 118p. biblio.

A sociological profile of today's college student—his attitudes, values, interests, and life goals.

408 Butz, Otto, ed. *To make a Difference: a Student Look at America: Its Values, Its Society, and Its Systems of Education.* New York, Harper, 1967. 174p.

A group of articulate young people criticize sharply the whole range of our social institutions and plead for humanity in an impersonal world. For students and the teachers and administrators who wish to understand them.

409 *Changing Patterns of Jewish Life on the Campus.* Washington, B'nai B'rith, 1961. 91p.

A symposium report on the future of the Hillel Foundation (an organization acting as a liason between the Jewish college student and the Jewish heritage, with many campus branches in the United States) in the light of the changing community.

410 Dennis, Lawrence F., and Kauffman, Joseph F., eds. *The College and the Student: an Assessment of Relationships and Responsibilities in Undergraduate Education, by Administrators, Faculty Members, and Public Officials.* Washington, ACE, 1966. 390p. biblio.

Except that students also contributed to this volume, the lengthy title is entirely accurate. An excellent, sound collection of up-to-date essays with a wide coverage of student interests and concerns.

411 Draper, Hal. *Berkeley: The New Student Revolt.* New York, Grove, 1965. 246p. biblio.

A somewhat student-oriented inspection of the commotion at Berkeley, with a step-by-step report of the preliminary problems, actions and reactions of students, faculty, and administration, and an analysis of the events. As this was a severe but not at all unique uprising, the book should provide some helpful insights.

412 Habein, Margaret L., ed. *Spotlight on the College Student.* Washington, ACE, 1959. 89p.

A report of a discussion by such men as Riesman, Jacob, and Sanford based on Jacob's *Changing Values in College*

(#415), which points to need for new approaches concerning student culture and capabilities, faculty values, and to understanding students.

413 Havemann, Ernest, and West, Patricia. *They Went to College: the College Graduate in America Today.* New York, Harcourt, 1952. 277p.

A survey of graduates to determine the effects of college education in all areas—social, economic, marital, political—of their lives, with comparisons among alumni of different types of programs. In many ways considerably out-of-date but still useful.

414 Hunt, Everett L. *The Revolt of the College Intellectual.* New York, Aldine, 1963. 172p. biblio.

A case study of Swarthmore College and its students in an attempt to describe its intellectual and emotional effect on personality growth.

415 Jacob, Philip E. *Changing Values in College: an Exploratory Study of the Impact of College Teaching.* New York, Harper, 1957. 174p. biblio.

A survey of the influence of social science courses on student values. Shows that most value changes occur outside of formal education and that little influence is exerted by course content, instructors, or methods of teaching.

416 Keniston, Kenneth. *The Uncommitted: Alienated Youth in American Society.* New York, Harcourt, 1965. 495p. biblio.

An inquiry into the root causes for alienation among youth who, presumably, have no apparent reasons for estrangement. Attempts to evaluate society psychologically to understand the social stresses of youth today.

417 Lipset, Seymour M., and Wolin, Sheldon S. *The Berkeley Student Revolt: Facts and Interpretations.* New York, Doubleday, 1965. 585p. biblio.

A collection of essays and documents attempting to convey the sense of the events on the Berkeley campus in 1964, when the student body defied the administration and, as a result, undergraduates across the country became the focus of attention and concern.

418   Lloyd-Jones, Esther M., and Estrin, Herman A., eds. *The American Student and His College.* Boston, Houghton Mifflin, 1967. 384p. biblio.

A collection of articles, primarily from newspapers, on current aspects of student concern, not including teaching and curriculum. Of importance especially to administrators and others involved with college students.

419   _____. *Social Competence and College Students* (Studies. Series VI, no. 3). Washington, ACE, 1940. 89p. biblio.

Emphasizes the importance of social development as a coordinate of the formal instructional program.

420   Lunn, Harry H., Jr. *The Students' Role in College Policy Making.* Washington, ACE, 1957. 100p. biblio.

In view of increasing student unrest today, this is a particularly apt report describing varying forms of student participation. Central to the approach is recognition of the individual student and the importance of a strong sense of the campus as a community.

421   Mallery, David. *Ferment on Campus: an Encounter with the New College Generation.* New York, Harper, 1966. 147p.

A seven-college survey of student attitudes on social, political, and academic questions. By means of student dialogue and author comments, topics of campus and world concern are considered, with the conclusion that present ferment is a hopeful sign, bringing youth to a new seriousness about and involvement with the world.

422   Morris, Richard T. *The Two-Way Mirror: National Status in Foreign Students' Adjustment.* Minneapolis, U of Minnesota P, 1960. 215p. biblio.

An exploration of the processes and determinants of adjustment, learning, and attitude formation in cross-cultural experience. Based on questionnaires sent to both graduate and undergraduate students from other countries studying in the United States, this points up difficulties and failures.

423   Newcomb, Theodore M., and others. *Persistence and Change: Bennington College and Its Students after Twenty-five Years.* New York, Wiley, 1967. 292p. biblio.

A restudy (see #424) of both the women and the college to determine whether the shifts in attitude have persisted and whether the college has changed with respect to its effect on student values.

424   _____. *Personality and Social Change: Attitude Formation in a Student Community.* New York, Dryden, 1943. 225p.

Public Affairs, of the effects of the college environment on student values, documenting attitude changes of prewar Bennington College women in the direction of greater liberalism.

A classic study, sponsored by the American Council on

425   Pervin, Lawrence A., and others, eds. *The College Dropout and the Utilization of Talent.* Princeton, N.J., Princeton UP, 1966. 260p.

The outgrowth of a 1964 conference that included participants from business, education, and medicine. An informative examination of the multi-faceted problems involved in avoiding the waste of talents of dropouts. A refreshing approach in which, however, the definition of dropout is perhaps too loose as it includes transfer students.

426   Raushenbush, Esther. *The Student and His Studies.* Middletown, Conn., Wesleyan UP, 1964. 185p.

An inspection in depth of the academic histories of four students, but primarily based on interviews with 170 students who face an increasingly competitive college atmosphere and who, according to this report, want most the time and opportunity for serious communication with the faculty.

427   Rivlin, Harry N., and others. *The First Years in College: Preparing Students for a Successful College Career.* Boston, Little Brown, 1965. 605p. biblio.

Hopefully helpful in a day when more students drop out of college than graduate. Leading scholars discuss the various disciplines in an effort to aid students to become familiar with them and their interrelationships.

428   Robinson, Francis P. *Effective Study,* rev. ed. New York, Harper, 1961. 278p. biblio.

An introduction to the techniques of effective study habits, which offers a basis for diagnosis and provides a means of recording progress.

429   Sanford, Nevitt, ed. *The American College: a Psychological and Sociological Interpretation of the Higher Learning.* New York, Wiley, 1962. 1,084p. biblio.

An analysis of college students—their culture, their performance, their interaction with educators—and the effects of education and its impact on society. The insights of the behavioral sciences are applied to the problems of learning and living in an academic community in a distinguished and important book.

430 ———, ed. *College and Character.* New York, Wiley, 1964. 308p.

A condensed version of *The American College* for the general reader as well as the specialist. Concerned with the student in relation to the college and recommends self-study by the colleges to improve their programs.

431 ———. *Where Colleges Fail: a Study of the Student as a Person.* San Francisco, Jossey-Bass, 1967. 229p. biblio.

Focusing on the student as a person rather than as an academic scholar, this points to the neglect of undergraduates, a failure to deal effectively with student discontent, and a failure to give sufficient attention to the long range effects of college education on the development of the student as a human being.

432 Wallace, Walter L. *Student Culture: Social Structure and Continuity in a Liberal Arts College.* Chicago, Aldine, 1966. 237p. biblio.

A sociological study of the assimilation of students into the culture of a small midwestern college. Socialization is rapid and appears to be transmission rather than re-creation of culture.

COMMUNITY COLLEGES see JUNIOR AND COMMUNITY COLLEGES

COMMUNITY ORGANIZATION

433 Dahl, Robert A. *Who Governs? Democracy and Power in an American City.* New Haven, Yale UP, 1961. 335p.

A classic on the pluralist approach to the study of community decision-making. Specific attention is given to public education in a discussion of the motivation of decision-making in New Haven.

434 Harper, Ernest B., and Dunham, Arthur, eds. *Community Organization in Action: Basic Literature and Critical Comments.* New York, Association, 1959. 543p.

Carefully selected and logically organized articles, many of them ephemeral materials otherwise not easily accessible. A useful reference work.

435   Hunter, Floyd. *Community Power Structure: a Study of Decision Makers.* Chapel Hill, U of North Carolina P, 1953. 297p. biblio.

A classic by the best known of the social scientists who study communities. A study of community decision-making, including methodology and a description of Regional City.

436   Vidich, Arthur J., and Bensman, Joseph. *Small Town and Mass Society: Class Power and Religion in a Rural Community.* New York, Doubleday, 1960. 329p.

A description of political interaction in a small town, with particular attention to education, religion, and social class.

COMPARATIVE EDUCATION
see also EDUCATION IN FOREIGN COUNTRIES

437   Bereday, George Z. *The Comparative Method in Education.* New York, Holt. 1964. 302p. biblio.

An introduction to a systematic study of comparative education by analysis of educational problems common to many systems.

438   Carmichael, Oliver C. *Universities: Commonwealth and American: a Comparative Study.* New York, Harper, 1959. 390p. biblio.

An attempt to show the depth as well as the breadth of higher education in a number of English-speaking countries. Britain, Canada, Australia, India, Pakistan, New Zealand, and the Union of South Africa are discussed and viewed as variations of a single system.

439   *A Collection of Excerpts and a Bibliography Relative to American Education and Certain Other Educational Systems.* (LC, Legislative Reference Service) Washington, GPO, 1958. 52p.

Prepared at the request of Senator Karl E. Mundt for the Second Session of the 85th Congress (Document no. 109), this is not notable for its excerpts—rather dull bits of speeches and magazine articles—but for its bibliography, which is indeed a notable listing.

440 Cramer, John F., and Browne, George S. *Contemporary Education: a Comparative Study of National Systems.* New York, Harcourt, 1956. 637p. biblio.

A study of the successes and failures of educational systems in other nations, which aims at a better understanding of one's own national system and the realization that educational dilemmas are not confined to any one country.

441 Foshay, Arthur W., and others. *Educational Achievements of 13-Year Olds in 12 Countries.* Hamburg, UNESCO Institute for Education, 1962. 68p.

Report of an international research project, 1959-1961, having the double purpose of throwing light on research in comparative education and of discerning patterns of intellectual functioning in certain basic subjects under varying conditions. Results are little more than suggestive but offer encouragement for future research.

442 Hans, Nicholas A. *Comparative Education: a Study of Educational Factors and Traditions,* 3rd ed. London, Routledge and Paul, 1967. 334p. biblio.

Defines comparative education and describes its scope. Discusses the natural, religious, and secular factors affecting education in several countries, democratic and not.

443 _____. *The Principles of Educational Policy: a Study in Comparative Education,* 2nd ed. London, King, 1933. 276p. biblio.

An attempt to summarize the results of education legislation in the larger countries and to evolve a system in conformity with a democratic state.

444 Holmes, Brian. *Problems in Education: a Comparative Approach.* New York, Humanities, 1965. 326p. biblio.

A study of methodology in comparative education. The conceptual framework is based largely on the writings of John Dewey and K. R. Popper. Includes national case studies of the U.S., England and Wales, U.S.S.R., and Japan.

445 Kandel, Isaac L. *The New Era in Education: a Comparative Study.* Boston, Houghton Mifflin, 1955. 388p.

A contribution to an understanding of current trends in education and the influences that have produced them, with reference to England, France, Russia, and the United States.

446 Kazamias, Andreas M., and Massialas, Byron G. *Tradition and Change in Education: a Comparative Study.* Englewood Cliffs, N.J., Prentice-Hall, 1965. 182p. biblio.

Includes discussion of comparative education as a field of study and of ancient, primitive, and Western and non-Western contemporary societies in an attempt to shed light on some substantive issues and problems in education and on the nature and scope of comparative education.

447 King, Edmund J. *Other Schools and Ours: a Comparative Study for Today,* 3rd ed. New York, Holt, 1967. 360p. biblio.

A comparison of social and educational thought and of school systems, focusing on problems in education by means of case studies. Reviews and analyzes recent world trends.

448 ———. *World Perspectives in Education.* Indianapolis, Bobbs Merrill, 1962. 380p. biblio.

Comparative education with a problems approach. Selects some perennial educational concerns and illustrates them with international examples.

449 Mallinson, Vernon. *An Introduction to the Study of Comparative Education,* 2nd ed. New York, Macmillan, 1960. 257p. biblio.

Educational policy and practice in contemporary Western Europe traced on a comparative basis. Explores how and why problems common to all are being tackled in different ways and with what results in Scandinavia, the Lowlands, France, Germany, and Italy.

450 Meyer, Adolph E. *The Development of Education in the Twentieth Century,* 2nd ed. Englewood Cliffs, N.J., Prentice-Hall, 1949. 609p. biblio.

An examination, from a comparative viewpoint, of the important individuals and developments in the modernizing of education and the educational systems of the larger Western nations.

451 Moehlman, Arthur H., and Roucek, Joseph S., eds. *Comparative Education.* New York, Dryden, 1952. 630p. biblio.

A collection of essays describing education in this country and various countries in Europe, Africa, Asia, and South America.

452 _____. *Comparative Educational Systems.* New York, CARE, 1963. 113p. biblio.

Explores certain basic questions essential to the understanding of educational systems as instruments of national policy. Investigates the factors shaping education, the principal trends in the development of systems, and the strengths and weaknesses of educational systems in various cultures.

453 Reller, Theodore L., and Morphet, Edgar L., eds. *Comparative Educational Administration.* Englewood Cliffs, N.J., Prentice-Hall, 1962. 438p. biblio.

Two authorities on educational developments outside of the United States identify and discuss major trends in organization and administration in other countries. Nations included represent varying philosophies and ways of dealing with educational problems.

454 Rickover, Hyman G. *Swiss Schools and Ours: Why Theirs Are Better.* Boston, Little Brown, 1962. 219p.

The controversial Admiral writes with vigor and frankness about the weaknesses of our educational system. He examines education in Switzerland in the belief that there are lessons for us in certain aspects of the Swiss system, particularly in their serious attitude toward education.

455 Sargent, John, ed. *Education and Society: Some Studies of Education Systems in Europe and America.* London, Batchworth, 1955. 176p. biblio.

Selections by acknowledged authorities with firsthand knowledge and experience offer concise descriptions of widely differing educational systems.

456 Smith, Henry L. *Comparative Education.* Bloomington, Ind., Educational Publications, 1941. 529p. biblio.

The educational systems of England, France, Germany, Italy, Russia, China, Japan, and the United States are explored in an attempt to reveal the relationship of education to the way of life of a people. Discusses the use of education in mapping out and developing national destiny.

457 Thut, I. N., and Adams, Don. *Educational Patterns in Contemporary Societies.* New York, McGraw-Hill, 1964. 494p. biblio.

A scholarly description of educational systems as they

function in a variety of cultural settings, including representative Western and Oriental patterns as well as those of newly emerging nations.

History

458   Fraser, Stewart. *Jullien's Plan for Comparative Education, 1816-1817*. New York, TC, Columbia, 1964. 147p. biblio.

The first fully annotated and analyzed edition in English of a historic classic in comparative education. Jullien proposed the establishment of an institute that would standardize teaching methods throughout Europe, using only the best practice, instructors, and texts. Includes an extensive pedagogical questionnaire drawn up by Jullien.

459   Kandel, Isaac L. *Comparative Education*. Boston, Houghton Mifflin, 1933. 922p. biblio.

A classic contribution to the philosophy of education in the light of both theory and practice in England, France, Germany, Italy, Russia, and the United States.

460   _____. *Essays in Comparative Education*. New York, TC, Columbia, 1930. 235p.

Lectures and articles on various phases of educational development, viewed from the comparative standpoint by a pioneer in the field.

461   Monroe, Paul. *Essays in Comparative Education: Republished Papers*, 2 vols., New York, TC, Columbia, 1932.

A collection of papers, many previously published elsewhere, republished as a record of changing conditions in the field of education. An evaluation of educational organizations and procedures based on the American experience and world-wide tendencies. The papers date from 1913-1931.

462   Sandiford, Peter, ed. *Comparative Education: Studies of the Educational Systems of Six Modern Nations*. Toronto, Dent, 1918. 500p. biblio.

Essays by five of the leaders of the time in the field analyze the factors determining the character of educational institutions of the United States, Germany, England, France, Canada, and Denmark. Educational principles and social, political, and economic factors are covered in a book that was important in its time and now has historic interest.

463   Ulich, Robert. *The Education of Nations: a Comparison in Historical Perspective.* Cambridge, Harvard UP, 1961. 325p. biblio.

Contributes to an understanding of the forces that have molded the educational ideals and systems of a number of nations. The combination of historical and comparative approach reveals many similarities in Western nations.

COMPOSITION see WRITING AND COMPOSITION

COMPUTERS IN EDUCATION
see also RESEARCH METHODS
TEACHING MACHINES

464   Bushnell, Donald D. *The Role of the Computer in Future Instructional Systems.* Washington, NEA, 1963. 70p. (Available from Johnson Reprint, New York.)

Descriptions of computer fundamentals, computer-based teaching, information retrieval in education, computer-based simulation, and the automated classroom of the System Development Corporation.

465   Caffrey, John, and Mosmann, Charles J. *Computers on Campus.* Washington, ACE, 1967. 207p. biblio.

A penetrating analysis, for the administrator, of the problems and issues associated with computer applications. A comprehensive study of the computer and its capabilities as an aid to efficient and effective administration, as a professional tool, as an aid to instruction and learning, and as a model of automata that will increasingly affect society. Glossary of technical terms.

466   Coulson, John E., ed. *Programmed Learning and Computer-Based Instruction.* New York, Wiley, 1962. 306p. biblio.

A collection of papers from the 1961 Conference on the Application of Digital Computers to Automated Instruction, on three topics: theory and experimentation in programed learning, computer-based instructional systems, and computer technology in automated teaching.

467   Crowley, Thomas H. *Understanding Computers.* New York, McGraw-Hill, 1967. 142p.

For the neophyte, educator or not, as technical detail is not stressed and explanations are clear and comprehensible.

468   Fuller, R. Buckminster. *Education Automation: Freeing the Scholar to Return to His Studies.* Carbondale, Southern Illinois UP, 1962. 88p.

A contemporary genius speculates on some of the potential for education after analyzing many of our current short-comings. A bit out of his field but stimulating and important.

469   Gerard, Ralph W., and others, eds. *Computers and Education.* New York, McGraw-Hill, 1967. 252p.

The report of a University of California conference. Covers learning and the technical aspects of computers, computer-aided learning, library storage of materials, the use of computers in university and college administration, and the establishment of university computerized networks.

470   Goodlad, John I., and others. *Computers and Information Systems.* New York, Harcourt, 1966. 152p. biblio.

A description for the uninitiated educator of the workings of computers and electronic machines and their present and potential applications in the schools.

471   Grossman, Alvin, and Howe, Robert L. *Data Processing for Educators.* Chicago, Aldine, 1965. 362p.

Most suitable as an introductory work for administrators and apprentice computer specialists in education. Details of computer mechanics and operation presented with pictures, diagrams, and samples of computer forms and reports. Based primarily on projects in California and other states.

472   Hirsch, Werner Z., ed. *Inventing Education for the Future.* San Francisco, Chandler, 1967. 384p.

A compilation of papers presented at the Educational Innovations Seminar at UCLA, involving scholars from a variety of fields. Coverage includes an overview of educational innovations, a study of the future and the implications for education, and some description of future potential, including the use of computers.

473   Kaimann, Richard A., and Marker, Robert W., eds. *Educational Data Processing: New Dimensions and Prospects.* Boston, Houghton Mifflin, 1967. 326p.

Over four dozen superior essays tackle everything from basic installation to integrated data banks. A high standard of authority for those concerned with judicious use of teacher energy.

474 Loughary, John W. *Man-Machine Systems in Education.* New York, Harper, 1966. 242p. biblio.

An introductory view of the potential use of computers in education. A man-machine system is defined as an integration of the two, producing a total greater than both parts. Useful in spite of its emphasis on administrative functions in relation to computers, with a corresponding lack of emphasis on the use of computers in teaching and learning.

CORE CURRICULUM

475 Faunce, Roland C., and Bossing, Nelson L. *Developing the Core Curriculum,* 2nd ed. Englewood Cliffs, N.J., Prentice-Hall, 1958. 386p. biblio.

It is hard to tell whether this book is of potential use currently or simply of historic interest as an example of a popular innovation that faded away in the face of an increasing emphasis on subject learning.

476 Lurry, Lucile L., and Alberty, Elsie J. *Developing a High School Core Program.* New York, Macmillan, 1957. 297p. biblio.

A plea for the reorganization of the high school on the basis of the core program, whose essence is concern for the worth of the individual, the value of the cooperative process, and the use of intelligence in the solution of common problems.

COUNSELING AND PSYCHOTHERAPY
see also GUIDANCE AND COUNSELING IN EDUCATION

477 Brammer, Lawrence M., and Shostrom, Everett L. *Therapeutic Psychology: Fundamentals of Counseling and Psychotherapy.* Englewood Cliffs, N.J., Prentice-Hall, 1960. 447p. biblio.

An advanced text describing methods of personal counseling and clinical psychology. Includes excerpts from case histories illustrating how techniques have developed from a study of non-pathological clients.

478   Cottle, William C., and Downie, Norville M. *Procedures and Preparation for Counseling*. Englewood Cliffs, N.J., Prentice-Hall, 1960. 330p. biblio.

A collation of information on interviewing and the preparation of counselors, which summarizes and reviews tools and techniques and discusses the use of statistics in the interpretation of client data.

479   Klapman, Jacob W. *Group Psychotherapy: Theory and Practice*, 2nd ed. New York, Grune and Stratton, 1959. 301p. biblio.

The methods and techniques of group psychotherapy and their application to minimal, moderate, and severe personality disorders. Discusses dynamics and assesses this form of psychotherapy.

480   Krumboltz, John D., ed. *Revolution in Counseling: Implications of Behavioral Science*. Boston, Houghton Mifflin, 1966. 121p. biblio.

The papers of the 1965 Cubberly Conference, which are a revolutionary attempt to propose systematically the application of behaviorism, and particularly of operant conditions, to the counseling process.

481   McGowan, John F., and Schmidt, Lyle D., eds. *Counseling: Readings in Theory and Practice*. New York, Holt, 1962. 623p. biblio.

Developments, techniques, and basic issues for students in counseling programs.

482   Patterson, Cecil H. *Counseling the Emotionally Disturbed*. New York, Harper, 1958. 458p. biblio.

A thorough coverage of all aspects of counseling the emotionally disturbed, including the nature and extent of disturbance, rehabilitation, the counselor, the selection of clients, the counseling process, and the training and employment of the emotionally disturbed.

483   _____. *Theories of Counseling and Psychotherapy*. New York, Harper, 1966. 518p. biblio.

A wide-ranging, clearly written survey of current theories with the greatest emphasis on the rational and learning approaches. Of particular merit is the discussion summarizing the similarities and differences among various theories.

484 Patterson, Charles H. *Counseling and Psychotherapy: Theory and Practice*. New York, Harper, 1959. 322p. biblio.

Text for an advanced course in counseling individuals with general personal, social, or emotional problems. A systematic point of view based upon phenomenological psychology and client-centered therapy.

485 Rogers, Carl R. *Client-Centered Therapy: Its Current Practice, Implications, and Theory*. Boston, Houghton Mifflin, 1951. 560p. biblio.

Clear exposition of the procedures by means of which individuals may be assisted through counseling to achieve for themselves new and more effective adjustments. Client-centered, non-directive counseling approach is discussed and evaluated with reference to basic philosophy.

486 _____. *Counseling and Psychotherapy*. Boston, Houghton Mifflin, 1942. 750p. biblio.

A practical book representing the author's own viewpoint and conviction that counseling can be a knowable, predictable, understandable process that can be learned, tested, refined, and improved.

487 _____. *On Becoming a Person: a Therapist's View of Psychotherapy*. Boston, Houghton Mifflin, 1961. 420p. biblio.

A collection of the author's papers that discuss his philosophy of the individual in relation to living, the role of the therapist, and the implications of the behavioral sciences.

488 Rosenbaum, Max, and Berger, Milton M., eds. *Group Psychotherapy and Group Function*. New York, Basic, 1963. 690p. biblio.

A collection of 51 papers having two aims: to give some idea of the vastness and historical roots of group psychotherapy and to stimulate an exchange of experience. Discusses the group function, the relation between group theory and therapy, and the training of therapists.

489 Sundberg, Norman D., and Tyler, Leona E. *Clinical Psychology: an Introduction to Research and Practice*. New York, Appleton, 1962. 564p. biblio.

An organized presentation of clinical inquiry and practice, introducing the student to the kind of thinking he can apply to the patients and situations with which he will work.

490 Thorne, Frederick C. *Principles of Personality Counseling: an Eclectic Viewpoint.* Brandon, Vt., Journal of Clinical Psychology, 1950. 491p. biblio.

An attempt to stimulate a comprehensive re-evaluation of the whole problem of the application of clinical psychology to the field of counseling and psychotherapy. Raises such controversial points as the role of self-control and of the intellect in the causation and treatment of personality disorders.

491 Tyler, Leona E. *The Work of the Counselor,* 2nd ed. New York, Appleton, 1961. 327p. biblio.

A book with theoretical depth and practical utility, covering the counselor's function, the use of records, tests and occupational information, psychotherapy, and decision-making interviews. Summaries and evaluation of research material at the end of each chapter.

CREATIVITY

see also **ART EDUCATION**
POETRY
WRITING AND COMPOSITION

492 Anderson, Harold H., ed. *Creativity and Its Cultivation.* New York, Harper, 1959. 293p. biblio.

A collection of 15 addresses presented at the Interdisciplinary Symposia at Michigan State University. Stimulating discussions from a variety of points of view.

493 Andrews, Gladys. *Creative Rhythmic Movement for Children.* Englewood Cliffs, N.J., Prentice-Hall, 1954. 198p. biblio.

Develops the thesis that the conditions necessary for experiencing creativity in movement are similar to the conditions essential for creativity in all areas of living. Stress is placed on ways of assisting children to think for themselves.

494 Getzels, Jacob W., and Jackson, Philip W. *Creativity and Intelligence: Explorations with Gifted Students.* New York, Wiley, 1962. 293p. biblio.

A forward thrust into the area of the relationship between what we have generally been calling intelligence and the specific trait of creativity. The findings raise important questions about some assumptions under which our schools have been operating.

495   Gowan, John C., and others, eds. *Creativity: Its Educational Implications*. New York, Wiley, 1967. 336p. biblio.

Thirty-six readings on the theory, research, and educational applications of what is known about creativity. A highly valuable collection, whose suggestions for developing creativity are invaluable. Chapter on research is significant.

496   Gruber, Howard E., and others, eds. *Contemporary Approaches to Creative Thinking*. New York, Atherton, 1962. 223p.

Papers of a 1958 symposium held at the University of Colorado. Each author focuses on a particular area in discussing aspects and methods.

497   Kagan, Jerome, comp. *Creativity and Learning*. Boston, Houghton Mifflin, 1967. 289p. biblio.

A collection of 16 articles by scholars in several disciplines, focusing on creativity in relation to science and to education.

498   Lehman, Harvey C. *Age and Achievement*. Princeton, N.J., Princeton UP, 1953. 358p. biblio.

A discussion of creativity with a plea for special attention to the education problems of the gifted, which sets forth the relationship between youth and creative performance.

499   Mearns, Hughes. *Creative Power: the Education of Youth in the Creative Arts*, rev. ed. New York, Dover, 1958. 272p.

A genuinely important book, a classic that presents challenging techniques for stimulating and releasing the creative power in young people.

500   Osborn, Alexander F. *Applied Imagination: Principles and Procedures of Creative Thinking*. New York, Scribner, 1953. 317p.

An examination of brainstorming and its implications for creative thinking.

501   Parnes, Sidney J., and Harding, Harold F., eds. *A Source Book for Creative Thinking*. New York, Scribner, 1962. 393p. biblio.

A collection of 29 articles and addresses and more than 75 research summaries concerned with creative thinking and creative problem-solving, especially as it concerns education. A fine resource with an excellent annotated bibliography.

502 Stein, Morris I., and Heinze, Shirley J., eds. *Creativity and the Individual: Summaries of Selected Literature in Psychology and Psychiatry.* New York, Free Press, 1960. 428p.

An annotated bibliography on the creative process, directed at both the academic and the business world. Includes books on the creative process in general, as well as in relation to various art forms, and on such factors as heredity, the nervous system, age, early experience, religion, and cognition.

503 Taylor, Calvin W., ed. *Creativity: Progress and Potential.* New York, McGraw-Hill, 1964. 241p. biblio.

A stock-taking report that is, in effect, the Fourth Utah Conference on the Identification of Creative Scientific Talent. Contains a summary of research findings in creativity to indicate promising leads and urgent needs.

504 _____, and Williams, Frank E., eds. *Instructional Media and Creativity.* New York, Wiley, 1966. 397p. biblio.

The proceedings of the Sixth Utah Conference in which behavioral scientists and specialists in the audiovisual field combine talents to discuss basic problems in teaching for creativity and the ways in which films and television can be useful in such teaching.

505 _____, and Barron, Frank, eds. *Scientific Creativity: Its Recognition and Development.* New York, Wiley, 1963. 419p. biblio.

A collection of 31 research papers from the First, Second, and Third Research Conferences on the Identification of Creative Scientific Talent. They discuss the fundamental nature of scientific creativity in an effort to develop means of measuring and of nurturing it with appropriate educational programs.

506 _____, ed. *Widening Horizons in Creativity.* New York, Wiley, 1964. 466p.

The papers of the Fifth Utah Conference on Creativity, which report on studies of the creative process, discuss education and the development of creativity, consider criteria and prediction, and examine creativity in such fields and settings as architecture, industry, and public relations.

507 Torrance, E. Paul. *Guiding Creative Talent.* Englewood Cliffs, N.J., Prentice-Hall, 1962. 278p. biblio.

A research-based discussion of highly creative children. Presents materials useful in guiding a wide range of creative talent at all ages and educational levels.

508 _____. *Rewarding Creative Behavior: Experiments in Classroom Creativity.* Englewood Cliffs, N.J., Prentice-Hall, 1965. 353p. biblio.

A discussion of creative behavior, treating the encouragement of it and with developing means of dealing with the problems related to rewarding it. Describes studies to measure creative behavior, analyzing and evaluating the findings, and the consequent potential for practical application.

CURRICULUM

509 Alberty, Harold B., and Elsie J. *Reorganizing the High School Curriculum,* 3rd ed. New York, Macmillan, 1962. 512p. biblio.

Designed to aid in understanding and interpreting the conflicts and issues in the present educational scene and in developing a consistent point of view toward them.

510 Alexander, William M., ed. *Changing Curriculum Content.* (ASCD) Washington, NEA, 1964. 26p.

The report of a 1963 conference that attempts to discover ways staff members and curriculum workers can complement and assist each other in modifying the curriculum.

511 _____, ed. *The Changing Secondary School Curriculum: Readings.* New York, Holt, 1967. 496p.

A collection of diverse opinions on complex and controversial curriculum issues, focusing on the need for continued, systematic change and the issues to be faced in improving the curriculum.

512 Ammons, Margaret, and Gilchrist, Robert F. *Assessing and Using Curriculum Content.* (ASCD) Washington, NEA, 1965. 30p.

A concise report with study questions of great value to the individual researcher as well as to the school system.

513   Anderson, Vernon E. *Principles and Procedures of Curriculum Improvement*, 2nd ed. New York, Ronald, 1965. 498p. biblio.
An extensively up-dated revision of a comprehensive graduate text, which is experience-centered and problem-solving in its focus.

514   Broudy, Harry S., and others. *Democracy and Excellence in American Secondary Education: a Study in Curriculum Theory*. Chicago, Rand McNally, 1964. 302p. biblio.
A discussion of secondary school curriculum from the point of view of the social and psychological, as well as the scholastic or logical, demands upon it and the need for the curriculum to be responsive to new demands.

515   Conner, Forrest E., and Ellena, William J., eds. *Curriculum Handbook for School Administrators*. (AASA) Washington, NEA, 1967. 323p.
Addressed to the dilemma of the school administrator who must make critical decisions based upon pertinent information but who is overwhelmed by the volume of new curricular concepts. Specialists and organizations in 15 curriculum areas prepared this handbook. Each chapter covers an aspect of the curriculum and offers an overview of current developments.

516   Crosby, Muriel. *Curriculum Development for Elementary Schools in a Changing Society*. Boston, Heath, 1964. 409p. biblio.
A new curriculum design, new in its focus on human relations education but rooted in historic principles of curriculum development. Offers numerous examples and illustrations.

517   Doll, Ronald C. *Curriculum Improvement: Decision-making and Process*. Boston, Allyn and Bacon, 1964. 337p. biblio.
Presents background analysis for the development of a theory of curriculum improvement, together with some very pertinent and helpful procedures for bringing about change.

518   Fleming, Robert S., ed. *Curriculum for Today's Boys and Girls*. Columbus, Merrill, 1963. 662p. biblio.
Proposes guiding learning experiences with children to encourage learning that lasts. Basic premise that such learning must be made active and real for the child through careful planning and effective use of the many materials available.

519 Fraser, Dorothy M., ed. *Deciding What to Teach.* Washington, NEA, 1963. 264p. biblio.

Identifies 12 significant areas of decision in education and makes appropriate recommendations for guiding decision-making in these areas.

520 Goodlad, John, and others. *The Changing School Curriculum.* New York, Ford Foundation, 1966. 122p. biblio.

An overview of curriculum change, summarizing the shaping forces, the characteristic features, and the authors' views of the major strengths and weaknesses. Description of the major change projects and problems and issues involved.

521 _____. *School, Curriculum, and the Individual.* Waltham, Mass., Blaisdell, 1966. 259p. biblio.

A collection of papers, all but one by Goodlad, focusing on the author's belief that human variability and potentiality demand new, alternative patterns of school and curriculum organization.

522 Herrick, Virgil E. *Strategies of Curriculum Development: the Works of Virgil E. Herrick.* (Compiled by Dan W. Anderson and others.) Columbus, Merrill, 1965. 196p. biblio.

A posthumous collection of hitherto unpublished essays that are remarkably current. For the graduate student and administrator, it offers specific examples and centers around three themes: the development of curriculum theory and design, the improvement of instructional theory and practice, and analysis of classroom episodes as a method of inquiry.

523 Inlow, Gail M. *The Emergent in Curriculum.* New York, Wiley, 1966. 353p. biblio.

Based on the philosophy of total personality development, this graduate level book deals in depth with directions and innovations and the forces that dictate them. Fine analyses of team teaching and the nongraded classroom.

524 King, Arthur R., Jr., and Brownell, John A. *The Curriculum and the Disciplines of Knowledge: a Theory of Curriculum Practice.* New York, Wiley, 1966. 221p.

A theory of curriculum practice based on the steps in intellectual development, the significance of inquiry, and the structures of the disciplines. Occasionally oversimplified but generally very stimulating.

525 Koopman, George R. *Curriculum Development*. New York, CARE, 1966. 120p. biblio.

A brief historical review is followed by a discussion of recent developments and basic concepts, the relationship of curriculum development to in-service education, organization, new practices, current issues, and future challenges.

526 Krug, Edward A. *Curriculum Planning*. New York, Harper, 1957. 336p. biblio.

Deals with curriculum planning practices and with the problems involved in making curriculum planning an effective process.

527 Lee, Johnathan M., and Dorris M. *The Child and His Curriculum*, 3rd ed. New York, Appleton, 1960. 596p.

A child development approach with a number of chapters on understanding children's needs and a chapter each on the major areas of the school program. A total picture of contemporary practice and generally advanced thinking at the time of publication.

528 Nesbitt, Marion. *A Public School for Tomorrow*. New York, Harper, 1953. 164p.

Describes an unusual curriculum design in a small mountain public school, where an "accent on the arts" was developed as a way of experiencing and learning all content.

529 Oliver, Albert I. *Curriculum Improvement: a Guide to Problems, Principles, and Procedures*. New York, Dodd, 1965. 504p. biblio.

All significant aspects of curriculum improvement are covered in this practical, specialized book, which includes sufficient discussion of theory to give an understanding of rationale.

530 Phenix, Philip H. *Realms of Meaning: a Philosophy of the Curriculum for General Education*. New York, McGraw-Hill, 1964. 391p.

The central thesis of this significant book is that the job of education is to introduce the student to the principal varieties of meaning as these are exhibited in the six principal domains of human intellectual activity. A pluralistic theory of meaning and of symbolic functioning, using the insights of philosophy and anthropology.

531 Saylor, John G., and Alexander, William M. *Curriculum Planning for Modern Schools*. New York, Holt, 1966. 534p. biblio.

A methodological resource with particular utility for the beginning instructional administrator.

532 Shuster, Albert H., and Ploghoft, Milton E. *The Emerging Elementary Curriculum*. Columbus, Ohio, Merrill, 1963. 577p.

An introductory text on elementary school curriculum development and design.

533 Smith, Bunnie O. *Fundamentals of Curriculum Development*, rev. ed. New York, World, 1957. 780p. biblio.

A scholarly analysis of curriculum development that continues to be sound and relevant.

534 Taba, Hilda. *Curriculum Development: Theory and Practice*. New York, Harcourt, 1962. 529p.

An outstanding work that is a highly cogent welding of research findings and curriculum development theory. A comprehensive and pertinent resource text helpful in understanding curricular bases, plans, and the action of change.

535 Tyler, Ralph W. *Basic Principles of Curriculum and Instruction*. Chicago, U of Chicago P, 1950. 83p.

A brief and classic exposition of curriculum theory whose sound principles continue to have pertinence and relevance.

536 ――――, and others. *Perspectives of Curriculum Evaluation* (AERA Monograph Series on Curriculum Evaluation, no. 1). Chicago, Rand McNally, 1967. 102p.

This first of a new series designed for the practitioner includes papers by Tyler, Robert Gagné, and Michael Scriven. Covers issues, methodology, problems, and possible solutions.

History

537 Seguel, Mary L. *The Curriculum Field: Its Formative Years*. New York, TC, Columbia, 1966. 203p. biblio.

An historical review covering the years 1895-1937 pointing up the relevance of each idea to current concerns. A clearly stated, evolutionary treatise of curriculum making as a field of specialization organized around seven major figures and their influences.

DEAF

see also **EXCEPTIONAL CHILDREN**
SPEECH PATHOLOGY
SPEECH THERAPY

538 Davis, Hallowell, and Silverman, S. Richard, eds. *Hearing and Deafness.*, rev. ed. New York, Holt, 1960. 573p. biblio.

Chapters by specialists in the various areas of audiology cover hearing testing, hearing aids, rehabilitation, and the social, educational, and psychological problems of those with impaired hearing.

539 Ewing, Alexander W., ed. *Educational Guidance and the Deaf Child.* Washington, Volta Bureau, 1957. 345p. biblio.

A thorough discussion of early diagnosis and prognosis of partial deafness, initial treatment, environmental requirements for effective education, and methods of assessing educational potentialities and achievement, based on experimental investigations.

540 _____, and Ethel C. *Teaching Deaf Children to Talk.* Washington, D.C., Volta Bureau, 1965. 254p.

Describes a multisensory approach to teaching speech to deaf and hard of hearing children.

541 Glorig, Aram, ed. *Audiometry: Principles and Practices.* Baltimore, Williams and Wilkins, 1965. 271p.

A basic text with chapters on audiology and otolaryngology, some devoted to experimental bases. Emphasis on clinical audiology.

542 Harris, Grace M. *Language for the Preschool Deaf Child,* 2nd ed. New York, Grune and Stratton, 1963. 354p. biblio.

Sound advice with suggestions for practical procedures are included with an appreciation of the child's problems of communication. Describes fundamental training activities for language development and considers parent education and nursery school attendance.

543 Hart, Beatrice O. *Teaching Reading to Deaf Children.* Washington, Volta Bureau, 1963. 132p.

A monograph on developmental programs of teaching reading to deaf children. Stresses the purpose rather than the process of reading and includes activity suggestions for each level from nursery through advanced.

544 Hirsh, Ira J. *Measurement of Hearing*. New York, McGraw-Hill, 1952. 364p.

Summarizes experimental areas basic to clinical and experimental audiology. Early psycho-acoustic studies are described and related to clinical methodology.

545 Jerger, James, ed. *Modern Developments in Audiology*. New York, Academic, 1963. 446p. biblio.

Contributors from the fields of audiology, otolaryngology, physics, and psychology present significant past experimental findings related to experimental and clinical audiology.

546 Lack, Agnes. *The Teaching of Language to Deaf Children: Based on the Natural Development of the Child*. London, Oxford UP, 1955. 380p.

A step-by-step description of the teaching of English to deaf children. Suggests methods as well as ways of correlating spoken and written language.

547 Lerman, Alan. *Vocational Adjustment and the Deaf: a Guide and Annotated Bibliography*. Washington, Volta Bureau, 1965. 60p.

A descriptive guide and an annotated listing of more than 200 journal articles, dissertations, books, and reports.

548 Levine, Edna S. *Psychology of Deafness: Techniques of Appraisal for Rehabilitation*. New York, Columbia UP, 1960. 383p. biblio.

A basic orientation to hearing-impaired individuals and their problems from the psychologist's point of view. Covers such topics as hearing and impaired-hearing, psychological practice in a rehabilitative setting, the psychological examination, and an evaluation of research.

549 _____. *Youth in a Soundless World: a Search for Personality*. New York, New York UP, 1956. 217p. biblio.

Points to the need for proper diagnostic and counseling methods for the deaf for effective occupational planning and rehabilitation and, as important, to help them develop as individuals.

550 Miller, Maurice H., and Polisar, Ira A. *Audiological Evaluation of the Pediatric Patient*. Springfield, Ill., Thomas, 1964. 117p. biblio.

Of value to the therapist although addressed to the physician, this presents various evaluative techniques and tests and emphasizes a team approach to total evaluation of the handicapped child.

551 Myklebust, Helmer R. *Auditory Disorders in Children: a Manual for Differential Diagnosis.* New York, Grune and Stratton, 1954. 367p. biblio.

A discussion of auditory disorders and language development and of such diagnostic procedures as differential history-taking and evaluation of behavioral symptomatology, which are supplemental to the examination of the child. Includes recommendations for training.

552 ———. *The Psychology of Deafness,* 2nd ed. New York, Grune and Stratton, 1964. 423p. biblio.

Explores learning and adjustment problems of the deaf.

553 Newby, Hayes A. *Audiology,* 2nd ed. New York, Appleton, 1964. 400p. biblio.

A basic text with step-by-step descriptions of basic audiometry as well as rehabilitative and professional information.

554 O'Neill, John J., and Oyer, Herbert J. *Applied Audiometry.* New York, Dodd, 1966. 368p. biblio.

A basic text in audiology for educators of the deaf as well as audiologists, otologists, psychologists, and nurses.

555 ———, and ———. *Visual Communication for the Hard of Hearing: History, Research, and Methods.* Englewood Cliffs, N.J., Prentice-Hall, 1961. 163p. biblio.

A comprehensive text in aural rehabilitation that includes a review of pertinent literature.

556 O'Neill, Veronica. *Teaching Arithmetic to Deaf Children.* Washington, Volta Bureau, 1961. 143p. biblio.

The suggestions and techniques presented focus on the interrelationships of arithmetical knowledge to provide enriching experiences that will lead the deaf child to a better understanding of the rationale of number work and the role of arithmetic in the world.

557 Quigley, Stephen P., ed. *The Preparation of Teachers of the Deaf* (USOE Bulletin No. 8). Washington, GPO, 1966. 63p.

Provides guidelines for the establishment, administration, and evaluation of teacher preparation programs and discusses recruitment, selection, and accreditation.

558 Stevens, Stanley S., and Davis, Hallowell. *Hearing: Its Psychology and Physiology.* New York, Wiley, 1938. 489p. biblio.
A now-classic analysis of hearing.

559 Streng, Alice, and others. *Hearing Therapy for Children,* 2nd ed. New York, Grune and Stratton, 1958. 353p. biblio.
For the teacher as well as the medical and speech specialists who deal with the deaf child, this describes the special skills and knowledge required to help the child whose growth and learning are hampered by a lack of auditory clues to the world around him.

History

560 Bell, Alexander G. *The Mechanism of Speech,* 6th ed. New York, Funk and Wagnalls, 1914. 133p.
A collection of lectures on the nature of the speech mechanism and methods of teaching speech to the deaf. Includes Bell's "visible speech" symbols and his theories on vowel production.

DEBATES AND DEBATING see RHETORIC AND PERSUASION

DISADVANTAGED
see also MINORITY PROBLEMS
URBAN PROBLEMS AND EDUCATION

561 Bereiter, Carl, and Englemann, Siegfried. *Teaching Disadvantaged Children in the Preschool.* Englewood Cliffs, N.J., Prentice-Hall, 1966. 312p. biblio.
Views cultural deprivation as primarily language deprivation, discusses the need for a new kind of preschool for the disadvantaged child, and describes specific teaching procedures and curricula.

562 Bernstein, Abraham A. *The Education of Urban Populations.* New York, Random, 1967. 398p. biblio.
Although focusing on the Negro secondary school student and his problems in relation to the school and the community, this also gives attention to other minority groups, both in metropolitan and rural areas, as well as to adult education. Makes some significant recommendations that would

tend to give the school and the larger community a larger share of the time of the school child and therefore a larger influence in his education.

563 Bloom, Benjamin S., and others. *Compensatory Education for Cultural Deprivation.* New York, Holt, 1965. 179p. biblio.

An excellent selection providing an annotated bibliography and report of recent research as well as discussions that took place at the Research Conference on Educational and Cultural Deprivation at the University of Chicago.

564 Booth, Robert E., and others. *Culturally Disadvantaged: a Bibliography and Key-Word-Out-of-Context (KWOC) Index.* Detroit, Wayne State UP, 1967. 803p.

An index to the literature, mostly through 1965 only, and a bibliography of the literature, comprised of some 1,400 selected references to books, journal articles, reports, etc. Key words derived from titles or body of text.

565 Corbin, Richard, and others, eds. *Language Programs for the Disadvantaged.* Champaign, Ill., NCTE, 1965. 327p. biblio.

A survey and discussion of more than 100 projects and programs in urban and rural disadvantaged areas covering all educational levels.

566 Cowles, Milly, ed. *Perspectives on the Education of Disadvantaged Children: a Multidisciplinary Approach.* Cleveland, World, 1967. 314p. biblio.

An exploration of basic concepts from the social sciences and medicine as they relate to the education of the disadvantaged, with a focus on the effects of poverty and the educational implications thereof.

567 Crow, Lester D., and others. *Educating the Culturally Disadvantaged Child: Principles and Programs.* New York, McKay, 1966. 306p. biblio.

An objective presentation of the sociological and psychological background necessary for understanding disadvantaged children and a discussion of the deficiencies in their experience with which the school must cope and attempt to compensate. Includes also summaries of some of the programs that have been developed in urban areas across the country.

568 Davis, Allison. *Social Class Influence upon Learning.* Cambridge, Harvard UP, 1948. 100p.

A classic presentation and early analysis of the effect of differences in social class values on educational motivation and achievement.

569 Deutsch, Martin, and others. *The Disadvantaged Child: Selected Papers.* New York, Basic, 1967. 400p. biblio.

A collection of papers on the education of the deprived members of our society by a pioneer in the development of compensatory programs and some of his associates.

570 Frost, Joe L., and Hawkes, Glenn R., eds. *The Disadvantaged Child: Issues and Innovations.* Boston, Houghton Mifflin, 1966. 445p. biblio.

Fifty-seven selections in which poverty is equated with cultural disadvantage. Puerto Ricans, Negroes, Appalachians, Indians, and Mexicans in the United States are discussed. Good material and bibliography.

571 Gordon, Edmund W., and Wilkerson, Doxey A. *Compensatory Education for the Disadvantaged: Programs and Practices: Preschool Through College.* New York, CEEB, 1966. 299p. biblio.

A significant contribution to the field of educating the deprived with descriptions of some of the on-going programs.

572 Gray, Susan W., and others. *Before First Grade: the Early Training Project for Culturally Disadvantaged Children.* New York, TC, Columbia, 1966. 128p.

Based on a program developed primarily for and successfully used in a Southern community, this is a well balanced, helpful approach to identifying the needs of the deprived preschool child and to teaching procedures to meet those needs.

573 Hamlin, Ruth, and others. *Schools for Young Disadvantaged Children.* New York, TC, Columbia, 1967. 178p. biblio.

A review of the problems of low socio-economic status as they relate to schooling, a discussion of needs, and a generous offering of practical suggestions.

574 Herriott, Robert E., and St. John, Nancy H. *Social Class and the Urban School: the Impact of Pupil Background on Teachers and Principals.* New York, Wiley, 1966. 289p.

A study of the socio-economic status of pupils, teachers, and administrators in schools of varying status and of their interrelationships and effects. Based on a survey of 490 schools in 41 large American cities.

575 Holbrook, David. *English for the Rejected: Training Literacy in Lower Streams of Secondary School.* New York, Cambridge UP, 1964. 291p. biblio.

A challenging discussion of goals and approaches to the teaching of English to slow and socially disadvantaged youngsters.

576 Keach, Everett T., Jr., and others, eds. *Education and Social Crisis: Perspectives on Teaching Disadvantaged Youth.* New York, Wiley, 1967. 413p.

A fine selection of brief articles crammed with hard facts on the cultural values of the culturally deprived, their challenge in the schoolroom, and their future.

577 Kontos, Peter G., and Murphy, James J., eds. *Teaching Urban Youth: a Source Book for Urban Educators.* New York, Wiley, 1967. 346p. biblio.

Based on the premise that students will respond when they feel that their response is valued, this volume defines, develops, and evaluates techniques for strengthening the skills of teachers of urban youth.

578 Kvaraceus, William C., and others, eds. *Poverty, Education, and Race Relations.* Boston, Allyn and Bacon, 1967. 248p. biblio.

An enlightening discussion of the educative process in relation to low motivation and achievement. Emphasizes the role of the school in helping the deprived child and his family and in providing interracial learning experiences.

579 Landes, Ruth. *Culture in American Education.* New York, Wiley, 1965. 330p.

The report of a two-year project in Southern California, sponsored by Claremont College, which sought to train educators to understand the social complexities of their task and modify their purposes and procedures accordingly. The recommendations stress the need for educators to acquire through active community associations an understanding of the cultural and family background of each child.

580 Lloyd, Francis V., Jr. *Forward to Teach*. Boston, Little Brown, 1967. 172p. biblio.
This is the opposite side of the coin of *The Blackboard Jungle*, wherein are described the joys and rewards of elementary school teaching, even in urban schools.

581 Loretan, Joseph O., and Umans, Shelley. *Teaching the Disadvantaged: New Curriculum Approaches*. New York, TC, Columbia, 1966. 242p. biblio.
A proposal to stimulate and motivate disadvantaged children by using the experimental curricula that have been developed recently for gifted children. The authors believe that culturally-deprived children have far greater intellectual capacity than commonly realized and should not be restricted to either an authoritarian or bland curriculum.

582 McGeoch, Dorothy M., and others. *Learning to Teach in Urban Schools*. New York, TC, Columbia, 1965. 140p.
Four young middle-class teachers describe their experiences in slum schools and conclude that, for them, the rewards are greater than the frustrations.

583 Manuel, Herschel T. *Spanish-Speaking Children of the Southwest: Their Education and the Public Welfare*. Austin, U of Texas P, 1965. 222p. biblio.
An excellent study of the cultural influences producing the problems that impede the education of these children. Indicates the universal problem of equal participation of all people for the common welfare.

584 Miller, Harry L., ed. *Education for the Disadvantaged: Current Issues and Research*. New York, Free Press, 1967. 302p. biblio.
More than four dozen articles reflecting findings from the behavioral sciences review current attitudes, research, and controversy in relation to the education of the socially disadvantaged child. Stressing urban and inner city problems in the schools, the articles discuss testing dilemmas, experimental projects, curriculum issues, teacher training, and new approaches to desegregation.

585 _____, and Smiley, Marjorie B., eds. *Education in the Metropolis.* New York, Free Press, 1967. 295p.

A collection of articles providing supplementary background material. The selections, such as those by Richard Wright and James Baldwin that effectively describe the plight of the minority, are out of the ordinary.

586 Moore, G. Alexander, Jr. *Realities of the Urban Classroom: Observations in Elementary Classrooms.* New York, Praeger, 1967. 188p.

Based on Project TRUE (Teachers and Resources for Urban Education at Hunter College, New York City), this is an interdisciplinary report of action studies and a perceptive study of teacher success and lack of success, which is focused on the class rather than on the individual student.

587 Passow, A. Harry, ed. *Education in Depressed Areas.* New York, TC, Columbia, 1963. 359p.

Papers presented at a 1962 conference on Curriculum and Teaching in Depressed Areas in which specialists discuss the problems relative to the education of the disadvantaged child. Although the focus is on urban education, consideration is given to rural and small town environments in which exist conditions fostering cultural deprivation.

588 _____, and others. *Education of the Disadvantaged: a Book of Readings.* New York, Holt, 1967. 512p.

Research-based articles by psychologists, sociologists, and educators focus on the special educational difficulties of the disadvantaged learner and cover such topics as teaching techniques and strategies, program development, and defining the task and roles for school and teacher.

589 Powledge, Fred. *To Change a Child.* Chicago, Quadrangle, 1968. 110p.

A description by Dr. Martin Deutsch and the staff of the Institute for Developmental Studies (New York University) of an experimental program in a handful of New York City public schools. "Massive intervention" is the key phrase used to describe the program, now covering preschool through grade three in four slum schools, that has small classes, each with two teachers and many aides, such as social workers, psychologists, and persons from the community. Findings to date indicate that early enrichment programs can produce long-range changes in the educational success of disadvantaged children.

590   Roberts, Joan I., ed. *School Children in the Urban Slum.* New York, Free Press, 1967. 626p. biblio.

A collection of readings designed to help the classroom teacher understand and deal with the differences that children from various backgrounds bring to the slum school, based on the assumption that children are influenced by their social and physical environments.

591   Strom, Robert D., and others. *The Inner-City Classroom: Teacher Behaviors.* Columbus, Merrill, 1966. 204p. biblio.

Specialists view the educational efforts of inner-city schools in terms of teacher perceptions and consequent behaviors. Includes teaching strategies and although most valuable for elementary teachers in urban schools, has considerable usefulness for anyone working with culturally disadvantaged children.

592   _____. *Teaching in the Slum School.* Columbus, Merrill, 1965. 116p. biblio.

An overview of the important factors that can influence failure or progress in the classroom, based on the belief that success is dependent upon teacher understanding of slum life and of differences in children as well as of the functions of the school specialists and the school's role in serving an unstructured community.

593   Taba, Hilda, and Elkins, Deborah. *Teaching Strategies for the Culturally Disadvantaged.* Chicago, Rand McNally, 1966. 295p. biblio.

A good book for teachers of preadolescent urban children, which includes some instructional strategies for teaching the culturally deprived.

594   Webster, Staten W., ed. *Educating the Disadvantaged Learner: Knowing, Understanding, Education.* San Francisco, Chandler, 1966. 644p. biblio.

A recommended collection of readings by scholars and practitioners. Identifies disadvantaged groups such as the Negro, the Mexican-American, Indian, urban, and rural, their educational problems, and offers some practical suggestions for teaching.

595 Witty, Paul A., ed. *The Educationally Retarded and Disadvantaged* (NSSE 66th Yearbook, Part I). Chicago, U of Chicago P, 1967. 384p. biblio.

With Wattenberg's *Social Deviancy among Youth* (#1444) and *Metropolitanism: a Challenge to Education* (1968), this forms a trio of studies concerned with what is now a rapidly expanding segment of school enrollment. Defining the educationally retarded as those who are slow in achieving traditional objectives, this examines the student, the program, some on-going compensatory programs, and the teacher, especially in relation to problems of morale.

596 Young, Ethel. *Nursery School Program for Culturally Different Children.* Menlo Park, Cal., Pacific Coast. 56p. biblio.

A framework for a nursery school curriculum for culturally deprived children that includes helping children develop first a concept of self and then skills in language, art, music, and drama. Working with parents is discussed, and the bibliography is excellent.

DISADVANTAGED — GHETTO SCHOOLS

597 Conant, James B. *Slums and Suburbs.* New York, McGraw-Hill, 1961. 147p.

A scholarly, consistent portrait of two totally different kinds of neighborhoods and the schools that serve them. The author's opinion, based on considerable research, is that the urban situation is "social dynamite" and requires urgent corrective attention.

598 Greene, Mary F., and Ryan, Orletta. *The Schoolchildren: Growing Up in the Slums.* New York, Pantheon, 1966. 227p.

A sympathetic, anecdotal picture of two New York City elementary schools and their pupils, which is absolutely horrifying. Offered objectively are the details of the crippling world in which these children live and the inability of the school program to reach or teach them.

599 Hentoff, Nat. *Our Children Are Dying.* New York, Viking, 1966. 141p.

A compelling portrait of a school in the heart of Harlem's slums, its children, its place in the community, the diversity of opinion and approach among its staff, and above all, its troubled, sympathetic, controversial, and non-iconoclastic principal, Elliott Shapiro.

600   Kohl, Herbert. *36 Children*. New York, New American Library, 1967. 256p.

A superb addition to the growing literature of first-hand accounts of teaching in slum schools. The author, a former sixth grade teacher in Harlem, depicts a defeating power system. Included are generous samplings of his pupils' writing, their own testimonial of their gifts.

601   Kozol, Jonathan. *Death at an Early Age: The Destruction of the Hearts and Minds of Negro Children in the Boston Public Schools*. Boston, Houghton Mifflin, 1967. 256p.

Recounts the author's personal observations and experiences of prejudice and cruelty during the year he taught in elementary schools in the ghetto section of Boston, concluding with his being fired for introducing a poem by Langston Hughes.

602   Schrag, Peter, *Village School Downtown: a Politics and Education—a Boston Report*. Boston, Beacon, 1967. 191p.

A study of the plight of the city child from which the author concludes that urban schools are pitifully anachronistic and bear little relation to the 20th century.

DISCIPLINE IN SCHOOLS

603   Hymes, James L., Jr. *Behavior and Misbehavior: a Teacher's Guide to Action*. Englewood Cliffs, N.J., Prentice-Hall, 1955. 140p.

A brief, provocative, perceptive discussion of "discipline." Focuses on understanding typical childhood behaviors and the causes of atypical behaviors and what to do about them. Though not specifically examined in the classroom setting, classroom applications are abundant.

604   Larson, Knute G., and Karpas, Melvin R. *Effective Secondary School Discipline*. Englewood Cliffs, N.J., Prentice-Hall, 1963. 206p.

A book offering some answers but no easy panaceas. Provides some background and brings together some of the best contemporary thinking on a complex subject.

605 McDonald, Blanche, and Nelson, Leslie W. *Successful Classroom Control.* Dubuque, Iowa, Brown, 1955. 157p.

A practical book containing many good hints on general classroom control in both the elementary and secondary school.

606 Parody, Ovid F. *The High School Principal and His Staff Deal with Discipline.* New York, TC, Columbia, 1958. 93p. biblio.

A positive approach to the problems faced by youth as they learn increasingly adult patterns of behavior. Develops a program based on study and experience focused on the junior high school.

607 Sheviakov, George V., and Redl, Fritz. *Discipline for Today's Children and Youth.* (ASCD) Washington, NEA, 1956. 64p.

A real contribution to thinking in the area of school discipline. Includes a practical application of psychological and pedagogical theory to the problems of children and youth.

DISCUSSION TECHNIQUES
see also ADULT EDUCATION—TEACHING AND TEACHING METHODS

608 Auer, J. Jeffery, and Ewbank, Henry L. *Handbook for Discussion Leaders,* rev. ed. New York, Harper, 1954. 153p. biblio.

Step-by-step procedures for planning, organizing, and leading group and public discussion.

609 Cortright, Rupert L., and Hinds, George L. *Creative Discussion.* New York, Macmillan, 1959. 303p. biblio.

A comprehensive treatise on discussion as a social instrument imperative for contemporary society. Techniques drawn from varied disciplines, such as semantics, psychology, sociology, and political science, are presented with suggested applications and implications.

610 Hill, Richard J. *A Comparative Study of Lecture and Discussion Methods.* White Plains, N.Y., Fund for Adult Education, 1960. 153p. biblio.

A pioneering attempt to apply the methods of social science research to the evaluation of adult education programs, with particular emphasis on study-discussion programs in the liberal arts.

DRAMATICS see STORYTELLING AND DRAMATICS

DRIVER EDUCATION

611   Aaron, James E., and Strasser, Marland K. *Driver and Traffic Safety Education: Content, Methods, and Organization.* New York, Macmillan, 1966. 401p. biblio.
A college text for use in teaching driver education.

612   Brody, Leon, and Stack, Herbert J. *Highway Safety and Driver Education.* Englewood Cliffs, N.J., Prentice-Hall, 1954. 464p. biblio.
A popular and reliable college text used to prepare teachers of driver education.

613   ————. *Personal Factors in Safe Operation of Motor Vehicles.* New York, Center for Safety Education, New York University. 1941. 96p.
Examines the relationships between accidents and the personal characteristics of drivers.

614   Kramer, Milton D., comp. *The Motor-Vehicle Driver: His Nature and Improvement.* Saugatuck, Conn., Eno Foundation for Highway Traffic Control, 1949. 165p.
An examination of the psycho-physical factors in the traffic environment.

615   McFarland, Ross A., and Moseley, Alfred L. *Human Factors in Highway Transport Safety.* Boston, School of Public Health, Harvard University, 1954. 295p.
Factual information on the role of human factors.

616   ————, and others. *Human Variables in Motor Accidents.* Boston, School of Public Health, Harvard University, 1955. 203p. biblio.
A study of the connection between personal variabilities and the occurrence of accidents.

617   *Policies and Guidelines for Teacher Preparation and Certifi-cation in Driver and Traffic Safety Education.* Washington, NEA, 1965. 52p.

Developed by the Safety Education Commission to affect improvements in teacher preparation and certification.

618   *The State of the Art of Traffic Safety: a Critical Review and Analysis of the Technical Information on Factors Affecting Traffic Safety.* Cambridge, Mass., Arthur D. Little, Inc., 1966. 624p.

A study sponsored by the American Automobile Manu-facturers Association, this has some industry bias but is a summary of the current state of knowledge. The excellent and remarkably complete bibliography is analyzed in the text and is an indispensable reference.

History

619   Stack, Herbert J. *The History of Driver Education in the United States.* Washington, NEA, 1966. 64p.

Comprehensive historical review.

DROPOUTS

620   Burchill, George W., ed. *Work Study Programs for Alienated Youth.* Chicago, SRA, 1962. 265p.

A description of nine work-study programs for secondary students in which eight public schools and one group of pri-vate individuals have combined classroom and job experi-ence in a preventive rather than remedial effort.

621   Cervantes, Lucius. *The Drop-Out: Causes and Cures.* Ann Arbor, U of Michigan P, 1965. 244p. biblio.

A study of 300 youths, of whom half finished high school and half dropped out, which investigated and analyzed social backgrounds, the "influential others," and personality char-acteristics in an effort to learn the causes and find the cures for the uneducated community reject in an age of automation.

622   Dentler, Robert A., and Warshauer, Mary E. *Big City Drop-outs and Illiterates.* New York, Center for Urban Education, 1965. 127p. biblio.

An important study of educational barriers to economic security, which compares high school dropouts and adult illiteracy in 131 of the largest United States cities and provides data showing that there is a continuing decline in the employment of the poorly educated because of the increasing demand for higher skills.

623 Greene, Bert I. *Preventing Student Dropouts.* Englewood Cliffs, N.J., Prentice-Hall, 1966. 223p. biblio.

A comprehensive coverage of a major problem. Discusses the nature of the problem, the characteristics of the dropout, and the roles of parents, school administrators, guidance counselors, and teachers.

624 Lichter, Solomon O., and others. *The Dropouts.* New York, Free Press, 1962. 302p.

The findings of a three-year treatment study, sponsored by the Scholarship and Guidance Association, of a group of intellectually capable Chicago youngsters who wanted to or who left high school. Extensive counseling proved to be useful in countering the primary reason for dropping out, which was serious emotional problems and difficulties at home.

625 Schreiber, Daniel, ed. *Profile of the School Dropout: a Reader on America's Major Educational Problem.* New York, Random, 1967. 393p. biblio.

A group of well-known educators, such as Riessman, Bettelheim, and Deutsch, examine the reasons why young people quit school, discuss some of the programs that have been designed to cope with this problem, and offer some challenging ideas.

626 Tannenbaum, Abraham J. *Dropout or Diploma: a Socio-Educational Analysis of Early School Withdrawal.* New York, TC, Columbia, 1966. 36p. biblio.

Much information and thought are packed into this small review of a large problem, which is seen as shared by the schools and by other agencies in the community, such as the labor unions, industry, and the military.

627 Torrance, E. Paul, and Strom, Robert D., eds. *Mental Health and Achievement: Increasing Potential and Reducing School Dropout.* New York, Wiley, 1966. 417p. biblio.

More than three dozen articles by professionals from various fields involving mental health. Covers home and community, the changing school and curriculum, learning, and evaluation.

ECONOMIC EDUCATION

628 Frankel, M. L. *Economic Education.* New York, CARE, 1965. 118p. biblio.

A recommendation that economic education begin in the early grades and be developed sequentially through senior high school. Descriptions of courses that will promote greater economic literacy are included.

629 Kazanjian Foundation. *Economic Education Experiences of Enterprising Teachers.* Vol. 1-   1963-   . New York, Joint Council on Economic Education.

Annual publications describing selected entries in the annual Kazanjian Foundation Awards Program for the Teaching of Economics. Covers kindergarten through college and is an excellent (free) aid to teachers looking for stimulating ideas.

630 Martin, Richard S., and Miller, Reuben G. *Economics and Its Significance.* Columbus, Merrill, 1965. 165p. biblio.

Two scholars discuss their field and consider methods of teaching economics in the schools.

631 National Task Force on Economic Education. *Economic Education in the Schools.* New York, Joint Council on Economic Education, 1961. 78p.

An examination of economic concepts and how they may be taught in the schools, with some curriculum recommendations. The *Teachers Guide to Developmental Economic Education Programs* (1964, the Council) is an explanation of the principal concepts and a guide to their introduction in the classroom at elementary and secondary levels.

ECONOMICS OF EDUCATION
see also HIGHER EDUCATION—ECONOMICS

632 Barach, Arnold B. *U.S.A. and Its Economic Future: a Twentieth Century Fund Survey.* New York, Macmillan, 1964. 148p. biblio.

A distinguished economist examines our economic system with emphasis on such aspects of living as housing, health, clothing, recreation, travel, and education, with some discussion of the effects of growing urbanization on colleges.

633 Benson, Charles S. *The Economics of Public Education.*
Boston, Houghton Mifflin, 1961. 580p.

A comprehensive analysis of the ways in which the tools
of economics may be used to study the revenues and expenditures of public education. School finance is seen as a
sub-area of public finance.

634 ———, ed. *Perspective on the Economics of Education:
Readings in School Finance and Business Management.* Boston, Houghton Mifflin, 1963. 477p.

Chapters by noted economists cover such topics as the
returns to education, the economic structure of education,
taxation for schools, grants-in-aid, and productivity.

635 Blaug, Mark. *The Economics of Education: a Selected Annotated Bibliography.* New York, Pergamon, 1966. 190p.

Contains some 800 published items in English, French,
and German, and unpublished papers from international
agencies and institutions. For scholars, research students, and
educators.

636 Burke, Arvid J., ed. *Financing Public Schools in the United
States,* rev. ed. New York, Harper, 1957. 679p.

A dated but still widely used textbook that deals with the
traditional topics of school finance. Chapters by specialists
in such areas as budgeting, transportation, insurance, and
purchasing.

637 Burkhead, Jesse, ed. *Public School Finance: Economics and
Politics.* Syracuse, N.Y., Syracuse UP, 1964. 394p.

The 11 chapters are summaries of monographs that stress
issues of public policy. Prepared by the Maxwell School at
Syracuse.

638 Casey, Leo M. *School Business Administration.* New York,
CARE, 1964. 117p. biblio.

A concise presentation of such topics as the budget, accounting, purchasing, insurance, operation and maintenance,
transportation, and food services, placed firmly within their
framework—that the function of school business is to expe-
dite instruction.

639 Hechinger, Fred M. *The Big Red Schoolhouse.* New York,
Doubleday, 1959. 240p.

A dramatic study by a well-informed journalist of the

need for less politics and more financial support of our schools, with a comparison of Russian and American post-World War II education.

640 Knezevich, Stephen J., and Fowlkes, John G. *Business Management of Local School Systems.* New York, Harper, 1960. 328p. biblio.

A thorough, practical manual on school financial management. Topics include school budgets, purchasing, payrolls, accounting, auditing, capital outlay, transportation, school plants, and financial reporting.

641 Schultz, Theodore W. *The Economic Value of Education.* New York, Columbia UP, 1963. 92p. biblio.

For school administrators, members of school boards, university trustees, and legislators concerned with determining the amount of public funds for education and the direction of their flow.

EDUCATION
see also EDUCATIONAL PHILOSOPHY

642 ASCD. *Yearbook.* 1944-   . Washington, NEA. biblio.

A notable series in which each volume covers a particular aspect of education. Generally composed of lengthy articles written for the volume by specialists, they occasionally, as in *Perceiving, Behaving, Becoming* (an especially distinguished yearbook), include discussion. Other recent titles: *Learning and Mental Health in the Schools* (1966), *Evaluation as Feedback and Guide* (1967), and *Youth Education: Problems, Perspectives, Promises (1968).*

643 Bandman, Bertram. *The Place of Reason in Education.* Columbus, Ohio State UP, 1966. 191p. biblio.

A philosophical examination of the crucial question in education, "What should be taught?" Attempts to arrive at a solution to the problem on the basis of argument and logic.

644 Belth, Marc. *Education as a Discipline: a Study of the Role of Models in Thinking.* Boston, Allyn and Bacon, 1965. 317p. biblio.

A stimulating, thought provoking, and possibly revolutionary thesis that requires careful study and develops the idea that education is the discipline of disciplines—the study of models and the development of the ability to use and invent different ones.

645 Benjamin, Harold. *Saber-Tooth Curriculum: Including Other Lectures in the History of Paleolithic Education.* New York, McGraw-Hill, 1939. 139p.

According to the title page, this is by J. Abner Peddiwell, Ph.D., who, with the help of "Tequila Daisies" in a Tijuana bar, delivers several hilarious lectures poking fun at every sacred cow in the field of education and a few in the American social scene as well. As devastating and thought-provoking a satire on educational goals and methods today as it was when Peddiwell downed his first drink.

646 Benne, Kenneth D. *Education for Tragedy: Essays on Disenchanted Hope for Modern Man.* Lexington, U of Kentucky P, 1967. 203p. biblio.

Essays on the contemporary human crisis in a world lacking personal identity and sense of community. Views education as man's strongest hope.

647 Benson, Charles S. *The Cheerful Prospect: a Statement on the Future of American Education.* Boston, Houghton Mifflin, 1965. 134p.

An argument for greater centralization of school control to equalize educational opportunity and genuinely permit the development of each child in accordance with his abilities and aptitudes. Provocative conclusions and recommendations.

648 Bereday, George Z., and Volpicelli, Luigi, eds. *Public Education in America: a New Interpretation of Purpose and Practice.* New York, Harper, 1958. 212p.

Based on a symposium undertaken at Professor Volpicelli's invitation, this book explores basic current issues and is an introduction to current educational problems in the U.S.

649 Blanshard, Brand, ed. *Education in the Age of Science.* New York, Basic, 1959. 302p.

Contributions by distinguished scholars from other disciplines, including the humanities and social sciences, discuss education today, its successes and failures, and the relation between the sciences and the humanities. Provocative, but no answers.

650 Booth, Wayne C., ed. *The Knowledge Most Worth Having.*
Chicago, U of Chicago P, 1967. 212p.

A stimulating collection of essays on human values, broadening interests, diversity, man's place in nature, and the scientific culture, intended to spur a rethinking of educational goals.

651 Brameld, Theodore. *The Cultural Foundations of Education: an Interdisciplinary Exploration.* New York, Harper, 1957. 330p.

A counterattack upon the intellectual celibacy of the contemporary world. Discusses educational theory in the light of ideas and facts from anthropology, philosophy, sociology, and other fields. Constructs a theory of democratic education that can give a consistent and dynamic direction to education in this age of revolutionary change.

652 ———. *Education as Power.* New York, Holt, 1965. 145p.

A reminder that this country's urgent educational problems and concerns are as crucial in other parts of the world, discussed on the basis of creativity, audacity, directiveness, convergence, commitment, confrontation, involvement, and control.

653 ———. *Education for the Emerging Age: Newer Ends and Stronger Means.* New York, Harper, 1950. 245p.

In strong words as applicable today as two decades ago, the author states that education "can and should dedicate itself to the task of reconstructing a culture which, left unreconstructed, will almost certainly collapse of its own frustrations and conflicts." A plea for transforming American schools into powerful institutions of cultural change toward a goal of planet-wide democratic order.

654 ———. *Ends and Means in Education: a Mid-century Appraisal.* New York, Harper, 1950. 244p.

An evaluation at midpoint in this century of the failures and successes of American and world education and an assessment of resources in planning for the next half-century. The author's theme is that education must dedicate itself to the task of reconstructing a culture that otherwise may collapse.

655 Brickman, William W., and Lehrer, Stanley, eds. *Automation, Education, and Human Values*. New York, School and Society, 1966. 419p. biblio.

Essays on the effects of technological change on the home training received in school, government, the American economy, employment, and the use of leisure time.

656 ———. *Educational Systems in the United States*. New York, CARE, 1964. 118p.

The origin, development, and organization of American lower schools seen by the author as the "dual system of education." Succinct description of the conflicts between the public and private elements concerning federal aid, church-state relations, private schools, and racial segregation.

657 Bruner, Jerome S. *On Knowing: Essays for the Left Hand*. Cambridge, Harvard UP, 1962. 165p.

Ten provocative essays by a lively student of learning and the learning process. Emphasizes intellectual learnings and the importance of enrichment for the individual as well as for society and seeks to identify and describe universal aspects of creating kowledge.

658 ———. *The Process of Education*. Cambridge, Harvard UP, 1960. 97p.

Essays of historic importance that probe deeply into some of the potential for increasing the effectiveness of the educational process and challenge the group-oriented conception of the teaching-learning process.

659 Conant, James B. *Education and Liberty: the Role of the Schools in a Modern Democracy*. Cambridge, Harvard UP, 1953. 168p.

Lectures that examine the degree of instruction in the mid-20th century that should be provided to all youth to ensure the safety of liberty. Considered is the education of youths from 12 to 20, a comparison of the British and American systems, the four-year liberal arts college and its influence on the secondary school, and the question of supporting private schools with public funds.

660 ———. *Shaping Educational Policy*. New York, McGraw-Hill, 1964. 139p. biblio.

A call for a nationwide educational policy supported by

both the states and the federal government that will serve as a standard for colleges and universities and for all publicly supported educational institutions.

661   Cremin, Lawrence A. *The American Common School: an Historic Conception.* New York, TC, Columbia, 1951. 248p. biblio.

An investigation of the fundamental principles and assumptions of the American public school based on social and intellectual factors and a study of the nature of the schools that have emerged.

662   _____. *The Genius of American Education.* Pittsburgh, U of Pittsburgh P, 1965. 122p. biblio.

An affirmation of faith in free schools. Deals with our commitment to popular education, the relationship between popular education and popular culture, and the politics of popular education. The 1965 Horace Mann Lecture.

663   Cressman, George R., and Benda, Harold W. *Public Education in America: a Foundations Course,* 3rd ed. New York, Appleton, 1966. 483p. biblio.

An up-to-the-minute, broadly comprehensive introduction to the American educational system. Accurate and well-organized.

664   Eble, Kenneth E. *A Perfect Education.* New York, Macmillan, 1967. 215p.

Discusses delight, feeling, and self-realization in the context of old and new educational practice. Good and bad are to be found in the old—Socrates, Thoreau and Whitehead—and in the new—teaching machines, test batteries, and TV.

665   Educational Conference, New York. *Report.* 1st-   1932- New York, Educational Records Bureau.

Starting out with an emphasis on measurement and progress in school, this annual conference has gradually broadened its scope to include instruction and guidance. In the last few years effort has been made to bring to the conference the contributions of research. Recent titles include: *Modern Educational Developments: Another Look* (1965), *Teacher Education: the Emerging Future* (1966), and *Climate for Learning: the Teacher as a Person* (1967).

666   Educational Policies Commission. *The Central Purpose of American Education.* Washington, NEA, 1961. 21p.

An examination of the central purpose of the school and the means of achieving it. Sees as necessary a commitment to a program suffused with creativeness and innovation rather than a narrow intellectualism. Emphasizes that thinking is the central outcome of education.

667   Ehlers, Henry, and Lee, Gordon C., eds. *Crucial Issues in Education,* 3rd ed. New York, Holt, 1964. 374p. biblio.

An anthology presenting opposing views on highly controversial issues in education. Chapters may be seen as dialogues between some of the outstanding minds of today.

668   Foshay, Arthur W., and others, eds. *The Rand McNally Handbook of Education.* Chicago, Rand McNally, 1963. 294p. biblio.

The principal facts about education in the United States and in those countries with whom we often compare ourselves. Presented in an effort to assist in decision-making and to provide a base on which a rationale of education can be built.

669   Full, Harold, ed. *Controversy in American Education: an Anthology of Crucial Issues.* New York, Macmillan, 1967. 488p. biblio.

A sampling of the discussion, debates, and disputes that characterize the controversy in American education today, with some reference to European schools. A provocative collection of articles that range over such topics as the changing nature of school authority, the problems of the teaching profession, the demands and pressures placed on schools and the schools' response.

670   Gardner, John W. *Excellence.* New York, Harper, 1961. 171p. biblio.

Explores the social context in which excellence may survive or be smothered in our democratic society and emphasizes that this issue cuts across all others.

671   _____. *Self Renewal: the Individual and the Innovative Society.* New York, Harper, 1964. 141p. biblio.

Discusses the need for personal renewal in contemporary

society and explores ways of fostering versatile and innovative men and women.

672 Goodlad, John I., ed. *The Changing American School.* (NSSE 65th Yearbook, Part II). Chicago, U of Chicago P, 1966. 319p.

Describes and analyzes a number of aspects of schooling that have emerged or undergone significant re-examination since World War II. An overview of current trends, with appraisals and reactions, and an attempt to relate the educational picture to contemporary societal forces.

673 Goodman, Paul. *Compulsory Mis-Education.* New York, Horizon, 1964. 189p.

An outspoken advocate of individualism and a controversial critic of the American scene decries and documents the ways in which our educational system denies individual freedom. A rigorous attack on goals and methods that seeks to promote an educational philosophy in which citizen means society-maker, not one participating in or adjusted to society.

674 Greene, Theodore M. *Liberal Education Reconsidered.* Cambridge, Harvard UP, 1953. 46p.

A redefinition of the goal of education to take into account man's social necessities and obligations. A Christian, neo-Kantian approach that maintains that the social purpose of education must be to prepare youth for responsible and cooperative participation in the overlapping social groups that constitute the structure of our society.

675 Gross, Ronald, and Murphy, Judith, eds. *The Revolution in the Schools.* New York, Harcourt, 1964. 250p. biblio.

A stimulating collection of reports by educators, behavioral and social scientists, and practicing teachers, who discuss with authority and imagination some new concepts and practices in education.

676 Haan, Aubrey, and Norma, eds. *Readings in Professional Education.* Boston, Allyn and Bacon, 1963. 379p.

An interdisciplinary and comparative approach to modern educational developments. Includes a discussion of education in selected areas of the world, the function of education in society, contributions of the behavioral sciences, and some explorations in contemporary thinking about education.

677 Hicks, William V., and Blackington, Frank H. *Introduction to Education: an Orientation to Teaching.* Columbus, Merrill, 1965. 148p. biblio.

A description of the state of the teaching profession as it is today as well as a picture of contemporary education in the United States.

678 Hopkins, Levi T. *Interaction: the Democratic Process.* Boston, Heath, 1941. 490p. biblio.

A classic definition of the educative experience. Explores the meaning of cooperative democratic action and its importance in the theory and practice of American education.

679 Hughes, James M. *Education in America,* 2nd ed. New York, Harper, 1965. 570p. biblio.

An introductory textbook that is generally inclusive. Considerable description of the professional education curriculum.

680 Keppel, Francis. *The Necessary Revolution in American Education.* New York, Harper, 1966. 201p.

A broad view of American education from a broad perspective. Needs can best be met and inequalities best be eliminated by cooperation between all levels of government, education, and business. An excellent explanation of the rationale behind federal support of public education.

681 Kerber, August, and Smith, Wilfred R., eds. *Educational Issues in a Changing Society,* 2nd ed. Detroit, Wayne State UP, 1964. 482p. biblio.

An informative sourcebook covering eight broad areas of problems in education. Each area contains readings by several authors with varying viewpoints.

682 Lieberman, Myron. *The Future of Public Education.* Chicago, U of Chicago P, 1960. 294p.

A highly opinionated attack on the "educational establishment." The author examines the "ineffectiveness" of lay control, teacher preparation, and teacher organizations, and presents a strategy for change.

683 McGrath, Earl J. *Education, the Wellspring of Democracy.* University, U of Alabama P, 1951. 139p.

Essays stressing the need for an educational system that cultivates the minds and spirits of free men and guards against the evil forces of totalitarianism and dictatorship.

684 Mayer, Martin. *The Schools.* New York, Harper, 1961. 446p.

An entertaining portrait of schooling today in Western Europe and across the United States, by a knowledgeable journalist who spices his prose with lively vignettes of classroom scenes. Some just and unjust criticisms as well as some reasonable suggestions and unreasonable panaceas.

685 Miles, Matthew B., ed. *Innovation in Education.* New York, TC, Columbia, 1964. 689p. biblio.

A compilation of case studies and conceptualizations concerning change in education.

686 Miller, Richard I. *Education in a Changing Society.* Washington, NEA, 1963. 166p. biblio.

Presents significant educational issues and numerous recommendations for their resolution.

687 Morphet, Edgar L., and Ryan, Charles O., eds. *Designing Education for the Future: an Eight State Project,* 4 vols. New York, Citation, 1967-1968. biblio.

The reports and papers of three major conferences: *Prospective Changes in Society by 1980* (1), *Implications for Education of Prospective Changes in Society* (2), *Planning and Effecting Needed Changes in Education* (3), and *Cooperative Planning for Education in 1980* (4), and a fifth to be published in 1968. A multidisciplinary approach, with contributions by prominent scholars. Explores in some depth the interrelationships of societal changes and education and provides concrete plans for modifying and improving the existing educational system.

688 Morse, Arthur D. *Schools of Tomorrow, Today.* New York, Doubleday, 1960. 191p.

A review of some forward-looking experiments covering a variety of different phases of the educational scene. Ten experiments in eight states, selected because they represent a cross section of experimentation and because their early results appeared promising, are examined intensively.

689 Norton, John K. *Critical Issues in American Public Education.* Pittsburgh, U of Pittsburgh P, 1965. 108p. biblio.

A lucid lecture on the values of education, the need for truly democratic control of education, the right of every child to an education that will develop his fullest potential, and the need to double our expenditures on education to achieve these ends.

690   NSSE. *Yearbook*. Chicago, U of Chicago P, 1st-   1902-
      After a halting start in 1895, this series took off in a gallop in 1902 and has been up front ever since. A yearbook published in at least two parts every year, each with a prominent editor, each consisting of original articles devoted to a particular aspect in the field of education, usually of current, crucial interest. (See index for titles of importance.)

691   Peters, Richard S. *Ethics and Education*. Chicago, Scott Foresman, 1967. 256p.
      Relates and applies current thought in ethics and social philosophy to concrete ethical issues and problems in education. Readable, non-technical style.

692   Power, Edward J. *Education for American Democracy: Foundations of Education*, 2nd ed. New York, McGraw-Hill, 1965. 518p. biblio.
      An introductory text with balanced perspectives. Less emphasis on systematizing education than on the importance to each individual of a liberal education and a humanistic approach.

693   *The Pursuit of Excellence: Education and the Future of America*. New York, Doubleday, 1958. 48p.
      A panel report of a special study project of the Rockefeller Brothers Fund, this attempts to assess the major problems and opportunities likely to confront the United States in the next decade or so. Addressed specifically to inherent contemporary problems—the inhibition or destruction of individuality and the difficulty of giving free expression to creativity.

694   Redl, Fritz. *When We Deal with Children: Selected Writings*. New York, Free Press, 1966. 511p. biblio.
      An eloquent discussion by a multidisciplinary practitioner, in a collection of articles written over a 25-year period. A challenging, stimulating application of psychoanalytical insights to numerous subjects, including education, child development, delinquency, classroom discipline, and sex education.

695   Rudy, Solomon W. *Schools in an Age of Mass Culture: an Exploration of Selected Themes in the History of 20th Cen-*

tury American Education. Englewood Cliffs, N.J., Prentice-Hall, 1965. 374p. biblio.

Probes the questions of why and how schools change by studying some basic questions. Chapters on the child-centered school, the school in the American social matrix, the adjusted child, education for all, church-state-and-school, integration, and evaluation of American education by those from other countries.

696   Russell, James E. *Change and Challenge in American Education.* Boston, Houghton Mifflin, 1965. 114p.

A stimulating analysis challenging much contemporary thinking about the route to be followed by our educational pattern. Controversial and provocative.

697   Thelen, Herbert A. *Education and the Human Quest.* New York, Harper, 1960. 224p.

The course of inquiry in education and its significance. Both individual and group inquiry processes are considered.

698   Van Til, William. *The Making of a Modern Educator.* Indianapolis, Bobbs Merrill, 1961. 252p.

A collection of essays that take issue with James Conant's preference for the child-centered elementary school and subject-centered secondary school and college. Proposes supporting at all levels "an education that deals with social realities and appropriate social demands."

699   Whitehead, Alfred N. *The Aims of Education.* New York, Macmillan, 1959. 248p.

A collection of lectures given between 1912 and 1928 and originally published in 1929, they are, in Whitehead's words, "a protest against dead knowledge and inert ideas." As "students are alive and the purpose of education is to stimulate and guide their self-development, therefore teachers also should be alive." The lectures cover technical education in relation to science and literature, the classics in education, the function of the university, etc.

700   Wynn, D. Richard. *Organization of Public Schools.* New York, CARE, 1964. 115p. biblio.

Deals with such moot questions as vertical vs. horizontal administrative and supervisory organization, the self-contained vs. the departmentally organized classroom, team teaching, and heterogeneous vs. homogeneous grouping. A lucid and balanced discussion that also covers the relation of the local school district to various levels of government.

EDUCATION IN FOREIGN COUNTRIES
see also COMPARATIVE EDUCATION
UNDERDEVELOPED COUNTRIES

701 Benton, William. *The Teachers and the Taught in the U.S.S.R.* New York, Atheneum, 1966. 174p.

A terse examination of Soviet educational objectives and organization by an experienced observer whose ambassadorial status enabled him to confer with top officials. His recommendations, based on Cold War competition, are for greater United States government effort.

702 Bereday, George Z., and others, eds. *The Changing Soviet School: the Comparative Education Society Field Study in the U.S.S.R.* Boston, Houghton Mifflin, 1960. 514p. biblio.

An outgrowth of an intensive tour of Russia in 1958, and visits to schools, colleges and universities, collective farms, and industrial plants. An analysis of Soviet educational practices viewed with reference to educational conditions existing prior to the 1917 Revolution.

703 Blyth, William A. *English Primary Education: a Sociological Description,* 2 vols. New York, Humanities, 1965. biblio.

An account of the whole social process of English primary education and its institutional framework, whose purpose is to stimulate social research in preparation for proposed changes in the English educational structure.

704 Burns, Donald C. *African Education: an Introductory Survey of Education in Commonwealth Countries.* New York, Oxford UP, 1965. 215p. biblio.

Covers primary, secondary, and university education as they have developed in relation to the differing social customs in Africa. Tabulated data based on reports of ministries and departments of education.

705 Castle, B. B. *Growing Up in East Africa.* New York, Oxford UP, 1966. 272p. biblio.

A comprehensive treatment of Africa's educational needs. Examines the social and cultural background, the existing educational resources, and teacher education. The conflict between Western and tribal values is discussed as it interferes with educational progress and principles for synthesizing the best elements of the two cultures are recommended.

706 Cowan, L. Gray, and others. *Education and Nation-Building in Africa.* New York, Praeger, 1965. 403p. biblio.

A coherent overview of African education in a series of articles and documents. Emphasis is more on education than on nation-building.

707 Curtis, S. J. *History of Education in Great Britain,* 5th ed. London, University Tutorial Press, 1963. 706p. biblio.

The origin and growth of primary and secondary schools, universities, and other educational institutions and agencies in England. Points out the important differences between the English and Scottish systems and the influence of each upon the other.

708 Dixon, Willis. *Society, Schools and Progress in Scandinavia.* New York, Pergamon, 1965. 193p. biblio.

Relates educational policy debates to basic issues of social policy and processes of political decision-making. An examination of educational systems undergoing radical changes in the direction of social equality.

709 Flack, Michael J. *Sources of Information on International Educational Activities.* Washington, ACE, 1958. 114p.

A survey of information clearinghouses and bureaus listing organizations, institutions, or projects that, as a primary service, compile or disseminate information on international activities of interest to American universities and colleges.

710 Hans, Nicholas A. *The Russian Tradition in Education.* London, Routledge and Paul, 1963. 196p. biblio.

By providing a history of Russian educational ideas and how they have been realized in the past and present, the author attempts to answer the question of whether the Soviet Union is the heir of the old Russian Empire not only in territory, population, and language, but also in ideas and traditions.

711 Havighurst, Robert J., and Moreira, J. Roberto. *Society and Education in Brazil.* Pittsburgh, U of Pittsburgh P, 1965. 263p. biblio.

A comprehensive and authoritative work on a rapidly changing and growing nation.

712   Hu, Chang-Tu, ed. *Chinese Education under Communism.* New York, TC, Columbia, 1962. 157p.

Selections by various Communist leaders focus on the fundamental educational considerations, principles, and policies operational in China today.

713   *International Yearbook of Education,* vol. 29. Geneva, International Bureau of Education, 1967.

An indispensable annual covering educational developments in nearly 100 countries. A sort of news-of-the-year-in-review, with listings of officials and useful statistics.

714   King, Edmund J., ed. *Communist Education.* Indianapolis, Bobbs Merrill, 1963. 309p. biblio.

The principal purpose of this collection of articles on education at various levels and in various areas of the Communist world is to present as objectively as possible the "inside story" as seen and studied by professional educators.

715   Kitchen, Helen A., ed. *The Educated African: a Country by Country Survey of Educational Development in Africa.* (Ruth Sloan Associates, Inc.) New York, Praeger, 1962. 542p. biblio.

A data source book, notable for its descriptions of educational systems.

716   Korol, Alexander G. *Soviet Education for Science and Technology.* New York, Wiley, 1957. 513p. biblio.

In the race between this country and Russia we face defeat from the Soviet challenge if we continue business as usual in education or any other field. For national survival there are indispensable goals that must be ranked ahead of individual propensities for conspicuous consumption.

717   Matthews, Roderic D., and Akrawi, Matt. *Education in the Arab Countries of the Near East: Egypt, Iraq, Palestine, Transjordan, Syria, and Lebanon.* Washington, ACE, 1949. 584p.

The report of a commission sponsored by the U.S. Department of State, its value lies in its intensive study and description of educational provisions in Arab-speaking countries two decades ago.

718 Moos, Elizabeth. *Soviet Education: Achievements and Goals.*
New York, National Council of American-Soviet Friendship,
1967. 127p. biblio.

An outline of educational development in Russia over the
past 50 years and a description of the schools in 1967, based
on Soviet education journals and documents and on the
author's observations and conversations with Soviet educators.

719 Noah, Harold J. *Financing Soviet Schools.* New York, TC,
Columbia, 1966. 294p. biblio.

A revision of the author's doctoral dissertation. Offers a
detailed analysis of school financing in Russia as well as a
study of provisions for education in that country.

720 Qubain, Fahim I. *Education and Science in the Arab World.*
Baltimore, Johns Hopkins UP, 1966. 539p. biblio.

A brief overview of the entire educational system and a
survey of the extent and quality of science training as well
as of manpower resources in the various Arab nations.

721 Ramanathan, Gopalakrishnan. *Educational Planning and National Development.* New York, Asia (Taplinger), 1965.
252p.

Linguistic diversity, the continued use of English as the
common language, and the problems of developing a national
language are part of this study of education in India. Concern
is expressed that education's goal is personal affluence and
that educational development and innovation will be hindered by traditionalists.

722 Redl, Helen B., ed. *Soviet Educators on Soviet Education.*
New York, Free Press, 1964. 252p.

A representative selection of old and recent materials,
focusing on the basic philosophy of child-rearing and education and its implementation.

723 Rudman, Herbert C. *The School and State in the USSR.* New
York, Macmillan, 1967. 286p.

An examination of the power and authority structure in the
highly centralized school system in Russia to determine how
decisions are made.

724 Sasnett, Martena, and Sepmeyer, Inez. *Educational Systems
of Africa: Interpretations for Use in the Evaluation of Aca-*

demic Credentials. Berkeley, U of California P, 1966. 1550p. biblio.

This mammoth undertaking is useful beyond its stated intent, as it is packed with historical, cultural, and political facts and statistics in addition to its charts and textual descriptions of educational systems. Extensive bibliography.

725 Scanlon, David G., ed. *Church, State and Education in Africa.* New York, TC, Columbia, 1966. 313p. biblio.

Discusses the transfer of church and school leadership from colonial to African hands in a group of essays that review past church-state relationships in relation to education, analyze existing arrangements, and comment on possible trends.

726 Shamsul Huq, Muhammad. *Education and Development Strategy in South and Southeast Asia.* Honolulu, East-West Center, 1965. 286p.

Partially a review of research and opinion about education in developing countries and for the rest an examination of education in India, Pakistan, Indonesia, and the Philippines, with a bit of attention given to primary education in other Asian countries. This is a thorough and scholarly work and a major contribution.

727 Weinberg, Ian. *The English Public Schools: the Sociology of Elite Education.* New York, Atherton, 1967. 225p. biblio.

Describes the development of a unique educational institution, its conservation of important values, and its relation to cultural tradition in the light of the pressure of the contemporary forces of social change.

728 *World Survey of Education,* 4 vols. Paris, UNESCO, 1955-66.

Without equal as a source of information on education in other countries of the world. Volume 1 (1955) is a handbook of educational organizations and statistics; volumes 2 (1958), 3 (1961), and 4 (1966) cover primary, secondary, and higher education. Information can be updated by using the *International Yearbook of Education* (#713).

729 *The World Yearbook of Education.* New York, Harcourt. 1932- .

Called the *Yearbook of Education* from 1932 to 1965, this annual covers a particular area in the field of education in each volume. Each contains articles by prominent educators in this country and in others. Recent titles have been: *The Education Explosion* (1965), *Church and State in Education* (1966), and *Educational Planning* (1967).

Higher Education Abroad

730 Ashby, Eric, and Anderson, Mary. *Universities: British, Indian, African: a Study in the Ecology of Higher Education.* Cambridge, Harvard UP, 1966. 558p. biblio.

An historian and administrator brilliantly analyzes the development of higher education in English-speaking tropical Africa and in India.

731 Bradby, Edward, ed. *The University Outside Europe: Essays on the Development of University Institutions in Fourteen Countries.* New York, Oxford UP, 1939. 332p.

The story of the impact of the European university on new or changing societies and of the modifications and adaptations the idea of the European university has undergone. Examines the fundamental issues faced by most universities and has as much pertinence today as when it was written.

732 Carr-Saunders, Alexander M. *New Universities Overseas.* London, Allen and Unwin, 1961. 260p. biblio.

Describes the latest phase (1945-1960) of the rise and development of universities in territories that have been under British rule, especially those that had colonial status in 1945 and at that time had few facilities for higher education.

733 *Commonwealth Universities Yearbook: a Directory to the Universities of the Commonwealth and the Handbook of Their Association.* London, The Association of Commonwealth Universities. 1st-   1914-

An annual directory to university institutions in all the Commonwealth countries, not restricted to the 157 that comprise the Association's membership. Includes general information, teaching and administrative staff, and recent events.

734 *Higher Education in the United Kingdom: a Handbook for Students from Overseas and Their Advisers.* London, Longmans, 1966. 304p.

A biennial guide that serves as a useful reference covering all areas of study, both academic and vocational.

735 *International Handbook of Universities and Other Institutions of Higher Education*, 3rd ed. Paris, International Association of Universities, 1965. 1034p.

A companion volume to *Commonwealth Universities Yearbook* (#733) and *American Universities and Colleges* (#1169) and an invaluable source of information on higher education in about one hundred countries and territories. Several hundred institutions are described in detail and another one thousand or so are mentioned briefly.

736 Kerr, Anthony. *Universities of Europe*. Westminster, Md., Canterbury, 1962. 235p.

A description of university organization, studies, and life throughout Europe. Chapters describe individual countries and their institutions.

EDUCATIONAL PHILOSOPHY
see also EDUCATION

737 Arnstine, Donald. *Philosophy of Education: Learning and Schooling*. New York, Harper, 1967. 388p.

A scholarly, well-written, and lively consideration of education as a total life experience and a proposal that schooling be characterized by esthetic experience, curiosity, and problem-solving. Stimulating definitions of learning as a change in disposition and thinking as the pursuit of discrepancies.

738 Bode, Boyd H. *Progressive Education at the Crossroads*. New York, Newson, 1938. 128p. biblio.

A defense of progressive education that seeks to contribute to a better understanding of its justification, its promise, and its potential in promoting a distinctive way of life.

739 Brauner, Charles J., and Burns, Hobert W. *Problems in Education and Philosophy*. Englewood Cliffs, N.J., Prentice-Hall, 1965. 114p.

Methods of philosophy applied to four problems of education: training the mind, progressive education, academic excellence and the dropout, and creativity and conformity. Soundly based and well-written.

740 Brown, L. M. *General Philosophy in Education*. New York, McGraw-Hill, 1966. 244p. biblio.

Application of logical positivism and linguistic analysis to educational objectives and to problems in philosophy relevant to education.

741 Brubacher, John S. *Modern Philosophies of Education,* 3rd ed. New York, McGraw-Hill, 1962. 373p. biblio.

A comparative study of the different philosophic approaches to educational problems.

742 Burns, Hobert W., and Brauner, Charles J., eds. *Philosophy of Education: Essays and Commentaries.* New York, Ronald, 1962. 442p. biblio.

Discursive essays on the nature of educational philosophy, the divisions of philosophy, philosophies of education, and the crucial issue of translating theory into practice.

743 Butler, J. Donald. *Four Philosophies and Their Practice in Education and Religion,* 3rd ed. New York, Harper, 1968. 528p. biblio.

An introduction to philosophy and to philosophy of education. Naturalism, idealism, realism, and pragmatism are studied, compared, and related to education and religion. Some attention given to existentialism. A systematically organized, thorough, and lucid book.

744 Childs, John L. *Education and Morals: an Experimental Philosophy of Education.* New York, Appleton, 1950. 299p. biblio.

The aim of education should be the growth and liberation of the child, not his subordination to an external and absolute system. This necessarily makes *method* in education a moral as well as a psychological and pedagogical affair.

745 Childs, John L. *Pragmatism and American Education.* New York, Appleton, 1956. 373p. biblio.

A thorough and critical examination of the pragmatists, their philosophy, ambiguities, and the cultural roots of their thinking.

746 Demiashkevich, Michael J. *Introduction to the Philosophy of Education.* New York, American, 1935. 449p. biblio.

An enlightening critique of past philosophies of education intended to help the student formulate his own philosophy intelligently.

747 Dewey, John. *The Child and the Curriculum.* Chicago, U of Chicago P, 1902. 31p.

One of the philosopher's influential essays, written just after his arrival at Teachers College. The focus is on the growing individual.

748 _____. *Democracy and Education: an Introduction to the Philosophy of Education.* New York, Free Press, 1966. 378p.

Originally published in 1916, this book investigates the ideas implicit in a democratic society and applies them to the problems of education. A discussion of the constructive aims and methods of public education and a critical evaluation of the theories of knowing and development that hamper the realization of the democratic ideal. (See also #757.)

749 _____. *Experience and Education.* New York, Collier, 1963. 116p.

Originally published in 1938, this Kappa Delta Pi Lecture is a lucid analysis of both traditional and progressive education, describing some fundamental defects of both. Calls attention to the larger and deeper issues and the need for a new conceptual framework to form an educational philosophy.

750 _____. *Lectures in the Philosophy of Education.* New York, Random, 1966. 366p. biblio.

Well-edited by Reginald D. Archambault, these hitherto unpublished 1898 and 1899 lectures provide background for Dewey's evolving philosophy and for *Democracy and Education* (#748), the great work of his mature years.

751 _____. *The School and Society,* rev. ed. Chicago, U of Chicago P, 1915. 164p.

Written in 1899 when Dewey's focus was an attack on the still entrenched and often unthinking educational system and revised later to incorporate modifications in Dewey's thinking and suggestions made by students and colleagues, this contains Dewey's basic ideas of progressive education.

752 Dupuis, Adrian M. *Philosophy of Education in Historical Perspective.* Chicago, Rand McNally, 1966. 308p. biblio.

An historical perspective on current conflicts in education that demonstrates that today's debates over educational goals are based on fundamental problems that have vexed past educators.

753 Frankena, William K. *Philosophy of Education.* New York, Macmillan, 1965. 165p. biblio.

A discussion of four philosophers: John Dewey, Alfred North Whitehead, Jacques Maritain, and Richard S. Peters, with selections from their works. The purpose is to assist the reader to reach an examined and intelligent position.

754 Frasier, George W. *An Introduction to the Study of Educa-tion*, 3rd ed. (Revised by James E. Frasier) New York, Harper, 1965. 303p. biblio.

A basic book with a well-written philosophical approach for the general reader and the prospective teacher.

755 Henderson, Stella V. *Introduction to Philosophy of Education.* Chicago, U of Chicago P, 1947. 401p. biblio.

A discussion of the need for teachers, to be successful in furthering human welfare, to apply philosophy to the study of educational problems, with the assumption that the ends and objectives of living determine educational aims.

756 Henry, Nelson B., ed. *Modern Philosophies and Education* (NSSE 53rd Yearbook, Part I). Chicago, U of Chicago P, 1954. 374p. biblio.

Authoritative opinions on the fundamental issues of edu-cational aims and procedures as interpreted by educational philosophers and by those having an interest in education.

757 Horne, Herman H. *The Democratic Philosophy of Education: Companion to Dewey's Democracy and Education: Exposi-tion and Comment.* New York, Macmillan, 1932. 547p.

Particularly valuable for those who may find Dewey's prose occasionally turgid, this follows the Dewey text and presents a clarifying exposition with interpretive and critical comment.

758 Johnston, Herbert. *A Philosophy of Education.* New York, McGraw-Hill, 1963. 362p.

The author's thesis is that the philosophy of education, far from being a static framework, is a dynamic approach to viewing educational problems in perspective.

759 Kneller, George E., ed. *Foundations of Education,* 2nd ed. New York, Wiley, 1967. 678p. biblio.

Believing that education is an intellectual discipline com-parable to other academic disciplines and that teaching is a rewarding profession but one that commands its price, the author presents basic methodological and theoretical prin-ciples necessary to the investigation and solution of such educational problems as transmitting knowledge and relating it to the interests and capacities of all students.

760 Lodge, Rupert C. *Philosophy of Education,* rev. ed. New York, Harper, 1947. 350p. biblio.

A philosopher presents creatively and sympathetically the three major schools in the philosophy of education: the realist, the idealist, and the pragmatic.

761 Maritain, Jacques. *Education at the Crossroads.* New Haven, Yale UP, 1943. 120p. biblio.

Lectures delivered by the French philosopher at Yale in 1943. He sees the crucial need and problem in education as the rejection of pragmatism in favor of a rediscovery of the natural faith of reason in truth.

762 Meiklejohn, Alexander. *Education Between Two Worlds.* New York, Atherton, 1966. 303p.

Originally published in 1942, this critically examines the theories of education of Rousseau and Dewey. Their strengths and deficiencies are developed in relation to current philosophical issues and educational decisions.

763 Morris, Van Cleve. *Existentialism in Education: What It Means.* New York, Harper, 1966. 163p.

A succinct review of existential philosophy and a discussion of its application to educational theory and practice.

764 Nash, Paul. *Authority and Freedom in Education: an Introduction to the Philosophy of Education.* New York, Wiley, 1966. 342p.

A philosophy of education with a wide range, going beyond the field of education into the larger social context. Scholarly and eloquent.

765 Neff, Frederick C. *Philosophy and American Education.* New York, CARE, 1966. 116p. biblio.

The leading ideas of five historic schools of philosophy (idealism, realism, pragmatism, analysis, and existentialism) are analyzed and evaluated in an attempt to consider their bearing on education. Emphasis on the need for philosophers of education to consider their ideas as part of the broad discipline of philosophy.

766 Park, Joe, ed. *Selected Readings in the Philosophy of Education,* 2nd ed. Cambridge, Harvard UP, 1963. 614p. biblio.

A collection of 26 selections makes available some of the best known works in the philosophy of education, including Dewey, Kneller, and others.

767   Peters, Richard S. *Authority, Responsibility, and Education.* New York, Atherton, 1966. 137p.

    A reprint of a 1960 title, based on talks delivered between 1956 and 1959. Discusses the changing face of authority, Freud, Marx, and responsibility in relation to the philosophy of education.

768   ———, and others. *The Concept of Education.* New York, Humanities, 1967. 224p.

    Based on lectures given in 1965 at the University of London Institute of Education by philosophers interested in education as an area for philosophical investigation and by educators interested in philosophy of education. Somewhat diverse approaches unified by the editor's introduction.

769   Price, Kingsley. *Education and Philosophical Thought,* 2nd ed. Boston, Allyn and Bacon, 1967. 605p. biblio.

    This considerably enlarged revision discusses the ideas of the great philosophers—Plato, Quintilian, St. Augustine, Comenius, Locke, Rousseau, Kant, Mill, Dewey—in terms of their influence on subsequent philosophies of education.

770   Rich, John M., ed. *Readings in the Philosophy of Education.* Belmont, Cal., Wadsworth, 1966. 393p.

    Twenty-eight essays examine educational aims, develop theories of human nature and their meaning for education and social life, philosophically formulate the place and function of education within the social order, and interpret educational values and their role in the development of youth.

771   Russell, Bertrand. *Education and the Good Life.* New York, Boni and Liveright, 1926. 319p.

    Considers the aims of education and the kinds of individuals and community we hope to see produced by education. Philosopher Russell is a crystal gazer who attached weight to psychological research showing that character is determined by early education to a much greater extent than believed by educators of earlier generations.

772   ———. *Education and the Social Order.* New York, Humanities, 1967. 150p.

    A collection of perceptive essays, first published in 1932, by the century's leading philosopher, who addresses himself to the question of whether education should train good individuals or good citizens.

773 Smith, Philip G. *Philosophy of Education: Introductory Studies.* New York, Harper, 1965. 276p. biblio.

A philosophy *of* education, comparable to the philosophy of science and distinguished from philosophies *and, in, and for* education.

774 Wegener, Frank C. *The Organic Philosophy of Education.* Dubuque, Iowa, Brown, 1957. 472p. biblio.

Recognizing the validity of two diverse educational doctrines (education as growth, development, and experience and education as a systematic intellectual and moral process), the author recommends that the two should be synthesized and coordinated into an organic philosophy that would provide a "school within a school" and the "formal within the informal."

775 Wingo, Max G. *The Philosophy of American Education.* Boston, Heath, 1965. 438p. biblio.

Primarily a descriptive study of contemporary thought in educational philosophy, posing the major questions and offering the variant answers that have been given.

EDUCATIONAL PSYCHOLOGY
see also LEARNING THEORY
PSYCHOLOGICAL THEORY

776 Bernard, Harold W., and Hickins, Wesley C., eds. *Readings in Human Development.* Boston, Allyn and Bacon, 1967. 368p. biblio.

An interdisciplinary approach covering the principles of development, intellectual development, group influences, and the role of the school.

777 Bower, Eli M., and Hollister, William G., eds. *Behavioral Frontiers in Education.* New York, Wiley, 1967. 539p. biblio.

An excellent collection of essays on the theory of human learning with emphasis on the application of ego processes to education.

778 Bruner, Jerome S. *Toward a Theory of Instruction.* Cambridge, Harvard UP, 1966. 176p.

Bruner manages to pack large punches into small volumes that have an enormous impact. A provocative discussion of the relationship between psychology and education and between teaching and learning, based on research in many fields and Bruner's own experiments.

779 Bugelski, B. R. *The Psychology of Learning Applied to Teaching.* Indianapolis, Bobbs Merrill, 1963. 278p. biblio.

Designed to familiarize the classroom teacher with those findings of psychology that pertain to the process of instruction, with emphasis on practical information rather than theoretical speculation.

780 Burton, William H., and others. *Education for Effective Thinking: an Introductory Text.* New York, Appleton, 1960. 508p.

An examination of the process of thinking and the application of thought processes within a school setting.

781 Carpenter, Finley, and Haddan, Eugene E. *Systematic Application of Psychology to Education.* New York, Macmillan, 1964. 270p.

An exposition of the situational nature and relevance of educational processes and the exercise of appropriate skills for sequential functions.

782 Craig, Robert C. *The Psychology of Learning in the Classroom.* New York, Macmillan, 1966. 85p. biblio.

An succinct yet comprehensive review of the major current learning theories with examples of their application to classroom teaching.

783 Cronbach, Lee J. *Educational Psychology,* 2nd ed. New York, Harcourt, 1963. 406p. biblio.

A lucid presentation of essential principles designed to assist teachers to perform more knowledgeably and therefore more intelligently.

784 DeCecco, John P., ed. *Human Learning in the School.* New York, Holt, 1963. 636p. biblio.

A balanced selection of articles that reflect the contributions of both educational and experimental psychology to our knowledge of how children learn and how they can be helped to learn.

785 Dewey, John. *How We Think: a Restatement of the Relation of the Reflective Thinking to the Educative Process.* Boston, Heath, 1933. 301p.

An admittedly idealized version of how people think with an emphasis on a problem-solving type of thinking. Originally published in 1910.

786   Eson, Morris E. *Psychological Foundations of Education.* New York, Holt, 1964. 563p. biblio.

Acting on the theory that no single school of psychological thought can cover the wide range of problems faced by the classroom teacher and that each school or system of psychology can contribute to the clarification of particular questions, the author considers each educational problem in the light of the most pertinent and insightful psychological viewpoint.

787   Fields, Morey R., ed. *Frontiers in Education.* New York, CARE, 1967. 116p. biblio.

Concerned with the problems, the research, and the implementation of research results in the areas of child development, learning, intellectual growth, and teaching.

788   Gagné, Robert M. *The Conditions of Learning.* New York, Holt, 1965. 308p. biblio.

A lucid and illuminating discussion of the process of learning intended for use in designing better education, based on the theory that complex forms of learning require simpler forms of behavior as prerequisites.

789   ————, ed. *Learning and Individual Differences.* Columbus, Merrill, 1967. 265p. biblio.

The report of a symposium of the Learning Research and Development Center at the University of Pittsburgh. Discusses in broad terms what kinds of ways people may be expected to differ in their learning and how these methods might be measured as individual differences.

790   Garry, Ralph. *The Psychology of Learning.* New York, CARE, 1963. 111p. biblio.

Research in the behavioral sciences and conceptual theory are integrated with practice. An honest confrontation of facts and ideas with the practical problems of application.

791   Glaser, Robert, ed. *Training Research and Education.* Pittsburgh, U of Pittsburgh P, 1962. 596p. biblio.

An examination of research by experimental psychologists in the field of training and a discussion of the implications of the findings in this field for education, based on the premise that the processes involved in education and in training have common elements.

792   Havighurst, Robert J. *Human Development and Education.* New York, McKay, 1953. 338p.

    A well-written basic reference that is an analysis of the meaning of the developmental task concept as it relates to education, with data and cases.

793   Hilgard, Ernest R., and Bower, Gordon H. *Theories of Learning,* 3rd ed. New York, Appleton, 1966. 661p. biblio.

    An orientation to the main influences on learning theory in the first half of the 20th century and an examination of how they are represented in contemporary experimentation and theorizing.

794   ———, ed. *Theories of Learning and Instruction* (NSSE 63rd Yearbook, Part I). Chicago, U of Chicago P, 1964. 430p.

    An overview and analysis of the present state of the art of understanding understanding. Relates what we know about how we learn to a theory of how we can best teach. Important not only for its presentation of major lines of contemporary thought, but also for the clear implications of what we do not know.

795   Holt, John C. *How Children Fail.* New York, Pitman, 1964. 181p.

    An eloquent critique, based on personal observation in the classroom, of standard educational practice. The author finds school an intellectually debilitating experience where children's curiosity is stifled as they acquire facilities that will somehow get them through their schooling.

796   ———. *How Children Learn.* New York, Pitman, 1967. 189p.

    A plea for permitting children to be in control of their own learning, with intelligent guidance, for dealing honestly with them, and granting them dignity. Idealistic and bound to be controversial, the book substantiates its original and acute thesis by offering many examples of the author's own teaching experiments.

797   Hullfish, H. Gordon, and Smith, Philip G. *Reflective Thinking: the Method of Education.* New York, Dodd, 1961. 273p. biblio.

    An analysis of the processes of thought that provides insights into the types of intellectual activities that contribute to reflective thinking, based on the thesis that the primary responsibility of the teacher in a free society is to help develop independently thinking citizens.

798 James, William. *Talks to Teachers on Psychology: and to Students on Some of Life's Ideals.* New York, Norton, 1958. 191p.

Originally published in 1899, this is of historic interest and not wholly applicable today.

799 Klausmeier, Herbert J., and Goodwin, William. *Learning and Human Abilities: Educational Psychology,* 2nd ed. New York, Harper, 1966. 720p. biblio.

The concept of emergent human abilities is evolved as a bridge between learning and development, which are not seen as separate entities. With an emphasis on learning-teaching processes, the authors discuss the principal variables affecting efficiency of learning and the conditions essential to efficient learning.

800 Krumboltz, John D., ed. *Learning and the Educational Process.* Chicago, Rand McNally, 1965. 277p. biblio.

Selected papers from the 1964 Stanford University Conference on Learning and the Educational Process. A fine sampling of the research approaches and findings on learning and motivation in the schools.

801 Loree, M. Ray. *Psychology of Education.* New York, Ronald, 1965. 620p.

Descriptions of pertinent research studies serve both to illuminate the principles, concepts, and theories of the teaching-learning process and to demonstrate the relevance of scientific method to the solution of actual classroom problems.

802 Melby, Ernest O. *The Teacher and Learning.* New York, CARE, 1963. 118p. biblio.

A bold, outspoken challenge by one of the country's most distinguished educators, which raises and attempts to answer some fundamental questions about the teaching-learning process.

803 Scheffler, Israel. *The Conditions of Knowledge: an Introduction to Epistemology and Education.* Chicago, Scott Foresman, 1965. 117p. biblio.

A brief but telling treatment of knowledge in relation to teaching, truth, evidence, belief, and skill.

804 Stephens, John M. *The Process of Schooling: a Psychological Examination*. New York, Holt, 1967. 168p. biblio.

A well-written and illuminating discussion of the conduct of education in the light of current psychological understanding.

805 ———. *The Psychology of Classroom Learning*. New York, Holt, 1965. 511p. biblio.

Applies psychological principles and data to the means used by teachers to direct academic achievement, to promote character development, and to aid in personal adjustment.

806 Stoddard, George D. *The Meaning of Intelligence*. New York, Macmillan, 1943. 504p. biblio.

Still an important book, this brings into focus various research findings on the broad questions of intelligence and attempts to relate technical issues to problems in modern life. Examines the nature, measurement, and growth of intelligence, the effects of heredity and environment, and educational and social implications.

807 Stones, E. *An Introduction to Educational Psychology*. New York, Barnes and Noble, 1966. 424p. biblio.

A clear exposition of teaching-learning theory and proven techniques by an experienced Englishman.

808 Thorndike, Edward L. *Educational Psychology*, 3 vols. New York, TC, Columbia, 1913-1914. biblio.

A classic study, with continuing relevance, of the nature of man, the psychology of learning, and of mental work, fatigue, and individual differences.

809 Travers, Robert M. W. *The Essentials of Learning: an Overview for Students of Education*, 2nd ed. New York, Macmillan, 1967. 560p. biblio.

Updated, revised, and partly rewritten, this is an improved version of Travers' 1963 book. Covers the field of learning as applied to the educational process. Analytical in tone and purpose and well-documented.

810 Whipple, Guy M., ed. *Intelligence: Its Nature and Nurture: Original Studies and Experiments* (NSSE 39th Yearbook, Part II). Chicago, U of Chicago P, 1940. 409p. biblio.

———. *Addresses and Discussions Presenting the Thirty-*

Ninth Yearbook "Intelligence: Its Nature and Nurture." Chicago, U of Chicago P, 1940. 84p.

The yearbook, a sequel to the famous 27th, is an exhaustive coverage of mental growth in children and the effects of schooling and other factors on the growth of intelligence. The *Addresses and Discussions* take up the problems of the issues emerging from the yearbook's reports and their social and educational implications.

811 _____, ed. *Nature and Nurture: Their Influence upon Intelligence* and *Their Influence upon Achievement* (NSSE 27th Yearbook, Part I and Part II in one volume). Chicago, U of Chicago P, 1928. 465p. and 397p. biblio.

Referred to as the "famous 27th," this examines and speculates on the effect of environment upon intelligence. If differences among children are due to controllable factors of environment and training, then theoretically, dull children can be turned into bright ones through appropriate educational procedures. If not, the schools must provide for differentiated training that will take into account native differences.

EDUCATIONAL SOCIOLOGY
see also GOVERNMENT AND EDUCATION
SOCIAL PSYCHOLOGY

812 Amidon, Edmund J., and Hough, John B., eds. *Interaction Analysis: Theory, Research, and Application.* Cambridge, Mass., Addison Wesley, 1967. 402p. biblio.

A collection of representative papers dealing with theory, research, and application of interaction analysis to the assessment of the socio-emotional climate of the classroom and to the problems of teacher education.

813 Brembeck, Cole S. *Social Foundations of Education: a Cross-Cultural Approach.* New York, Wiley, 1966. 540p. biblio.

A well-organized text covering the social aspects of teaching, the educational aspects of environment, social class influences on learning, the social function of the schools, the teacher, and the educational problems of a changing society.

814 Brookover, Wilbur B., and Gottlieb, David. *A Sociology of Education*, 2nd ed. New York, American, 1964. 488p. biblio.

A theoretical discussion of education in society, the school society, and socialization in the school system. Develops an interaction theory of school learning and analyzes education in relation to social change, economic growth, and basic American goals and values.

815 Charters, W. W., Jr., and Gage, Nathaniel L., eds. *Readings in the Social Psychology of Education*. Boston, Allyn and Bacon, 1963. 350p.

Analyzes the forces that affect students and teachers in the educational setting: those arising outside the classroom and inside the classroom that influence students and those that act upon the adult in the school.

816 Cicourel, Aaron V., and Kitsuse, John I. *The Educational Decision-Makers*. Indianapolis. Bobbs Merrill, 1963. 178p.

A penetrating analysis of the school as a mechanism of social differentiation. Discusses ascription of parental and student college aspirations, organizational differentiation of incoming freshmen, bureaucratization of the counseling system, high school bureaucracy, and social mobility.

817 Clark, Burton R. *Educating the Expert Society*. San Francisco, Chandler, 1962. 301p. biblio.

Deals with issues relating to the educational structure in the light of educational control, formal organization of school and college, and student culture. The author's thesis is that a changing society calls for changing schools.

818 Corwin, Ronald G. *A Sociology of Education: Emerging Patterns of Class, Status, and Power in the Public Schools*. New York, Appleton, 1965. 454p. biblio.

Based primarily on the growing sociological literature on educational systems. School systems are viewed from various perspectives as complex bureaucratic organizations unavoidably involved in the rapid changes occurring in our society.

819 Doll, Ronald C., and Fleming, Robert S., eds. *Children Under Pressure*. Columbus, Merrill, 1966. 109p.

A description of the scholastic pressures affecting children today, a plea for permitting children some time and freedom for living, and suggestions on how to accomplish this.

820 Edgar, Earl E. *Social Foundations of Education*. New York, CARE, 1965. 118p. biblio.

An examination of the role of the school and its task, in

relation to some of the significant forces that aid or hinder its performance within the socio-cultural framework.

821 Goslin, David A. *The School in Contemporary Society*. Glenview, Ill., Scott Foresman, 1965. 173p. biblio.

An incisive analysis of the school and of the major sociological phenomena affecting educational structure and practice. Concise, well-written, convincing, and well-documented with research.

822 Grambs, Jean D. *Schools, Scholars, and Society*. Englewood Cliffs, N.J., Prentice-Hall, 1965. 181p. biblio.

A provocative consideration of the educational process in relation to society. Discusses such topics as "whose school is it?," "society as educator," "education for limbo," "stainless steel ivory towers," and the culture of the secondary school and the college.

823 Havighurst, Robert J., and others. *Society and Education: a Book of Readings*, 3rd ed. Boston, Allyn and Bacon, 1967. 364p.

Intended to provide supplementary readings for courses in educational sociology and to provide depth by including two or three articles on each of the successive topics regarded as central in importance.

824 Hodgkinson, Harold L. *Education, Interaction, and Social Change*. Englewood Cliffs, N.J., Prentice-Hall, 1967. 256p.

An argument for the use of sociology as a means of analyzing change, which is seen as the basic force in operation today in all educational institutions, public and private, kindergarten to graduate school.

825 Jensen, Gale E. *Educational Sociology*. New York, CARE, 1965. 112p. biblio.

A clear picture of the sociological aspects of educational problems. Defines several related clusters of problems in terms of pertinent sociological knowledge and places particular emphasis on small groups and formal organization.

826 Lutz, Frank W., and Iannaccone, Laurence. *Understanding Educational Organizations*. Columbus, Merrill, 1968. 200p. biblio.

An examination of research methods in community study in relation to education and of methods of studying power in educational systems. Attempts to make up for the lack of theory in most books in this subject.

827 MacLean, Malcolm S., and Lee, Edwin A. *Change and Process in Education*. New York, Dryden, 1956. 520p. biblio.

Discusses the public schools as a basic agency in a democratic society, covering the relationships between school and society, society's effects on education, and the teaching profession's attempt to meet current societal demands.

828 McLendon, Jonathon C., ed. *Social Foundations of Education: Current Readings from the Behavioral Sciences*. New York, Macmillan, 1966. 382p.

Articles by scholars in psychology, sociology, anthropology, communications, government, history, and philosophy that focus on the schools as social institutions.

829 Musgrove, F. *The Family, Education and Society*. New York, Humanities, 1966. 156p. biblio.

A provocative book capable of stirring considerable controversy as a result of its British author's unorthodox views in favor of competitive examinations for the young and strengthening the school at the expense of family ties. He offers some genuinely constructive suggestions for the improvement of the school system and society.

830 Page, Charles H., ed. *Sociology and Contemporary Education*. New York, Random, 1964. 138p. biblio.

Essays presented at the 1962 meetings of the American Sociological Association that discuss sociology as an educational enterprise, sociology and general education, the conventional wisdom of education and sociology, and popular sociology.

831 Sexton, Patricia C. *The American School: a Sociological Analysis*. Englewood Cliffs, N.J., Prentice-Hall, 1967. 122p. biblio.

A brief and lucid survey of the social factors that affect the school: power, the economy, social class, bureaucracy, cultural values and ideology, youth culture, and the city and community.

832 _____, ed. *Readings on the School in Society*. Englewood Cliffs, N.J., Prentice-Hall, 1968. 288p.

A collection of stimulating, provocative readings examining

the nature of public education and its isolation from the mainstream of society. An approach to studying and solving the problems of American schools through analyzing the social forces that shape the schools and the flaws that exist within the school system.

833 Spindler, George D., ed. *Education and Culture: Anthropological Approaches.* New York, Holt, 1963. 571p.

A purposeful exploration of a frontier area—the application of anthropology to education.

834 Thayer, Vivian T. *The Role of the School in American Society*, 2nd ed. New York, Dodd, 1966. 589p. biblio.

An analysis of the essential characteristics of the heritage of our system of public education that identifies the critical issues that threaten to destroy it.

835 Westby-Gibson, Dorothy, ed. *Social Foundations of Education.* New York, Free Press, 1967. 256p.

Important new research done by a wide range of social critics and educators. Covers pressures on students, the social role of education, pressures on socially disadvantaged youth, and the growing status of educators.

ELEMENTARY SCHOOLS

836 Frazier, Alexander, ed. *The New Elementary School.* Washington, NEA, 1967. 160p.

The papers of a 1967 conference jointly sponsored by ASCD and the Department of Elementary School Principals. Reviews new knowledge about learning and new approaches in school organization and curriculum, and gives attention to the teacher and in-service education. A useful overview of elementary education today.

837 Kearney, Nolan C. *Elementary School Objectives.* New York, Russell Sage Foundation, 1953. 189p. biblio.

A report prepared for the Mid-Century Committee on Outcomes in Elementary Education, in which the specific objectives of elementary education are outlined by a distinguished group of consultants and evaluated by selected critics. Emphasis on obtainable objectives rather than on curriculum problems or instructional methods.

838   Lambert, Hazel M. *Elementary Education*. New York, CARE, 1963. 117p. biblio.

     A skillful and brief review of history, learning theory, curriculum trends and innovations, and of organizational practices, which places the elementary school in the contemporary social context.

839   Manolakes, George. *The Elementary School We Need*. (ASCD) Washington, NEA, 1965. 40p.

     Reflects a broad perspective of thinking about the needs of children and possible ways to fulfill these needs through teaching approaches and school organization.

840   Neill, Alexander S. *Summerhill: a Radical Approach to Child Rearing*. New York, Hart, 1960. 392p.

     A widely read, influential description of a unique philosophy and of the school in which it is implemented, a place where children are raised not to have or to use much, but to be much, where freedom replaces authority, and where learning takes place as the result of spontaneous curiosity and as the result of the mutual respect of teacher and child.

841   Wolf, William C., Jr., and Loomer, Bradley M. *Elementary School: a Perspective*. Chicago, Rand McNally, 1966. 310p. biblio.

     Today's elementary school, its evolving nature, its children, and its teachers are the focus of this soundly-based attempt "to portray a 'Gestalt' known as the elementary school." Past and future are sketched, and the present is vividly brought to life by the introduction of a fictitious teacher and her real-life experiences in an urban classroom.

EMOTIONALLY DISTURBED CHILDREN
see also EXCEPTIONAL CHILDREN
PSYCHOPATHOLOGY

842   Axline, Virginia M. *Dibs: In Search of Self*. Boston, Houghton Mifflin, 1964. 186p.

     A case history demonstrating the effectiveness of play therapy, which, although it deals with one small boy, has more universal application.

843   Berkowitz, Pearl H., and Rotham, Esther P. *The Disturbed Child: Recognition and Psychoeducational Therapy in the Classroom*. New York, New York UP, 1960. 204p. biblio.

Starting with the premise that the teacher is in the most favored position for detecting maladjustment in children, the authors discuss the need for recognizing disturbances and the teacher's potential for helping in the therapeutic process. Some suggestions for curriculum adaptation and the use of the creative arts.

844 Bettelheim, Bruno. *The Empty Fortress: Infantile Autism and the Birth of Self.* New York, Free Press, 1967. 498p.

Documents an "experiment in nature" that probed the complex responses of autistic children to illuminate many basic aspects of normal and abnormal behavior and development. Includes case histories. Findings based on 20 years of intensive research.

845 _____. *Love Is Not Enough: the Treatment of Emotionally Disturbed Children.* New York, Free Press, 1950. 386p. biblio.

A report, with a psychoanalytic approach, on the daily life at an institution for treating emotionally disturbed children. An elaboration and implementation of the author's thinking about the education and treatment of these children.

846 _____. *Truants from Life: the Rehabilitation of Emotionally Disturbed Children.* New York, Free Press, 1955. 511p. biblio.

Discusses the rehabilitation of the severely disturbed institutionalized child, with reference to individual cases and their progress after leaving the institution.

847 Bower, Eli M. *Early Identification of Emotionally Handicapped Children in School.* Springfield, Ill., Thomas, 1960. 120p. biblio.

A research study for use by teachers in the early diagnosis of incipient disturbances in the emotional development of their pupils.

848 Caplan, Gerald, ed. *Emotional Problems of Early Childhood.* New York, Basic, 1955. 544p. biblio.

Twenty-four reports from an international symposium on the emotional problems of children under age six provide an account of thinking and practice in the areas of prevention, diagnosis, and treatment of psychological disorders in the very young.

849 _____, ed. *Prevention of Mental Disorders in Children.* New York, Basic, 1961. 425p. biblio.

A valuable source book on preventive psychiatry, with three chapters devoted to the school's role in reducing mental disorders among children.

850 Chess, Stella. *An Introduction to Child Psychiatry.* New York, Grune and Stratton, 1959. 254p. biblio.

An excellent introductory survey covering the practitioner and the patient, the child and his parents, the diagnostic process, diagnosis, and treatment.

851 D'Evelyn, Katherine E. *Meeting Children's Emotional Needs: a Guide for Teachers.* Englewood Cliffs, N.J., Prentice-Hall, 1957. 169p. biblio.

Constructive assistance for the classroom teacher at all grade levels in meeting average emotional needs and dealing with disturbed children. Specific symptomatic problems are discussed with case histories.

852 Freud, Anna. *Normality and Pathology in Childhood: Assessments of Development.* New York, International Universities, 1965. 273p. biblio.

A psychoanalytic view of childhood and a discussion of the relation between analysis of children and adults. Appraisals of normality, pathology, and therapy, based on experience in London's Hampstead Child Therapy Clinic.

853 ———. *The Psycho-Analytic Treatment of Children: Technical Lectures and Essays.* New York, Schocken, 1964. 114p.

A series of lectures (1926-1945) originally published in 1946, translated from the German. Highly technical in subject and language, they cover advances in understanding and evaluating infantile neuroses.

854 Ginott, Haim G. *Group Psychotherapy with Children: the Theory and Practice of Play Therapy.* New York, McGraw-Hill, 1961. 208p. biblio.

Clear descriptions of play therapy techniques and of the rationales that support them. Emphasizes concreteness in dealing with problems and specificity in suggesting solutions.

855 Grossman, Herbert. *Teaching the Emotionally Disturbed: a Casebook.* New York, Holt, 1965. 184p.

Using three case studies as a frame of reference, the author examines educational procedures for emotionally dis-

turbed children and induces some general principles relating
the insights of psychology to their education.

856 Haring, Norris G., and Phillips, E. Lakin. *Educating Emo-*
tionally Disturbed Children. New York, McGraw-Hill, 1962.
322p. biblio.

A translation of theoretical problems and positions into a
practical therapeutic program. Offers data on what happens
to hyperactive, emotionally disturbed children in an on-going
public school program when they are provided with adequate
diagnostic personnel and an educational program based on
a realistic learning theory.

857 Kessler, Jane W. *Psychopathology of Childhood.* Englewood
Cliffs, N.J., Prentice-Hall, 1966. 533p. biblio.

A survey of the clinical, research, and theoretical aspects
of the diagnosis and treatment of the psychopathological
child. An interdisciplinary, problem-centered approach that
emphasizes the psychological factors responsible for deviations.

858 Krugman, Morris, ed. *Orthopsychiatry and the School.* New
York, American Orthopsychiatric Association, 1958. 265p.
biblio.

A collection of 26 papers portraying a wide variety of
approaches and projects involving the prevention of emotional and behavioral disorders in the schools, from preschool
to post-graduate level.

859 Lennhoff, Frederick G. *Exceptional Children: Residential*
Treatment of Emotionally Disturbed Boys at Shotton Hall.
New York, Taplinger, 1962. 201p.

A description of an unusual school that "combines the
functions of informal education with those of a psychological
first-aid post, a child guidance unit, a treatment center, a
psychic convalescent home, and a psychological laboratory."

860 Lippman, Hyman S. *Treatment of the Child in Emotional*
Conflict, 2nd ed. New York, McGraw-Hill, 1962. 367p. biblio.

A sympathetic approach to the treatment of the emotionally disturbed child. Discusses group therapy, the neurotic
child, children with learning and personality problems, aggressive children, and those with a tenuous hold on reality.

861 Long, Nichols J., and others, eds. *Conflict in the Classroom: the Education of Emotionally Disturbed Children*. Belmont, Cal., Wadsworth, 1965. 515p. biblio.

An empathetic approach, using illustrations from the writings of authors such as Capote, McCullers, Chekhov, Dostoyevsky, and Cather, attempts to show how it *feels* to be emotionally disturbed. In addition, an excellent practical guide to the diagnosis, treatment, and education of the "child in conflict."

862 Morse, William C., and others. *Public School Classes for the Emotionally Handicapped: a Research Analysis*. Washington, Council for Exceptional Children, 1964. 142p. biblio.

Describes existing programs in special public school classes, provides illustrative case histories, evaluates the effects of the programs, and discusses the need for improvement.

863 Moustakas, Clark E. *Children in Play Therapy*. New York, McGraw-Hill, 1953. 218p. biblio.

An attempt to expand perception of children's feelings and attitudes and to promote more effective responsiveness to children's emotions by portraying experiences in play therapy with both well adjusted and disturbed children.

864 Redl, Fritz, and Wineman, David. *The Aggressive Child*. New York, Free Press, 1957. 575p. biblio.

A one volume edition of *Children Who Hate: the Disorganization and Breakdown of Behavior Controls* and *Controls from Within: Techniques for the Treatment of the Aggressive Child*. A sympathetic description of the treatment of the more severe forms of childhood aggression with a plea for better facilities for the care of such children and for more intensive research into the origin of hate.

865 Rimland, Bernard. *Infantile Autism: the Syndrome and Its Application for a Neural Theory of Behavior*. New York, Appleton, 1964. 282p. biblio.

A comprehensive coverage of present knowledge about infantile autism. Presents a theory of its origin and nature and suggests an evaluative research program.

866 Rogers, Carl R. *The Clinical Treatment of the Problem Child*. Boston, Houghton Mifflin, 1939. 393p. biblio.

A classic on understanding and helping the problem youngster. Discusses environment in relation to treatment and covers specific interviewing techniques.

ENGLISH TEACHING
see also LANGUAGE AND LINGUISTICS
LANGUAGE ARTS
LITERARY CRITICISM
SPELLING
WRITING AND COMPOSITION

867 Bernstein, Abraham. *Teaching English in High School.* New York, Random, 1961. 470p. biblio.

A stimulating approach based on classroom discussion with an emphasis on question techniques. Includes discussion material for classroom use.

868 Berry, Elizabeth. *Guiding Students in the English Class.* New York, Appleton, 1957. 438p. biblio.

Illuminates the relationship between the classroom teaching of English and the development of values and personality in the adolescent. Presents creative units in literature and composition.

869 Burton, Dwight L. *Literature Study in the High School,* rev. ed. New York, Holt, 1964. 312p. biblio.

A useful survey of transitional literature for adolescents. Offers insight into the relationship between the literary work and adolescent development.

870 Dixon, John. *Growth Through English: a Report to the Profession from the Anglo-American Conference at Dartmouth College on New Concepts for Teaching English in Elementary and Secondary Schools.* London, National Association for Teaching of English, 1967. 150p. (Dist. by NCTE and MLA.)

Discusses for the teaching profession a new model for English teaching based on the recommendations of a majority of the Dartmouth participants. A detailed consideration of linguistic and imaginative growth and implications for teachers and teacher education. Complementary to Muller's *The Uses of English* (#1533).

871 *The English Language Arts in the Secondary School* (NCTE Curriculum Series, vol. III). New York, Appleton, 1956. 488p. biblio.

Specific guidance in curriculum development, with chapters on literature, reading, writing, speaking, listening, grammar, spelling, usage, meeting college entrance requirements, and other subjects.

872   Evans, William H., and Walker, Jerry L. *New Trends in the Teaching of English in Secondary Schools.* Chicago, Rand McNally, 1966. 129p.

A brief and easily read guide for the classroom teacher. Starting with an historical overview, points out significant achievements and the national background against which major changes in emphasis have occurred.

873   *Freedom and Discipline in English.* New York, CEEB, 1965. 190p. biblio.

A report of the CEEB's Commission on English, which culminates a five-year study. Analyzes the conditions and practices of English teaching in America's secondary schools, makes specific recommendations for improvement in the areas of teacher preparation, teaching conditions, curriculum, language, literature, and composition. Contains advice on approaches and methods.

874   Gordon, Edward J., and Noyes, Edward S., eds. *Essays on the Teaching of English.* New York, Appleton, 1960. 356p. biblio.

The report of the Yale University Conferences on the Teaching of English, which attempted to answer some questions: what sort of language teaching should be going on in secondary schools? how can writing and literature best be taught? how to evaluate expository prose? Cites examples.

875   Holbrook, David. *English for Maturity: English in the Secondary School.* New York, Cambridge UP, 1961. 255p. biblio.

A fine exploration of the value of teaching English that relates experiences of British teachers of English and offers many practical teaching suggestions.

876   Hook, Julius N. *The Teaching of High School English,* 3rd ed. New York, Ronald, 1965. 488p. biblio.

Practical rather than theoretical, presenting numerous suggestions and tested classroom procedures for teaching language and literature.

877   La Brant, Lou L. *We Teach English.* New York, Harcourt, 1951. 342p. biblio.

Formulates a school program for promoting language growth with reference to philosophy, psychology, and scholarship in the field of teaching language and literature.

878 Loban, Walter D., and others. *Teaching Language and Literature, Grades 7-12.* New York, Harcourt, 1961. 748p.

An excellent basic text in secondary school English methods, containing useful illustrative teaching units for both junior and senior high school.

879 Marckwardt, Albert H. *Linguistics and the Teaching of English.* Bloomington, Indiana UP, 1966. 151p. biblio.

An introduction to current approaches to English grammar, language usage, and the part played by linguistics in teaching composition, spelling, reading, and literature.

880 Pilgrim, Geneva H. *Learning and Teaching Practices in English.* New York, CARE, 1966. 117p. biblio.

A graphic description of problems and practices in teaching competence in reading, writing, speaking, and spelling to high school students. Evaluates current patterns of teaching and discusses trends in teaching literature, composition, grammar, vocabulary, and the other language skills.

881 Pooley, Robert C., ed. *Perspectives on English.* New York, Appleton, 1960. 328p.

Includes a report of the 1959 Conference on Basic Issues in the Teaching of English and selected essays examining and clarifying some major problems.

882 ———. *Teaching English Usage.* Champaign, Ill., NCTE, 1946. 265p.

An influential book that discusses changes in English usage and offers apt suggestions for teaching current usage in non-technical language.

883 Postman, Neil M. *Television and the Teaching of English.* Champaign, Ill., NCTE, 1961. 138p.

Comprehensive and replete with suggestions for the use of television, especially drama, in the classroom.

884 Rosenblatt, Louise M. *Literature as Exploration.* New York, Appleton, 1938. 340p. biblio.

A clarification of the relation between literary appreciation and social understanding and a philosophy for high school and college teachers to help young people gain the pleasures and understanding that literature can yield. (A revised and rewritten edition of this unique book is being published in 1968 by Noble and Noble, New York.)

885 Ryan, Margaret A. *Teaching the Novel in Paperback*. New York, Macmillan, 1963. 253p.

A lucid discussion of 14 novels available in paperback and popular with high school students (Steinbeck's *The Pearl*, Buck's *The Good Earth*, etc.). Provides questions, study guides, and suggested essay topics for each.

886 Sauer, Edwin H. *English in the Secondary School*. New York, Holt, 1961. 245p.

Views the many activities lumped under the general heading of "English" and emphasizes the interrelationships of the parts. Studies the question of what is meant by proficiency in language.

887 Stone, George W., ed. *Issues, Problems, and Approaches in the Teaching of English*. New York, Holt, 1961. 246p. biblio.

A provocative collection of essays designed to emphasize the importance of rethinking the goals and values of English teaching in American schools.

888 Wolfe, Don M. *Creative Ways to Teach English: Grades 7-12*, 2nd ed. New York, Odyssey, 1966. 554p. biblio.

Emphasis on ways and means of improving the writing of high school students. Suggests many new resources in various fields. Annotated bibliographies following each chapter.

Colleges and Universities

889 Gerber, John C., ed. *The College Teaching of English* (NCTE Curriculum Series, vol. IV). New York, Appleton, 1965. 312p.

A collection of essays on the most important aspects of teaching college English. Crucial needs and present activities are surveyed.

890 Kitzhaber, Albert R. *Themes, Theories, and Therapy: the Teaching of Writing in College*. New York, McGraw-Hill, 1963. 175p. biblio.

A report of a two-year study of the teaching of composition at Dartmouth College, with recommendations.

891 McGrath, Earl J. *Communication in General Education*. Dubuque, Iowa, Brown, 1949. 244p.

A study of communications skills programs at a number of United States undergraduate institutions, bringing together a variety of points of view and courses. Of assistance to those considering revision of traditional courses.

892 Rowland, J. Carter, and others. *An Annotated Bibliography on the College Teaching of English: 1957-1963*. Champaign, Ill., NCTE, 1966. 56p.

A useful collection of 481 items.

ENGLISH AS A SECOND LANGUAGE

893 Aickman, Dorothy. *Rhymes for Speech and Action*, 2 vols. London, U of London P, 1960.

A collection of graded rhymes designed to provide oral practice for children at the introductory level of English. Teacher's book gives suggestions for use of the material and notes on each rhyme.

894 Allen, Harold B., ed. *Teaching English as a Second Language: a Book of Readings*. New York, McGraw-Hill, 1965. 406p. biblio.

A collection of 50 articles by authorities in the field, divided into sections dealing with theories and approaches; teaching speech, structures, vocabulary, usage, composition, reading, and literature; methods and techniques; audiovisual aids; testing.

895 Allen, Virginia F., and Forman, Sidney. *English as a Second Language: a Comprehensive Bibliography*. New York, TC, Columbia, 1967. 255p.

A subject arranged purchase guide that gives full bibliographic information, including price and language of publication. Author, title, and publisher indexes.

896 ———, ed. *On Teaching English to Speakers of Other Languages*. Champaign, Ill., NCTE, 1965. 158p.

Papers read at the 1964 conference on Teaching English as a Second Language. Covers the subject as a professional entity, reports on special programs, key concepts, and current concerns, the preparation and use of materials, and classroom techniques.

897 Allen, Walter P. *Selecting Reading Materials for Foreign Students: a Technique for Selecting Reading Materials Which Provide Cultural Background for Learning English*. Washington, Washington Publications, 1955. 73p. biblio.

Based on the author's findings that patterns in the learner's culture may interfere with his understanding of fiction written in English. Suggests procedures for selecting and teaching American literature to advanced students.

898 Bumpass, Faye L. *Teaching Young Students English as a Foreign Language.* New York, American, 1963. 198p. biblio.

Thorough coverage of many topics, including teaching a foreign language early in school, the linguistic and psychological aspects of foreign language teaching in the elementary grades, audio-lingual mastery of a language, the use of audio-visual aids, and the preparation of structured drills.

899 Close, R. A. *English as a Foreign Language: Grammar and Syntax for Teachers and Advanced Students.* Cambridge, Harvard UP, 1962. 177p.

Discusses the structure of English from the point of view of the non-native learner. Intended for the advanced student.

900 Dacanay, Fe R. *Techniques and Procedures in Second Language Teaching.* Dobbs Ferry, N.Y., Oceana, 1963. 538p.

Published originally in the Philippines, this deals with the structure of English and is a practical coverage of types of drill, pronunciation drills, reading, writing, spelling, and testing. Contains suggestions on the presentation of materials with sample lessons and pictures.

901 English-Teaching Information Centre. *English-Teaching Bibliography.* London, The British Council, 1964. 163p.

An annotated bibliography primarily for teachers of English as a second language. Deals with such areas as psychology, linguistic theory, audiovisual aids, tests, and dictionaries. Sections on courses and textbooks contain mostly British titles. 1965 supplement has been published.

902 Frisby, A. W. *Teaching English: Notes and Comments on Teaching English Overseas.* New York, Longmans, 1957. 352p. biblio.

Deals with English phonology and expansion and control of vocabulary. An oral approach based on the work of Fries and Palmer. Contains suggestions for teachers.

903 Finocchiaro, Mary B. *Teaching English as a Second Language: In Elementary and Secondary Schools.* New York, Harper, 1958. 335p.

Relates theories of general education to foreign language teaching and to teaching English as a second language. Emphasis on activities approach and cultural orientation, with some attention to applied linguistics and drill techniques.

904 Fries, Charles C. *Teaching and Learning English as a Foreign Language.* Ann Arbor, U of Michigan P, 1945. 153p. biblio.
A classic in this field and an early application of linguistics to the teaching of English as a foreign language.

905 Gauntlett, John O. *Teaching English as a Foreign Language,* rev. ed. New York, St. Martin's, 1961. 124p. biblio.
For teachers of English and the advanced student whose mother tongue is not English. Covers methods, psychological problems, phonetics, intonation, vocabulary, structural forms, reading, and organizational problems.

906 Hornby, Albert S. *The Teaching of Structural Words and Sentence Patterns,* 4 vols. New York, Oxford UP, 1959-1966.
The four books are four stages in the teaching of English. Techniques for teaching structures of English to children over ten years of age. Items are graded in terms of the difficulties caused by the learner's native tongue. Include intonation guides and cumulative indexes of structural and heavy duty words.

907 *Language Learning: Series I and Series II,* 2 vols. Ann Arbor, Mich., Research Club in Language Learning, 1953 and 1963.
Both volumes include articles by well known authorities. The first, *English as a Foreign Language,* explores the methods of structural linguistics as applied to language teaching. The second, *Theory and Practice in English as a Foreign Language,* covers teacher education and such practical aspects as grammar and pronunciation.

908 MacNamara, John T. *Bilingualism and Primary Education: a Study of Irish Experience.* Chicago, Aldine, 1966. 173p. biblio.
A technical report based on a research study that is distinguished for its clarity and conciseness. Covers not only the problems of Irish children, but reports also on 77 research studies from all parts of the world on the problems and effects of bilingualism on linguistic skills and arithmetic.

909 Ohannessian, Sirarpi, ed. *Reference List of Materials for English as a Second Language. Part I: Texts, Readers, Dictionaries, Tests. Part II: Background Materials, Methodology,* 2 vols. Washington, CAL, 1964-66.

An annotated bibliography covering the years 1953-63; an exhaustive coverage of every aspect of the field.

910 Press, John, ed. *The Teaching of English Literature Overseas.* London, Methuen, 1963. 181p.

Extracts from the proceedings of a 1962 conference. Includes techniques, syllabi, and examinations for use in universities, adult education, and for training teachers of English.

911 Shen, Yao, and Crymes, Ruth H. *Teaching English as a Second Language: a Selected Bibliography.* Honolulu, East-West Center, 1965. 110p.

Prepared to meet the needs of teacher trainees at the University of Hawaii. Items are classified under phonology, grammar, methodology, and journals. The 874 entries are, unfortunately, not annotated.

912 Stevick, Earl W. *Helping People Learn English: a Manual for Teachers of English as a Second Language.* Nashville, Abingdon, 1957. 138p. biblio.

Intended for untrained Americans called upon to teach English to foreigners. A simple, direct, and practical guide that includes sample lessons.

913 ———. *A Workbook in Language Teaching: with Special Reference to English as a Foreign Language.* Nashville, Abingdon, 1963. 127p. biblio.

Covers English phonology, grammar fundamentals, and basic types of drill. A practical handbook with exercises and discussion questions to help the student evaluate his progress in acquiring skills.

914 *University Resources in the United States for Linguistics and Teacher Training in English as a Foreign Language,* 5th ed. Washington, CAL, 1966. 130p.

Lists courses, staff, research projects, programs, teacher training in English as a foreign language, and English for foreign students at nearly 100 United States colleges and universities. Revised frequently.

915   Wallace, Betty J. *The Pronunciation of American English for Teachers of English as a Second Language.* Ann Arbor, Mich., Wahr, 1957. 91p. biblio.

Prepared originally for Puerto Rican teachers of English. Contains general information on problems of pronunciation and phonology and practice exercises.

916   West, Michael P. *Teaching English in Difficult Circumstances: Teaching English as a Foreign Language, with Notes on the Technique of Textbook Construction.* London, Longmans, 1960. 136p.

A practical guide for those teaching English in unusual circumstances or out-of-the-way places. Suggestions for handling problems of class size, climate, classroom facilities, and teacher training.

EXCEPTIONAL CHILDREN

917   Baker, Harry J. *Introduction to Exceptional Children,* 3rd ed. New York, Macmillan, 1959. 523p. biblio.

A comprehensive coverage of what research and experience offer school personnel in the effort to understand the causes and nature of conditions that handicap or facilitate the learning of exceptional children.

918   Barbe, Walter B. *The Exceptional Child.* New York, CARE, 1963. 117p. biblio.

A meticulous, well-documented examination of all areas of exceptionality that is both succinct and comprehensive.

919   Connor, Frances P. *Education of Homebound or Hospitalized Children.* New York, TC, Columbia, 1964. 125p.

Discusses the particular problems of the out-of-school child in relation to program content, learning problems, pupil participation, self-realization, and socialization. Stresses the importance of the instructor's role and analyzes the professional background necessary.

920   Connor, Leo E. *Administration of Special Education Programs.* New York, TC, Columbia, 1961. 123p. biblio.

Examines administrative problems in the area of special education: the identification of pupils needing special attention, teacher recruitment, and selection of supervisory personnel. Examples of successfully operated programs.

921 Cruickshank, William M., and Johnson, G. Orville, eds. *Education of Exceptional Children and Youth*, 2nd ed. Englewood Cliffs, N.J., Prentice-Hall, 1967. 730p. biblio.

This new edition reflects the advances made in concept and method for recognition of problems in the curriculum, in teaching techniques, and in administration. A comprehensive discussion of nine primary areas of exceptionality.

922 *Directory for Exceptional Children*, 5th ed. Boston, Sargent, 1965. 702p.

An invaluable and comprehensive handbook listing schools, homes, clinics, hospitals, and services for the many kinds of socially, mentally, and physically handicapped children. Revised every several years.

923 Dunn, Lloyd M., ed. *Exceptional Children in the Schools*. New York, Holt, 1963. 580p. biblio.

A basic reference in which each chapter is devoted to a particular area of exception, including the gifted as well as the handicapped, with a description of the specialized school programs they need.

924 Frampton, Merle E., and Gall, Elena D., eds. *Special Education for the Exceptional*, 3 vols. Boston, Sargent, 1955.

The three volumes are: *Introduction and Problems, The Physically Handicapped and Special Health Problems,* and *Emotional and Mental Deviates and Special Problems.* A thorough resume of objectives and procedures for teaching the exceptional child and adult with informative data on various specialized services.

925 Garrison, Karl C., and Force, Dewey G., Jr. *The Psychology of Exceptional Children*, 4th ed. New York, Ronald, 1965. 571p. biblio.

Emphasis is placed on the contributions that the classroom teacher can make to the education and welfare of the exceptional child. Chapters discuss types of mental, emotional, and physical disabilities, and social and emotional adjustment.

926 Goldberg, I. Ignacy. *Selected Bibliography of Special Education.* New York, TC, Columbia, 1967. 127p.

More than 2,000 articles and books, unfortunately not annotated, are arranged according to the principal disabilities they cover. An exhaustive list.

927 Gowan, John C., and Demos, George D., eds. *The Guidance of Exceptional Children: a Book of Readings*. New York, McKay, 1965. 404p. biblio.

Articles, most based on research studies, arranged in accordance with particular disabilities and concerned primarily with the practical and the specific rather than the theoretical. An excellent resource.

928 Haring, Norris G., and others. *Attitudes of Educators Toward Exceptional Children*. Syracuse, N.Y., Syracuse UP, 1958. 238p. biblio.

A report of research and testing done because of the increasing placement of exceptional children in regular classrooms. A series of supportive workshops were instrumental in modifying attitudes toward greater acceptance of these children.

929 Haring, Norris G., and Schiefelbusch, Richard L., eds. *Methods in Special Education*. New York, McGraw-Hill, 1967. 430p. biblio.

An effort to find behavior patterns common to different disabilities and to develop methods that focus on this behavior rather than on the handicap. Reviews current research on the behavior and learning of exceptional children.

930 Heck, Arch O. *The Education of Exceptional Children: Its Challenge to Teachers, Parents, and Laymen*. New York, McGraw-Hill, 1953. 513p. biblio.

The proper care and education of socially, physically, and mentally handicapped children. Develops some basic principles, considers some practical problems, outlines the responsibilities of home and school, and describes several programs across the country.

931 Hellmuth, Jerome, ed. *Educational Therapy*, vol. 1. Seattle, Special Child, 1966. 468p. biblio.

Excellent articles on the role of special education and its relationship to the total educational endeavor.

932 Kirk, Samuel A., and Weiner, Bluma B., eds. *Behavioral Research on Exceptional Children*. Washington, Council for Exceptional Children, 1963. 369p. biblio.

Selected reviews of relevant studies in each major category of exceptionality. Focuses on contemporary problems and issues in the education of children who require special services.

933 _____. *Educating Exceptional Children.* Boston, Houghton Mifflin, 1962. 415p. biblio.

An integrated approach to the education of exceptional children. Interprets the characteristics of such children and describes suitable modifications of educational practice.

934 Lord, F. E., and Isenberg, Robert M., eds. *Cooperative Programs in Special Education.* Washington, NEA, 1964. 60p. biblio.

A broad look at the concept of interdistrict services in the United States, with descriptions of some representative approaches and cooperative programs.

935 Louttit, Chauncey M., and others. *Clinical Psychology of Exceptional Children,* 3rd ed. New York, Harper, 1957. 537p.

An examination of the problems of exceptional children, defined as all who are atypical in ability (including the gifted and the subnormal), those who show deviation in social behavior and personality, and those who have speech defects or other physical handicaps.

936 Magary, James F., and Eichorn, John R., eds. *The Exceptional Child: a Book of Readings.* New York, Holt, 1960. 575p. biblio.

A cooperative endeavor, drawing on the writings of specialists in education, psychology, social work, and medicine, that discusses the psychology, education, and rehabilitation of the exceptional child.

937 Magnifico, L. X. *Education for the Exceptional Child.* New York, McKay, 1958. 371p. biblio.

An excellent survey of the field, with chapters on the problems of socially and physically handicapped children, gifted children, the need for educational specialists, and the psychology of teaching the exceptional child.

938 Michal-Smith, Harold, ed. *Management of the Handicapped Child: Diagnosis, Treatment, and Rehabilitation.* New York, Grune and Stratton, 1957. 276p. biblio.

An authoritative survey of developments in the sciences and in community services that affect those children needing special assistance, treatment, and habilitation.

939 ———, and Kastein, Shulamith. *The Special Child: Diagnosis, Treatment, Habilitation.* Seattle, Special Child, 1962. 334p. biblio.

A group of selected papers by the authors on the special problems of the exceptional child. Covers the diagnosis, treatment and rehabilitation of the mentally retarded, brain injured, cerebral palsied, and those with communication disorders and emotional disturbances.

940 Trapp, E. Philip, and Himelstein, Philip, eds. *Readings on the Exceptional Child: Research and Theory.* New York, Appleton, 1962. 674p. biblio.

Nearly 50 essays, reports of experimental studies, and critical reviews of studies cover three areas of exceptionality: intellectual, sensory and motor, and emotional.

FACULTY IN COLLEGES AND UNIVERSITIES
see also TEACHERS
TEACHING—Colleges and Universities

941 Brown, David G. *The Mobile Professors.* Washington, ACE, 1967. 220p.

A study based on information supplied by college presidents and a nationwide sampling of more than 13,000 college teachers. Shows how, where, and why college professors move about within the academic labor market. Sponsored by the U.S. Office of Manpower and directed by an economist, this has numerous recommendations for more effective use of academic labor, including a register of available positions and personnel.

942 Caplow, Theodore, and McGee, Reece J. *The Academic Marketplace.* New York, Basic, 1958. 262p.

A witty look at mobility in the academic labor market, faculty vacancies, evaluation of performance, departmental strategy, recruitment, and supply and demand. Expresses some concern about current practices and trends and offers specific recommendations.

943 Dennison, Charles P. *Faculty Rights and Obligations in Eight Independent Liberal Arts Colleges.* New York, TC, Columbia, 1955. 186p. biblio.

A study of formal provisions, their adoption and operation, and opinions about them. Extensive synopsis of personal and professional status practices.

944 Dobbins, Charles G., ed. *Expanding Resources for College Teaching*. Washington, ACE, 1956. 137p. biblio.

A conference report directed toward recruitment and utilization of faculty, which, with its discussion of ways of improving quality, is still pertinent today.

945 Eells, Walter C., comp. *College Teachers and College Teaching: an Annotated Bibliography on College and University Faculty Members and Instructional Methods*. Atlanta, Southern Regional Education Board, 1957. 282p.

Books, articles, and dissertations, topically arranged. Supplements published in 1959 and 1962.

946 Greenough, William C., and King, Francis P. *Retirement and Insurance Plans in American Colleges*. New York, Columbia UP, 1959. 480p.

Benefit plans described, analyzed, and compared.

947 Herge, Henry C. *The College Teacher*. New York, CARE, 1965. 118p. biblio.

A succinct study of the traits and functions of a teacher, instructional techniques, and professional preparation, focusing on policies and practices, internships, and trends.

948 Ingraham, Mark H., and King, Francis P. *The Outer Fringe: Faculty Benefits Other than Annuities and Insurance*. Madison, U of Wisconsin P, 1965. 304p.

Presents facts, with advantages and disadvantages, of benefits such as housing, educational privileges, health services, loans, leaves, travel, retirement, and (seriously) parking. Appendixes of data.

949 McGrath, Earl J. *The Quantity and Quality of College Teachers*. New York, TC, Columbia, 1962. 24p.

An inquiry into the supply and demand of teachers for liberal arts colleges. Recommends more adequate salaries, teaching internships, a broader graduate educational base, financial aid plans, and revision of college personnel policies to stimulate supply of more adequately prepared teachers.

950 Rogers, James F. *Staffing American Colleges and Universities: the Demand for Faculty and Other Professional Staff in Higher Education, November 1963 Through October 1969*. (USOE) Washington, GPO, 1967. 220p.

A study of demand with projections to 1969. Covers all personnel in instruction, administration, research, and service.

951   Wilson, Logan. *The Academic Man: a Study in the Sociology of a Profession.* New York, Oxford UP, 1942. 248p.

The role of the professor in the occupational culture of the university is analyzed in terms of status, salaries, the university social system, and staff functions, with discussion of the conflicts between structure and functions.

FAMILY LIFE EDUCATION see HOME ECONOMICS

FEDERAL AID TO EDUCATION
see also ECONOMICS OF EDUCATION

952   Axt, Richard G. *The Federal Government and Financing Higher Education.* New York, Columbia UP, 1952. 295p. biblio.

A description of those federal programs that have had the greatest impact on the colleges and universities, a consideration of long-term development of federal policies affecting the financial support of higher education, and a presentation of the major issues of the time involving relations between the federal government and the institutions.

953   Blum, Virgil C. *Freedom in Education: Federal Aid for All Children.* New York, Doubleday, 1965. 235p.

Outlines the present acute financial problems of schools conducted by religious groups, the definite contribution these schools are making to the welfare of the democratic society, and the constitutionality of the precedents for government aid to the children attending these schools.

954   Dobbins, Charles G., ed. *Higher Education and the Federal Government.* Washington, ACE, 1963. 126p. biblio.

Principal addresses and papers from the Council's 45th annual meeting in 1962. Examines thoroughly the role of the federal government and its impact on higher education.

955   Educational Policies Commission. *Educational Responsibilities of the Federal Government.* Washington, NEA, 1964. 30p.

A brief but compelling statement that maintains that

federal educational policies fall short of federal educational responsibilities and that the present federal administrative structure helps to perpetuate that inadequacy.

956 *Guide to Federal Assistance for Education.* New York, Appleton, 1966- .

An expensive but useful reference work composed of letter-size folders, in metal file box, arranged under nearly 200 subjects. It guides the information-seeker through the maze of forms, sources, and reports on all federally assisted programs affecting education. Supplementary service keeps system reasonably current.

957 Jones, Howard R. *Financing Public Elementary and Secondary Education.* New York, CARE, 1966. 116p. biblio.

A lucid examination of the federal aid measures passed by Congress in recent years and their effect on public school programs.

958 Knight, Douglas M., ed. *The Federal Government and Higher Education.* Englewood Cliffs, N.J., Prentice-Hall, 1960. 205p.

Background reading on federal aid aimed at developing a national policy compatible with both educational and national goals.

959 McGarry, Daniel D., and Ward, Leo, eds. *Educational Freedom and the Case for Government Aid to Students in Independent Schools.* Milwaukee, Bruce, 1966. 226p. biblio.

A comprehensive view of a controversial subject in a collection of essays by men in the field of education and some who are not.

960 Orlans, Harold. *The Effects of Federal Programs on Higher Education: a Study of 36 Universities and Colleges.* Washington, Brookings Institution, 1962. 361p. biblio.

Concludes that federal support is beneficial, having considerable effect on the sciences, some on the social sciences, and nearly none on the humanities. A plea for quality is included with recommendations for continuance of present programs and extension to other institutions.

961 Roney, Ruth A. *The Doubleday Guide to Federal Aid Programs, 1967-68.* New York, Doubleday, 1967. 240p.

Provides information regarding major types of federal assistance available to schools and libraries. Outlines eligibility requirements and methods of application. For elementary and secondary schools, and school libraries.

962 Steel, Ronald, ed. *Federal Aid to Education.* New York, Wilson, 1961. 207p. biblio.

Articles attempting to place the problems of federal aid to education in perspective. Covers aid to elementary, secondary, public, and non-public schools as well as to colleges and universities.

963 Tiedt, Sidney W. *The Role of the Federal Government in Education.* New York, Oxford UP, 1966. 243p. biblio.

Deals with the general ideas implicit in the role of the federal government in education, with explanations and implications of some of the larger programs.

FOREIGN LANGUAGE TEACHING
see also ENGLISH AS A SECOND LANGUAGE
LANGUAGE AND LINGUISTICS

964 Abercrombie, David. *Problems and Principles in Language Study,* 2nd ed. London, Longmans, 1963. 83p.

A collection of essays on such topics as the relation of language to man and society, designing a beginner's course, and teaching pronunciation.

965 Brooks, Nelson H. *Language and Language Learning: Theory and Practice,* 2nd ed. New York, Harcourt, 1964. 300p. biblio.

A close examination of what language is, how it works, and how it is learned. Theoretical and practical aspects of learning are reviewed from the viewpoint of the teacher and the learner.

966 Childers, James W. *Foreign Language Teaching.* New York, CARE, 1964. 120p. biblio.

A brief review of the history of the changing status of foreign language teaching in this country and the principal methods in use today. Covers research in the field to show how research has influenced teaching.

967 Cornfield, Ruth R. *Foreign Language Instruction: Dimensions and Horizons.* New York, Appleton, 1966. 183p. biblio.

An overview relying considerably on the work of others in

the field but nevertheless a good resource on what and how to teach in a foreign language class.

968 Dodson, Charles J. *Language Teaching and the Bilingual Method.* London, Pitman, 1967. 182p.

Describes a new approach to foreign language teaching that is applicable at all levels of schooling and is especially useful in those areas where there is a problem of bilingualism. A direct and practical guide.

969 Ferguson, Charles A., and Stewart, William A. *Linguistic Reading Lists for Teachers of Modern Languages.* Washington, CAL, 1963. 114p. biblio.

More than 800 annotated entries of works on linguistics and language study: French, German, Italian, Russian, and Spanish.

970 Hagboldt, Peter. *Language Learning: Some Reflections from Teaching Experience.* Chicago, Chicago P, 1935. 165p. biblio.

An outgrowth of a series of university lectures, this is a philosophical study of language learning. Deals with concepts, the nature of some fundamental language learning processes, their psychological implications, and devices whereby these principles may be put into operation.

971 Huebener, Theodore. *Audio-Visual Techniques in Teaching Foreign Languages: a Practical Handbook,* rev. ed. New York, New York UP, 1967. 179p. biblio.

Intended for language teachers, the topics include the blackboard, dramatization, pictures, films, filmstrips, phonograph records, tape recorders, radio, television and language laboratories. Includes a bibliography of language laboratories.

972 _____. *How to Teach Foreign Languages Effectively,* rev. ed. New York, New York UP, 1965. 240p. biblio.

Not particularly imaginative but a useful and practical text, well-organized, and offering many examples.

973 Lado, Robert. *Language Teaching: a Scientific Approach.* New York, McGraw-Hill, 1964. 239p. biblio.

An introduction for the language teacher to the major areas of scientific approach to language and language learning, language teaching, and technological aids.

974 _____. *Language Testing: the Construction and Use of Foreign Language Tests.* New York, McGraw-Hill, 1961. 389p.

Based on the theory that items of difficulty can be identified through differential analysis of the mother tongue and the target language. Covers theory and practice of refining and standardizing tests, theory and strategy of language testing, testing the elements of language, and testing integrated skills.

975 _____. *Linguistics Across Cultures: Applied Linguistics for Language Teachers.* Ann Arbor, U of Michigan P, 1957. 141p. biblio.

An approach to language learning that combines the study of applied linguistics and culture analysis by comparing any two languages and cultures to discover and describe the problems that speakers of one of the languages will have in learning the other.

976 Nida, Eugene A. *Learning a Foreign Language: a Handbook for Missionaries,* rev. ed. New York, Friendship, 1957. 212p. biblio.

A practical, non-technical guide to principles and procedures in language study and fundamental features of language. Although designed for missionaries and illustrated with linguistic problems experienced by missionaries, this has more universal usefulness, especially for those concerned with learning one or more of the less common languages.

977 Northeast Conference on the Teaching of Foreign Languages. *Committee Reports.* 1st-   1954-   . New York, MLA.

An annual publication, with varying editors, on topics relating to teaching foreign languages. Recent titles include: *Challenges to the Profession* (1965), *Language Teaching: Broader Concepts* (1966), and *Foreign Languages: Reading, Literature, Requirements* (1967).

978 Nostrand, Howard L., and others. *Research on Language Teaching: an Annotated International Bibliography, 1945-1964,* 2nd ed. Seattle, U of Washington P, 1965. 373p.

An indispensable tool for the researcher that lists bibliographies, journals, and serials. A list of organizations in the field is included. Some research is abstracted.

979 Politzer, Robert L. *Foreign Language Learning: a Linguistic Introduction.* Englewood Cliffs, N.J., Prentice-Hall, 1965. 155p. biblio.

A basic discussion that examines such questions as: What is language? What are the problems involved in foreign language learning? What are the ways of dealing with these problems?

980 Remer, Ilo M. *A Handbook for Guiding Students in Modern Foreign Languages* (USOE Bulletin no. 26). Washington, 1963. 105p. biblio.

A source of information about foreign language study for guidance workers, teachers, principals, and parents. Deals with foreign language programs fitted to the needs and abilities of students and is designed to help in planning student programs.

981 Rivers, Wilga. *The Psychologist and the Foreign Language Teacher.* Chicago, U of Chicago P, 1964. 212p. biblio.

A critical evaluation of the current audio-lingual method of foreign language teaching and the role of the language teacher.

982 Valdman, Albert, ed. *Trends in Language Teaching.* New York, McGraw-Hill, 1966. 298p. biblio.

Contributions by linguists, psychologists, and language teachers present views on current theory and practice in foreign language teaching at all levels of instruction.

983 West, Michael. *Learning to Read a Foreign Language and Other Essays on Language Teaching.* London, Longmans, 1955. 100p.

Illuminating articles on teaching grammar and testing as well as reading.

Elementary Schools

984 Finocchiaro, Mary B. *Teaching Children Foreign Languages.* New York, McGraw-Hill, 1964. 210p. biblio.

Discusses the theory and practice of effective programs in elementary schools and emphasizes the need to stimulate in children the desire to pursue the study of languages.

985 Keesee, Elizabeth. *Modern Foreign Languages in the Elementary School: Teaching Techniques* (USOE Bulletin, no. 29). Washington, GPO, 1960. 65p.

Describes a variety of foreign language teaching techniques now in use and offers examples of types of materials that have been developed for elementary school use.

Secondary Schools

986 Hamlin, Donald J., and others. *Good Teaching Practices: a Survey of High School Foreign Language Classes.* New York, MLA, 1961. 37p.

Description of good teaching practices observed by a team of five evaluators who traveled all over the country visiting classes.

987 Johnston, Marjorie C., ed. *Modern Foreign Languages in the High School* (USOE Bulletin no. 16). Washington, GPO, 1958. 166p.

The papers and summaries of discussions of a 1957 conference whose aim was redesigning high school programs to better serve the national need. Includes an evaluation of programs and of teacher preparation.

988 O'Connor, Patricia. *Modern Foreign Languages in High School: Pre-Reading Instruction* (USOE Bulletin No. 9). Washington, GPO, 1960. 50p. biblio.

Provides the rationale for a preliminary period of aural-oral work in beginning foreign language instruction. Offers practical ways of planning and conducting pre-reading instruction. Many of the principles and formulations were developed in connection with an English language teaching project in Japan in 1957-58.

FOREIGN LANGUAGE TEACHING—INDIVIDUAL LANGUAGES

French

989 De Sauzé, Emile B., and Condon, Vesta. *The Cleveland Plan for the Teaching of Modern Languages: with Special Reference to French.* New York, Holt, 1953. 82p.

Outlines an experimental program conducted in the Cleveland public schools and discusses objectives and principles of modern language teaching, giving teaching suggestions, lesson plans, and assignments.

990 Dunkel, Harold B., and Pillet, Roger A. *French in the Elementary School: Five Years' Experience.* Chicago, U of Chicago P, 1962. 150p. biblio.

Includes program planning, methods and materials, formulation of instruction (with sample lesson plans), problems, and conclusions.

991 Politzer, Robert L. *Teaching French: an Introduction to Applied Linguistics,* 2nd ed. New York, Blaisdell, 1965. 181p. biblio.

Deals with general methodological considerations and linguistic concepts. Aims at increasing awareness of pattern conflicts between French and English and provides remedies as offered by the linguistic teaching method.

German

992 Kufner, Herbert L. *The Grammatical Structure of English and German: a Contrastive Sketch.* Chicago, U of Chicago P, 1962. 95p.

The tendency for a student to transfer the rules of his own language to the language he is learning is dealt with by outlining the differences and similarities between English and German grammar. An excellent reference for the preparation of lessons and the improvement of teaching techniques.

Greek and Latin

993 Buck, Carl D. *A Comparative Grammar of Greek and Latin.* Chicago, U of Chicago P, 1933. 405p. biblio.

A basic text including linguistic history, phonology, inflection, and formation.

Italian

994 Agard, Frederick B., and Di Pietro, Robert J. *The Grammatical Structures of English and Italian.* Chicago, U of Chicago P, 1965. 91p.

Outlines the similarities and differences between the two grammars and includes reference work for preparation of lessons and improvement of teaching techniques.

995 _____, and _____. *The Sounds of English and Italian.* Chicago, U of Chicago P, 1965. 76p.

A companion volume to #994. A detailed account of one of the major impediments to the learning of a second language, namely the interference caused by the structural differences between the mother tongue and the foreign language.

Spanish and Portuguese

996   Bull, William E. *Spanish for Teachers: Applied Linguistics.*
       New York, Ronald, 1965. 306p.
          A discussion of basic facts and fundamentals, Spanish
       sounds and their spelling, and the correlation of phonetic,
       phonemic, and graphemic systems, which bridges the gap
       between theoretical knowledge and actual classroom practice.

997   Doyle, Henry G., ed. *A Handbook on the Teaching of Spanish
       and Portuguese: with Special Reference to Latin America.*
       Boston, Heath, 1945. 395p. biblio.
          A practical guide that is still helpful in many ways, such
       as its advice to students and teachers and its suggestions for
       help available from governmental and semi-public agencies.
       The lists of books, articles, and other materials are outdated.

998   Kany, Charles E. *American-Spanish Syntax,* 2nd ed. Chicago,
       U of Chicago P, 1951. 467p. biblio.
          A compendium of the chief syntactical peculiarities of
       American-Spanish and their divergence from recognized
       standard or Castilian usage.

999   Politzer, Robert L., and Staubach, Charles N. *Teaching
       Spanish: a Linguistic Orientation,* rev. ed. New York, Blais-
       dell, 1965. 198p. biblio.
          For high school and college level, a text aimed at develop-
       ing awareness of the pattern conflicts between Spanish and
       English. Provides remedies offered by the linguistic method.

1000   Stockwell, Robert P., and others. *The Grammatical Structure
       of English and Spanish.* Chicago, U of Chicago P, 1965. 328p.
       biblio.
          An examination of the structure of English and Spanish,
       which assumes Spanish to be the language to be learned, in
       terms of the conflicts in their structure. Covers basic sentence
       patterns, noun phrases, and verb forms.

1001   _____, and Bowen, J. Donald. *The Sounds of English and
       Spanish.* Chicago, U of Chicago P, 1965. 168p. biblio.
          Emphasizing an aural-oral or audio-lingual approach to
       teaching Spanish, this explains theory as it relates to errors
       in pronunciation and covers sound systems, stress, rhythm,
       intonation patterns, and articulation of vowels and consonants.

History

1002   Palmer, Harold E. *The Oral Method of Teaching Languages: a Monograph on Conversational Methods Together with a Full Description and Abundant Examples of Fifty Appropriate Forms of Work.* Cambridge, Heffer, 1922. 134p.

An early British work with considerable validity today. Emphasizes the value of the oral method and gives examples of classroom exercises.

1003   _____. *The Principles of Language-Study.* London, Oxford UP, 1964. 182p.

Originally published in 1917, this is a classic study on the teaching and learning of foreign languages. Discusses the spontaneous and studial capacities for acquiring speech, the principles of language teaching, and the idea of language study as a habit-forming process.

1004   Sweet, Henry. *The Practical Study of Languages: a Guide for Teachers and Learners.* New York, Oxford UP, 1964. 276p.

Originally published in 1899, this is a classic study of the general principles and theoretical framework of foreign language teaching. Discusses the selection of language to be taught and the modification of principles and method to variant circumstances and learners.

FRUSTRATION

1005   Barker, Roger G., and others. *Frustration and Aggression: an Experiment with Young Children* (Studies in Child Welfare, vol. 18, no. 1). Iowa City, Iowa UP, 1941. 314p. biblio.

A study that, assuming that for the child constructive play is the best indicator of normality and adjustment, demonstrated that frustration leads to primitive and regressive behavior.

1006   Dollard, John, and others. *Frustration and Aggression.* New Haven, Yale UP, 1939. 209p. biblio.

A collection of articles providing a conceptual framework for understanding aggression, socialization in America, adolescence, and several varying political and social structures.

1007   Maier, Norman R. *Frustration: the Study of Behavior without a Goal.* New York, McGraw-Hill, 1949. 264p. biblio.

The report of a ten-year experimental research program on

frustration in which data on human subjects from other studies were compared with tests on animals and reinterpreted in the light of findings from subhuman forms.

GAMES FOR CLASSROOM USE
see also PLAY AND GAMES

1008   Crescimbeni, Joseph. *Arithmetic Enrichment Activities for Elementary School Children: a Collection of Practical Classroom Procedures and Activities for Enrichment of Arithmetic Teaching.* West Nyack, N.Y., Parker, 1965. 224p.

A handbook of brain teasers, learning devices, games, puzzles, manipulative equipment, and bulletin board stimulators whose purpose is to help make arithmetic teaching socially vital and practical through the use of many forms of sensory aids.

1009   Garroway, Dave. *Fun on Wheels.* New York, McGraw-Hill, 1960. 125p.

Many practical games and puzzles, including word games, numeral puzzles, and drawing games. Designed for elementary grades and easily adaptable to enhance almost any curriculum area.

1010   Meyer, Jerome S. *Puzzle, Quiz, and Stunt Fun.* New York, Dover, 1956. 249p.

Puzzles and quizzes in mathematics, language arts, and social studies for intermediate and upper grades. Ingenious illustrations for setting up teacher-made puzzles and quizzes.

1011   Roy, Mary M. *Spark.* Benton Harbor, Mich., Educational Service, Inc., 1965. 260p.

A compilation of games and activities arranged by social studies areas but amenable to correlation with arithmetic and language arts. Clear directions, grade level indications, and lists of sources of free materials.

1012   Russell, David H., and Elizabeth F. *Listening Aids Through the Grades: One Hundred Ninety Listening Activities.* New York, TC, Columbia, 1959. 108p.

Based on the belief that the ability to listen to spoken language with comprehension is clearly needed and that this ability can be developed and reinforced by systematic instruction.

1013 _____, and Karp, Etta E. *Reading Aids Through the Grades: Three Hundred Developmental Reading Activities*, rev. ed. New York, TC, Columbia, 1951. 120p. biblio.

An organized collection of successful devices to stimulate reading and help overcome reading difficulties.

1014 Tiedt, Sidney W., and Iris M. *Elementary Teacher's Complete Ideas Handbook*. Englewood Cliffs, N.J., Prentice-Hall, 1965. 298p.

A tremendous assortment of games and activities covering all curriculum areas and grade levels.

GEOGRAPHY TEACHING

1015 Hanna, Paul R., and others. *Geography in the Teaching of Social Studies: Concepts and Skills*. Boston, Houghton, Mifflin, 1966. 511p. biblio.

A practical guide to understandings and skills and to designing a social studies program with geography as the central theme. Includes materials and aids.

1016 Peattie, Roderick. *The Teaching of Geography: a Dynamic Approach*. New York, Appleton, 1950. 185p. biblio.

A practical guide for the high school teacher. Covers maps and map reading, the earth, climates and seasons, the sea, forests, the geography of mining, energy sources, the materials of industry, and so forth.

1017 Thralls, Zoe A. *The Teaching of Geography*. New York, Appleton, 1958. 339p. biblio.

A step-by-step description of the development of specific skills and abilities in the acquisition of geographic knowledge, including the teaching of the use of globes, maps, pictures, and graphs.

GHETTO SCHOOLS see DISADVANTAGED—GHETTO SCHOOLS

GIFTED CHILDREN
see also EXCEPTIONAL CHILDREN

1018 Abraham, Willard. *Common Sense about Gifted Children*. New York, Harper, 1958. 268p. biblio.

An easily read, well-documented book.

1019   Barbe, Walter B., ed. *Psychology and Education of the Gifted: Selected Readings.* New York, Appleton, 1965. 534p.

     Articles covering significant research and describing on-going programs. Includes all levels of schooling.

1020   Bray, Douglas W. *Issues in the Study of Talent.* New York, Columbia UP, 1954. 65p.

     Consideration of existing theory and empirical data in relation to talent, with discussion of the factors contributing to superior performance and the relative importance of capacity, opportunity, and personality.

1021   Cohen, Joseph W., ed. *The Superior Student in American Higher Education.* New York, McGraw-Hill, 1966. 299p.

     Describes and evaluates honors programs in the light of providing all superior students with a special and different learning experience, leading to integration of learning and thinking.

1022   Crow, Lester D., and Alice, eds. *Educating the Academically Able: a Book of Readings.* New York, McKay, 1963. 433p. biblio.

     Articles examining basic principles and practices and describing various types of programs in operation across the country.

1023   Cutts, Norma E., and Moseley, Nicholas. *Teaching the Bright and Gifted.* Englewood Cliffs, N.J., Prentice-Hall, 1957. 268p.

     Comprehensive coverage including identification, enrichment, acceleration, grouping, the use of community resources, motivation of underachievers, mental hygiene, and working with parents.

1024   DeHaan, Robert F. *Accelerated Learning Programs.* New York, CARE, 1963. 120p. biblio.

     For the average school with average resources. Describes programs now in action with elementary and secondary schools and, for contrast, visits a school that is doing nearly nothing to encourage the potential of its gifted students.

1025   ———, and Havighurst, Robert J. *Educating Gifted Children.* Chicago, U of Chicago P, 1957. 275p.

     A thorough discussion that includes screening programs, grouping, motivation, and family relationships.

1026   Everett, Samuel. *Programs for the Gifted: a Case Book in Secondary Education.* New York, Harper, 1961. 299p. biblio.

This 15th yearbook of the John Dewey Society contains a dozen or so chapters on what is being done in other countries to encourage the talented and describes many programs in operation in cities and rural and suburban areas.

1027   Freehill, Maurice F. *Gifted Children: Their Psychology and Education.* New York, Macmillan, 1961. 412p. biblio.

A comprehensive coverage of all aspects of working with gifted children in the schools. Includes vocational planning and emotional development.

1028   French, Joseph L., ed. *Educating the Gifted: A Book of Readings,* 3rd ed. New York, Holt, 1964. 514p. biblio.

Numerous excellent articles and original studies on all aspects of educating the gifted, arranged by category.

1029   Gallagher, James J. *Teaching the Gifted Child.* Boston, Allyn and Bacon, 1964. 330p. biblio.

Discusses the scope of the problem to aid teachers in organizing their thinking and illustrates a wide range of individual differences among gifted children. Includes needed curriculum changes, matters of style and pedagogy, and special provisions for the gifted achiever and underachiever.

1030   Gold, Milton J. *Education of the Intellectually Gifted.* Columbus, Merrill, 1965. 472p. biblio.

A comprehensive and authoritative coverage of the psychology and education of the intellectually superior youngster. Includes virtually all of the significant studies to date dealing with giftedness and educational provisions for the gifted. Offers critical appraisal and creative suggestions.

1031   Goldberg, Miriam L. *Research on the Talented.* New York, TC, Columbia, 1965. 72p. biblio.

A product of the Talented Youth Project of the Horace Mann-Lincoln Institute of School Experimentation, this brief book manages to be a comprehensive and objective review of research.

1032   Henry, Nelson B., ed. *Education for the Gifted* (NSSE 57th Yearbook, Part II). Chicago, U of Chicago P, 1958. 420p.

A collection of authoritative articles focusing on social factors, and on the gifted and their education.

1033 Hildreth, Gertrude H. *Introduction to the Gifted*. New York, McGraw-Hill, 1966. 572p. biblio.

Although not based on the most recent research and maintaining a rather neutral position on many issues such as ability grouping, this pioneer in the field has produced a scholarly and comprehensive text.

1034 Kough, Jack. *Practical Programs for the Gifted*. Chicago, SRA, 1960. 192p.

Much useful and practical material in discussions of the identification and motivation of the gifted. Covers administration, the consultant's role, special activities, and describes some significant programs.

1035 Project on the Academically Talented Student. Washington, NEA, 1959-1961. biblio.

A series of publications, many the reports of conferences jointly sponsored by the NEA and subject-oriented associations. Contain general recommendations as well as provisions for aiding teachers and administrators. The more than a dozen reports cover the various subject areas at the secondary level and the elementary school and include a report of research and an annotated bibliography.

1036 Sumption, Merle R., and Luecking, Evelyn M. *Education of the Gifted*. New York, Ronald, 1960. 499p. biblio.

Collects, coordinates, and interprets the major research findings with regard to educating gifted children. Emphasizes the need for and the uses of various types of educational programs, facilities, and equipment designed to foster optimum educational development.

1037 Thomas, George I. *Guiding the Gifted Child*. New York, Random, 1966. 206p. biblio.

Discusses the needs, expectations, and problems encountered in the classroom in dealing with gifted children as well as procedures other than intelligence tests that may be used for identifying the gifted. Presents a plan of action for meeting the needs of these pupils.

1038 Torrance, E. Paul, ed. *Talent and Education: Present Status and Future Directions*. Minneapolis, U of Minnesota P, 1960. 210p. biblio.

The report of a 1958 conference on gifted children that

is concerned with the identification, development, and utilization of talent.

1039   Ward, Virgil S. *Educating the Gifted: an Axiomatic Approach.* Columbus, Merrill, 1961. 240p. biblio.

Develops a systematic theory of differential educational experiences for the gifted, predicated on behavioral characteristics and upon their anticipated adult roles. Emphasizes the quality of educational experience in general education as distinguished from specific training for particular aptitudes.

1040   Witty, Paul A., ed. *The Gifted Child.* Boston, Heath, 1951. 338p. biblio.

A general work, with an excellent annotated bibliography, by a leader whose work stimulated a widening interest in education of the academically talented.

GOVERNMENT AND EDUCATION
see also ECONOMICS OF EDUCATION
FEDERAL AID TO EDUCATION
LAWS AND LEGISLATION

1041   Campbell, Roald F., and others. *The Organization and Control of American Schools.* Columbus, Merrill, 1965. 553p.

A thorough and perceptive analysis of governmental controls at all levels. Provocative discussion of non-governmental influences.

1042   *The Federal Government and Public Schools.* Washington, AASA, 1965. 72p.

The report of a commission of distinguished educators charged with examining the emerging relationships among local, state, and federal governments as they affect the public schools. Intended to provide a basis for study and understanding of the problems and issues inherent in the changing relationships among various levels of government.

1043   Glenny, Lyman A. *The Autonomy of Public Colleges: the Challenge of Coordination.* New York, McGraw-Hill, 1959. 325p.

Concerned with the state agencies and officers charged with the responsibility of higher education.

1044   Iannaccone, Laurence. *Politics of Education.* New York, CARE, 1967. 112p. biblio.

A realistic appraisal of the interrelation of politics and

education and an exploration of their connection through case studies on the local and state level.

1045 Kimbrough, Ralph B. *Political Power and Educational Decision Making*. Chicago, Rand McNally, 1964. 307p.

An extensive work describing a number of methods of community study and offering brief examples.

1046 Masters, Nicholas A., and others. *State Politics and the Public Schools: an Exploratory Analysis*. New York, Knopf, 1964. 319p.

An examination of the policies of three states (Missouri, Illinois, and Michigan) in terms of governmental decisions affecting the public schools, stressing the fact that, although public schools are thought of as being under local control and considerable discretionary authority is delegated to the local school district, primary control really rests with the state government.

1047 Moos, Malcolm, and Rourke, Francis E. *The Campus and the State*. Baltimore, Johns Hopkins UP, 1959. 414p. biblio.

Concerned with the impact of state administrative controls upon the management of state colleges and universities. Also deals with the effect of the politics of the legislature and the governor's office upon the operating climate of the campus.

1048 Pierce, Truman M. *Federal, State and Local Government in Education*. New York, CARE, 1965. 120p. biblio.

A readable discussion of the relationship between the schools and the various levels of government. Includes descriptions and analyses of federal and state constitutions as they influence education, the role of the legislatures and courts, and the impact of Congress.

1049 *School District Organization*. (AASA) Washington, NEA, 1958. 323p.

The report of the Commission on School District Reorganization. Reviews trends and makes recommendations.

1050 Thurston, Lee M., and Roe, William H. *State School Administration*. New York, Harper, 1957. 427p.

The principal treatment of this subject in recent decades. Includes two chapters on federal relationships and one on the nonpublic school.

1051   Walsh, John E. *Education and Political Power*. New York, CARE, 1964. 113p. biblio.

A simply and clearly written statement of the reciprocal relations between education and democracy.

GRADUATE EDUCATION
see also HIGHER EDUCATION

1052   Berelson, Bernard. *Graduate Education in the United States*. New York, McGraw-Hill, 1960. 346p.

A critical review and interpretation of current trends and issues, primarily in relation to doctoral programs, with numerous recommendations for tighter requirements, re-examination of requirements such as the oral and foreign language examinations, and an intermediate degree.

1053   Cartter, Allan M., ed. *An Assessment of Quality in Graduate Education*. Washington, ACE, 1966. 131p.

The informed opinions of 4,000 scholars in 106 universities in an appraisal of doctoral study in the humanities, the social sciences, biological and physical sciences, and engineering. A valiant and pioneering effort to achieve an almost impossible task.

1054   Graham, Jane, ed. *A Guide to Graduate Study: Programs Leading to the Ph.D. Degree*, 3rd ed. Washington, ACE, 1965. 610p. biblio.

A comprehensive guide to and directory of programs in 211 American colleges and universities.

1055   Grigg, Charles M. *Graduate Education*. New York, CARE, 1965. 115p. biblio.

A critical examination of the graduate school in relation to undergraduate education. Covers language requirements, the dissertation, the place of the masters degree, and the relationship between research and teaching.

1056   Livesey, Herbert B., and Robbins, Gene A. *Guide to American Graduate Schools*. New York, Viking, 1967. 357p.

A comprehensive guide to over 600 accredited graduate and professional institutions in the United States. Separate descriptions of each school give admission requirements and standards, fields of study, degree requirements, and such practical information as tuition, housing fees, and financial aid opportunities. Alphabetically arranged.

1057 McGlothlin, William J. *Patterns of Professional Education.* New York, Putnam, 1960. 288p. biblio.

A comparative study of the educational programs of ten professions, ranging from medicine to engineering. Analyzes the programs in terms of their aims, curricula, methods of instruction, the qualities sought in their faculties, and the criteria and procedures used in the recruitment and selection of students.

1058 ————. *The Professional Schools.* New York, CARE, 1964. 118p. biblio.

An analysis of the acute problems facing the professional schools within the university community: the need for training more professionals while admission qualifications become stricter, mounting costs, and the nearly impossible task of incorporating more liberal education into the program while the amount of information in each professional field continues to increase almost unmanageably.

1059 McGrath, Earl J. *The Graduate School and the Decline of Liberal Education.* New York, TC, Columbia, 1959. 65p.

An essay on the objectives of a liberal arts education, its current state of confusion and aimlessness, and subjection to graduate school domination. Proposes reforms in several areas.

1060 Ness, Frederic W., and James, Benjamin D. *Graduate Study in the Liberal Arts Colleges.* Washington, Association of American Colleges, 1962. 182p. biblio. (Dist. by ACE).

An examination and evaluation of existing programs and a search for criteria for improving the quality and vitality of master's degree programs.

1061 Ulich, Robert. *Professional Education as a Humane Study.* New York, Macmillan, 1956. 145p.

An appeal to educators to see their mission as "part of mankind's eternal endeavor to create the right knowledge conditions, and institutions in which free men can work together for the pursuit of their finest aspirations."

1062   Walters, Everett, ed. *Graduate Education Today.* Washington, ACE, 1965. 246p. biblio.

Chapters by 13 graduate school deans candidly discuss the complex process of graduate education, past, present, and future.

History

1063   Storr, Richard. *The Beginnings of Graduate Education in America.* Chicago, U of Chicago P, 1953. 195p. biblio.

Today's population explosion in the graduate schools had modest beginnings. This book traces the early, pre-Civil War traditions, the subsequent expansion of learning, and the profound German influence on this level of study.

GRAMMAR see LANGUAGE AND LINGUISTICS

GROUP RELATIONSHIPS

1064   Bany, Mary A., and Johnson, Lois V. *Classroom Group Behavior: Group Dynamics in Education.* New York, Macmillan, 1964. 412p. biblio.

Although the individual child and individualized instruction are still major emphases, some recognition is being given to the fact that classroom group setting and class group interaction have an important influence on learning and behavior. This is a significant contribution to that emerging concept.

1065   Bonner, Hubert. *Group Dynamics: Principles and Applications.* New York, Ronald, 1959. 531p. biblio.

A comprehensive discussion of the dynamics of small group behavior, offering insights into the relation of individuals to the group and conflict and adjustment within the group.

1066   Cartwright, Dorwin, and Zander, Alvin, eds. *Group Dynamics: Research and Theory,* 2nd ed. New York, Harper, 1960. 826p. biblio.

A standard, comprehensive reference covering history, theory, methods, group pressures, goals, performance, individual motives, and the structural properties of groups.

1067   Homans, George C. *The Human Group.* New York, Harcourt, 1950. 484p.

A presentation of the elements of general systems theory: activity, interaction, sentiment, and norms.

1068 Jennings, Helen H. *Sociometry in Group Relations: a Manual for Teachers*, 2nd ed. Washington, ACE, 1951. 155p.

A useful manual based on research and experience. Describes a method of studying the interactions of children.

1069 Lifton, Walter M. *Working with Groups: a Group Process and Individual Growth*, 2nd ed. New York, Wiley, 1966. 288p. biblio.

Although written primarily for social workers, the author's thesis that greater emphasis should be placed on the prevention of problems and on group rather than individual therapy has relevance for counselors.

1070 Moreno, Jacob L. *Who Shall Survive? a New Approach to the Problem of Human Relations*, rev. ed. New York, Beacon House, 1953. 763p. biblio.

A study of interpersonal relations among individuals in a social group and the techniques developed by the author to bring about social and psychological changes. An original theory incorporating original methods in sociometry, sociodrama, and group evolution.

1071 Thelen, Herbert A. *The Dynamics of Groups at Work*. Chicago, U of Chicago P, 1954. 379p.

An examination, based on theory and practice, of the methods and principles of small group operation.

1072 Thibault, John W., and Kelley, Harold H. *The Social Psychology of Groups*. New York, Wiley, 1959. 313p. biblio.

A theory of interpersonal relationships, both dyadic and complex, and of group functioning, based on a single set of concepts.

GROUPING IN SCHOOLS
see also TEAM TEACHING

1073 Beggs, David W., and Buffie, Edward G., eds. *Nongraded Schools in Action: Bold New Venture*. Bloomington, Indiana UP, 1967. 270p. biblio.

A discussion of ability grouping with descriptions of programs in operation.

1074 Borg, Walter R. *Ability Grouping in the Public Schools: a Field Study*. Madison, Wisc., Dembar, 1966. 97p. biblio.

A reworking of an earlier report of a research study at

Utah State University. Homogeneously and heterogeneously grouped classes with enrichment opportunities were studied. Conclusions were drawn from data, but no general conclusions were formulated.

1075   Brown, B. Frank. *The Nongraded High School*. West Nyack, N.Y., Parker, 1963. 223p.

The author, with some years of experience as the principal of a nongraded high school in Melbourne, Florida, discusses the need for innovation and change and offers dynamic plans and an imaginative organization.

1076   _____. *The Appropriate Placement School: a Sophisticated Nongraded Curriculum*. West Nyack, N.Y., Parker, 1965. 198p.

A complete school system design for elementary and secondary levels, based upon student achievement in particular subjects and convenient arrangements for mobile learning that are built into the curriculum. Coverage includes physical plant innovations and consideration of dropouts and the disadvantaged student.

1077   Cook, Walter W. *Grouping and Promotion in the Elementary School*. Minneapolis, U of Minnesota P, 1941. 65p. biblio.

The accommodation of individual differences by promotion methods, teaching methods, intra-class grouping, and homogeneous grouping.

1078   Dufay, Frank B. *Ungrading the Elementary School*. West Nyack, N.Y., Parker, 1966. 230p.

A discussion, based upon experience and analysis, which includes definition, practices such as ability grouping, team teaching and teacher specialists, and the most effective manner of changing from graded to ungraded.

1079   Franklin, Marian P., ed. *School Organization: Theory and Practice*. Chicago, Rand McNally, 1967. 489p. biblio.

A comprehensive examination of the various ways of organizing schools for instructional purposes. Covers grading and nongrading, multigrading, the self-contained classroom, departmentalization, and homogeneous vs. heterogeneous grouping.

1080   Franseth, Jane, and Koury, Rose. *Survey of Research on Grouping as Related to Pupil Learning*. (USOE) Washington, GPO, 1966. 64p.

A comprehensive review of the effectiveness and effects of ability grouping. Covers the subject from 12 aspects, including theories, concepts, and studies of practices.

1081   Goldberg, Miriam L., and others. *The Effects of Ability Grouping.* New York, TC, Columbia, 1966. 254p. biblio.

The first large-scale formal experiment (as reported by the Horace Mann-Lincoln Institute of School Experimentation) shows that ability grouping has no important effect on academic achievement. Also reported are a series of findings dealing with the relevance of the teacher's knowledge to the accomplishment of the students.

1082   Goodlad, John I., and Anderson, Robert H. *The Nongraded Elementary School,* rev. ed. New York, Harcourt, 1963. 248p.

A handbook designed to provide information on the nongraded school movement and to help those interested in creating nongraded schools. Included are problems of promotion and retention, reporting of pupil progress, the relation of the nongraded school to theories of curriculum, procedures, and some evaluation.

1083   Heathers, Glen. *Organizing Schools Through the Dual Progress Plan: Tryouts of a New Plan for Elementary and Middle Schools.* Danville, Ill., Interstate, 1967. 228p.

A detailed analysis of all aspects and an evaluation of a six-year trial in several schools of the controversial Dual Progress Plan. (See also #1092.)

1084   Hillson, Maurie, and Karlson, Ramona, eds. *Change and Innovation in Elementary School Organization.* New York, Holt, 1965. 387p. biblio.

Deals with organizational problems of current concern, such as grouping, team teaching, dual progress plans, and nongrading. Tends to see administrative reshuffling as solution of educational problems but provides good coverage.

1085   Keliher, Alice V. *A Critical Study of Homogeneous Grouping: with a Critique of Measurement as the Basis for Classification.* New York, TC, Columbia, 1935. 165p. biblio.

Part I describes the evolution of some of the significant concepts involved in school provisions for individual differences. Part II is a critical analysis of the basic implied assumptions involved in homogeneous grouping and measurement as the basis for grouping.

1086   Manlove, Donald C., and Beggs, David W. *Flexible Scheduling Using the IndiFlexS Model: Bold New Venture.* Bloomington, Indiana UP, 1965. 191p. biblio.

A way of adjusting the means (the organization for learning) to achieve the end (individualized teaching) by abandoning the traditional class group in favor of flexible scheduling. Included is a survey of 33 schools using some form of flexible scheduling and three using all the elements of IndiFlexS.

1087   Miller, Richard I., ed. *The Nongraded School: Analysis and Study.* New York, Harper, 1967. 289p. biblio.

A study that analyzes procedures, offers useful strategies for implementing processes, and carefully evaluates this innovation. Additional points of view contributed in 11 commentaries by people with experience in nongraded schools.

1088   Morgenstern, Anne, ed. *Grouping in the Elementary School.* New York, Pitman, 1966. 118p. biblio.

Timely selections present research data, provide better understanding of present grouping practices, urge intelligent evaluation, and suggest further studies.

1089   Pressey, Sidney L. *Educational Acceleration: Appraisals and Basic Problems* (Bureau of Educational Research Monograph no. 31). Columbus, Ohio State U, 1949. 153p. biblio.

A report of a study undertaken at Ohio State University between 1942 and 1947. Explores the effects of accelerated programs on academic accomplishments, health, social adjustment, and later career success.

1090   Rasmussen, Margaret, ed. *Toward Effective Grouping.* Washington, ACEI, 1962. 56p.

A thorough review of research into effectiveness and effects of ability grouping and a discussion of interage and multigrade grouping, continuous progress, ungraded primary schooling, and the problems of promotion and retention.

1091   Snyder, Edith R., ed. *The Self-Contained Classroom.* (ASCD) Washington, NEA, 1960. 88p.

A defense of the self-contained classroom in a day of increasing criticism of its isolation, rigidities, and limitations.

1092 Stoddard, George D. *The Dual Progress Plan: a New Philosophy and Program in Elementary Education.* New York, Harper, 1961. 225p.

A report of the first two years of the implementation of the plan in the elementary schools of Ossining and Long Beach, New York, gives substance to this proposal for semi-departmentalization in the elementary school in the areas of language arts, social studies, health and physical education, with nongraded, departmentalized teaching of mathematics, science, art, music, and foreign languages.

1093 Tewksbury, John L. *Nongrading in the Elementary School.* Columbus, Merrill, 1967. 138p. biblio.

A specific and concise statement of procedures for initiating a nongraded program. Discusses the need to reconsider teaching procedures and emphasizes the importance of carefully planned student-teacher assignments.

1094 Thelen, Herbert A., and others. *Classroom Grouping for Teachability.* New York, Wiley, 1967. 274p. biblio.

A detailed report of a three-year research investigation of classroom grouping for compatibility and effectiveness in achieving educational objectives. An important book that places the study in historical context and offers practical advice for initiating similar programs.

1095 West, Parl. *A Study of Ability Grouping in the Elementary School in Terms of Variability of Achievement, the Teaching Problem, and Pupil Adjustment.* New York, TC, Columbia, 1933. 70p.

Achievement test scores from 143 ability groups in eight elementary schools showed that the variability of achievement and the problems of pupil adjustment were slightly reduced in ability groups while the problems of pupil adjustment were occasionally increased.

1096 Yates, Alfred E. *Grouping in Education.* New York, Wiley, 1966. 314p. biblio.

A report sponsored by the UNESCO Institute for Education, Hamburg, which covers the major aspects of educational grouping practice in the United States, Great Britain, Israel, and Western and Northern Europe. Synthesizes results of research and summarizes current practice to stimulate policy makers in undeveloped countries as well as assisting in a reconsideration of present principles.

GUIDANCE AND COUNSELING IN EDUCATION
see also COUNSELING AND PSYCHOTHERAPY

1097 Arbuckle, Dugald S. *Counseling: an Introduction.* Boston, Allyn and Bacon, 1961. 349p.

Written from a client-centered viewpoint, offers a broad picture of the field of counseling and psychotherapy, covering basic issues and a description of the actual counseling experience.

1098 ———. *Guidance and Counseling in the Classroom.* Boston, Allyn and Bacon, 1957. 397p.

The philosophy, practice, and importance of the personal relationship between teacher and child in the school.

1099 ———. *Pupil Personnel Services in the Modern School.* Boston, Allyn and Bacon, 1966. 404p. biblio.

A practical and realistic presentation of the philosophy of pupil personnel work, based on the author's experience. A rewritten, new, and improved version of an earlier book.

1100 Barry, Ruth E., and Wolf, Beverly. *Modern Issues in Guidance Personnel Work.* New York, TC, Columbia, 1963. 256p.

An analysis of historical developments in an effort to find a way out of traditional conflicts, disagreements, illogicalities, and paradoxes. An outline of issues about which each guidance-personnel worker must attempt to reach some decisions.

1101 Bennett, Margaret E. *Guidance and Counseling in Groups,* 2nd ed. New York, McGraw-Hill, 1963. 421p. biblio.

Based on the assumption that the total school staff is involved in a group guidance program. Describes a plan for distributing functions on the basis of competencies.

1102 Berdie, Ralph F., and others. *Testing in Guidance and Counseling.* New York, McGraw-Hill, 1963. 288p.

Focuses on testing as an important part of counseling, emphasizing that it is neither the entire counseling process nor merely an adjunct.

1103 Buchheimer, Arnold, and Balogh, S. C. *The Counseling Relationship: a Casebook.* Chicago, SRA, 1961. 234p. biblio.

An attempt to clarify the problems involved in establishing a counseling relationship. Many styles are examined.

1104 Byrne, Richard H. *The School Counselor*. Boston, Houghton Mifflin, 1963. 295p. biblio.

Provides a thorough and forward-looking analysis of the counselor's task within the context of a realistic consideration of the total school program.

1105 Campbell, David P. *The Results of Counseling: Twenty-Five Years Later*. Philadelphia, Saunders, 1966. 205p. biblio.

Based on follow-up studies, this important and significant contribution reveals that, with due consideration of all factors, counseled students are more successful and, in comparison with the controls, still seeking greater achievement.

1106 *Directory of Approved Counseling Agencies*. Washington, American Board on Counseling Services, 1967. 193p.

A geographically arranged, often revised, listing of agencies offering counseling on educational progress, occupations and careers, and "other personal concerns not requiring prolonged and intensive psychotherapy." Includes detailed information. Could be even more valuable if the criteria for inclusion stipulated that the agencies evaluate their services by a follow-up of clients.

1107 Gibson, Robert L., and Higgins, Robert E. *Techniques of Guidance: an Approach to Pupil Analysis*. Chicago, SRA, 1966. 264p. biblio.

An introductory discussion of analytic principles and techniques.

1108 Gordon, Ira J. *The Teacher as a Guidance Worker: Human Development Concepts and Their Application in the Classroom*. New York, Harper, 1956. 350p.

A comprehensive treatment, presenting a sound theory as a basis for effective practice and emphasizing that guidance is a major part of a teacher's work.

1109 Hahn, Milton E., and MacLean, Malcolm S. *Counseling Psychology*, 2nd ed. New York, McGraw-Hill, 1955. 302p.

Thorough coverage of the field, including history, ethics, philosophy, tools and techniques, skills and aptitudes, and so forth, that reflect the ferment and the many changes in today's theory and practice.

1110 Hill, George E. *Management and Improvement of Guidance*. New York, Appleton, 1965. 508p. biblio.

A rationale for the management of guidance that stresses reliance on research.

1111 Hutson, Percival W. *The Guidance Function in Education.* New York, Appleton, 1958. 680p.

A contribution to guidance theory and practice drawn from the author's search for values. Research reported with ample data and methodological detail.

1112 Johnson, Walter F., and others. *Pupil Personnel and Guidance Services.* New York, McGraw-Hill, 1961. 407p.

Reviews the role of the counselor, simpler techniques for dealing with pupils, and looks into the future.

1113 Landy, Edward, and Perry, Paul A., eds. *Guidance in American Education: Selected Papers.* 1st-   1963-   Cambridge, Harvard Graduate School of Education.

The papers of the Summer Institutes for Administrators of Pupil Personnel Services, which provide an opportunity for practicing administrators to examine their roles in an atmosphere and at a level divorced from the daily minutiae of their jobs. Invited participants contribute to each institute; each has a distinctive title such as *Backgrounds and Prospects* and *Current Issues and Suggested Action.*

1114 Lee, James M., and Pallone, Nathaniel J., eds. *Readings in Guidance and Counseling.* New York, Sheed and Ward, 1966. 562p. biblio.

Intended to encourage more Catholic educators to join the guidance movement. Relies heavily upon deduction and essay rather than upon research-oriented writing.

1115 Litwack, Lawrence, and others. *Critical Issues in Student Personnel Work.* Chicago, Rand McNally, 1965. 105p. biblio.

Forty-five real problem situations in schools and colleges bridge the gap between theory and practice. The approach is problem-solving through the case study method, with cases representing the community, the school, and the individual.

1116 McKown, Harry C. *Homeroom Guidance,* 2nd ed. New York, McGraw-Hill, 1946. 521p.

Philosophy, purposes and principles of organization, administration, and presentation and evaluation of homeroom programs and activities. Theory is kept at a minimum and practice at a maximum.

1117 Mathewson, Robert H. *Guidance Policy and Practice*, 3rd ed. New York, Harper, 1962. 397p.
      Formulates a conceptual view of the field of guidance on an comprehensive and elevated plane while providing help for practice.

1118 Miller, Carroll H. *Foundations of Guidance*. New York, Harper, 1961. 464p.
      Emphasis on concepts rather than specific techniques, but the theoretical depth is combined with practical utility.

1119 Miller, Frank W. *Guidance Principles and Services*. Columbus, Merrill, 1961. 426p.
      Basic premises of guidance work. Theoretical concepts related to present day guidance services.

1120 Patterson, Cecil H. *Counseling and Guidance in Schools: a First Course*. New York, Harper, 1962. 382p.
      Emphasis on principles and problems rather than on procedures and techniques. Client-centered approach.

1121 Pearman, Jean R., and Burrows, Albert H. *Social Services in the School*. Washington, Public Affairs Press, 1955. 218p.
      For school administrators, teachers, public and private agency social workers, welfare board members, and others concerned with the problems of young people.

1122 Peters, Herman J., and Farwell, Gail F. *Guidance: a Developmental Approach*. Chicago, Rand McNally, 1959. 507p.
      A useful resource emphasizing sound principles and the various determinants that underlie the guidance discipline. Covers tools, techniques, and resources.

1123 ———, and Shertzer, Bruce. *Guidance: Program Development and Management*. Columbus, Merrill, 1963. 608p.
      Provides principles, procedures, and plans for initiating, developing, and evaluating a modern guidance program. Emphasizes that the unique characteristics of the individual school system must be considered.

1124 *Preparing School Counselors in Educational Guidance*. New York, CEEB, 1967. 146p.
      The papers presented at a 1966 invitational conference focusing on content in counselor education, problems and practices in guidance, and theoretical applications to im-

prove practices. An effort to re-examine the role of the counselor to bring about needed changes in the field.

1125 Roeber, Edward C. *The School Counselor*. New York, CARE, 1963. 107p. biblio.

A full coverage of the philosophy, responsibilities, rationale, role, and skills of the school counselor. Takes into consideration that the effective person is both guide and counselor to a wide range of youth with a wide range of problems, both normal and abnormal.

1126 Sachs, Benjamin M. *The Student, the Interview, and the Curriculum: Dynamics of Counseling in the School*. Boston, Houghton Mifflin, 1966. 302p. biblio.

Emphasis on the importance of the classroom teacher in accomplishing non-academic goals. Discussion of the roles, responsibilities, and relationships of various school personnel in guiding pupil development from the psychoanalytic and phenomenological points of view.

1127 Sechrest, Carolyn A. *New Dimensions in Counseling Students: a Case Approach*. New York, TC, Columbia, 1958. 119p. biblio.

Cases exemplify how the student being counseled may be helped to see the infinite possibilities that each moment brings, the self-mobility he can learn, and the command he can and must exercise over the directions his life can take.

1128 Shank, Donald J., and others. *The Teacher as Counselor* (Studies, series VI, no. 10). Washington, ACE, 1948. 48p.

Examines the faculty's role as an agency in counseling, the use of institutional resources, student needs, and the improvement of teacher counseling.

1129 Williamson, Edmund G. *How to Counsel Students: a Manual of Techniques for Clinical Counselors*. New York, McGraw-Hill, 1939. 562p.

Designed for a graduate level clinical course for counselors, this is a comprehensive survey of techniques of diagnosis and counseling.

1130 ———, and others. *Student Personnel Work: an Outline of Clinical Procedures*. New York, McGraw-Hill, 1937. 313p. biblio.

Emphasizes educational importance of guidance, with focus on educational and vocational adjustment.

1131 Wrenn, Charles G. *The Counselor in a Changing World.* Washington, American Personnel and Guidance Association, 1962. 195p.

Report of a questionnaire study of the preparation and role of the professional counselor.

1132 Zeran, Franklin R., and Riccio, A. O. *Organization and Administration of Guidance Services.* Chicago, Rand McNally, 1962. 302p.

The roles and responsibilities of all school personnel in relation to guidance are considered. Authors see guidance as a developmental process on a long-term basis and discuss the responsibility of the individual student for his own potential.

Elementary Schools

1133 Kowitz, Gerald T., and Norma G. *Guidance in the Elementary Classroom.* New York, McGraw-Hill, 1959. 314p.

The philosophy of guidance and its practical relationship to mental hygiene, child development, and to teaching and learning. Proposes and discusses specific techniques for teachers to help children meet and solve their problems.

1134 Peters, Herman J., and others. *Guidance in Elementary Schools.* Chicago, Rand McNally, 1965. 278p. biblio.

Well-written from the developmental point of view, it includes theory, instruments and functions, program development, and management. The book is unique, and its weaknesses are those of the field it covers, which has not yet developed a firm structure and rationale.

1135 Willey, Ray D. *Guidance in Elementary Education,* rev. ed. New York, Harper, 1960. 462p.

A textbook for use in introducing elementary school guidance. Techniques included for use by the classroom teacher.

Secondary Schools

1136 Horowitz, Alice H., ed. *The Outlook for Youth* (The Reference Shelf, vol. 34, no. 1). New York, Wilson, 1962. 216p. biblio.

Traces general trends and reveals attitudes of high school and college students.

1137   Loughary, John W. *Counseling in Secondary Schools: a Frame of Reference.* New York, Harper, 1961. 153p.

The frame of reference is for school counselors, and the thesis is that counseling is the most important function of the school counselor, far outweighing non-counseling guidance procedures.

1138   Strang, Ruth. *Counseling Technics in College and Secondary School,* 2nd ed. New York, Harper, 1949. 302p. biblio.

Underlying assumption is that counseling techniques can be taught. Discussion of counselor's personal qualifications, his relationship with the student being counseled, and the intelligent and flexible use of the various techniques.

1139   Williamson, Edmund G. *Counseling Adolescents.* New York, McGraw-Hill, 1950. 548p. biblio.

Stresses counseling as a form of personalized and individualized assistance to adolescents as they develop their full personalities in a societal and school context and as a democratic society's means of utilizing human resources to their utmost.

Colleges and Universities

1140   Arbuckle, Dugald S. *Student Personnel Services in Higher Education.* New York, McGraw-Hill, 1953. 352p.

Addressed to faculty to increase understanding of student personnel services. Emphasizes concern for the individual student and the need for continual evaluation. Includes a helpful appendix of forms used by counselors.

1141   Ayers, Archie R., and others. *Student Services Administration in Higher Education* (USOE Bulletin no. 16). Washington, GPO, 1966. 290p.

An up-to-date, comprehensive study of personnel, allocation of functions, policy development and implementation, and patterns of organization and operation. Contains much data useful for comparative purposes.

1142   Farnsworth, Dana L. *Mental Health in Colleges and Universities.* Cambridge, Harvard UP, 1957. 244p. biblio.

Discusses a matter of increasing concern—the responsibility of the college for the mental health of its students and what can be done about it.

1143   Hardee, Melvene D. *The Faculty in College Counseling.* New York, McGraw-Hill, 1959. 391p.

Describes the coordination of counseling by faculty members with other aspects of counseling.

1144 Lloyd-Jones, Esther M., and Smith, Margaret R., eds. *Student Personnel Work as Deeper Teaching*. New York, Harper, 1954. 361p.

A conception of personnel work as the extension and deepening of the educational program to develop whole men prepared for life in a democratic society. An appeal for cooperative programs with faculty, personnel workers, and students.

1145 Mueller, Kate H. *Student Personnel Work in Higher Education*. Cambridge, Riverside, 1961. 570p. biblio.

A theoretical and practical view that presents background perspectives and relevant concepts, describes services, and examines the nature of the profession.

1146 Shaffer, Robert H., and Martinson, William B. *Student Personnel Services in Higher Education*. New York, CARE, 1966. 115p. biblio.

With attention given to the current issue of student freedom and to directing student energies into productive channels, this deals also with such practical matters as financial aid, health services, counseling, housing, and organized student activities.

1147 Williamson, Edmund G. *Student Personnel Services in Colleges and Universities*. New York, McGraw-Hill, 1961. 474p. biblio.

Discusses the processes of the day-to-day operation and management of services to students. Views the administrative services of colleges and universities as educative and stresses the need for understanding the societal context within which institutional programs operate.

HANDICAPPED see EXCEPTIONAL CHILDREN
RECREATION FOR THE HANDICAPPED
REHABILITATION

HEALTH EDUCATION

1148 Anderson, Carl L. *School Health Practice*, 3rd ed. St. Louis, Mosby, 1964. 530p. biblio.

Includes all aspects of the school health program: elementary and secondary health instruction, school health services, and healthful school environment.

1149 Byrd, Oliver E. *School Health Administration*. Philadelphia, Saunders, 1964. 491p.

An all-inclusive description of the total school health program, plus court decisions on school health cases, medical abstracts of pupil and teacher health problems, administrative checklists, and problem-solving situations to stimulate the improvement of school health programs.

1150 Coops, Helen L. *Health Education in Elementary Schools*. Cranbury, N.J., Barnes, 1950. 279p.

Intended for the elementary school classroom teacher to help in planning a health education program.

1151 Grout, Ruth E. *Health Teaching in Schools*, 4th ed. Philadelphia, Saunders, 1963. 415p.

Topics include health education in elementary and secondary schools, audiovisual materials, evaluation, and the health needs of home, school, and community.

1152 Haag, Jessie H. *School Health Program*, rev. ed. New York, Holt, 1965. 395p.

All aspects of the school health program are covered: health services, healthful school living, and health education.

1153 Hanlon, John L., and McHose, Elizabeth. *Design for Health: the Teacher, the School, the Community*. Philadelphia, Lea and Febiger, 1963. 390p.

A discussion of community health problems and programs, with emphasis on the school health program.

1154 Irwin, Leslie W., and others. *Methods and Materials in School Health Education*. St. Louis, Mosby, 1956. 367p.

Covers both elementary and secondary school health teaching, with considerable stress on various teaching methods.

1155 Kilander, H. Frederick. *School Health Education*. New York, Macmillan, 1963. 500p.

Considers the content, methods, and materials in a school health education program.

1156 LaSalle, Dorothy, and Geer, Gladys. *Health Instruction in Today's Schools*. Englewood Cliffs, N.J., Prentice-Hall, 1963. 359p.

Presents philosophy, objectives, and methods. Strong on problem-solving method.

1157 Moss, Bernice R., and others, eds. *Health Education: a Guide for Teachers and a Text for Teacher Education,* 5th ed. Washington, NEA, 1961. 429p.

A project of the NEA and the American Medical Association, this is a source book not only for teachers but also for school physicians and other professionals involved in school health programs. A guide to the changing concepts of teaching in the health field.

1158 Nemir, Alma. *The School Health Program,* 2nd ed. Philadelphia, Saunders, 1965. 418p.

Considers the normal health status of the school child and his common health problems. Emphasis on school health services, with one chapter each devoted to healthful school living and school health education.

1159 Oberteuffer, Delbert, and Beyrer, Mary K. *School Health Education,* 3rd ed. New York, Harper, 1965. 454p.

A comprehensive view of the school health program covering foundations, the curriculum, teaching, administration, and activities.

1160 Schneider, Robert E. *Methods and Materials of Health Education.* Philadelphia, Saunders, 1958. 382p.

Methods, materials, and the organization of the elementary and secondary school health education program.

1161 Smith, Helen N., and Wolverton, Mary E. *Health Education in the Elementary School.* New York, Ronald, 1959. 315p.

A practical text that includes teaching units for the classroom teacher.

1162 Turner, Clair E., and others. *School Health and Health Education,* 5th ed. St. Louis, Mosby, 1966. 411p. biblio.

Organization, methods, and procedures in health education, including safety education. Considers administrative relationships and educational opportunities of school physicians, nurses, dentists, dental hygienists, physical educators, and others.

1163 Van Dalen, Deobald B. *Health and Safety Education.* New York, CARE, 1963. 117p. biblio.

Health and safety education are related to basic learning, and learnings that will carry into adulthood are stressed.

1164 Veenker, Harold C., ed. *School Health Education Study: Synthesis of Research in Selected Areas of Health Instruction.*

Washington, Association for Health, Physical Education, and Recreation (NEA), 1963. 192p. biblio.

A study of existing practices in a random sample of United States public school districts and of students' knowledge of health in grades 6, 9, and 12. Includes 14 topics by various authors, based on a review of research.

1165 Wheatley, George M., and Hallock, Grace T. *Health Observation of School Children: a Guide for Helping Teachers and Others to Observe and Understand the School Child in Health and Illness*, 3rd ed. New York, McGraw-Hill, 1965. 527p.

An aid to identifying health problems for teachers and school nurses. With knowledge drawn from all the sciences, the authors cover all aspects of sickness and health, including growth and emotional disturbance.

1166 Willgoose, Carl E. *Health Education in the Elementary School*, 2nd ed. Philadelphia, Saunders, 1964. 364p. biblio.

A methods and materials text for the elementary school classroom teacher.

1167 Williams, Jesse F., and others. *Administration of Health Education and Physical Education*, 6th ed. Philadelphia, Saunders, 1964. 349p. biblio.

A text stressing the problems of the schools. Covers the administration of large city schools and school systems as well as the small or rural community.

1168 Wilson, Charles C., ed. *School Health Services*. Washington, NEA, 1964. 424p.

Sponsored by a joint committee of the NEA and the American Medical Association, this is a comprehensive guide to school health services. Contains specific recommendations and practical illustrations.

HIGH SCHOOLS see JUNIOR HIGH SCHOOLS
SECONDARY EDUCATION

HIGHER EDUCATION

1169 *American Universities and Colleges*, 9th ed. Washington, ACE, 1964. 1339p.

Published approximately every four years since 1928, this

directory of accredited higher institutions in the United States is an indispensable handbook and source of information. Updated by the semiannual *Accredited Institutions of Higher Education*. Tenth edition planned for 1968.

1170   Baskin, Samuel, ed. *Higher Education: Some Newer Developments*. New York, McGraw-Hill, 1965. 342p. biblio.

An optimistic view of progress in all areas of higher education, with a review of new programs, curriculum revisions, uses of independent study and off-campus experiences, and new technological developments. Includes improvements in teaching, administrations, use and design of facilities, and financing.

1171   Brown, Hugh S., and Mayhew, Lewis B. *American Higher Education*. New York, CARE, 117p. biblio.

A broad view of types of institutions and of programs, students, faculty, and administrative structures. Describes some experimental programs.

1172   Brubacher, John S. *Bases for Policy in Higher Education*. New York, McGraw-Hill, 1965. 144p. biblio.

A comparative account of theories of higher education regarding who should go to college, general and specialized education, and ethical considerations.

1173   Chambers, Merritt M. *Freedom and Repression in Higher Education*. Bloomington, Ind., Bloomcroft, 1965. 126p.

A review of higher education that sees a need for greater coordination between private and public institutions and proposes decentralization of state systems. Disagrees with Conant's *Shaping Educational Policy* (#660) regarding public higher education.

1174   Conant, James B. *The Citadel of Learning*. New Haven, Yale UP, 1956. 79p.

Three essays on the role and functions of the university. Presents some basic problems confronting American education and the American citizen.

1175   *Current Issues in Higher Education* (Association for Higher Education. National Conference on Higher Education. Proceedings). 1st-   1946-   . Washington, NEA.

True to its title, each volume in the series of annual publications reflects issues of current concern. Recent titles: *Undergraduate Education* (1964), *Pressures and Priorities in Higher Education* (1965), and *Higher Education Reflects: on Itself and on the Larger Society* (1966).

1176   Dadson, D. F., ed. *On Higher Education: Five Lectures.* Toronto, U of Toronto, 1966. 149p.

A stimulating, multilateral discussion of the conduct of university affairs and the relation of the university to the state.

1177   DeVane, William C. *The American University in the Twentieth Century.* Baton Rouge, Louisiana State UP, 1957. 72p.

A challenge to private institutions to set standards, maintain quality, and brush aside ivory tower traditions. Discusses the scope and function of the university, the role of the college, the liberalization of studies, and the relation of the university to the national culture.

1178   Dobbins, Charles G., ed. *The Strength to Meet Our National Need: a Statement.* Washington, ACE, 1956. 125p. biblio.

A statement approved by the constituent membership of the ACE for presentation to the President's Committee on Education Beyond the High School, plus some conference addresses. Included are the demand for educational opportunities, manpower needs, the responsibilities of the federal government, and the essential funds to meet these needs.

1179   Dressel, Paul L. *The Undergraduate Curriculum in Higher Education.* New York, CARE, 1963. 110p. biblio.

An analysis of present curriculums and their underlying premises and a proposal for much-needed reforms as a result of environmental pressures, student demands, the needs of society, and the necessity for economical operations.

1180   Eells, Walter C. *Degrees in Higher Education.* New York, CARE, 1963. 118p. biblio.

An objective analysis and evaluation of academic degrees, which vary in character, acceptance, and recognition.

1181   Ferre, Nels. *Christian Faith and Higher Education.* New York, Harper, 1954. 251p.

Proposes a relation between education and religion in terms of the Christian faith that attempts to protect the integrity of both. Surveys the field of higher education from this perspective in the areas of the natural sciences, the social sciences, and the humanities.

1182 Freedman, Morris. *Chaos in Our Colleges*. New York, McKay, 1963. 241p.

A perspicacious essay on some perennial issues that are becoming increasingly acute, including faculty tenure, automation, academic wealth, and publish-or-perish. The author foresees dramatic changes for the future.

1183 Harris, Seymour E., ed. *Education and Public Policy*. Berkeley, Cal., McCutchan, 1965. 347p. biblio.

An illuminating debate on some issues of current concern —political, economic, and such qualitative problems as research, accreditation, and admission.

1184 Havighurst, Robert J. *American Higher Education in the 1960's*. Columbus, Ohio State UP, 1960, 92p.

Predicts "that the future of higher education will be shaped by the forces of economy, demography, and ideology" and offers supporting projections of social goals, numbers of students, and opportunities.

1185 Hofstadter, Richard, and Hardy, C. DeWitt. *The Development and Scope of Higher Education in the United States*. New York, Columbia UP, 1952. 254p. biblio.

Written just after the first impact of the higher educational population explosion became evident, this historical treatment shows the relationship of education to its environment. Stresses the need for intellectual freedom, for intense and relevant learning, and generous financial support.

1186 Kerr, Clark. *The Uses of the University*. Cambridge, Harvard UP, 1963. 140p. biblio.

A witty and scholarly scrutiny of the university of today, the numerous communities of the "multiversity" it has become, the influence of federal money, and the recognition that, with all the changes that have occurred, knowledge remains the university's primary product.

1187 Lineberry, William P., ed. *Colleges at the Crossroads*. New York, Wilson, 1966. 196p. biblio.

Authoritative data provide the base for these informative

reprints of journal articles by leading educators who provide a critical treatment of the controversies, events, and problems intrinsic to the transformation overtaking American higher education today.

1188 McGrath, Earl J., ed. *Cooperative Long-Range Planning in Liberal Arts Colleges.* New York, TC, Columbia, 1964. 108p. biblio.

A practical approach to re-evaluation and analysis, on a continuing basis, of policies and practices concerning the quality and cost of education, institutional research, tuition, admissions, faculty, and programs and objectives in general. Points out the benefits of cooperative efforts.

1189 _____. *The Liberal Arts College and the Emergent Caste System.* New York, TC, Columbia, 1966. 69p. biblio.

Lectures that clarify the peculiar place of the independent liberal arts college in the constellation of institutions of higher education, argue that future strength is dependent upon concern for teaching rather than research, and warn against the creation of an academic elite. Small liberal arts colleges must be supported to avoid domination by a small group of powerful institutions, which receive the lion's share of government appropriations and are interested only in the brightest students.

1190 _____, ed. *Universal Higher Education.* New York, McGraw-Hill, 1966. 258p. biblio.

The report of a 1964 conference with predictions for the next two decades. Universal education is seen as a reality with individual and collective goals, necessitating a redefinition of high school functions, of existing programs and policies, and the development of various types of schools.

1191 Madsen, David. *The National University: Enduring Dream of the USA.* Detroit, Wayne State UP, 1966. 178p. biblio.

A utopian proposal for a Congress-created national graduate institution in Washington, with a faculty of the highest competence, little or no tuition, a minimum of formal instruction, no granting of degrees, and a focus on research.

1192 Mayhew, Lewis B., ed. *Higher Education in the Revolutionary Decades.* Berkeley, Cal., McCutchan, 1967. 476p.

Considers the dynamics of establishing goals, developing

administrative patterns, and coping with alienation during a period of rapid technological and social change. A collection of high-quality essays by eminent scholars.

1193 _____. *The Smaller Liberal Arts College.* New York, CARE, 1962. 113p. biblio.

A discussion of the problems of existence and identity of small independent colleges today and their difficulty in maintaining the traditions that for so long made them a vital part of the educational scene.

1194 Nevins, John F. *A Study of the Organization and Operation of the Voluntary Accreditation Agencies.* Washington, Catholic U of America P, 1959. 403p. biblio.

An intensive study covering the origins, structure, policies, and evaluation procedures of the accrediting agencies. The author concludes that many changes are needed to coordinate the agencies and to improve their role as watchdog.

1195 Patterson, Franklin, and Longsworth, Charles R. *The Making of a College: Plans for a New Departure in Higher Education.* Cambridge, MIT Press, 1966. 364p.

A working paper on the establishment of the new four-year Hampshire College, a cooperative venture on the part of Amherst, Smith, Mount Holyoke, and the University of Massachusetts that is scheduled to open its doors in the fall of 1969. The report serves as a review of recent thinking about undergraduate education because Hampshire proposes to implement many of the best of the newer ideas.

1196 Perkins, James A. *The University in Transition.* Princeton, N.J., Princeton UP, 1966. 89p.

Eloquent lectures by Cornell's president discuss the increasing importance of the university and its role in the social structure and some current intra-university problems such as over-specialization and the influence of graduate schools on undergraduate education. Sees the university as obligated to make the benefits of civilization available to all.

1197 Peterson, George H. *The New England College in the Age of the University.* Amherst, Mass., Amherst College P, 1964. 260p. biblio.

A study of the effect of the university revolution on the small, traditional New England colleges. Has larger implications in relation to the problem of the survival of all independent colleges in the face of public and private university expansion.

1198 Riesman, David. *Constraint and Variety in American Education.* New York, Doubleday, 1958. 174p.

Several essays on the educational functioning of American colleges and universities, including a study of some experiments in higher education, such as Bennington and Reed, that points out that avant-garde models affect other institutions only slowly.

1199 Schmidt, George P. *The Liberal Arts College: a Chapter in American Cultural History.* New Brunswick, N.J., Rutgers UP, 1957. 310p. biblio.

A sampling of the "most important" liberal arts colleges is examined historically in an era when they are trying to maintain their identity and keep from being smothered by the dynamic growth of the universities and their professional schools.

1200 Smith, Huston. *The Purposes of Higher Education.* New York, Harper, 1955. 218p.

A presentation of the principles that should shape the college curriculum so that education can "relate itself constructively to the basic value questions of our age."

1201 Stickler, W. Hugh, ed. *Experimental Colleges: Their Role in American Higher Education.* Tallahassee, Florida State U, 1964. 185p. biblio.

With an accent on innovation, this offers a brief examination of experiments in higher education, both recent and not so recent, of such places as Antioch, Michigan State University, New College (Florida), and Parsons.

1202 Tannenbaum, Frank, ed. *A Community of Scholars: the University Seminars at Columbia.* New York, Praeger, 1965. 177p.

Papers of the interdisciplinary seminars at Columbia, by the editor and other scholars both from Columbia and from other institutions. A significant contribution to the attempt to increase communication between and among the various disciplines.

1203   Taylor, Harold. *On Education and Freedom*. New York, Abe-
       lard Schuman, 1954. 320p.

       A thought-provoking essay on the "value of critical intelli-
       gence" and the failure of educational reform to achieve it.
       A plea for educators to assume more responsibility for engag-
       ing students in the process of knowledge.

1204   von Hoffman, Nicholas. *The Multiversity: a Personal Report
       on What Happens to Today's Students at American Uni-
       versities*. New York, Holt, 1966. 201p. biblio.

       A self-described journalistic book of travel that attempts
       to see what the educational experience means to the indi-
       vidual in the university. The scene and people at the
       University of Illinois are examined in detail with the idea
       of generalizing from that study. Emphasis on pressures and
       the need for institutions to be responsive and have the
       capacity for change.

1205   Wahlquist, John T., and Thornton, James W., Jr. *State
       Colleges and Universities*. New York, CARE, 1964. 117p.
       biblio.

       Explores imaginatively various ways in which the state
       college may attempt to survive, faced with the problem of
       maintaining quality of education while somehow absorbing
       the growing tidal wave of enrollment.

1206   Williams, George G. *Some of My Best Friends Are Profes-
       sors: a Critical Commentary on Higher Education*. New York,
       Abelard Schuman, 1958. 250p.

       Reflections on the failings of universities and faculties.
       Profound self-criticism is necessary if higher education is to
       be improved so that the university can truly be a service
       institution, exercise rational judgment, contribute to the needs
       of human beings as individuals, and express joy in learning.

1207   Wilson, Logan, ed. *Emerging Patterns in American Higher
       Education*. Washington, ACE, 1965. 292p.

       Three dozen well-known leaders in education describe and
       interpret new developments in the structure and function
       of colleges and universities as well as the impact of outside
       influences. Covers also new state systems, cooperative ar-
       rangements, professional associations, and government roles.

History

1208   Brickman, William W., and Lehrer, Stanley. *A Century of Higher Education: Classical Citadel to Collegiate Colossus.* New York, Society for the Advancement of Education, 1962. 293p.

   An examination of the forces of change, the needs, and the demands that have influenced the growth of higher education in America and elsewhere.

1209   Brubacher, John S., and Rudy, Solomon W. *Higher Education in Transition, 1636-1956.* New York, Harper, 1958. 494p. biblio.

   A documented history that covers student life, professional education, federal relationships, curriculum, and academic freedom.

1210   Cattell, James M. *University Control.* New York, Science Press, 1913. 484p.

   A case study demonstrating the need for more democratic administration and control. Even though different viewpoints appear in the many articles and letters included, the need for change was clear in 1913.

1211   Clapp, Margaret, ed. *The Modern University.* Ithaca, N.Y., Cornell UP, 1950. 115p. biblio.

   A developmental view of ideas and functions in Europe and the United States in the 19th and early 20th centuries. Discusses the conflict of concepts between the two centuries and their impact.

1212   Earnest, Ernest. *Academic Procession: an Informal History of the American College, 1636-1953.* Indianapolis, Bobbs Merrill, 1953. 368p. biblio.

   The history of the American college viewed as a record of conflict between inherited tradition and the needs and desires of a restless, dynamic society. Emphasis on typical and influential men and institutions.

1213   Eells, Walter C. *Surveys of American Higher Education.* New York, Carnegie Foundation, 1947. 538p. biblio.

   Useful now on an historical basis, this evaluates 230 published surveys conducted from 1903 to 1933 and some others that were not officially published.

1214   Eliot, Charles W. *Educational Reform: Essays and Addresses.* New York, Century, 1898. 418p.

A chronologically arranged collection of lectures, addresses, and speeches covering the years 1869 to 1897, setting forth the educational reforms in higher education that Eliot, then president of Harvard, brought about in his own university and that had a profound influence on the rest of the country.

1215 ———. *University Administration*. Boston. Houghton Mifflin, 1908. 266p.

A study of role, responsibilities, and power of trustees, faculty, president, general administration, and alumni. Includes descriptions of the elective system, methods of instruction, and social organization.

1216 Haskins, Charles H. *The Rise of the Universities*. New York, Holt, 1923. 134p. biblio.

An introductory examination of the earliest universities and the medieval professor and student.

1217 Hofstadter, Richard, and Smith, Wilson, eds., 2 vols. *American Higher Education: a Documentary History*. Chicago, U of Chicago P, 1961. 474p.

Traces the establishment of the early American colleges and the quest of higher education for an adequate educational system. Considers also the question of freedom and repression in past centuries. The second volume covers the growth of the university and the development of the elective system, of faculties and university control, and of academic freedom.

1218 Leonard, Eugenie A. *Origins of Personnel Services in American Higher Education*. Minneapolis, U of Minnesota P, 1956. 146p. biblio.

An historical study, from the early 17th century to mid-19th, covering the development of personnel services from their formless beginnings to their emergence as a separate administrative unit. Discusses student welfare, board and housing, supervision, discipline, educational guidance, financial aid, and health services.

1219 Lindsay, Ernest E., and Holland, Ernest O. *College and University Administration*. New York, Macmillan, 1930. 666p. biblio.

Material from many sources is brought together in this comprehensive historical study, ranging from classical times to this century, of all phases of administration.

1220 Newman, John Henry. *The Idea of a University Defined and Illustrated.* (Edited by Martin Svaglic) New York, Holt, 1959. 520p. biblio.

Nine lectures delivered during the 1850's while Newman was rector of the newly established Catholic university in Dublin. Although the perspective is religious, this remains not only some of Newman's most effective writing but a fine example of mid-19th century thought about higher education.

1221 Rashdall, Hastings. *The Universities of Europe in the Middle Ages,* 3 vols. New York, Oxford UP, 1936. biblio.

First published in 1895, this monumental work is an authoritative resource. Volume I describes in great detail the three archetypal universities: Bologna, Paris, and Oxford. Volume II deals with the universities of Spain, Germany, Poland, Hungary, Denmark, Sweden, and Scotland. Volume III describes the universities of England and their relationship with the Church and student life in the Middle Ages.

1222 Rudolph, Frederick. *The American College and University: a History.* New York, Knopf, 1962. 516p. biblio.

A study of colleges from their beginnings in Colonial America. Shows how, why, and with what consequences the colleges and universities have developed.

1223 Thwing, Charles. *College Administration.* New York, Century, 1900. 321p.

An early book in the field, based on personal observation, which affords an opportunity to compare conditions then and now.

1224 ———. *The College President.* New York, Macmillan, 1926. 345p. biblio.

A pleasant and, for today, nostalgic discourse on the perils, rewards, and responsibilities of a college president.

1225 Veysey, Laurence R. *The Emergence of the American University.* Chicago, U of Chicago P, 1965. 505p. biblio.

Considers the principal academic philosophies that vied for dominance in higher learning during the decades after 1865. Describes the academic structure that came into being after 1890 and offers brief illustrative analyses of the leaders associated with each philosophy.

1226 Wieruszowski, Helene. *The Medieval University: Masters, Students, Learning.* Princeton, N.J., Van Nostrand, 1966. 207p. biblio.

Documents illustrate this brief and scholarly introduction to the development of the medieval university.

HIGHER EDUCATION—ADMINISTRATION

1227 Arden, Kelvin J., and Whalen, William J. *Effective Publications for Colleges and Universities.* West Lafayette, Ind., Balt, 1965. 125p. biblio.

In a day of increasing reliance on public relations, this serves a useful purpose. A handbook that examines college publications and gives practical advice on organizing a publications office, editing, uses of art and photography, mailing, and economies.

1228 Ayers, Archie R., and Russel, John H. *Internal Structure: Organization and Administration of Institutions of Higher Education* (USOE Bulletin no. 9). Washington, GPO, 1962. 123p.

Suggests organizational structure, outlines administrative functions and levels of control, and offers guidelines for continual improvement. Accents need for involvement of personnel and for adequate communication.

1229 Benjamin, Harold, ed. *Democracy in the Administration of Higher Education.* New York, Harper, 1950. 240p. biblio.

The 10th yearbook of the John Dewey Society, stressing human relationships rather than mechanics and viewing the university as an integrated unit. Offers some practical suggestions.

1230 Blackwell, Thomas E. *College and University Administration.* New York, CARE, 1966. 116p. biblio.

A brief but comprehensive treatment analyzing administrative functions and the need for trained administrators. Surveys all divisions and areas of collegiate institutions, pointing out that there is considerable difference between the administrative problems of tax-supported institutions and those of private colleges and universities.

1231 Bolman, Frederick deW. *How College Presidents Are Chosen.* Washington, ACE, 1965. 60p.

A look at the process of selecting qualified individuals for top academic posts. Based on a survey of over 100 cases and on interviews.

1232 Burns, Gerald P., ed. *Administrators in Higher Education: Their Functions and Coordination.* New York, Harper, 1962. 236p.

A plea for an academically-oriented administration for the enhancement of academic programs. Chapters by educational leaders offer philosophical and pragmatic guidelines.

1233 _____. *Trustees in Higher Education: Their Functions and Coordination.* New York, Independent College Funds of America, 1966. 194p.

Directed toward the college trustee in an effort to assist him in more expert performance of his responsibilities. Examines the developing role and function of the college trustee and defines past and present status.

1234 Capen, Samuel P. *The Management of Universities.* Buffalo, N.Y., Foster and Stewart, 1953. 287p.

A plea for formal and informal cooperation and a proposal for joint management by boards, presidents, and faculties, which is not unrealistic and recognizes the obstacles.

1235 *College and University Business Administration,* rev. ed. Washington, ACE, 1968. 400p. biblio.

Sponsored by the National Committee on the Revision of College and University Business Administration, this guide is intended to provide information and guidance to the business officers of a college or university in those areas in which they have primary responsibility.

1236 Corson, John J. *The Governance of Colleges and Universities.* New York, McGraw-Hill, 1960. 209p.

A close and critical study by a professional management consultant who defines the college function and the roles of faculty and administration and considers the pressures.

1237 De Ferrari, Roy J., ed. *The Problems of Administration in the American College.* Washington, Catholic U of America P, 1956. 191p. biblio.

Proceedings of a workshop on selected administrative problems. Discussions of aims, purposes, curriculum, and specific college office roles and procedures.

1238 Demerath, Nicholas J., and others. *Power, Presidents, and Professors.* New York, Basic, 1967. 275p. biblio.

A sociological, research-based study of 45 major universities as managed organizations. Professional manager executives are recommended for greater innovation and excellence. Appendixes of questionnaires and tables for self-study.

1239 Dodds, Harold W., and others. *The Academic President: Educator or Caretaker.* New York, McGraw-Hill, 1962. 294p.

A description of the changing role of the college president and a search for a better definition of his function. Includes a prescription for the ideal president who, among other things, must be healthy, wise, energetic, inspire confidence, and, of course, get along with people.

1240 Durham, Milton W., and De Busk, Manuel. *Handbook for University and College Regents.* Denver, Golden Bell, 1964. 69p. biblio.

Prepared for the Association of Governing Boards of Universities and Colleges, this is a question-and-answer attempt to stimulate regents, trustees, and board members to become better informed and more deeply involved in institutional affairs.

1241 Duryea, E. D. *The Management of Learning* (USOE New Dimensions in Higher Education no. 5). Washington, GPO, 1960. 37p.

A brief but significant report reviewing published and unpublished studies that develops new insights into the theory, the process, and the operations of college and university administration.

1242 Eells, Walter C., and Hollis, Ernest V. *Administration of Higher Education: an Annotated Bibliography* (USOE Bulletin no. 7). Washington, GPO, 1960. 410p.

Books, articles, and dissertations, primarily from 1950-1959, selected for their value to administrators and containing more than 2,700 entries topically arranged.

1243 Farnsworth, Dana L. *College Health Administration.* New York, Appleton, 1964. 250p. biblio.

An intensive examination of all aspects of a college health program. Covers services for students and employees in medicine, surgery, dentistry, and psychiatry and discusses preventive programs and administrative problems.

1244 Gibson, Raymond C. *The Challenge of Leadership in Higher Education.* Dubuque, Iowa, Brown, 1964. 362p. biblio.

A plea for sound management by liberally educated, socially and technically skilled administrators who can help create a free academic society with full participation by all.

1245 Harkness, Charles A. *College Staff Personnel Administration.* Urbana, Ill., College and University Personnel Association, 1965. 130p.

A guide for the administrator covering placement, position classification and salaries, employee evaluation, orientation and training, vacations, and the like.

1246 Harris, Seymour E., and others., eds. *Challenge and Change in American Education.* Berkeley, Cal., McCutchan, 1965. 346p. biblio.

Educational policy and management in higher education are explored, and management roles and responsibilities are defined and criticized where appropriate. Some remedies and challenges offered. Papers of a seminar held at Harvard.

1247 Henderson, Algo D. *Policies and Practices in Higher Education.* New York, Harper, 1960. 338p. biblio.

A comprehensive analysis of trends and problems in administration, covering purposes and objectives in relation to students, faculty, administration, and program. Attempts to identify changes and future directions.

1248 Hungate, Thad L. *Management in Higher Education.* New York, TC, Columbia, 1964. 348p. biblio.

An analysis of management, its functions, interactions, efficient use of faculty, and other abilities. Extensive appendix of quotations from authorities.

1249 Martorana, Sebastian V. *College Boards of Trustees.* New York, CARE, 1963. 115p. biblio.

Useful both to college boards and to administrators, this describes the different types of boards in the various kinds of institutions of higher education, the wide span of issues and problems for which they are responsible, and the areas in which more knowledge and research are needed.

1250 Meeth, Louis R. *Selected Issues in Higher Education: an Annotated Bibliography.* New York, TC, Columbia, 1965. 212p.

Books, parts of books, journal articles, and doctoral dissertations are included in this topically arranged list that principally focuses on the various administrative aspects of higher education. The annotations are oriented toward administrative usefulness.

1251 Millett, John D. *The Academic Community: an Essay on Organization.* New York, McGraw-Hill, 1962. 265p.

A political scientist's view of college organization and the differences between it and other social institutions. Discusses the concept of shared power through shared respect in a company of individual scholars with collective responsibility and leadership carrying consensus but no absolute power.

1252 Prator, Ralph. *The College President.* New York, CARE, 1963. 118p. biblio.

An examination of the role of the college president as leader and decision-maker, with consideration of the nature of the office. Recommends formal preparatory training.

1253 Rourke, Francis E., and Brooks, Glenn E. *The Managerial Revolution in Higher Education.* Baltimore, Johns Hopkins UP, 1966. 184p. biblio.

Charts the extent to which new managerial practices have been introduced into higher education and assesses their effects. Based on questionnaires from four-year institutions, both private and publicly supported.

1254 Sammartino, Peter. *Multiple Campuses.* Rutherford, N.J., Fairleigh Dickinson UP, 1964. 129p.

Addressed to a growing phenomenon and its particular problems, this discusses the administrative aspects of multiple campuses in such areas as finance, libraries, student services, budgeting, and setting up new campuses.

1255 ———. *The President of a Small College.* Rutherford, N.J., Fairleigh Dickinson College P, 1954. 163p.

Not a study in depth but a pleasant and practical account by a college president of his working life—the college organization, public relations, evaluation of instructors, student guidance, fund raising, parents and alumni, and the library.

1256   Stoke, Harold W. *The American College President*. New York, Harper, 1959. 180p. biblio.

An interpretation of the president's unique position, as seen through personal observation, and a description of both the pleasures and the pains of his job.

1257   Stroup, Herbert. *Bureaucracy in Higher Education*. New York, Free Press, 1966. 242p.

A study attempting to formulate principles through comparison with other institutions. Sets no guidelines but does offer some generalizations.

1258   Thompson, Ronald B. *Enrollment Projections for Higher Education, 1961-1978*. Washington, ACE, 1961. 36p.

Prepared for the American Association of Collegiate Registrars and Admissions Officers, this is a vital tool for planning. Presents maps and graphs by states.

1259   Williams, Robert L. *The Administration of Academic Affairs in Higher Education*. Ann Arbor, U of Michigan P, 1966. 182p.

An attempt to place the administrative task in its educational context. Describes existing policies and suggests improvements in such areas as budgets, space utilization, and red tape cutting.

1260   Woodburne, Lloyd S. *Principles of College and University Administration*. Stanford, Cal., Stanford UP, 1958. 197p. biblio.

A practical, comprehensive guide that is a functional analysis of all phases of administrative procedure.

HIGHER EDUCATION—ECONOMICS

1261   Burchard, John E., ed. *Mid-Century: the Social Implications of Scientific Progress*. Cambridge, MIT Press, 1950.

Papers on the control of higher education, financial problems, endowment, federal support, which have relevance to today's explosive needs and pressing problems.

1262   Chambers, Merritt M. *Financing Higher Education*. New York, CARE, 1963. 117p. biblio.

Where the money comes from and where it goes. A timely discussion of philanthropy, public support, fees, and financial aid to students. Some cogent comments on the need for greater efficiency to counteract rising operational costs.

1263   Curti, Merle, and Nash, Roderick. *Philanthropy in the Shaping of American Higher Education.* New Brunswick, N.J., Rutgers UP, 1965. 340p. biblio.

A chronological assessment of philanthropy as both creative giving and coercion. "Together, the idea, the leader, and the dollar brought about change in response to changing conditions."

1264   Danière, André. *Higher Education in the American Economy.* New York, Random, 1964. 206p.

Examines the relationship between all levels of higher education and national economic resources.

1265   *The Economics of Higher Education.* New York, CEEB, 1967. 100p.

The papers of the Third College Scholarship Service Colloquium. They cover the broad economic problems of higher education, financing higher education, the relationships between public and private institutions, and public support of private institutions.

1266   Harris, Seymour E., ed. *Higher Education in the United States: the Economic Problems.* Cambridge, Harvard UP, 1960. 252p.

Seminar papers (1958 and 1959) presenting diverse views and reviews of current practices concerning economic issues in higher education and their relationship to educational problems and values.

1267   _____. *Higher Education: Resources and Finance.* New York, McGraw-Hill, 1962. 713p. biblio.

A thorough examination of the economics of higher education. Covers all forms of income, efficient management of monies, and effective use of resources.

1268   _____. *More Resources for Education.* New York, Harper, 1960. 86p.

A proposal that education receive a greater share of the gross national income and that education programs be revised for more efficient use of resources to increase educational productivity.

1269   Keezer, Dexter M., ed. *Financing Higher Education, 1960-1970.* New York, McGraw-Hill, 1959. 304p.

With an accent on long-range planning, this predicts college costs and discusses research, management, student fees, and both government and private support.

1270 McGrath, Earl J. *Memo to a College Faculty Member.* New York, TC, Columbia, 1961. 54p.

A report of 14 independent liberal arts colleges on curriculum and instructional costs, emphasizing the need for faculty participation and leadership in more economical management of curriculum and staff time.

1271 Mushkin, Selma J., ed. *The Economics of Higher Education* (USOE Bulletin no. 5). Washington, GPO, 1962. 406p. biblio.

Economists discuss the supply and demand of college personnel, higher education as an investment in people, financial resources, and economic research.

1272 Nance, Paul. *Business Management Practices in Selected Colleges and Universities* (USOE Bulletin no. 12). Washington, GPO, 1966. 125p. biblio.

A case study report for use by colleges and universities in evaluating and revising their operations. Provides suggestions and guidelines for institutional self-study.

1273 _____, and others. *Guide to College and University Business Management* (USOE Bulletin no. 30). Washington, GPO, 1965. 169p. biblio.

A guide for business managers, dealing with role, functions, and determinants of effectiveness. Numerous subheadings aid in quick location of items.

1274 Pollard, John A. *Fund-Raising for Higher Education.* New York, Harper, 1958. 255p.

For development officers, alumni, and others concerned with the voluntary support of colleges and universities. The thesis stated is that an institution must have a "good case" before it can successfully raise money or have good public relations.

1275 Ruml, Beardsley, and Morrison, Donald H. *Memo to a College Trustee: a Report on Financial and Structural Problems of the Liberal College.* New York, McGraw-Hill, 1959. 94p. biblio.

The crisis faced today by even the best-endowed institutions makes this book of even greater interest now than when it was published. A discussion of the economic, financial, and structural issues that must be resolved if the liberal college is to maintain its strength and freedom.

1276 Schoenfeld, Clarence A. *The University and Its Publics: Approaches to a Public Relations Program for Colleges and Universities.* New York, Harper, 1954. 284p.

The need for greater public support for both private and public institutions becomes increasingly crucial. This book is concerned with the human realities in effecting harmony between the college and its publics.

1277 Tickton, Sidney G. *Needed: a Ten Year College Budget.* New York, FAE, 1961. 40p.

An argument for long-term planning to replace, or at least relieve, annual crises, which includes advice on how to plan as well as outlining procedures. Detailed case history of one college's planning.

1278 Williams, Harry. *Planning for Effective Resources Allocation in Universities.* Washington, ACE, 1966. 80p.

An important study on program budgeting as a basic planning tool, emphasizing that budgets should derive from plans, not determine them.

HISTORY OF EDUCATION
see also subdivision within subjects

1279 Bailyn, Bernard. *Education in the Forming of the American Society: Needs and Opportunities for Study.* New York, Random (Vintage), 1960. 147p. biblio.

A pathbreaking essay envisioning the development of education in this country as contributing to the more comprehensive sweep of cultural history.

1280 Bolgar, R. R. *The Classical Heritage and Its Beneficiaries.* New York, Harper, 1954. 592p. biblio.

An analysis of the cultural unity of the classical heritage and its role in the shaping of European culture, as well as of those changes in educational philosophy that represent departures from the classical tradition.

1281 Brubacher, John S. *A History of the Problems of Education,* 2nd ed. New York, McGraw-Hill, 1966. 659p. biblio.

Current problems are examined in the light of their historical development and the relationship of the past to the present. An encyclopedic account of the interplay between economic, political, and social forces and of the philosophies of individuals who sought to interpret the educational needs of their day.

1282 Butts, R. Freeman. *A Cultural History of Western Education: Its Social and Intellectual Foundations,* 2nd ed. New York, McGraw-Hill, 1955. 645p. biblio.

Based on the assumption that education is affected by the dominant institutions and beliefs of a culture and that education in turn affects that culture. Traces the history of Western education from ancient times, utilizing findings from the fields of philosophy, psychology, and the social sciences.

1283 ———, and Cremin, Lawrence A. *A History of Education in American Culture.* New York, Holt, 1953. 628p. biblio.

A cultural approach based on recent scholarship in social history, intellectual history, philosophy, and other social sciences in which the development of education is shown to be an integral part of the total sweep of American history.

1284 Carlton, Frank T. *Economic Influences upon Educational Progress in the United States, 1820-1850.* New York, TC, Columbia, 1966. 165p. biblio.

A reissue of a 1908 doctoral dissertation, whose thesis is that "the trend of educational advance is determined by economic evolution." Has additional interest in the light it throws on the writing of the history of education.

1285 Cremin, Lawrence A. *The Transformation of the School.* New York, Knopf, 1961. 387p.

An historical perspective on the development and emergence of the school of today through a detailed examination of progressivism from 1876 to 1957.

1286 Dewey, John, and Evelyn. *Schools of Tomorrow.* New York, Dutton, 1915. 316p.

A hardy perennial, still in print, this attempts to show what happened when schools put into practice some of the more widely accepted views of educational reformers. A picture of the direction in which education was going in the early years of this century.

1287 Eby, Frederick, and Arrowood, Charles F. *The Development of Modern Education: Theory, Organization, and Practice*, 2nd ed. Englewood Cliffs, N.J., Prentice-Hall, 1952. 719p.

A comprehensive and scholarly survey of the educational theories of Locke, Rousseau, Pestalozzi, Froebel, Hall, and Dewey from both a philosophical and a psychological point of view with reference to their influence on American education.

1288 Higson, C. W. J., ed. *Sources for the History of Education*. London, Library Association, 1967. 206p.

A complete bibliography of books in libraries of British Institutes and Schools of Education. Includes titles on education, school textbooks, and children's books from the 15th century to 1870, and government publications to 1917.

1289 Jaeger, Werner W. *Paideia: the Ideals of Greek Culture*, 3 vols. New York, Oxford, 1945.

Translated by Gilbert Highet, these volumes are a definitive chronological study of the foundation, growth, and crises of Greek culture through the age of Plato.

1290 Jernegan, Marcus W. *Laboring and Dependent Classes in Colonial America, 1607-1783: Studies of the Economic, Educational, and Social Significance of Slaves, Servants, and Poor Folk*. Chicago, U of Chicago P, 1931. 256p. biblio.

A significant work for the student of American history. Part 4, "Public Schools in New England," and Part 5, "Public Schools in the Southern States," are of particular interest.

1291 Johnson, Clifton. *Old Time Schools and School Books*. New York, Macmillan, 1904. 381p. (Dover, 1963.)

Traces the early history of education in America from the first Colonial efforts in Massachusetts to establish public and private ways to instruct children to 1850. Focuses on New England but includes information about developments from New York to Virginia and in the Midwest.

1292 Kandel, Isaac L., ed. *Twenty-Five Years of American Education: Collected Essays*. New York, Macmillan, 1924. 469p. biblio.

A collection that summarizes achievements during the

first quarter of the 20th century and indicates areas still remaining to be developed. Of particular interest are the essays on education in the South and of the Negro.

1293   Karier, Clarence J. *Man, Society, and Education: a History of American Educational Ideas.* Glenview, Ill., Scott Foresman, 1967. 334p. biblio.

Analytic essays, chronologically arranged, describe the shaping of American education by examining major intellectual themes and ideas, the men most influential in translating them into action, and the institutions they created.

1294   Knight, Edgar W., ed. *A Documentary History of Education in the South before 1860,* 5 vols. Chapel Hill, U of North Carolina P, 1953.

Deals with Colonial education, the emergence of a system of public education of a distinctively American and non-European character, the rise of the state universities, the private and denominational academies and colleges, and the problems and practices that distinguish Southern education from that of the North. An exhaustive coverage that is not merely an array of documents but has a point of view.

1295   _____, ed. *Readings in American Educational History.* New York, Appleton, 1951. 799p. biblio.

A collection of documents from Colonial times to 1950.

1296   Krug, Edward A. *Salient Dates in American Education: 1635-1964.* New York, Harper, 1966. 159p. biblio.

Using primary sources, records and interprets 35 of the most significant developments in American education, providing a chronological framework.

1297   Marrou, H. I. *A History of Education in Antiquity.* New York, Sheed and Ward, 1956. 466p. biblio.

Translated from the French, this is an intensive review of the origins of classical education in Homeric times and a discussion of classical education in both Greece and Rome.

1298   Mayer, Frederick. *A History of Educational Thought,* 2nd. ed. Columbus, Merrill, 1966. biblio.

A scholarly and eminently readable compendium of educational ideas from ancient times until today, inclusive of the Orient. The effects of the ideas on subsequent practice are analyzed, and the general thesis is a search for the development of creativity in education and educational thought.

1299 Medlin, William K. *The History of Educational Ideas in the West.* New York, CARE, 1964. 118p. biblio.

An introductory survey from classical times through the 19th century, distinguished for its excellent organization and clarity of exposition.

1300 Meyer, Adolph E. *An Educational History of the American People,* 2nd ed. New York, McGraw-Hill, 1967. 516p.

An historical review of the landmarks in the history of United States education, with particular emphasis on such events and issues of recent years as integration, the growing strength of teacher unions, the Conant reports, Supreme Court decisions, and numerous innovations.

1301 Nash, Paul, and others, eds. *The Educated Man: Studies in the History of Educational Thought.* New York, Wiley, 1965. 421p. biblio.

Views on education of 15 eminent philosophers from Plato to Buber, with judgments of various commentators. Not an easy book but stimulating, especially for discussion purposes.

1302 Park, Joe. *The Rise of American Education: an Annotated Bibliography.* Evanston, Ill., Northwestern UP, 1965. 216p.

A valuable reference for the researcher as it includes books in the history of education plus related Early American imprints, microprints of books, pamphlets and broadsides published from 1639 to 1800, and doctoral dissertations.

1303 Parsons, Elsie Worthington Clews. *Educational Legislation and Administration of Colonial Governments.* New York, Macmillan, 1899. 524p. biblio.

An account of the educational legislation of the central governments during the Colonial period. Presents records of legislative interest, which were at times the formulation of and stimulus to the colonists' efforts.

1304 Perkinson, Henry J. *The Imperfect Panacea: American Faith in Education 1865-1965.* New York, Random, 1968. 200p. biblio.

An illuminating and very pertinent examination of the central role played by American schools and of the different ways Americans have used the schools to try to solve their political and social problems.

1305 Power, Edward J. *Main Currents in the History of Education.* New York, McGraw-Hill, 1962. 522p. biblio.

An excellent and readable history of education with interesting sections on early American education as well as more recent developments.

1306 Rossello, Pedro. *Forerunners of the International Bureau of Education: a Hitherto Unrecorded Aspect of the History of Education and of International Institutions.* London, Evans, 1944. 120p.

An abridged translation of the first comprehensive survey of all the efforts that were made for more than a century to create an international organization for the service of education.

1307 Rusk, Robert R. *The Doctrines of the Great Educators,* 3rd ed. New York, St. Martin's, 1966. 336p.

Major personalities from Plato to Dewey are considered in a brief but scholarly fashion. Comments and evaluations weave a pattern demonstrating the influence of these thinkers in today's approaches and philosophies.

1308 Small, Walter H. *Early New England Schools.* Boston, Ginn, 1914. 401p. biblio.

A history of 17th and 18th century schools, based on primary sources that are liberally quoted. Offers some fascinating insights into the task of the schoolmaster, his salary and responsibilities, schoolhouses, the education of the female, curriculum, and school laws. Proves that school business has been community business in this country from the very beginning.

1309 Ulich, Robert. *Education in Western Culture.* New York, Harcourt, 1965. 136p. biblio.

A succinct, and perhaps overly compressed, review of education as a part of social history. A chronological study of the development of education.

1310 _____, ed. *Three Thousand Years of Educational Wisdom: Selections from Great Documents.* 2nd ed. Cambridge, Harvard UP, 1954. 668p.

A comprehensive collection selected and arranged in such

a way as to demonstrate the development of ideas of general human significance. A critical edition of primary sources.

1311   Vassar, Rena L., ed. *Social History of American Education,* 2 vols. Chicago, Rand McNally, 1965.

There is a minimum of commentary in this collection of historical documents and writings that is organized around four major themes as well as on a chronological basis. The four themes: free universal education, the role of the school in a changing social order, the reflection of the social and economic order in the schools, and the ultimate problems of mass education in a complex society.

1312   Welter, Rush. *Popular Education and Democratic Thought in America.* New York, Columbia UP, 1962. 473p. biblio.

Traces the evolution of the American belief in education by focusing on representative schools of political and social theory from Colonial times to the present.

1313   Wesley, Edgar B. *NEA: the First Hundred Years: the Building of the Teaching Profession.* New York, Harper, 1957. 419p.

A description of the growth and development of the NEA that is, in its reflection of trends, a history of American education.

HISTORY OF EDUCATION—EDUCATORS AND PHILOSOPHERS

1314   Arnold, Matthew. *Culture and Anarchy.* Cambridge, The UP, 1946. 241p.

A penetrating examination of the educational problems generated by the democratization of English society in the 19th century. Originally published in 1869.

1315   Ascham, Roger. *The Schoolmaster (1570).* Ithaca, N.Y., Cornell UP, 1967. 167p.

Edited by Lawrence V. Ryan and with an introduction by him, this modernized version of an old classic is amply annotated and eminently readable.

1316   Augustine, Saint. *Concerning the Teacher.* New York, Appleton, 1938. 88p.

A translation of the 5th century *De Magistro,* a dialogue between Augustine and his son in which the philosopher states that all knowledge comes directly or indirectly from God.

1317 Carter, James G. *Essays upon Popular Education: Containing a Particular Examination of the Schools of Massachusetts and an Outline of an Institution for the Education of Teachers.* Boston, Bowles, 1826. 60p.

Written to focus public attention on the failure of the free schools to provide education as good as that of the private academies, this proposed reforms that included the education and preparation of teachers.

1318 Durkheim, Emile. *Education and Sociology.* New York, Free Press, 1956. 163p.

Originally published posthumously in 1922, this is a collection of lectures by the "father of sociology," who argued that the mental life of the individual comes from his social environment and that therefore education is a "filling-up" process as well as a "drawing-out." Translated from the French.

1319 Elyot, Thomas. *The Book Named the Governor.* (Edited by S. E. Lehmburg) New York, Dutton, 1963. 241p.

First published in 1531, this is a composite treatise dealing with political theory, education, and moral philosophy, whose purpose was to set out a way of life for members of the English ruling class.

1320 Emerson, Ralph W. *The American Scholar.* New York, American, 1893. 108p. (Available AMS Reprints.)

Reflections on education by America's foremost transcendentalist.

1321 Franklin, Benjamin. *Benjamin Franklin on Education.* (Edited by John H. Best) New York, TC, Columbia, 1962. 174p. biblio.

Selections and quotations from Franklin's letters, papers, speeches, and published writings are placed against the background of his extraordinary variety of careers.

1322 Froebel, Friedrich. *The Education of Man.* New York, Appleton, 1887. 332p.

The philosophy and fundamental principles on which Froebel based the kindergarten system.

1323 Gentile, Giovanni. *The Reform of Education.* New York, Harper, 1922. 250p.

Translated from the Italian, this is based on a series of lectures to Trieste teachers. Explores the philosophical basis of education and argues in favor of education of the spirit.

1324   Hall, G. Stanley. *Health, Growth, and Heredity.* (Edited by Charles E. Strickland and Charles Burgess) New York, TC, Columbia, 1965. 187p.

An original thinker, who first introduced psychology into the field of education, is fairly presented in this selection of his principal ideas. Of interest to the student of educational history as his ideas have been largely repudiated.

1325   Heafford, Michael. *Pestalozzi: His Thought and Its Relevance Today.* New York, Barnes and Noble, 1967. 100p. biblio.

A welcome addition to the meager literature on Pestalozzi in English. Drawn from primary sources, this shows the Swiss master's application of new methods to intellectual, moral, physical, and industrial education.

1326   Herbart, Johann F. *The Science of Education: Its General Principles Deduced from Its Aims and the Aesthetic Revelation of the World.* Boston, Heath, 1900. 268p.

A translation of the early 19th century German philosopher's chief educational work, which deals in detail with the aim of education, which he considered to be the cultivation of good will and the formation of character.

1327   Horne, Herman H. *Idealism in Education: Or First Principles in the Making of Men and Women.* New York, Macmillan, 1910. 183p. biblio.

Idealism in education is defined as combining both science and philosophy in the practical aim of "man-making." The transition from scientific ethical idealism to philosophic idealism.

1328   Isocrates. *Orations,* 3 vols. Cambridge, Harvard UP (Loeb Classical Library).

One of Athens' great 4th century B.C. teachers sets forth his views on education in several of his orations. A proponent of the "discipline of discourse" whose course of instruction was a system of general culture based on rhetorical composition. Greek text with English translation on facing pages.

1329 Jefferson, Thomas. *Crusade Against Ignorance: Thomas Jefferson on Education.* (Edited by Gordon C. Lee) New York, TC, Columbia, 1962. 167p.

Selections from Jefferson's writings present his conception of the education appropriate to a free people and demonstrate that many of his ideas continue to be relevant today.

1330 Jeffreys, M. V. C. *John Locke: Prophet of Common Sense.* New York, Barnes and Noble, 1967. 120p.

An interpretation of Locke that minimizes his influence on Rousseau and sees him as emphasizing habit rather than stressing learning how to learn. An enjoyable book, paying due homage to a master.

1331 Locke, John. *John Locke on Education.* (Edited by Peter Gay) New York, TC, Columbia, 1964. 176p.

Lockean theories of knowledge and learning had a profound influence on the subsequent course of educational philosophy. His precepts on the subordination of information and facts to the formation of character and intelligence and on the need for the teacher to be wise rather than simply learned. Republished with an enlightening introduction.

1332 _____. *Some Thoughts Concerning Education.* (Edited by F. W. Garforth) Woodbury, N.Y., Barron's. 240p.

An educational classic by the 17th century English philosopher, based on letters about the education of a friend's children. He opposed rote learning and beginning the study of language with grammar.

1333 Mann, Horace. *Horace Mann on the Crisis in Education.* (Edited by Louis Filler) Yellow Springs, Ohio, Antioch Press, 1965. 243p.

Selections and extracts from the five-volume edition of Mann's life and works, freely edited to present Mann's views with clarity and their greatest relevance to education today.

1334 _____. *Lectures on Education.* Boston, Fowle and Capen, 1845. 338p.

Seven lectures by Mann delivered while he was Secretary of the Massachusetts State Board of Education. Presents his views on the means and objects of the common school, preparation of teachers, the necessity of education, school libraries, and school discipline.

1335   Mill, John Stuart. *John Stuart Mill: a Selection of His Works.*
        New York, St. Martin's, 1966. 471p.

        John and brother James were 19th century utilitarian
        philosophers and outspoken critics of traditional English
        education as well as the final exponents of the Lockean
        school.

1336   Milton, John. *Milton on Education: the Tractate of Educa-
        tion.* (Edited by Oliver M. Ainsworth) Ithaca, N.Y., Cornell
        UP, 1928. 369p.

        An imaginative and fantastic educational scheme incor-
        porating the "old" and the "new" education.

1337   Mulcaster, Richard. *Positions.* Oxford, Oxford UP, 1888.
        309p.

        A discourse on the training of children either for "skill in
        their booke or health in their bodie," written in 1581 by the
        first headmaster of England's Merchant Taylor School.

1338   Nietzsche, Friedrich W. *On the Future of Our Educational
        Institutions,* vol. 3. New York, Russell, 1964.

        Incisive criticism of pedagogues and pedagogy by the 19th
        century German philosopher, forerunner of modern existen-
        tialism and critic of all existing institutions. Translated from
        the German.

1339   Parker, Francis W. *Talks on Pedagogics: an Outline of the
        Theory of Concentration.* Chicago, Kellogg, 1894. 491p.

        A development of lectures given in 1891 that discuss the
        doctrine of concentration, student government, and instruc-
        tion in history and the natural sciences in the primary school.

1340   Pestalozzi, Johann H. *How Gertrude Teaches Her Children:
        an Attempt to Help Mothers to Teach Their Own Children
        and an Account of the Method.* London, Allen and Unwin,
        1915. 256p.

        A principal work of the Swiss educational reformer, first
        published in 1801, which describes his ideas on education.
        His method is to begin with observation, to pass from obser-
        vation to consciousness, from that to speech, and thence to
        more formal instruction.

1341   Plato. *The Republic.* (Edited and translated by I. A. Rich-
        ards) New York, Cambridge UP, 1966. 194p.

        A remarkably small book, especially when one considers

that, to paraphrase Whitehead, "all educational thought is but a footnote to Plato's *Republic*."

1342   Plutarch. *Moralia*. Cambridge, Harvard UP, 1927.
        Included is "A Discourse Touching the Training of Children," an outline of Roman educational theory with its emphasis on character training.

1343   Rousseau, Jean Jacques. *Emile: or Education*. New York, Dutton. 444p.
        Published in 1762 in reaction to those who saw education as training in aristocratic superficialities, this was the charter of the rights of childhood and the validity of children's feelings. A durable classic whose publication forced the author to flee France, it has been of profound influence on the subsequent course of educational philosophy.

1344   Spencer, Herbert. *Herbert Spencer on Education*. (Edited by Andreas M. Kazamias) New York, TC, Columbia, 1966. 228p. biblio.
        An attempt to separate what Spencer actually said from what his disciples and critics have inferred. Aims at gaining a critical perspective on Spencer's ideas, which have become part of our conventional educational wisdom.

1345   Thomas Aquinas, Saint. *The Teacher*. Chicago, Regnery, 1959. 227p.
        Selections from the works of the 13th century philosopher and theologian's *De Magistro* discuss the question of whether one man can teach another. (Published in this edition with *The Mind* and *The Truth*.)

1346   Vives, Juan Luis. *Vives on Education: a Translation of De Tradendis Disciplinis*. Cambridge, The UP, 1913. 328p.
        A translation, with an introduction by Foster Watson. A study of Vives' idea on education and the full text of *The Transmission of Knowledge* (published in 1531), presented to establish the significance of Vives' thinking.

1347   Williams, Edward I. F. *Horace Mann, Educational Statesman*. New York, Macmillan, 1937. 367p. biblio.
        A biography of the man who, more than any other, was responsible for the growth of the common school. Places Mann's accomplishments in the social, religious, political, and educational context of his time.

1348 Woodward, William H. *Desiderius Erasmus Concerning the Aim and Method of Education.* New York, TC, Columbia, 1964. 244p. biblio.

A classic volume of text and commentary documenting the decisive influence of Erasmus on Western educational thought.

HISTORY TEACHING

1349 Krug, Mark M. *History and the Social Sciences: New Approaches to the Teaching of Social Studies.* Waltham, Mass., Blaisdell, 1967. 292p. biblio.

A judicious and intelligent evaluation of current approaches to the teaching of history and social studies that is a refreshingly skeptical survey.

1350 Tooze, Ruth, and Krone, Beatrice P. *Literature and Music as Resources for Social Studies.* Englewood Cliffs, N.J., Prentice-Hall, 1955. 457p. biblio.

An imaginative approach to the use of poetry, song, and story to expand and deepen children's learning and understanding of facts. Offers generous amounts of suggestions and, although primarily focused on teaching history, is adaptable to other areas of the curriculum.

HOME ECONOMICS

1351 Arny, Clara M. *Evaluation in Home Economics.* New York, Appleton, 1953. 378p. biblio.

The objectives of a modern home economics education program are described to offer a basis for evaluating methods of appraising individual growth. Numerous illustrations of techniques for measuring various kinds of learning.

1352 Budewig, Caroline, and others. *The Field of Home Economics: What It Is.* Washington, American Home Economics Association, 1964. 64p. biblio.

Four papers attempt to define the profession and the professional in historical perspective and in relation to the contributions of sociology to the field.

1353 Coon, Beulah I. *Home Economics Instruction in the Secondary Schools.* New York, CARE, 1965. 115p. biblio.

A review of the historical background and the purposes of

home economics education as well as a practical guide to curriculum design, instruction, and the planning and equipping of home economics centers in the schools.

1354 Fleck, Henrietta, and others. *Exploring Home and Family Living*, 2nd ed. Englewood Cliffs, N.J., Prentice-Hall, 1965. 419p.

Designed to give a clear understanding of the responsibilities of family living and the relation these bear to society. A practical guide covering family relationships, nutrition, and the like.

1355 Force, Elizabeth S. *Teaching Family Life Education: the Toms River Program.* New York, TC, Columbia, 1962. 38p.

An attempt to dispel some misconceptions about the aims and content of family life education by describing and evaluating the Toms River program from its inception as an experiment through its development and implementation as an ongoing program.

1356 Garrett, Pauline G., ed. *Contemporary Issues in Home Economics.* Washington, NEA, 1965. 129p.

A conference report that examines selected issues in home economics education. Considers bases for commitment to the issues and discusses ways to develop sensitivity and professional responsibility to them. Issues include provision for homemaking education, for employment, needed facilities, and objectives.

1357 Hall, Olive A. *Research Handbook for Home Economics Education.* Minneapolis, Burgess, 1962. 165p. biblio.

Provides assistance in recognizing and solving problems and in making evaluations, with considerations of important issues and research methods.

1358 ———, and Paolucci, Beatrice. *Teaching Home Economics.* New York, Wiley, 1961. 397p. biblio.

Describes home economics programs in a variety of school situations, defines the role of the home economics teacher and the various aspects of her job, and offers specific aids.

1359 Hatcher, Hazel M., and Andrews, Mildred E. *The Teaching of Home Economics*, 2nd ed. Boston, Houghton Mifflin, 1963. 486p.

A comprehensive survey of procedures, techniques, instructional resources, curriculum planning, department management, and the significance of the federal Vocational Education Act in relation to the teaching of home economics.

1360 *Homemaking Education Programs for Adults* (USOE Vocational Division Bulletin no. 268). Washington, GPO, 1958. 62p. biblio.

Planned for state and local departments of education having responsibility for developing and administering programs of adult education in home and family living. Covers curriculum, methods, evaluation, administration, and teacher education.

1361 Lee, Jeanette A., and Dressel, Paul L. *Liberal Education and Home Economics.* New York, TC, Columbia, 1963. 108p. biblio.

A report of a study of home economics education in undergraduate professional schools and liberal arts colleges. Based on a variety of investigative techniques, including interviews, questionnaires, and analysis of data.

1362 Mather, Mary E. *A Manual for Student Teaching in Home Economics.* Danville, Ill., Interstate, 1962. 84p. biblio.

A guide for student teachers and supervisors that includes samples of report forms. Several assignments are based on Hall and Paolucci (see #1358).

1363 Porter, Thelma, ed. *Home Economics in Higher Education.* East Lansing, College of Home Economics, Michigan State U, 1960. 67p. biblio.

The papers and discussions of a 1960 workshop whose broad topics included: the purposes of higher education, the roles of women, college students' values, and the organization of the professional component in home economics. The consensus of the workshop, on the latter point, was that university home economics programs should prepare students for professional careers.

1364 Williamson, Maude, and Lyle, Mary S. *Homemaking Education in the High School,* 4th ed. New York, Appleton, 1961. 351p. biblio.

An introductory text that includes basic philosophy and emphasizes problem-solving approaches and helping students develop concepts.

INDEPENDENT STUDY

1365 Alexander, William M., and Hines, Vynce A. *Independent Study in Secondary Schools.* New York, Holt, 1967. 208p. biblio.

Based on firsthand examination of independent study practices. Describes and illustrates "self-directed learning activity" and offers five patterns with factual material about practices and steps to be taken in the development of programs. Appendix lists schools with independent study plans in operation.

1366 Beggs, David W., ed. *Independent Study: Bold New Venture.* Bloomington, Indiana UP, 1965. 236p. biblio.

Articles discussing independent study at elementary and secondary levels, emphasizing the how as well as the why.

INDIVIDUALIZED INSTRUCTION
see READING INSTRUCTION —INDIVIDUALIZED APPROACH

INDUSTRIAL ARTS EDUCATION
see also VOCATIONAL EDUCATION

1367 American Council on Industrial Arts Education. *Yearbook.* 1st- 1952- . Bloomington, Ind., McKnight.

Primarily concerned with technical education, each volume has a distinctive title and covers a specific area of the field. Recent titles: *Approaches and Procedures in Industrial Arts* (14th, 1965), *Status of Research in Industrial Arts* (15th, 1966), *Evaluation Guidelines for Contemporary Industrial Arts Programs* (16th, 1967).

1368 Bakamis, William A. *Improving Instruction in Industrial Arts.* Milwaukee, Bruce, 1966. 269p. biblio.

A philosophic approach to the problems of supervision.

1369 Bonser, Frederick, and Mossman, Lois C. *Industrial Arts for Elementary Schools.* New York, Macmillan, 1923. 491p.

A durable book outlining the principles of organizing and teaching industrial arts in elementary schools. Applications of principles to activities in which children may engage.

1370 Duffy, Joseph W. *Power: Prime Mover of Technology. Teacher's Manual.* Bloomington, Ind., McKnight, 1965. 144p.

A textbook more than a manual, this covers course organization, facilities, audiovisual materials, a course of study, and a shop layout as well as course content.

1371 Earl, Arthur W. *Experiments with Materials and Products of Industry.* Bloomington, Ind., McKnight, 1960. 351p. biblio.
An approach to the teaching of industrial arts based on research and experimentation.

1372 Ericson, Emanuel E., and Seefeld, Kermit. *Teaching the Industrial Arts.* Peoria, Ill., Manual Arts Press, 1946. 384p. biblio.
Practical suggestions for dealing with a wide range of problems in teaching industrial arts.

1373 Feirer, John L., and Lindbeck, John R. *Industrial Arts Education.* New York, CARE, 1964. 116p. biblio.
A useful and comprehensive guide to and overview of industrial arts education past, present, and future. Views industrial arts as a part of the total school program.

1374 _____, and Williams, William A. *Course Making in Industrial Education,* 3rd ed. Peoria, Ill., Bennett, 1966. 301p.
A practical guide for industrial arts and vocational education teachers for planning each study phase and for correlating subject matter with instructional methods. Includes information on federal legislation and other background information for course planning.

1375 Fryklund, Verne C. *Analysis Technique for Instructors.* Milwaukee, Bruce, 1965. 178p. biblio.
The analysis technique—how to analyze occupational areas into teachable components—is extended to industrial arts.

1376 Gerbracht, Carl, and Babcock, Robert J. *Industrial Arts for Grades K-6.* Milwaukee, Bruce, 1959. 160p.
An aid to understanding the functions and methods of industrial arts activities in the elementary grades.

1377 _____, and Robinson. Frank E. *Understanding America's Industries.* Bloomington, Ind., McKnight, 1962. 274p.
A description of the country's major industries, designed to acquaint young people with their organization and relationships.

1378　Giachino, Joseph W., and Gallington, Ralph O. *Course Construction in Industrial Arts and Vocational Education,* 2nd ed. Chicago, American Technical Society, 1961. 234p.

The fundamental principles of writing a practical course of study and of adjusting it to changing needs and conditions.

1379　Gilbert, Harold G. *Children Study American Industry.* Dubuque, Iowa, Brown, 1966. 211p. biblio.

An aid to elementary teachers in directing learning activities that involve the tools, machines, materials, and processes of industry.

1380　Jones, Walter B. *Problems in Teaching Industrial Arts and Vocational Education: a Job Analysis and Suggested Solutions.* Milwaukee, Bruce, 1958. 213p.

Offers practical answers and solutions to common problems in the teaching of industrial arts and vocational and technical education.

1381　Kidd, Donald M., and Leighbody, Gerald B. *Methods of Teaching Shop and Technical Subjects.* Albany, N.Y., Delmar, 1966. 201p.

Covers basics of teaching shop and related subjects.

1382　Kigin, Denis J. *Teacher Liability in School Shop Accidents.* Ann Arbor, Mich., Prakken, 1963. 128p. biblio.

Provides answers to the problems of liability for shop accidents and recommendations for procedures for safeguarding the pupil, the teacher, and the school.

1383　Littrell, Joseph J. *Guide to Industrial Arts Teaching.* Peoria, Ill., Bennett, 1966. 192p. biblio.

Guiding principles of early secondary school teaching applied to vocational and technical education.

1384　Mason, Ralph E., and Haines, Peter G. *Cooperative Occupational Education and Work Experience in the Curriculum.* Danville, Ill., Interstate, 1965. 525p. biblio.

A guide to the fundamental methods of organizing and operating high school level cooperative education programs for school administrators, supervisory personnel, guidance personnel, and directors of vocational education.

1385　Miller, Rex, and Smalley, Lee H., eds. *Selected Readings for Industrial Arts.* Bloomington, Ind., McKnight, 1963. 357p.

A well chosen collection of 34 articles comprehensively cover the contributions of pioneers in the field, content and organization, and teaching techniques.

1386   Silvius, George H., and Curry, Estell H. *Teaching Successfully the Industrial Arts and Vocational Subjects*, 2nd ed. Bloomington, Ind., McKnight, 1967. 339p.

Describes and evaluates basic methods of successful shop teachers in fundamental teaching activities and examines specific situations.

1387   Struck, Ferdinand T. *Creative Teaching: Industrial Arts and Vocational Education*. New York, Wiley, 1938. 623p.

An aid to new and to experienced teachers in refining their art.

1388   Weaver, Gilbert G. *Shop Organization and Management for Vocational and Industrial Arts Teachers*. New York, Pitman, 1959, 183p.

For the teacher needing help in setting up and maintaining an efficient shop. Methods and techniques examined and discussed.

1389   Wilber, Gordon O. *Industrial Arts in General Education*. Scranton, Pa., International Textbook, 1959. 216p.

Encourages thinking and rethinking concerning the relationship of the industrial arts program to the overall curriculum.

INITIAL TEACHING ALPHABET

1390   Downing, John A. *The Initial Teaching Alphabet: Explained and Illustrated*. New York, Macmillan, 1962. 150p. biblio.

An explanation of i.t.a., devised by Sir James Pitman as a device for successfully teaching beginning readers, by a devoted disciple. The discussion includes the what, why, and how of i.t.a. and a chapter on its use in teaching English as a second language.

1391   _____. *The i.t.a. Reading Experiment: Three Lectures on the Research in Infant Schools with Sir James Pitman's Initial Teaching Alphabet*. London, Evans, 1964. 143p. biblio.

The results of investigations to see whether children could learn to read more easily through i.t.a. before transferring to the normal alphabet. Discusses the ways in which i.t.a. can be helpful in conjunction with other teaching methods, such as phonics, and concludes that i.t.a. appears to make learning reading easier as it seems better adapted to the child's natural approach.

1392 ———. *The i.t.a. Symposium: Research Report on the British Experiment with i.t.a.* New York, New York UP, 1968. 168p. biblio.

Based on a controlled study of 4,000 children, of whom half used i.t.a., the report concludes that in spite of a setback during the stage of transition from i.t.a. to the traditional orthography, the latter is a serious cause of difficulty in the early stages of learning to read and i.t.a. produces superior results.

1393 Harrison, Maurice. *The Story of the Initial Teaching Alphabet.* New York, Pitman, 1964. 213p. biblio.

Provides historical background and discusses recent work done with this revolutionary teaching alphabet. Describes its experimental use in British schools, detailing the results and evaluating the children's progress in reading and writing.

INTEGRATION AND SEGREGATION
see also ATTITUDES AND PREJUDICE
DISADVANTAGED—GHETTO SCHOOLS
MINORITY PROBLEMS

1394 Coleman, James S., and others. *Survey of Equality of Educational Opportunity,* 2 vols. (USOE) Washington, GPO, 1966.

A massive survey of more than 3,000 schools representing about 650,000 students in grades 1, 3, 6, 9, and 12, to assess the lack of availability of equal educational opportunities by reason of race, color, religion, or national origin. Ordered by the U.S. Civil Rights Commission Act of 1964, the study suffers from the two-year limitation put upon it. It contains some questionable hypotheses and statistics, some incomplete measurements, and has been to some extent misinterpreted. It does substantiate the existence of segregation in the North as well as the South and differences in educational achievements in racial and ethnic groups. It should stimulate new research into the complex relationships among family, school, community, and educational outcomes.

1395 Coles, Robert. *Children of Crisis: a Study of Courage and Fear*. Boston, Little Brown, 1967. 401p. biblio.

A child psychiatrist's stirring and revealing firsthand study of the effects of integration in the South on 20 individuals, black and white, pro and con.

1396 Dentler, Robert A., and others. *The Urban R's: Race Relations as the Problem in Urban Education*. New York, Praeger, 1967. 304p. biblio.

Published for the Center for Urban Education in New York City, this is an examination of racial self-consciousness and of segregation in urban schools, both seen as inhibiting educational factors.

1397 Giles, H. Harry. *The Integrated Classroom*. New York, Basic, 1959. 338p. biblio.

An examination of the background of racial conflict in the schools and a report of a 13-state survey made on mixed-class patterns. The author analyzes social attitudes and suggests procedures and teaching aids for dealing with the integrated class.

1398 Humphrey, Hubert H., ed. *Integration vs Segregation*. New York, Crowell, 1964. 314p. biblio.

A variety of documents and articles offering insight into the legal, political, sociological, and psychological factors, with some consideration of geographical variations that influence and are pertinent to the problem of integration.

1399 Klopf, Gordon J., and Laster, Israel A., eds. *Integrating the Urban School*. New York, Columbia UP, 1963. 126p.

The proceedings of the Conference on Integration in the New York City Public Schools. In a brief space it covers the school's role, the need for a clear policy, and special training of all school personnel. It questions the validity of ability grouping and recommends increased guidance services. A blueprint for all concerned with integrating the schools.

1400 McGrath, Earl J. *The Predominantly Negro Colleges and Universities in Transition*. New York, TC, Columbia, 1965. 204p. biblio.

A comprehensive factual study sponsored by the Carnegie Foundation, of the needs of Negro institutions of higher learning, with recommendations that emphasize the necessity for massive private and federal financial support to accomplish necessary improvements, fulfill potentials, and maintain identities.

1401 Miller, Arthur S. *Racial Discrimination and Private Education: a Legal Analysis.* Chapel Hill, U of North Carolina P, 1957. 136p. biblio.

A study of the legal problems involved in the racial desegregation of denominational and other private schools, undertaken because attention had been justifiably focused almost entirely on the public schools.

1402 Noar, Gertrude. *The Teacher and Integration.* Washington, NEA, 1966. 112p.

Presents specific, practical, and positive aids with respect to race, race relations, and integration in education. Offers help to teachers in applying facts and insights to achieve a truly integrated classroom.

1403 *Racial Isolation in the Public Schools,* 2 vols. (US Commission on Civil Rights) Washington, GPO, 1967.

A report, of which volume 2 contains the statistical data. The study concludes that racial isolation is widespread and that it results in increasing disparities in education. While concluding that there is no sure remedy, it provides valuable analyses of some of the compensatory programs.

1404 Sarratt, Reed. *The Ordeal of Desegregation: the First Decade.* New York, Harper, 1966. 374p.

A journalistic account of desegregation between 1954 and 1964, with a focus on the actions and words of the people directly and significantly involved. Reportorial, not judgmental.

1405 Sexton, Patricia C. *Education and Income: Inequalities of Opportunity in Our Public Schools.* New York, Viking, 1961. 298p.

A sociologist presents data based on a study of an industrial city in the Middle West to support the contention that less quality is provided in the educational resources available to children in low income areas and that stratification exists in the public school system, making it virtually impossible for slum children to compete with those not similarly deprived.

1406 Weinberg, Meyer, ed. *School Integration*. Chicago, Integrated Education Associates, 1967. 137p.

A comprehensive bibliography of 3,100 references on various aspects of integration.

History

1407 Bond, Horace Mann. *The Education of the Negro in the American Social Order*, rev. ed. New York, Octagon, 1966. 531p. biblio.

When published originally in 1934, this set forth a vision and a plan for equality of educational expenditures that would gradually lessen the gap between the "separate but equal" facilities for white and negro children. This revised edition has a new retrospective chapter.

1408 Bullock, Henry A. *A History of Negro Education in the South: from 1619 to the Present*. Cambridge, Harvard UP, 1967. 339p. biblio.

Sweeping changes in the last decade have made this review of the past particularly pertinent.

INTERNATIONAL EDUCATION AND EXCHANGE

1409 Bidwell, Percy W. *Undergraduate Education in Foreign Affairs*. New York, Columbia UP, 1962. 215p.

A study indicating that we fail to interest and inform students about world events. Shows also that teachers as a group are not very well informed themselves.

1410 Cleveland, Harlan, and others. *The Overseas Americans*. New York, McGraw-Hill, 1960. 316p.

Notable because it is the only study to date of how Americans operate abroad. Fallacies that faculties are guilty of quoting are listed, and educational recommendations offered.

1411 Education and World Affairs. *The University Looks Abroad: Approaches to World Affairs at Six American Universities*. New York, Walker, 1965. 300p.

A Carnegie Corporation sponsored study finds much room for improvement and makes numerous recommendations.

1412 Fraser, Stewart, ed. *Governmental Policy and International Education*. New York, Wiley, 1965. 373p. biblio.

Outgrowth of a conference jointly sponsored by Phi Delta

Kappa, the National Association for Foreign Student Affairs, and the Comparative Education Society in 1964.

1413 Houle, Cyril O., and Nelson, Charles A. *The University, the Citizen and World Affairs*. Washington, ACE, 1956. 179p.

An examination of successful practices in educating adults for greater understanding of world affairs and participation in the shaping of American foreign policy.

1414 Kenworthy, Leonard S. *Introducing Children to the World: in Elementary and Junior High Schools*. New York, Harper, 1956. 268p. biblio.

A practical guide to social studies themes stressing learning about the world. For all grade levels. Extensive lists of teaching materials.

1415 Long, Harold M., and King, Robert N. *Improving the Teaching of World Affairs: the Glens Falls Story* (NCSS Bulletin no. 35). Washington, NEA, 1964. 101p. biblio.

An account of the ways in which a New York state school system assisted its elementary school children to understand more about their relationship to the world and other societies.

1416 Mudd, Stuart, ed. *Conflict Resolution and World Education*. Bloomington, Indiana UP, 1967. 294p.

A proposal for a world university as a means of reducing world conflict. A collection of papers from a symposium held in Rome, at which war and its effects on society and the relation of education to war and its prevention were discussed.

1417 Speakman, Cummins E. *International Exchange in Education*. New York, CARE, 1966. 115p. biblio.

A useful reference for Americans seeking educational experience abroad and for citizens of other countries wishing to come to the United States for study, teaching, or research.

1418 *The University and World Affairs* and *The College and World Affairs*. New York, Ford Foundation, 1960 and 1964. 84p. and 74p.

Studies of the role of the university in world affairs. States the goal of liberal education and recommends the study of world affairs as an integral part of the undergraduate curriculum. Suggests the development of special programs for foreign exchange students and greater cooperation with foreign universities. The 1964 title supplements the earlier.

1419 Weidner, Edward W. *The World Role of Universities.* New York, McGraw-Hill, 1962. 366p. biblio.

Provides data useful for evaluating present international exchange programs at American universities. A comprehensive examination of criteria for such programs, of the educational structures of different countries, their faculties and student bodies, American programs abroad, and the entire question of foreign policy and university exchange.

History

1420 Scanlon, David G., ed. *International Education: a Documentary History.* New York, TC, Columbia, 1960. 196p. biblio.

Concerned with the phenomena and dimensions of the field of international education. Covers governmental cultural programs, the promotion of mutual understanding among nations, educational assistance to underdeveloped regions, cross-cultural education, and international communication.

JEWISH EDUCATION
see also RELIGIOUS EDUCATION

1421 Alper, Michael. *Reconstructing Jewish Education.* New York, Reconstructionist Press, 1957. 156p.

Deals with the principles of reconstructionism as applied to Jewish education, pointing the way by which Jewish education can prepare Jewish youth to live as Jews in the American environment. Does justice to both the Jewish and American heritage.

1422 Cohen, Jack J. *Jewish Education in a Democratic Society.* New York, Reconstructionist Press, 1964. 350p.

Not a philosophy of education but the formulation of a theory of practical use to educators and an objective analysis of some controversial issues in Jewish education today.

1423 Pilch, Judah, and Ben-Horin, Meir, eds. *Judaism and the Jewish Schools: Selected Essays on the Direction and Purpose of Jewish Education.* New York, Bloch, 1966. 336p.

A guide to the varieties of Jewish educational thinking.

1424 Winter, Nathan H. *Jewish Education in a Pluralistic Society: Samson Benderly and Jewish Education in the United States.* New York, New York UP, 1966. 262p. biblio.

A study of the philosophy and work of Benderly, a pioneer in American Jewish education. Describes the conditions prevailing in the United States in Jewish education at the turn of the century, Benderly's educational program, and the influence of his theories and practices.

JUNIOR AND COMMUNITY COLLEGES

1425 *American Junior Colleges*, 7th ed. Washington, ACE, 1967. 950p.

A directory of recognized institutions, numbering 751 in 1967 and arranged by states, giving full information for prospective students and counselors. Lists those providing on-campus housing, various curricula, and church relationships, if any.

1426 Blocker, Clyde E., and others. *The Two-Year College: a Social Synthesis.* Englewood Cliffs, N.J., Prentice-Hall, 1965. 298p. biblio.

A thorough and critical analysis of the growing pains of expanding two-year colleges. Proposes new approaches to the role of the junior college and its relationship to society.

1427 Educational Policies Commission. *Universal Opportunity for Education beyond the High School.* Washington, NEA, 1964. 36p.

With the goal of encouraging mature, independent minds, this proposes expansion of universal education to include two years beyond high school for all high school graduates.

1428 Hillway, Tyrus. *The American Two-Year College.* New York, Harper, 1958. 276p. biblio.

A comprehensive description of the nature, development, function, and growth potential of the two-year college with an analysis of its place in our educational system.

1429 Knoell, Dorothy M., and Medsker, Leland L. *From Junior to Senior College: a National Study of the Transfer Student.* Washington, ACE, 1965. 102p.

The report of a 10-state research study involving some 10,000 students, 345 two-year institutions, and 43 senior colleges and universities. In view of soaring enrollments, this study of the major factors affecting the success or failure of the transfer student, with its recommendations for improvements in coordination and articulation, is of great importance.

1430 Medsker, Leland L. *The Junior College: Progress and Prospect.* New York, McGraw-Hill, 1960. 367p.

An investigation of patterns of control, finance, administration, and functions of 76 public, two-year colleges in 15 states. Present status described and evaluated, trends are traced, and evolving patterns presented, looking forward to the next stages of development.

1431 Rarig, Emory W., ed. *The Community Junior College: an Annotated Bibliography.* New York, TC, Columbia, 1966. 114p.

A topically arranged collection of books, parts of books, pamphlets, and journal articles intended to be of use primarily to the administrator.

1432 Reynolds, James W. *The Junior College.* New York, CARE, 1965. 111p. biblio.

A brief, comprehensive picture of the development, purposes, curriculum, and standards of junior colleges. Students, staff, and organization are described as is the place of the two-year college in the context of higher education.

1433 Thornton, James W., Jr. *The Community Junior College,* 2nd ed. New York, Wiley, 1966. 300p. biblio.

A definitive study of the philosophy and organization of the two-year community colleges, their place in the community, curriculum, administration, students, and future opportunities.

JUNIOR HIGH SCHOOLS
see also SECONDARY EDUCATION

1434 Brimm, R. P. *The Junior High School.* New York, CARE, 1963. 115p. biblio.

A stimulating, informative, and well-organized book covering everything from the instructional and extraclass programs to school services and reporting pupil progress, from staffing and team teaching to homework and evaluation.

1435   Conant, James B. *Recommendations for Education in the Junior High School: a Memorandum to School Boards.* Princeton, N.J., Educational Testing Service, 1960. 46p.

A sequel to *The American High School Today* (#2415), containing 14 recommendations to improve the functioning of the junior high school.

1436   Van Til, William, and others. *Modern Education for the Junior High School Years,* 2nd ed. Indianapolis, Bobbs Merrill, 1967. 592p. biblio.

Treats substantive issues in junior high school education from a frame of reference based on sociological, psychological, and philosophical foundations, and more specifically, on social realities, adolescent personal and social needs, and democratic values.

JUVENILE DELINQUENCY
see also ADOLESCENCE

1437   Cloward, Richard A., and Ohlin, Lloyd E. *Delinquency and Opportunity: a Theory of Delinquent Groups.* New York, Free Press, 1960. 220p. biblio.

Explores the development of delinquent norms and rules of conduct as well as the conditions that account for the distinctive content of various systems of delinquent norms. Offers a theory of differential opportunity that provides a constructive way of studying deviancy.

1438   Cohen, Albert K. *Delinquent Boys: the Culture of the Gang.* New York, Free Press, 1955. 202p.

A discussion of the subculture of juvenile delinquents. Includes exploration of a general theory of subculture, various aspects of growing up in a class-structured society, and the origin and persistence of the delinquent culture in our society.

1439   Conger, John J., and others. *Personality, Social Class, and Delinquency.* New York, Wiley, 1966. 249p. biblio.

A well-written study of young urban delinquents in which psychological and sociological variables are examined and their interaction in the determination of delinquent behavior is emphasized.

1440 Henry, Nelson B., ed. *Juvenile Delinquency an the School* (NSSE 47th Yearbook, Part I). Chicago, U of Chicago P, 1948. 280p. biblio.

The role of the school in promoting remedial and preventive measures in relation to juvenile delinquency. From the point of view of the needs of the child rather than in terms of adult sanctions and authoritative control.

1441 Kvaraceus, William C., and others. *Delinquent Behavior*, 2 vols. Washington, NEA, 1959. biblio.

Individual titles are *Culture and the Individual* and *Principles and Practices*. Focuses on the role of the school in dealing effectively with the aggressively troublesome youngster and offers suggestions for early identification of potential delinquents as well as specific practices for prevention and control.

1442 _____. *Dynamics of Delinquency*. Columbus, Merrill, 1966. 291p. biblio.

An informative and challenging book that argues that the school has both the opportunity and the responsibility to change and to improve the personal-social behavior of children and youth. Includes an extensive discussion of the role of the school as agent for change and of the international aspects of delinquency.

1443 Quay, Herbert C., ed. *Juvenile Delinquency: Research and Theory*. Princeton, N.J., Van Nostrand, 1965. 350p. biblio.

A comprehensive and critical survey of theory and research. Examines the delinquent in relation to social disorganization and delinquent subcultures, family interaction, intellectual and personality factors, community action, institutional treatment, and the role of the school.

1444 Wattenberg, William W., ed. *Social Deviancy among Youth* (NSSE 65th Yearbook, Part I). Chicago, U of Chicago P, 1966. 434p. biblio.

Since 1948 when the last yearbook on this subject was published, there has been increasing recognition that juvenile delinquency is one symptom of a cluster of problems related to the alienation of youth from our culture and its established institutions. This summarizes major developments in thinking, research efforts, and programs. (See also #595.)

264 • LANGUAGE AND LINGUISTICS — 1445

KINDERGARTEN see PRESCHOOL EDUCATION
LANGUAGE AND LINGUISTICS
see also FOREIGN LANGUAGE TEACHING

1445   Allen, Harold B., ed. *Readings in Applied English Linguistics*, 2nd ed. New York, Appleton, 1964. 535p.

All-inclusive coverage including 62 introductory and advanced articles. Principal topics in addition to historical background are dialect differences, usage, and the application of linguistics to composition and literature.

1446   Bronstein, Arthur J. *The Pronunciation of American English: an Introduction to Phonetics*. New York, Appleton, 1960. 320p.

American English presented mainly in articulatory phonetic terms. Deals with basic concepts and terminology, standard and other usage, dialects, sounds, stress, and pitch. Includes diagrams, charts, maps, and study guides.

1447   Brown, Roger W. *Words and Things*. New York, Free Press, 1958. 395p.

A general overview of psycholinguistics. Discusses the nature of meaning, the language of animals, the relation between language and thought, primitive language, phonetic symbolism, persuasion, and the development of language in children.

1448   Dean, Leonard F., and Wilson, Kenneth G., eds. *Essays on Language and Usage*, 2nd ed. New York, Oxford UP, 1963. 400p.

Excellent introduction to the study of language from varied points of view provided by authorities in linguistics, lexicography, usage, history, and semantics.

1449   Emig, Janet A., and others, eds. *Language and Learning*. New York, Harcourt, 1966. 301p. biblio.

Based on essays appearing in a special 1964 edition of the *Harvard Educational Review*. Linguistic studies dealing with current problems in the teaching of a first language at all academic levels.

1450   Fodor, Jerry A., and Katz, Jerrold J., eds. *The Structure of Language: Readings in the Philosophy of Language*. Englewood Cliffs, N.J., Prentice-Hall, 1964. 612p. biblio.

A collection of pioneer studies, mostly technical and chiefly using the transformational model.

1451   Francis, W. Nelson. *The Structure of American English.* New York, Ronald, 1958. 614p. biblio.

Structural linguistics related to the teaching of English. For advanced students. Includes chapters on grammar, phonology, and one by Raven McDavid that continues to be the best study of American dialects.

1452   Fries, Charles C. *American English Grammar: the Grammatical Structure of Present-Day American English with Especial Reference to Social Differences or Class Dialects.* New York, Appleton, 1940. 313p.

The report of an investigation sponsored by NCTE, MLA, and the Linguistic Society of America. An analysis of the actual grammar in use by Americans by a study of 3,000 letters by writers of varying educational and social status.

1453   _____. *The Structure of English: an Introduction to the Construction of English Sentences.* New York, Harcourt, 1952. 304p.

A pioneer work, on an advanced level, dealing with the grammar of structure. An approach to the problems of sentence analysis that differs in point of view and emphasis from the usual treatment of syntax.

1454   Gray, Louis H. *Foundations of Language.* New York, Macmillan, 1939. 530p.

An important basic study, with examples from some 200 languages, attempting to summarize the state of linguistic knowledge at the time, to set forth hypotheses, and to draw boundaries between the generally accepted, the inferred, and the unknown.

1455   Greenberg, Joseph H. *Essays in Linguistics.* Chicago, U of Chicago P, 1957. 108p. biblio.

Discusses a variety of approaches to the analysis of linguistic phenomena with insights derived from other disciplines.

1456   Hamp, Eric P., and others, eds. *Readings in Linguistics II.* Chicago, U of Chicago P, 1966. 395p. biblio.

Thirty-nine seminal articles written during the formative period of 20th century linguistics, brought together for the first time in a comprehensive sourcebook. Companion volume to Joos (#1463).

1457   Hayakawa, S. I. *Language in Thought and Action,* 2nd ed. New York, Harcourt, 1964. 350p. biblio.

An analysis of thought and language with suggestions for secondary school teachers.

1458   Hoenigswald, Henry M. *Language Change and Linguistic Reconstruction.* Chicago, U of Chicago P, 1959. 168p. biblio.

The application of the methods of science to the study of language. Establishes a typology of linguistic change of considerable importance.

1459   Hoijer, Harry, ed. *Language in Culture.* Chicago, U of Chicago P, 1954. 286p. biblio.

Papers of a conference on the interrelationships of language and other aspects of culture.

1460   Hughes, John P. *The Science of Language: an Introduction to Linguistics.* New York, Random, 1962. 305p. biblio.

A topical presentation of fundamentals with a full discussion of each.

1461   Jakobson, Roman, and Halle, Morris. *Fundamentals of Language.* The Hague, Mouton, 1956. 87p. biblio.

A "non-Bloomfield-ian" approach to phonology and phonetics. Includes a discussion of aphasic disturbances. The bibliography is a selected list of studies in general phonology from 1931-1955.

1462   Jones, Daniel. *Everyman's Pronouncing Dictionary, Containing over 58,000 Words in International Phonetic Transcription,* 12th ed. New York, Dutton, 1964. 539p.

Formerly published as *An English Pronouncing Dictionary,* this includes some material on the characteristics of American pronunciation, although primarily British. Covers stress, assimilation, and intonation as well as several techniques for teaching English to the foreign born.

1463   Joos, Martin, ed. *Readings in Linguistics I: the Development of Linguistics in America, 1925-1956,* 4th ed. Chicago, U of Chicago P, 1966. 421p.

Originally published in 1958 and containing theoretical viewpoints other than those included in Hamp (#1456), this has 43 articles illustrating the scope and growth of linguistics in the United States. Some coverage of European and Asiatic languages.

1464   Kenyon, John S., and Knott, Thomas A. *A Pronouncing Dictionary of American English*, 2nd ed. Springfield, Mass., Merriam, 1953. 484p.

A dictionary of colloquial English with a vocabulary intended to include the great body of common words in use today and based on actual cultivated usage.

1465   Lamb, Sidney M. *Outline of Stratificational Grammar*, rev. ed. Washington, Georgetown UP, 1966. 109p.

The most recent theory of grammar in a field that has evolved several in the past few years, by the person most active in developing it.

1466   Lees, Robert B. *The Grammar of English Nominalizations*. The Hague, Mouton, 1966. 205p. biblio.

A summary of the rules of transformational grammar of English as illustrated in the creation of new nouns for the purpose of identifying the problems involved in constructing an adequate theory of English sentences.

1467   Lenneberg, Eric H., ed. *New Directions in the Study of Languages*. Cambridge, MIT Press, 1964. 194p. biblio.

A collection of papers by outstanding scientists, read at the 17th International Congress of Psychology held in 1963, which discusses the phenomenon of language. Offers a wide view of language problems with broad implications for many disciplines.

1468   Mackey, William F. *Language Teaching Analysis*. London, Longmans, 1966. 554p. biblio.

The relationship of language theories to the analysis and evolution of language courses. Emphasis on identifying quantifiable features of a language for processing by computer, an instrument for analysis.

1469   Malmstrom, Jean. *Language in Society*. New York, Hayden, 1965. 176p.

An introductory discussion offering insights into the phenomenon of language. Gives a brief world view of language, examines the differences between speech and writing in American English, some history of the English language, and traces the increasing influence of our language abroad.

1470   Miller, George A. *Language and Communication*. New York, McGraw-Hill, 1951. 298p.

An examination of the psychology of speech and communication, covering the various approaches to language study and the relation of verbal behavior to thinking and social interaction. No longer up-to-date but still useful.

1471 Moulton, William G. *A Linguistic Guide to Language Learning.* New York, MLA, 1966. 144p.

A lucid and authoritative statement of the principles of linguistics as they apply to learning a language. Of use to English teachers as well as foreign language teachers because of the discussion of contrastive linguistics.

1472 Ogden, Charles K., and Richards, I. A. *The Meaning of Meaning: a Study of the Influence of Language upon Thought and of the Science of Symbolism,* 8th ed. New York, Harcourt, 1959. 363p. biblio.

An illuminating analysis of human interpretations of language, signs, signals, and symbols. Discusses the symbolic meanings in verbal and non-verbal communication. An important book of special interest to language art teachers.

1473 Osgood, Charles E., and others. *The Measurement of Meaning.* Urbana, U of Illinois P, 1957. 342p. biblio.

A progress report of language research in the development of an objective measure of meaning. Deals with the logic of semantic differentiation, the dimensionality of semantic space, and the semantic differential as a measuring instrument.

1474 Parker, William R. *The Language Curtain and Other Essays on American Education.* New York, MLA, 1966. 227p. biblio.

A collection of speeches and articles on the place of English and the modern foreign languages in 20th century society and American education.

1475 Pei, Mario. *Invitation to Linguistics: a Basic Introduction to the Science of Linguistics.* New York, Doubleday, 1965. 266p. biblio.

A scholar who has written many popular books on language presents in a delightfully understandable form the basic facts of linguistics, the subject matter, terminology, and methodology of descriptive linguistics, historical linguistics, and geolinguistics.

1476   ———, ed. *Language Today: a Survey of Current Linguistic Thought.* New York, Funk and Wagnalls, 1967. 150p.

A lucid exploration of today's English. Includes articles by Pei, Katherine Le Mée, Don Nilsen, and William Marquardt on modern grammar, semantics, and gesture. Includes a provocative discussion of good usage.

1477   Pooley, Robert C. *Teaching English Grammar.* New York, Appleton, 1957. 207p. biblio.

A readable clarification of some of the existing confusions in grammar instruction, distinguishing the particular contribution grammar may make to the education of young people and presenting a plan for accomplishing these goals.

1478   Postman, Neil M., and Weingartner, Charles. *Linguistics: a Revolution in Teaching.* New York, Delacorte, 1966. 209p.

An engagingly written definition and rationale for the linguistic approach to the teaching of language. Discusses the contributions of the great linguistic scholars and, stressing the pervasive influence of language on the individual, clearly suggests that all teachers should know more about language.

1479   Roberts, Paul. *Patterns of English.* New York, Harcourt, 1956. 314p. biblio.

An analysis of the form, structure, and patterns of English sentences, with discussion of intonation and punctuation.

1480   ———. *Understanding Grammar.* New York, Harper, 1954. 550p. biblio.

A basic and introductory account of the grammatical forms in use by educated Americans today. A traditional approach.

1481   Russell, Bertrand. *Human Knowledge: Its Scope and Limits.* New York, Simon and Schuster, 1948. 524p.

Historically comprehensive in its treatment of epistemology and the limits of semantics and logic. An excellent introduction to the subject.

1482   Rycenga, John A., and Schwartz, Joseph, eds. *Perspectives on Language: an Anthology.* New York, Ronald, 1963. 356p.

Thirty-one essays on language organized in a carefully structured progressive sequence. Deals with the definition and history of language, grammar, linguistics, and usage.

1483   Sapir, Edward. *Culture, Language, and Personality*. (Edited by David G. Mandlebaum) Berkeley, U of California P, 1962. 207p.

An illuminating examination of the social and cultural implications of language, stimulating in concept and brilliantly written. A superb book whose contents were selected from a 1949 collection of Sapir's essays.

1484   _____. *Language: an Introduction to the Study of Speech*. New York, Harcourt, 1921. 258p.

An illuminating and eloquent basic study of language, what it is, its variability in place and time, and its relation to other fundamental human interests such as the problem of thought, the nature of historical process, race, culture, and art.

1485   Saporta, Sol, and Bastian, J. R., eds. *Psycholinguistics: a Book of Readings*. New York, Holt, 1961. 551p.

A collection of scholarly essays on the psychological aspects of linguistics, including theory of language, speech perception, semantics, bilingualism, language acquisition, language pathologies, and linguistic relativity.

1486   Skinner, Burrhus F. *Verbal Behavior*. New York, Appleton, 1957. 478p.

A study of the processes involved in verbal behavior from a behavioristic point of view, with consideration of the implications for teaching.

1487   Sledd, James, and Ebbitt, Wilma R. *Dictionaries and That Dictionary: a Casebook on the Aims of Lexicographers and the Targets of Reviewers*. Chicago, Scott Foresman, 1962. 273p.

Some of the furor and controversy over *Webster's Third International Dictionary* (1961) has abated, but this remains a good source of information on lexicography.

1488   Sturtevant, Edgar H. *An Introduction to Linguistic Science*. New Haven, Yale UP, 1947. 173p.

An introductory consideration of phonetics and phonemes, the relation of writing to speech, the origin of language, descriptive linguistics, and the empirical basis of phonetic laws.

1489   Trager, George I., and Smith, Henry L., Jr. *An Outline of English Structure*. Norman, Okla., Battenburg, 1951. 92p.

A significant analysis of English structure, especially

phonology and morphology, which is the basis for the phonemic transcription and structural descriptions of many language teaching manuals published since.

History

1490 Baugh, Albert C. *A History of the English Language,* rev. ed. New York, Appleton, 1957. 506p.

A basic historical study of the development of the English language, including both British and American English. In this day of rapid language change, the section dealing with attitudes toward language and language change is especially interesting.

1491 Marckwardt, Albert H. *American English.* New York, Oxford UP, 1958. 194p.

An analysis of the development of American English as it has led to the differences between American and British English, which are seen, however, as minor and reflective of cultural variations. Traces the contributions of the various cultural and linguistic groups and their influence on the divergence between the two branches of the language.

1492 Mencken, Henry L. *The American Language: an Inquiry into the Development of English in the United States,* 4th ed., and *Supplements I* and *II,* 3 vols. (Abridged, revised, and some new material added by Raven I. McDavid, Jr.) New York, Knopf, 1963.

The diverse coverage is a lively account of history and usage. Indispensable for an understanding of our language.

1493 Pedersen, Holger. *The Discovery of Language.* Bloomington, Indiana UP, 1962. 360p.

Translated by John W. Spargo, this was first published as *Linguistic Science in the 19th Century* in 1931. A summary of the development of historical linguistics for the advanced student.

1494 Pyles, Thomas. *The Origins and Development of the English Language.* New York, Harcourt, 1964. 388p. biblio.

An advanced text covering the internal history of the English language in a chronological treatment of its phonological and grammatical development. Some discussion of British and American differences.

1495 Sturtevant, Edgar H. *Linguistic Change: an Introduction to the Historical Study of Language.* Chicago, U of Chicago P, 1961. 185p.

Excellent source of motivational material. Includes a wealth of examples drawn from firsthand knowledge, in depth, of classical languages and culture. First published in 1917.

1496 Waterman, John T. *Perspectives in Linguistics: an Account of the Background of Modern Linguistics.* Chicago, U of Chicago P, 1963. 105p. biblio.

A survey of linguistic thought from the earliest recorded beginnings to the contemporary "Bloomfield-ian" era. Concerned too with the source of ideas and theories and with their significance for today's linguistic studies.

LANGUAGE ARTS
see also ENGLISH TEACHING
LANGUAGE AND LINGUISTICS READING

1497 Anderson, Paul S. *Language Skills in Elementary Education.* New York, Macmillan, 1964. 447p. biblio.

For beginning teachers "who need to know how to work and also to understand why." Set up in the form of answers to questions and contains many practical ideas and plans. Includes lists of materials.

1498 Anderson Verna D., and others. *Readings in the Language Arts.* New York, Macmillan, 1964. 503p. biblio.

A review of current trends in teaching the various aspects of the language arts and specific suggestions for implementing them.

1499 Applegate, Mauree. *Easy in English: an Imaginative Approach to the Teaching of the Language Arts.* New York, Harper, 1960. 564p.

As breezy as its title, which almost disguises the soundness of the content. The author's thesis is that most children, parents, and teachers are distinctly uneasy with the English language, and he offers a comfortable what-to-teach and how-to-teach it.

1500 Burns, Paul C., and Lowe, Alberta L. *The Language Arts in Childhood Education.* Chicago, Rand McNally, 1966. 419p. biblio.

Describes a guided discovery method of instruction based

on modern concepts of learning and child development. Raises issues and questions needing serious study by those concerned with children's language development.

1501 Cutforth, John A. *English in the Primary School*. Oxford, Blackwell, 1964. 108p.

Proof, if any were needed, that teachers face the same problems everywhere. Although intended for British teachers, this discussion of reading, poetry, drama, language, and written work (based on visits to hundreds of schools) is universally applicable. Examples of children's work.

1502 Dawson, Mildred A., and others. *Guiding Language Learning*, 2nd ed. New York, Harcourt, 1963. 430p.

A methods book for use in enlivening and enlightening language instruction in the elementary grades.

1503 ———, and Newman, Georgiana C. *Language Teaching in Kindergarten and the Early Primary Grades*, rev. ed. New York, Harcourt, 1966. 162p. biblio.

A revision of a 1957 book, this is concerned with language and not with reading. A concise and useful book with listings of materials and sources.

1504 Deighton, Lee C. *Vocabulary Development in the Classroom*. New York, TC, Columbia, 1959. 62p.

A provocative approach to vocabulary growth that questions the use of context and word analysis methods and proposes the study of word parts with fixed meanings.

1505 *The English Language Arts* (NCTE Curriculum Series, vol. I). New York, Appleton, 1952. 501p. biblio.

An overview of planning at all levels. Considers goals, English in the total school program, modern grammar, speech, and writing.

1506 Goldstein, Mildred B. *The Teaching of Language in Our Schools*. New York, Macmillan, 1966. 192p. biblio.

An excellent, thoughtful analysis providing insights into the teaching of language. Discusses literacy, grammar, and usage, emphasizing new knowledge rather than devices or methods.

1507 Greene, Harry A., and Petty, Walter T. *Developing Language Skills in the Elementary Schools*, 2nd ed. Boston, Allyn and Bacon, 1963. 572p.

A comprehensive coverage of educational philosophy as

it affects language teaching, objectives, techniques and methods, special aspects of the language program, and evaluation.

1508 Herrick, Virgil E., and Jacobs, Leland B., eds. *Children and the Language Arts*. Englewood Cliffs, N.J., Prentice-Hall, 1955. 524p. biblio.

Chapters by leaders in the field cover the broad role of language in the elementary school, modern teaching practices, and organization of language arts programs. Emphasis is on practical experiences based on sound philosophic foundations.

1509 *Language Arts for Today's Children* (NCTE Curriculum Series, vol. II). New York, Appleton, 1954. 431p.

Language development, listening, speaking, writing, and reading are covered. Offers broad units for interrelating all four and describes the characteristics of a good program.

1510 Loban, Walter D. *The Language of Elementary School Children: a Study of the Use and Control of Language Effectiveness in Communication, and the Relations among Speaking, Reading, Writing, and Listening*. Champaign, Ill., NCTE, 1963. 92p.

A longitudinal study that followed 338 children through 11 years of schooling. Systematic analysis of examples over the years revealed the kinds of growth and showed correlations among intelligence, general language ability, socio-economic level, reading, writing, and so forth. Of particular interest is the effect of social class differences on the child's acquisition of language.

1511 MacCampbell, James C. *Readings in the Language Arts in the Elementary School*. Boston, Heath, 1964. 470p. biblio.

Recognized authorities and practitioners have contributed to this collection of articles and essays on the most important aspects of language arts instruction.

1512 May, Frank B. *Teaching Language as Communication to Children*. Columbus, Merrill, 1967. 227p. biblio.

A scholarly and research-based discussion of the problems of communication. Covers the environmental experiences that influence spoken language, the structure of American English, and the teaching of generative grammar. Insights from psychology illuminate the discussion of individual and mass problems in communication. Describes characteristics and criteria for high quality written and oral communication and for creative teachers.

1513 Muller, Herbert J., ed. *The Uses of English: Guidelines for the Teaching of English from the Anglo-American Conference at Dartmouth College.* New York, Holt, 1967. 208p.

An analytical assessment of the discussions and resulting decisions of the 1966 month-long conference on content, curriculum, continuity and sequence, the role of the teacher, and methods of teaching, with particular emphasis on programs for children up to age 16. The 46 American and British specialists formed an impressive and diversified group, deeply concerned with the state of language arts programs here and abroad. Complementary to Dixon's *Growth Through English* (#870).

1514 Petty, Walter T. *The Language Arts in Elementary Schools.* New York, CARE, 1962. 116p. biblio.

A summary of the problems confronting teacher and pupil in developing in the latter a mastery of the rudiments of oral and written expression. A thoughtful study of the issues and difficulties that hamper language arts education with enlightened practical advice on overcoming them.

1515 Smith, James A. *Creative Teaching of the Language Arts in the Elementary School.* Boston, Allyn and Bacon, 1967. 304p.

A rationale for the language arts derived from an analysis of the nature of creative teaching and creative communication. Theoretical and practical coverage of all aspects of the language arts.

1516 Strickland, Ruth. *The Language Arts in the Elementary School,* 2nd ed. Boston, Heath, 1957. 464p.

An authority in the field discusses the various aspects of the language arts, oral and written, and ways to teach them. Emphasizes language as communication and draws heavily from research.

1517 Trauger, Wilmer K. *Language Arts in the Elementary School.* New York, McGraw-Hill, 1963. 392p. biblio.

A practical, rather than theoretical, book based on the author's own experiences and experiments in teaching communication, language, and literature.

LANGUAGE DEVELOPMENT IN CHILDREN
see also CHILD DEVELOPMENT

1518 Fisher, Mary S. *Language Patterns of Preschool Children.*
New York, TC, Columbia, 1934. 88p. biblio.

A classic observational study of preschool children during
the period of sentence development, based on verbatim
records of 72 children. Reveals the various stages through
which children pass in gaining linguistic control.

1519 McCarthy, Dorothea A. *The Language Development of the
Preschool Child.* Minneapolis, U of Minnesota P, 1930. 174p.
biblio.

A study of the length and structure of the sentence and
the use of various parts of speech in a representative group
of preschool children. Investigates the relationship of language processes to age, sex, socio-economic status, intelligence, position in the family, and other factors.

1520 Thorndike, Edward L., and Lorge, Irving. *The Teacher's
Word Book of 30,000 Words.* New York, TC, Columbia, 1944.
274p.

An extension of Thorndike's two earlier versions, this is an
alphabetical listing of the words found most frequently in
children's literature, the Bible, the English classics, elementary school textbooks, newspapers, and other reasonably
common sources. Although probably somewhat out of date
now, this remains a basic source of vocabulary.

LANGUAGE LABORATORIES
see also TEACHING MACHINES

1521 Adam, James B., and Shawcross, Arthur J. *The Language
Laboratory.* London, Pitman, 1963. 72p.

New material on tapes, teaching and learning methods,
and other new technical developments are described by two
people who are responsible for considerable research and
experimentation in oral methods of language teaching.

1522 Hayes, Alfred S. *Language Laboratory Facilities: Technical Guide for the Selection, Purchase, Use, and Maintenance* (USOE Bulletin no. 37). Washington, GPO, 1963. 119p.

Educators and representatives of the electronics industry discuss the pedagogical and technical matters that affect the language laboratory user.

1523 Hocking, Elton. *Language Laboratory and Language Learning*, 2nd ed. (DAVI) Washington, NEA, 1967. 211p. biblio.

A non-technical discussion in depth of the language laboratory as an instructional device. Revised edition has revised bibliography and lists of language tests, materials centers, and films relating to language teaching methodology.

1524 Iodice, Don R. *Guidelines to Language Teaching in Classroom and Laboratory*. Washington, Electronic Teaching Laboratories, 1961. 60p. biblio.

A thorough, succinct guide for the teacher covering philosophy, administration, the function of the language laboratory, and the evaluation of classroom and laboratory programs.

1525 *The Language Laboratory: Selected Readings.* New York, MLA, 1966. 148p.

A packaged collection of reprinted articles covering the planning, operation (use and misuse), and effectiveness of language laboratories in both high school and college.

1526 Stack, Edward M. *The Language Laboratory and Modern Language Teaching*, rev. ed. New York, Oxford UP, 1966. 234p. biblio.

This enlarged revision includes recent improvements in the technology of the language laboratory.

LAWS AND LEGISLATION
see also CHURCH AND STATE
GOVERNMENT AND EDUCATION
FEDERAL AID TO EDUCATION

1527 Blackwell, Thomas E. *College Law: a Guide for Administrators*. Washington, ACE, 1961. 347p. biblio.

A practical, working handbook for college attorneys and administrators emphasizing the importance of reviewing procedures to ensure inclusion of legal safeguards. Appendix of court actions.

1528 Chambers, Merritt M. *The Colleges and the Courts: Recent Judicial Decisions Regarding Higher Education in the United States,* 3 vols. New York, Carnegie Foundation, 1941-52.

1529 ———. *The Colleges and the Courts Since 1950.* Danville, Ill., Interstate, 1964. 246p.
Important reference and research tools.

1530 Drury, Robert L., and Ray, Kenneth C. *Principles of School Law.* New York, Appleton, 1965. 356p. biblio.
Concise presentation of broad principles, combined with cases for illustration. Broad overview of the entire field.

1531 Edwards, Newton. *The Courts and the Public Schools: the Legal Basis of School Organization,* rev. ed. Chicago, U of Chicago P, 1955. 622p.
Focuses on cases to illustrate principles of school law. Presents many citations, case principles, and excerpts of opinions combined with textual treatment.

1532 Fellman, David., ed. *The Supreme Court and Education.* New York, TC, Columbia, 1960. 131p.
The Court's decisions and dissents on 14 crucial cases involving religious education, academic freedom, and segregation.

1533 Gauerke, Warren E. *School Law.* New York, CARE, 1965. 116p. biblio.
In addition to being a study of the legal structure of public education, this covers such topics as liability and negligence, not usually found in books on school law.

1534 Hageny, William J. *Handbook of New York State Education Law.* Albany, N.Y., New York State School Boards Association, 19- .
Revised biennially, this is a model of clarity and simplicity, organized to answer the most frequently asked questions of school boards and administrators. Recommended for other states to follow.

1535 Hamilton, Robert R., and Mort, Paul R. *The Law and Public Education, with Cases.* Chicago, Foundation Press, 1941. 579p.
A how-to book whose date of publication is of little significance. Facilitates a case study approach and emphasizes

study of factual situations and court reasoning. Textual material provides background. Discussion notes follow cases.

1536   Nolte, Mervin C., and Linn, John P. *School Law for Teachers.* Danville, Ill., Interstate, 1963. 343p. biblio.

Utilizes 350 court cases to illustrate the application of legal principles to areas of concern to teachers.

1537   Rezny, Arthur A., and Remmlein, Madeline, eds. *A School-man in the Law Library.* Danville, Ill., Interstate, 1962. 64p. biblio.

Introduces law books and their use to educators. Research sources are explained and illustrated with exercises for practice.

1538   Seitz, Reynolds C., ed. *Law and the School Principal.* Cincinnati, Anderson, 1961. 226p.

Focuses on the basic legal principles applicable to the administrative functions and responsibilities of the school principal.

1539   Spurlock, Clark. *Education and the Supreme Court.* Urbana, U of Illinois P, 1955. 252p. biblio.

Covers 39 cases decided from 1789 to 1953. Includes practically all those concerned primarily with education and other representative cases on issues affecting it.

1540   *Yearbook of School Law.* Danville, Ill., Interstate, 1933-   .

Published annually and edited recently by Lee Garber. Includes digests of case law. Provides an annotated bibliography of selected research studies in the field as well as feature articles on specific areas of school law.

LEADERSHIP
see also GROUP RELATIONSHIPS

1541   Fiedler, Fred E. *Leader Attitudes and Group Effectiveness.* Urbana, U of Illinois P, 1958. 69p. biblio.

A summary of the findings of a six-year research project designed to identify the psychological factors underlying group effectiveness. Develops a theory regarding the part played by interpersonal perception in making groups productive.

1542 Gordon, Thomas. *Group-Centered Leadership: a Way of Releasing the Creative Power of Groups.* Boston, Houghton Mifflin, 1956. 366p. biblio.

A philosophy of group dynamics stressing a constructive leadership. Illustrated by the effects of a particular group's experience on its members' attitudes and behavior.

1543 Klein, Alan F. *Role Playing in Leadership Training and Group Problem Solving.* New York, Association, 1956. 176p.

A complete, definitive, step-by-step guide to when, where, and how to use role-playing. Covers the job of the leader, values, and dangers and includes case illustrations.

1544 Lippitt, Gordon L., ed. *Leadership in Action.* (National Training Laboratories) Washington, NEA, 1961. 96p. biblio.

A collection of articles published between 1945 and 1961 that have made significant contributions to the study of leadership.

1545 Ross, Murray G., and Hendry, Charles E. *New Understandings of Leadership.* New York, Association, 1957. 158p. biblio.

A discussion of leadership theory and research findings regarding the role of the leader and the group factors that affect leadership.

1546 Weber, Clarence A., and Mary E. *Fundamentals of Educational Leadership,* 2nd ed. New York, Exposition, 1961. 278p. biblio.

A handbook on leadership that analyzes the qualities requisite for effective leadership. Addressed not to those in administration but to parents, teachers, and school board members.

LEARNING DISABILITIES
see also READING PROBLEMS
SLOW LEARNING CHILDREN

1547 Frierson, Edward C., and Barbe, Walter B., eds. *Educating Children with Learning Disabilities: Selected Readings.* New York, Appleton, 1967. 502p. biblio.

A compilation of 42 readings from a variety of sources. Provides ready reference in the diagnosis and teaching of children with learning disorders. By (perhaps unwittingly) demonstrating the gaps between analyses of learning problems and the remedial techniques in use by educators, it may serve as a guide for future research and feedback.

1548   Harris, Irving D. *Emotional Blocks to Learning: a Study of the Reasons for Failure in School.* New York, Free Press, 1961. 210p. biblio.

Focuses on the emotional stresses that interfere with the learning process, with particular emphasis on the home environment.

1549   Hellmuth, Jerome, ed. *Learning Disorders,* 2 vols. Seattle, Special Child, 1965-66. biblio.

A comprehensive anthology of philosophy and research, with contributions by scientists and educators. Covers the diagnosis and treatment of children with learning disorders and explores the conditions necessary for learning. A significant, well-illustrated work with an attractive format.

1550   _____, ed. *The Special Child in Century 21.* Seattle, Special Child, 1964. 370p.

The papers of a 1962 conference, which, in spite of the title, is a good compilation of 20th century methods of dealing with learning disabilities. A survey in depth, addressed to medical men, psychologists, and practitioners in the field of special education.

1551   Johnson, Doris J., and Myklebust, Helmer R. *Learning Disabilities: Educational Principles and Practices.* New York, Grune and Stratton, 1967. 336p.

Presents a frame of reference, principles, and practices developed during 15 years of active work with children having deficiencies in the development of speech and in their ability to learn to read, write, spell, or handle numerical concepts. A notable and important contribution emphasizing the role of the clinical teacher in relation to the deviant learning patterns of the child.

1552   Myklebust, Helmer R. *Development and Disorders of Written Language,* 2 vols. New York, Grune and Stratton, 1965 and 1968. biblio.

Provides a standardized procedure for appraising normal facility with the written word as well as for studying, diagnosing, and categorizing disorders. Includes the Picture Story Language Test, instructions for use, and data on validity and reliability as well as normative data and illustrations of typical disorders. Volume 1: *Picture Story Language Test;* Volume 2: *Studies in Learning Disorders.*

1553 Peter, Laurence J. *Prescriptive Teaching.* New York, Mc-Graw-Hill, 1965. 246p. biblio.

Provides a rationale for efforts to coordinate and implement data from psychological tests and case histories so that children referred for special services can be more adequately helped in the context of the school. A systematic, direct approach to meeting the needs of the child having educational difficulties in the regular or special class.

1554 Young, Milton A. *Teaching Children with Special Learning Needs: a Problem-Solving Approach.* New York, Day, 1967. 244p.

Offers a deductive method of teaching each child as an individual. Creative solutions to particular problems that emphasize problem-solving or diagnostic teaching.

LEARNING THEORY
see also **CHILD DEVELOPMENT**
EDUCATIONAL PSYCHOLOGY
PSYCHOLOGICAL THEORY

1555 Almy, Millie C., and others. *Young Children's Thinking: Studies of Some Aspects of Piaget's Theory.* New York, TC, Columbia, 1966. 141p. biblio.

The report of a cross-sectional and longitudinal study of 65 primary school children from lower- and middle-class backgrounds, designed to investigate the development of some aspects of Piaget's theories, particularly conservation. A clear description of procedures and results and of the study's educational implications. By and large the study is a corroboration of Piaget.

1556 Bartlett, Frederic C. *Thinking: an Experimental and Social Study.* New York, Basic, 1958. 203p. biblio.

Systematic and adventurous thinking are discussed as natural developments of earlier established forms of bodily skilled behavior. Illustrated with objective experiments and their results.

1557   Bigge, Morris L., and Hunt, Maurice P. *Psychological Foundations of Education: an Introduction to Human Development and Learning*, 2nd ed. New York, Harper, 1968. 588p.

A readable account of the various schools of psychology
and their relation to learning theory.

1558   Bruner, Jerome S., ed. *Learning about Learning* (USOE Cooperative Research Monograph no. 15). Washington, GPO,
1966. 276p.

The report of a 1963 conference of distinguished specialists in learning theory. Papers on attitudinal, affective, and
cognitive skills. An important document in the basic search
for answers to the root question, "How do children learn?"

1559   _____, and others. *Studies in Cognitive Growth*. New York,
Wiley, 1966. 343p. biblio.

A report of a program of research by members of the
Harvard Center for Cognitive Studies. Based primarily on
Piaget's concepts, a discussion of theory is followed by study
reports, which are imaginative, well-written, and do not
always support Piaget. An important examination of the
processes as well as the achievements of cognition.

1560   _____, and others. *A Study of Thinking*. New York, Wiley,
1956. 330p. biblio.

An effort to deal with categorizing or conceptualizing, a
deceptively simple cognitive phenomenon, by describing and
attempting to analyze the processes involved when people
try to sort out the environment and organize information.

1561   Cantor, Nathaniel F. *The Dynamics of Learning*, 3rd ed.
Buffalo, N.Y., Stewart, 1956. 296p.

Based on the premise that significant learning stems from
the self-directed motivation of the learner.

1562   Church, Joseph. *Language and the Discovery of Reality: a
Developmental Psychology of Cognition*. New York, Random,
1961. 245p. biblio.

A provocative presentation of the author's views on the
psychological aspects of language and cognitive development.

1563   Dollard, John, and Miller, Neal E. *Personality and Psychotherapy: an Analysis in Terms of Learning, Thinking, and
Culture*. New York, McGraw-Hill, 1950. 488p. biblio.

With a focus on normal personality and adjustment mechanisms in relation to Freudian therapy, this covers the basic principles of learning, the normal use of the mind in solving emotional problems, how neurosis is learned, new conditions of therapeutic learning, conflict, special aspects of therapy, and applications to normal living.

1564 Estes, William K., and others. *Modern Learning Theory: a Critical Analysis of Five Examples*. New York, Appleton, 1954. 379p. biblio.

Five essays reviewing and evaluating the learning theories of Hull, Tolman, Skinner, Lewin, and Guthrie, chosen because of their dominance and their influence on current writing and research.

1565 Flavell, John H. *The Developmental Psychology of Jean Piaget*. Princeton, N.J., Van Nostrand, 1963. 472p.

A lucid, detailed, and integrated summary of the work of the man on whose thinking and research much of today's contributions are based.

1566 Gardner, Riley W., and others. *Cognitive Control: a Study of Individual Consistencies in Cognitive Behavior*. New York, International Universities, 1959. 185p. biblio.

A study drawing attention to structural constants—cognitive controls and styles—that condition and limit the influence of environmental forces and of tensions provoked by motives. Discusses such topics as aims and theoretical perspectives, field dependence-independence, and cognitive controls and defenses.

1567 Guthrie, Edwin R. *The Psychology of Learning*, rev. ed. New York, Harper, 1952. 310p. biblio.

An exploration of the field of learning to discover the nature of the phenomenon of association and the limits of its use in the explanation of learning.

1568 Humphrey, George. *Thinking: an Introduction to Its Experimental Psychology*. New York, Wiley, 1951. 331p. biblio.

A scholarly review of the study of human intellectual processes concerned primarily with the work of such Germans as Selz and Kulpe and covering thought theory, thought and motor reactions, and language and thought.

1569 Hunt, Earl B. *Concept Learning: an Information Processing Problem*. New York, Wiley, 1962. 286p. biblio.

Treats concept learning from a problem-oriented point of view and develops a theory based on electronic computer theory and computer programing.

1570 Hunt, Joseph McV. *Intelligence and Experience.* New York, Ronald, 1961. 416p. biblio.

An examination of recent research that suggests that intelligence is not fixed or predetermined but is crucially affected by life experience. An attempt to develop a theory based on this transformation of concept, which has important implications in the education of young children, especially those who are disadvantaged.

1571 Inhelder, Bärbel, and Piaget, Jean. *The Growth of Logical Thinking from Childhood to Adolescence: an Essay on the Construction of Formal Operational Structures.* New York, Basic, 1958. 356p.

An investigation of the formal psychological structures that mark the completion of the operational development of intelligence. Includes observational and experimental studies.

1572 Johnson, Donald M. *The Psychology of Thought and Judgment.* New York, Harper, 1955. 515p. biblio.

An attempt to systematize a hitherto ill-defined field of investigation, which examines the known and points the way for further research. Central to the discussion is the idea of problem-solving as a major activity of the socialized human being.

1573 Johnson, G. Orville, and Blake, Kathryn A. *Learning Performance of Retarded and Normal Children.* Syracuse, N.Y., Syracuse UP, 1960. 216p. biblio.

Reports two comparative studies, one of learning characteristics and the other of task performance involving learning and transfer. One conclusion: in situations involving direct sensorimotor learning, the retarded performed more adequately than the normal.

1574 Kimble, G. A. *Conditioning and Learning,* 2nd ed. New York, Appleton, 1961. 590p. biblio.

A detailed review of the facts and alternative concepts of the nature of learning, which attempts to place them in some sort of order rather than to present a theory of learning. In part a revision of the same title by Hilgard and Marquis, published in 1940.

1575 Klausmeier, Herbert J., and Harris, Chester W., eds. *Analysis of Concept Learning*. New York, Academic, 1966. 272p. biblio.

Sixteen eminent scholars, including psychologists and philosophers, deal with four topics: schemes for classifying and relating concepts, the learning of concepts, the learning-teaching process, and concepts in various subject fields. The report of the Conference on Analysis of Concept Learning, 1965.

1576 McGeoch, John A. *The Psychology of Human Learning*, 2nd ed. New York, McKay, 1958. 633p. biblio.

A comprehensive, technical reference that organizes the diverse material in the field of animal and human learning in a systematic fashion, pointing out the pros and cons, the type of research needed, noting the unreliable, inadequate, and apparently conflicting data, and making some justifiable generalizations.

1577 Miller, Neal E., and Dollard, John. *Social Learning and Imitation*. New Haven, Yale UP, 1941. 341p. biblio.

A detailed discussion of the necessity of imitative tendencies that, if they are not instinctive, must be learned. A fresh attack upon the problem of learning with a set of concepts that are particularly relevant.

1578 Mowrer, Orval H. *Learning Theory and Behavior*. New York, Wiley, 1960. 555p. biblio.

A high level synthesis of the psychology of learning with an examination of both research and conjecture in a broadly historical context. Based primarily on experiments with animals.

1579 ———. *Learning Theory and Personality Dynamics*. New York, Ronald, 1950. 776p. biblio.

An examination of current problems and issues in a rapidly changing field, discussed in historical perspective and with an accent on the "felicitous contemporary state of relative unity" as opposed to the era when psychology was considered in terms of "schools."

1580 ———. *Learning Theory and the Symbolic Processes*. New York, Wiley, 1960. 473p. biblio.

A description and interpretation of the symbolic processes

and the influence of cybernetics on the shaping of contemporary thought. A companion to *Learning Theory and Behavior* (#1578), this discusses learning in relation to language, thought and insight, memory and attention, and imagery.

1581   Niblett, William R., ed. *How and Why Do We Learn?* New York, Humanities, 1966. 196p.

Based on lectures given at the University of London. A fresh approach by psychologists and educators with some original, imaginative ideas.

1582   Piaget, Jean. *The Construction of Reality in the Child.* New York, Basic, 1954. 386p.

A basic treatise on the development of orientation in reality and in thinking during infancy.

1583   ———. *The Origins of Intelligence in Children.* New York, International Universities, 1952. 419p.

Describes the development of intelligence by tracing the various manifestations of sensorimotor intelligence and the most elementary forms of expression. Concerned with the formation of sensorimotor schemata and the mechanism of mental assimilation with implications for theories of intelligence.

1584   Rapaport, David., ed. and translator. *Organization and Pathology of Thought: Selected Sources.* New York, Columbia UP, 1951. 786p. biblio.

Selections from frequently quoted French and German authorities, such as Buehler, Lewen, Piaget, Freud, and Fenichel, with comments on each and a description of the editor's own theory of thinking.

1585   Russell, David H. *Children's Thinking.* New York, Ginn, 1956. 449p.

A refreshing and pioneering study of cognition in children. Has recently been receiving deserved recognition.

1586   Skinner, Burrhus F. *The Behavior of Organisms: an Experimental Analysis.* New York, Appleton, 1938. 457p. biblio.

Experiments with rats provide the base for this study of the conditioning of behavior and its implications for concepts of learning.

1587 Smith, Karl U., and Smith, Margaret F. *Cybernetic Principles of Learning and Educational Design*. New York, Holt, 1966. 529p. biblio.

A pioneering work that applies cybernetic principles to the psychology of learning on an extended scale. Particular stress on input media forms.

1588 Thorndike, Edward L. *Human Learning*. Cambridge, MIT Press, 1931. 206p.

Lectures containing "certain facts and theories concerning the nature and evolution of human learning," which, through reference to conditioned reflexes and frequency of situations in relation to learning, describe the author's associationistic views.

1589 Tolman, Edward C. *Purposive Behavior in Animals and Men*. New York, Century, 1932. 463p. biblio.

Developed out of experimental interest in animal learning, this discusses behaviorism, the rat in the maze, cats, apes, and men, motivation, and learning in a complex and influential system of psychology defining concepts in relation to laboratory procedures.

1590 Vygotsky, Lev S. *Thought and Language*. Cambridge, MIT Press, 1962. 168p. biblio.

A study of the interrelation between thought and language, based on experimental studies by the author, an influential Russian psychologist. Originally published in 1934 and here translated and edited, this discusses the ways that word meanings undergo evolution during childhood in relation to the development of thinking.

1591 Wallach, Michael A., and Kogan, Nathan. *Modes of Thinking in Young Children: a Study of the Creativity-Intelligence Distinction*. New York, Holt, 1965. 357p. biblio.

Characterizes groups of children in terms of thinking styles that seem to possess a sufficient degree of pervasiveness in the children's cognitive behavior. Then studies the correlates of these modes of thinking in other significant aspects of the children's lives.

1592 Werner, Heinz. *Comparative Psychology of Mental Development*. New York, International Universities, 1957. 564p.

An examination of early forms of thought in children, demonstrating their global aspects and relating them to the thinking of primitive and abnormal minds that have not developed to the plane of differentiation and abstraction.

1593 Wertheimer, Max. *Productive Thinking*, enl. ed. New York, Harper, 1959. 302p. biblio.

A Gestalt interpretation of thinking, which also examines traditional views by way of pointing out that these have ignored important characteristics of the thought processes. Illustrated by experiments and examples of thinking.

LIBERAL EDUCATION

1594 Bantock, G. H. *Education and Values: Essays in the Theory of Education*. New York, Humanities, 1966. 182p.

An Englishman pleads for the humanities and their insights in an increasingly scientific world, with specific reference to the goals and purpose of education.

1595 Bell, Daniel. *The Reforming of General Education: the Columbia College Experience in Its National Setting*. New York, Columbia UP, 1966. 320p. biblio.

A scholarly and beautifully written survey of general education in this country, its present status, and future potential. Discusses the sociological forces and philosophical implications impinging on curricular decisions on secondary and college levels. A plea for education for self-education.

1596 Griswold, A. Whitney. *Liberal Education and the Democratic Ideal, and Other Essays*, 2nd ed. New Haven, Yale UP, 1962. 206p.

A Jeffersonian defense of liberal education as the source of enlightenment for the individual and as the backbone and defender of freedom and democracy.

1597 Hook, Sidney. *Education for Modern Man: a New Perspective*, enl. ed. New York, Knopf, 1963. 235p.

An essay by a distinguished philosopher on what constitutes a liberal education in the modern world. Asks some fundamental questions and is concerned with the relation of the ends and means of education to a democratic social order.

1598 Hutchins, Robert M. *The Conflict in Education in a Democratic Society*. New York, Harper, 1953. 112p.

One of education's gadflies analyzes the shortcomings of

higher education both in philosophy and practice and offers a new interpretation of liberal education with a coherent general philosophy.

1599 ———. *The Great Conversation: the Substance of a Liberal Education.* Chicago, Encyclopaedia Britannica, 1955. 131p.

The first volume of the "Great Books of the Western World" series. Although it is focused on the series, it critically evaluates liberal education.

1600 ———. *The Higher Learning in America.* New Haven, Yale UP, 1936. 119p.

A classic essay that views the university as the home of liberal arts and of intellectual pursuits rather than of vocational training.

1601 McGrath, Earl J., ed. *The Humanities in General Education.* Dubuque, Iowa, Brown, 1949. 308p.

An examination of the purpose, content, and organization of humanities programs at 20 private and publicly supported colleges, which were selected somewhat arbitrarily but chiefly for the vitality of the faculty in developing new courses for non-humanities students.

1602 Starkey, Margaret M., ed. *The Education of Modern Man.* New York, Pitman, 1966. 203p.

A stimulating collection of essays, paired for contrasting views, on three aspects of modern education: the sciences in relation to the humanities, the pros and cons of a liberal education, and the place of vocational training in education. Eminent 19th century writers and 20th century educational leaders are included.

1603 Van Doren, Mark. *Liberal Education.* New York, Holt, 1943. 186p. biblio.

An essay on the idea of a college, "the arts of teaching and being taught," and on the "mutually humane" arts of language and science.

LIBRARIES IN THE SCHOOLS
see also CHILDREN'S LITERATURE

1604 Ellsworth, Ralph E. *The School Library.* New York, CARE, 1965. 116p. biblio.

A stimulating and thought-provoking examination of the goals of the library in the school of tomorrow by a university librarian interested in school architecture, who defers to those in the field but offers some new insights.

1605   Fargo, Lucile F. *The Library in the School,* 4th ed. Chicago, ALA, 1947. 405p. biblio.

Although no longer entirely up-to-date, this remains a standard guide to the secondary school library, its functions and activities, its personnel and management, its materials and equipment, and its organization and administration.

1606   Rossoff, Martin. *The Library in High School Teaching,* 2nd ed. New York, Wilson, 1961. 166p.

Directed to teachers to help them become familiar with the merits of the school library as a resource in teaching. Cites examples of teachers' use of the library to enhance their own teaching performance.

1607   Rufsvold, Margaret I. *Audio-Visual School Library Service.* Chicago, ALA, 1949. 116p. biblio.

Special attention is given to two neglected areas: the reference uses of audiovisual materials and the cataloging, organizing, and distributing of these instructional materials.

LITERARY CRITICISM AND ANALYSIS

1608   Abrams, Meyer H. *The Mirror and the Lamp: Romantic Theory and the Critical Tradition.* New York, Oxford UP, 1953. 406p.

A study of romantic critical theory that provides valuable insight into alternative critical approaches.

1609   Bentley, Eric R. *The Playwright as Thinker: a Study of Drama in Modern Times.* New York, Reynal and Hitchcock, 1946. 382p.

A survey of the contemporary theater and of 20th century drama, including such men as Ibsen, Shaw, Strindberg, Sartre, and Brecht. Of particular value to the secondary English teacher is the discussion of the playwright's ideas.

1610   Blackmur, Richard P. *Language as Gesture: Essays in Poetry.* New York, Harcourt, 1952. 440p.

An analysis of the importance of gesture in architecture, literature, sculpture, painting, and dancing. Discusses the role of gesture in poems by many authors, including Dickinson, Hardy, Yeats, Pound, Eliot, Stevens, Moore, Lawrence, and others.

1611   Boas, George. *A Primer for Critics.* Baltimore, Johns Hopkins UP, 1937. 153p.

A clear exposition of basic theoretical problems in the area of criticism and aesthetics.

1612   Bodkin, Maud. *Archetypal Patterns in Poetry: Psychological Studies of Imagination.* London, Oxford UP, 1934. 340p.

A balanced application of the psychological approach to the study of poetry and imagination. Provides fresh critical insights.

1613   Booth, Wayne C. *The Rhetoric of Fiction.* Chicago, U of Chicago P, 1961. 455p. biblio.

An important critical analysis of the novel, with emphasis on the question of point of view.

1614   Brooks, Cleanth, and Warren, Robert Penn. *Understanding Poetry,* 3rd ed. New York, Holt, 1960. 584p.

A very influential work, first published in 1938, which is the "new criticism" exemplified, demonstrating the close or analytic reading of poetry. Available also with a tape recording, *Conversations on the Craft of Poetry,* by the authors, with Robert Frost and others.

1615   _____. *The Well Wrought Urn: Studies in the Structure of Poetry.* New York, Harcourt, 1947. 270p.

An analysis of a number of celebrated English poems, by an eminent critic, in chronological order from the Elizabethan period to the present. Attempts to develop a common approach to different kinds of poetry.

1616   Crane, Ronald S., and others, ed. *Critics and Criticism: Ancient and Modern.* Chicago, U of Chicago P, 1952. 647p. biblio.

Presents the "neo-Aristotelian" point of view and is sharply critical of the "new criticism."

1617   Daiches, David. *A Study of Literature for Readers and Critics.* Ithaca, N.Y., Cornell UP, 1948. 240p.

An examination of the nature of fiction, poetry, and the literature of history and science by an eminent critic and scholar whose aim is to help the reader interpret and discriminate.

1618   Eliot, T. S. *Essays, Ancient and Modern.* New York, Harcourt, 1936. 203p.

     A collection by the very influential poet and critic. Includes essays on Baudelaire, the humanism of Irving Babbitt, religion, literature, modern education, and the classics.

1619   Fergusson, Francis. *The Idea of a Theatre: a Study of Ten Plays: the Art of Drama in a Changing Perspective.* Princeton, N.J., Princeton UP, 1949. 239p.

     An historical and critical examination of some tragedies provides a well-known poet-scholar with a base for the development of a theory of the drama.

1620   Forster, E. M. *Aspects of the Novel.* New York, Harcourt, 1927. 250p.

     Lectures delivered at Cambridge University by one of this century's influential novelists. He analyzes the novel in terms of story, characters, and plot and delves into fantasy, pattern, and rhythm as well.

1621   Frye, Northrup. *The Educated Imagination.* Bloomington, Indiana UP, 1964. 159p.

     Develops a myth-centered theory of literature and discusses how to teach it to children.

1622   Goldberg, Gerald J., and Nancy M., eds. *The Modern Critical Spectrum.* Englewood Cliffs, N.J., Prentice-Hall, 1962. 344p.

     An anthology of essays illustrating various approaches to literary criticism.

1623   James, Henry. *The Art of the Novel: Critical Prefaces.* New York, Scribner, 1934. 348p.

     A collection of the novelist's prefaces that constitute an essay in general criticism and a reference on the technical aspects of the art of fiction. They are, at the same time, descriptive of James' artistic consciousness and the character of his work.

1624   Langer, Susanne K. *Philosophy in a New Key: a Study in the Symbolism of Reason, Rite and Art,* 3rd ed. Cambridge, Harvard UP, 1957. 313p.

     One of our most original thinkers discusses signs and symbols, forms, language, and the fabric of meaning as she presents a theoretical framework for recent developments in criticism.

1625   Lubbock, Percy. *The Craft of Fiction.* New York, Viking, 1957. 276p.

   First published in 1929, this is a clear exposition of the theory of the novel as exemplified by Henry James.

1626   Richards, I. A. *Practical Criticism: a Study of Literary Judgment.* New York, Harcourt, 1929. 375p.

   Required reading for every teacher of English, as Richards' works constitute the most important 20th century treatment of the problems of literary interpretation.

1627   _____. *Principles of Literary Criticism.* New York, Harcourt, 1961. 298p.

   Originally published in 1928, this has been an immensely influential book. An exploration of values, communication, and psychology in the development of principles of literary criticism.

1628   Schorer, Mark, and others. *Criticism: the Foundations of Modern Literary Judgment,* rev. ed. New York, Harcourt, 1958. 553p. biblio.

   An anthology of literary criticism, ranging from Plato to the 20th century.

1629   Smith, James H., and Parks, Edd W., eds. *The Great Critics: an Anthology of Literary Criticism,* 3rd ed. New York, Norton, 1951. 952p. biblio.

   An historical survey that includes thoughts on criticism of many creative writers, such as Wordsworth and Lope de Vega, not ordinarily considered "critics."

1630   Van Ghent, Dorothy. *The English Novel: Form and Function.* New York, Harper, 1961. 276p.

   First published in 1955, this is a series of studies designed to accompany the rereading of 18 classics in the field of fiction, almost all of them English novels.

1631   Wellek, Rene, and Warren, Austin. *Theory of Literature,* 3rd ed. New York, Harcourt, 1956. 375p. biblio.

   An analysis of major problems in critical theory. Reflects the reaction against the social and historical approaches to literature.

1632   Wimsatt, William K., and Brooks, Cleanth. *Literary Criticism: a Short History.* New York, Knopf, 1957. 755p. biblio.

   A history of ideas about verbal art, its elucidation, and

criticism, illustrated with selections from many countries and centuries.

MANAGEMENT see ORGANIZATIONAL THEORY AND MANAGEMENT

MANPOWER NEEDS AND EDUCATION
see also UNDERDEVELOPED COUNTRIES
VOCATIONAL EDUCATION
VOCATIONAL GUIDANCE

1633 Caplow, Theodore. *The Sociology of Work.* Minneapolis, U of Minnesota P, 1954. 330p. biblio.

An essay on the division of labor, with reference to research on causes and consequences of occupational differentiation.

1634 David, Henry, ed. *Education and Manpower.* New York, Columbia UP, 1960. 326p.

A selection of articles from the publications of the National Manpower Council, including some on the relationship of manpower and vocational education.

1635 Educational Policies Commission. *Manpower and Education.* Washington, NEA, 1956. 128p. biblio.

Facts concerning the country's manpower situation and recommendations for education to remedy shortages and under-used potentials.

1636 Evans, Luther H., and Arnstein, George E., eds. *Automation and the Challenge to Education.* Washington, NEA, 1962. 190p.

Proceedings of a symposium sponsored by the NEA. Representatives of the fields of education, economics, political science, labor, and management submitted papers on how education can best answer the challenge of automation.

1637 Harris, Seymour E., ed. *The Economic Aspects of Higher Education.* Paris, Organization for Economic Cooperation and Development, 1964. 252p. biblio.

A summary of papers and discussions of the 1962 Study Group on the Economics of Education. Deals with the general problems in education and manpower and the special aspects of higher education in relation to manpower.

1638   Herzberg, Frederick. *Work and the Nature of Man*. Cleveland, World, 1966. 203p. biblio.

A development of the motivation-hygiene theory of work.

1639   Kahler, Alfred, and Hamburger, Ernest. *Education for an Industrial Age*. Ithaca, N.Y., Cornell UP, 1948. 334p.

Published for the Institute of World Affairs, this is an evaluation of vocational education and training in this country as they relate to the mobility of the labor force and employment stability. Selected European countries' apprenticeships and other in-service training programs were studied as comparisons.

1640   Rosenberg, Jerry. *Automation, Manpower and Education*. New York, Random, 1966. 179p. biblio.

A discussion of education's responsibility in relation to automation, use of manpower resources, changing job markets, and the social and psychological effects of automation on the individual. Suggests adapting the educational system and raises questions regarding the future.

1641   Thorndike, Robert L., and Hagen, Elizabeth. *Ten Thousand Careers*. New York, Wiley, 1959. 346p.

A study based on Air Force testing during World War II. Attempts to arrive at conclusions regarding the most effective use of manpower through detailed analysis of present occupations of previously tested veterans.

1642   Venn, Grant. *Man, Education and Work: Post-Secondary Vocational and Technical Education*. Washington, ACE, 1964. 184p. biblio.

The report of a 1962 conference. An assessment of the place of occupational education within the increasingly technological economy and a recognition that American education must respond to growing needs and challenges.

1643   Wolfle, Dael, ed. *America's Resources of Specialized Talent: a Current Appraisal and a Look Ahead*. New York, Harper, 1954. 332p. biblio.

The report of the Commission on Human Resources and Advanced Training provides a broader context within which

to view specialized manpower and a larger correlation of relevant data than previously available. Deals with fields of specialization, college graduation trends, occupational distribution of college graduates, and supply and demand in specialized fields.

MATHEMATICS AND MATHEMATICS TEACHING

1644   Allen, Frank B., ed. *The Revolution in School Mathematics: a Challenge for Administrators and Teachers.* Washington, NCTM, 1960. 90p. biblio.

A report of regional orientation conferences, this is a quick overview, or starting point for further study. The bibliography is substantial.

1645   *An Analysis of New Mathematics Programs.* (NCTM) Washington, NEA, 1963. 72p.

The report of an NCTM committee that analyzes eight programs for content and method.

1646   Courant, Richard, and Robbins, Herbert. *What Is Mathematics? an Elementary Approach to Ideas and Methods.* New York, Oxford UP, 1941. 521p. biblio.

A classic that should be in the library of every mathematics teacher.

1647   DeVault, M. Vere, and others. *Administrative Responsibility for Improving Mathematics Programs.* Washington, NEA, 1965. 24p. biblio.

A report of a joint project sponsored by the NCTM, the AASA, ASCD, and the NASSP, which makes suggestions for planning, organizing, implementing, and evaluating curricular changes in mathematics. Helpful bibliography.

1648   Fehr, Howard F., ed. *Mathematical Education in the Americas.* New York, TC, Columbia, 1962. 180p.

A report of the First Inter-American Conference on Mathematical Education, held in Bogota, Colombia in 1961. A collection of addresses by eminent mathematicians and mathematical educators about new developments in mathematics and mathematics education. Includes a brief survey of mathematics education in the Americas.

1649   Husen, Torsten, and others, eds. *International Study of Achievement in Mathematics: a Comparison of Twelve Countries,* 2 vols. New York, Wiley, 1967. biblio.

A large-scale comparative study that examines the productivity of various school systems. The findings are not necessarily conclusive, but the study does point the way for future research.

1650 Johnson, Wendell G., and Zaccaro, Luke N. *Modern Introductory Mathematics.* New York, McGraw-Hill, 1966. 576p.

An introduction for the non-mathematician to fundamental concepts, problem-solving, set theory, logic, real numbers, mathematical induction, algebra and algebraic functions, equations, and vectors.

1651 Nahikian, Howard M. *Topics in Modern Mathematics.* New York, Macmillan, 1966. 262p. biblio.

An introduction to finite mathematics, set theory, probability, and vector spaces (with no calculus) for the mathematical training of those in the physical and life sciences.

1652 NCTM. *Yearbook.* Washington, NEA. 1st-   1926-

A significant series of which each volume's articles are devoted to a particular aspect of the teaching of mathematics. Some notable recent titles have been *Insights into Modern Mathematics* (23rd, 1957) and *Topics in Mathematics for Elementary School Teachers* (29th, 1964). Regrettably not published regularly; the 30th will probably appear in 1968.

1653 *New Thinking in School Mathematics.* Paris, Organization for European Economic Cooperation, 1961. 246p. biblio.

Specifying the purposes of mathematical education, desirable changes in curriculum content, new goals, new materials, new methods of instruction, and the further teacher training necessary for reform, this report clarifies and summarizes the foremost thinking on elementary and secondary mathematics and the areas in which research needs are apparent.

1654 Newman, James R., ed. *The World of Mathematics,* 4 vols. New York, Simon and Schuster, 1956.

This collection of essays and excerpts from the works of great mathematicians and others with an interest in mathematics should be in the library of every mathematics teacher. The range of interest is great, the magnitude of the survey impressive, and the editor's comments superb.

1655 Polya, George. *How To Solve It: a New Aspect of Mathematical Method,* 2nd ed. New York, Doubleday, 1957. 253p.

First published in 1945 and probably the best book ever written on the topic of problem-solving. Should be read by every teacher of mathematics.

1656 Schult, Veryl G., and Abell, Theodore L. *Inservice Mathematics Education: Promising Practices for Elementary and Secondary Teachers* (USOE Bulletin no. 36). Washington, GPO, 1964. 129p. biblio.

The report of a joint USOE and NCTM conference that describes recent developments in mathematics education.

1657 Stanton, Ralph G., and Dryer, Kenneth D., eds. *Topics in Modern Mathematics*. Englewood Cliffs, N.J., Prentice-Hall, 1964. 187p.

Based on a series of 1959 seminars, but considerably updated and amplified, this volume covers a lot of ground. Discusses groups and fields, set theory, Boolean algebra, logic and computing, numerical analysis, the functions of a single variable, and probability theory and statistics. Not introductory.

1658 Woodby, Lauren G. *The Low Achiever in Mathematics* (USOE Bulletin no. 31). Washington, GPO, 1965. 95p. biblio.

A report of a joint NCTM and USOE conference. Includes papers presented at the conference, a summary of discussions, and a set of recommendations for action.

1659 Wooton, William. *SMSG: the Making of a Curriculum*. New Haven, Yale UP, 1965. 182p.

Describes the origins and activities of the School Mathematics Study Group, one of the most significant of the curricular reform groups. Includes a good chapter on the history of mathematics and mathematics teaching from 1890 to 1960.

Elementary Schools

1660 Adler, Irving. *A New Look at Arithmetic*. New York, New American Library, 1965. 309p.

Some basic contemporary notions of the real number system by a writer experienced in making mathematics comprehensible. Within the author's chosen, and possibly debatable context, concepts are elucidated for the student and elementary school teacher.

1661 Buswell, Guy T., and Judd, Charles H. *A Summary of Educational Investigations Relating to Arithmetic.* Chicago, U of Chicago P, 1925. 212p. biblio.

A summary of early psychological experiments of such men as Thorndike and Judd. Includes investigations of interest such as J. M. Rice's 1902 report showing that the amount of time children spent on arithmetic was not necessarily related to how much they learned.

1662 Copeland, Richard W. *Mathematics and the Elementary Teacher.* Philadelphia, Saunders, 1966. 355p. biblio.

A well-written combination of method and subject matter. Covers basic operations and geometry.

1663 Crouch, Ralph B., and Baldwin, George B. *Mathematics for Elementary Teachers.* New York, Wiley, 1964. 352p.

A study of the mathematical concepts underlying the elementary school mathematics program. Includes number systems from the natural numbers to the reals and work with simple concepts of geometry.

1664 Deans, Edwina. *Elementary School Mathematics: New Directions* (USOE Bulletin no. 13). Washington, GPO, 1963. 116p.

Reviews many of the newer programs.

1665 Dienes, Z. P. *An Experimental Study of Mathematics-Learning.* New York, Humanities, 1964. 206p. biblio.

The logistics of methodology relative to elementary school mathematics, dealing with specific basics of mathematics. Not for the beginner.

1666 Exner, Robert M., and Rosskopf, Myron F. *Logic in Elementary Mathematics.* New York, McGraw-Hill, 1959. 274p.

An introduction to the important ideas of logic for secondary school teachers of mathematics. Correct and easy to read.

1667 Fehr, Howard F., and McKeeby, Jo. *Teaching Modern Math in the Elementary School.* Reading, Mass., Addison Wesley, 1967. 448p. biblio.

The organization of elementary mathematics into a learning sequence to build a structure of knowledge that can serve as a base for subsequent study. Suggestions and illustrations of skills, concepts, and principles.

1668   Flournoy, Frances. *Elementary School Mathematics*. New York, CARE, 1964. 111p. biblio.

A lucid and perceptive account of the last decade's changes in arithmetic instruction, with explanations of the rationale of new math and practical advice for teachers on how to present arithmetic in such a way as to make the pupil think and discover for himself the underlying principles.

1669   Garstens, Helen L., and Jackson, Stanley B. *Mathematics for Elementary School Teachers*. New York, Macmillan, 1967. 500p.

Modern mathematical concepts are defined, illustrated, and developed in a book that assumes some mathematical background and sophistication.

1670   Howard, Charles F., and Dumas, Enoch. *Teaching Contemporary Mathematics in the Elementary School*. New York, Harper, 1966. 309p. biblio.

A thorough coverage of modern mathematical concepts in an excellent book. Gives some attention to teaching procedures and materials, but main emphasis is content.

1671   Lay, L. Clark. *The Study of Arithmetic*. New York, Macmillan, 1966. 590p. biblio.

A complete, sound development of the real number system and binary operations.

1672   McFarland, Dora, and Lewis, Eunice M. *Introduction to Modern Mathematics for Elementary Teachers*. Boston, Heath, 1966. 406p. biblio.

Well-written and comprehensive coverage. Notable for clarity of language, illustrations, and diagrams.

1673   Marks, John L., and others. *Teaching Elementary School Mathematics for Understanding*, 2nd ed. New York, McGraw-Hill, 1965. 500p. biblio.

For teachers of grades one through six. Well organized and readable, covering curriculum design, procedures for presenting modern content, methods, and evaluation.

1674   Piaget, Jean, and others. *The Child's Conception of Geometry*. New York, Basic, 1960. 411p.

A study of the psychogenesis of metrical notions in children, a psychological approach with potential practical applications in teaching. Covers spontaneous reactions, conservation and measurement, and metrical construction of angles and curves.

1675 ———. *The Child's Conception of Number.* New York, Humanities, 1952. 248p.

A classic investigation of the development of mathematical concepts in the young child. Includes observational and experimental studies.

1676 Rappaport, David. *Understanding and Teaching Elementary School Mathematics.* New York, Wiley, 1966. 227p. biblio.

Readable discussion of basic content, principles, curricular change, learning theory, the role of the teacher, and the different theories of mathematics, all as related to mathematics. A highly recommended comprehensive text.

1677 Scott, Lloyd. *Trends in Elementary School Mathematics.* Chicago, Rand McNally, 1966. 215p.

An overview of modern elementary school mathematics with particular attention to the practical needs of teachers. The material is sound and quite comprehensive.

1678 Willerding, Margaret F. *Elementary Mathematics: Its Structure and Concepts.* New York, Wiley, 1966. 298p.

Essential mathematics content for elementary school teachers, covering the newer concepts in the teaching of addition, subtraction, multiplication, division, and some algebra.

Secondary Schools

1679 Beberman, Max. *An Emerging Program of Secondary School Mathematics.* Cambridge, Harvard UP, 1958. 44p.

A report on the first six years of the University of Illinois Committee on School Mathematics, which was the first and one of the most exciting experiments with the teaching of modern mathematics in the secondary schools.

1680 Butler, Charles H., and Wren, F. Lynwood. *The Teaching of Secondary Mathematics,* 4th ed. New York, McGraw-Hill, 1965. 612p. biblio.

A readable, substantial text, well revised to include modern mathematical concepts. Covers relevant educational problems, practices, issues, subject matter, and methods.

1681 Dienes, Z. P. *The Power of Mathematics: a Study of the Transition from the Constructive to the Analytical Phase of Mathematical Thinking in Children.* New York, Humanities, 1964. 176p. biblio.

An enlightening and academically challenging analysis of the methodology of teaching mathematics in secondary schools. Basic concepts handled with clarity but a bit complex for the neophyte.

1682 Dubisch, Roy, and Howes, Vernon E. *The Teaching of Mathematics.* New York, Wiley, 1963. 136p. biblio.

An excellent book on teaching advanced high school and elementary college mathematics. Style is informal, ideas thought-provoking, and the bibliography substantial. Covers algebra, trigonometry and logarithms, analytic geometry, differential and integral calculus.

1683 Kinsella, John J. *Secondary School Mathematics.* New York, CARE, 1965. 116p. biblio.

The nature of changes in mathematics and revisions in curricula are discussed and evaluated. Examines the content and teaching of mathematics in grades 7 through 12 and the education of mathematics teachers in the light of current innovations.

1684 McCoy, Neal H. *Introduction to Modern Algebra.* Boston, Allyn and Bacon, 1960. 304p.

An elementary introduction to modern and linear algebra for the teacher with little exposure to modern mathematics.

1685 *Program for College Preparatory Mathematics.* New York, CEEB, 1959. 12p.

A report of the Commission on Mathematics. A proposal for reorganizing school mathematics at the secondary level that points up the need for additional teacher training. The appendices offer materials for use by teachers to familiarize themselves with a new approach.

1686 Sawyer, Walter W. *A Path to Modern Mathematics.* New York, Penguin, 1967. 223p.

Clearly presents the concepts needed in teaching high school math. Easy to read and mathematically accurate.

1687   Willoughby, Stephen S. *Contemporary Teaching of Second-ary School Mathematics.* New York, Wiley, 1966. 430p. biblio.

A methods book explaining modern mathematics and the teaching of secondary school mathematics, each in the light of the other. The coverage is thorough and the style delightfully informal.

Colleges and Universities

1688   May, Kenneth O. *Programed Learning and Mathematical Education.* San Francisco, Mathematical Association of America, 1964. 24p. biblio.

A review of programed learning and programs in mathematics at the college level. Concludes that there is a need for better programs to encourage more independent study and for more experimentation with all forms of auxiliary materials.

MATHEMATICS AND SCIENCE TEACHING

1689   Brown, Kenneth E., and Johnson, Philip G. *Education for the Talented in Mathematics and Science* (USOE Bulletin no. 15). Washington, GPO, 1952. 34p. biblio.

The report of a conference jointly sponsored by the USOE and AAAS. Focuses on identifying high school students with a high potential in mathematics and science and on providing opportunities for their development.

1690   *Mathematics and Science Education in U.S. Public Schools* (USOE Circular no. 533). Washington, GPO, 1958. 97p.

The report of a 1958 joint conference of the AASA, NASSP, and AAAS, which defined mathematics and science as methods of inquiry as well as bodies of knowledge. Seeing a need for improvement of courses of study and teaching, it develops guidelines for program appraisal and evaluating proposals for change.

1691   *Purchase Guide for Programs in Science and Mathematics.* Boston, Ginn, 1965. 466p.

Provides lists of equipment for elementary schools, with descriptions of each. A valuable guide with suggestions for storing materials. A project of the Council of Chief State School Officers.

MEASUREMENT AND EVALUATION IN EDUCATION
see also TESTS AND TESTING

1692   Ahmann, J. Stanley, and Glock, Marvin D. *Evaluating Pupil Growth, Principles of Tests and Measurements,* 2nd ed. Boston, Allyn and Bacon, 1963. 640p.

     A thorough and comprehensive discussion of evaluation that is practical as well as theoretical.

1693   ———. *Testing Student Achievement and Aptitudes.* New York, CARE, 1962. 118p. biblio.

     An overview of standardized tests and testing. Discusses the principles on which tests are built, their proper use, interpretation of results, and their utility in the educational process.

1694   Almy, Millie C. *Ways of Studying Children: a Manual for Teachers.* New York, TC, Columbia, 1959. 226p.

     A compilation of teaching experiences at the Horace Mann-Lincoln Institute of School Experimentation. Describes the various ways teachers collect evidence about how children behave, think, and feel and discusses some difficulties and practical applications of findings.

1695   Anastasi, Anne. *Psychological Testing,* 2nd ed. New York, Macmillan, 1961. 657p.

     A comprehensive examination of tests and testing problems that is intended to assist educators in interpreting the scores of intelligence and personality tests.

1696   ———, ed. *Testing Problems in Perspective.* Washington, ACE, 1966. 671p.

     A selection of major papers presented at the Invitational Conferences on Testing Problems from 1947 to 1964. Catalogs the specific contributions made in educational and psychological measurement during those years.

1697   Bartz, Albert E. *Elementary Statistical Methods for Educational Measurement.* Minneapolis, Burgess, 1966. 109p.

     An introductory text for the average classroom situation. Explains statistical methods and computations, frequency distributions, measures of central tendency, percentiles, norms, measures of variability, correlation, and the evaluation and interpretation of tests. Illustrative examples given with full explanation of calculations involved.

1698   Bonney, Merl E., and Hampleman, Richard S. *Personal-Social Evaluation Techniques*. New York, CARE, 1962. 114p. biblio.

Covers evaluation of pupil growth and behavior by all methods except testing. Discusses observational, sociometric, and projective techniques as well as pupil evaluation, personality rating, and evaluation of class attitudes. A useful book directed to the classroom teacher.

1699   Brewer, John M. *Mental Measurement in Educational and Vocational Guidance*. Cambridge, Harvard UP, 1924. 46p. biblio.

An early landmark in the field that is a comprehensive survey and review of findings at that time.

1700   Chauncey, Henry, and Dobbin, John E. *Testing: Its Place in Education Today*. New York, Harper, 1963. 223p.

An overview, rather than a technical manual, of current educational testing developments. Provides a broad picture of testing in schools and colleges and its place in the teaching and learning process.

1701   *College Testing: a Guide to Programs and Practices*. Washington, ACE, 1959. 189p.

For the college teacher and administrator without formal training in the techniques of testing but who is nevertheless concerned with testing procedures and results.

1702   Davis, Frederick B. *Educational Measurements and Their Interpretation*. Belmont, Cal., Wadsworth, 1964. 422p. biblio.

An excellent, well-written, well-organized presentation of the practical uses of tests and other evaluative instruments in schools and clinics. Includes a generous dose of statistics, analyzed and interpreted.

1703   Ebel, Robert L. *Measuring Educational Achievement*. Englewood Cliffs, N.J., Prentice-Hall, 1965. 481p. biblio.

Examines the background of testing and discusses techniques for preparing and using tests in the classroom.

1704   Elsbree, Willard S. *Pupil Progress in the Elementary School*. New York, TC, Columbia, 1941. 86p.

A brief but complete discussion of theory and practice as related to school policies and other variables. Remains a valuable resource.

1705   Fleck, Henrietta. *How to Evaluate Students.* Bloomington, Ind., McKnight, 1953. 85p. biblio.

An overview of the essential points to consider in the process of evaluating and appreciating the total individual. Addressed to the classroom teacher. Helpful methods and materials are discussed.

1706   Greer, Edith S., comp. *Pupil Marks and School Marking Systems: a Selected Bibliography* (USOE) Washington, GPO, 1963. 22p.

A valuable reference in a sparsely covered field. Includes journal articles and parts of books. An annotated sampling of published reports of research and current practice.

1707   Gronlund, Norman E. *Measurement and Evaluation in Teaching.* New York, Macmillan, 1965. 420p. biblio.

Presents background and techniques for preparing and using tests in the classroom. Particularly strong on principles of evaluation and on a variety of evaluative techniques other than multiple-choice or essay exams.

1708   Lindeman, Richard H. *Educational Measurement.* Chicago, Scott Foresman, 1967. 181p.

An introductory treatment of tests and measurements offering practical guidance for evaluating, using, and interpreting the results of both standardized and teacher-made tests. Stresses the influence of the teacher-made test on student attitudes.

1709   Lindquist, Everett F., ed. *Educational Measurement.* Washington, ACE, 1951. 819p. biblio.

A classic on educational measurement whose theoretical considerations are still relevant. Contributions by specialists discuss ideas, experiences, and research in this comprehensive handbook.

1710   Nunnally, Jum C. *Educational Measurement and Evaluation.* New York, McGraw-Hill, 1964. 440p. biblio.

A well-organized, readable discussion that includes chapters on teacher-made tests, basic statistical concepts, and standardized tests.

1711   Otto, Henry J., and others. *Four Methods of Reporting to Parents.* Austin, U of Texas P, 1957. 247p.

A report of a study conducted in six schools with four

different reporting plans. Findings were that marks based on rankings and standards were not as satisfactory or adequate in reporting to parents as were marks based on achievement in relation to individual ability.

1712   Remmers, Hermann H., and others. *A Practical Introduction to Measurement and Evaluation,* 2nd ed. New York, Harper, 1965. 390p. biblio.

Consists in part of a reprinting of some of a 1943 publication (*Educational Measurement and Evaluation*), plus material added for updating in the light of the changing educational scene. Not a handbook for guidance but concerned rather with providing the statistical methods and techniques for obtaining the facts and evaluative data necessary for valid guidance.

1713   Rothney, John W. *Evaluating and Reporting Pupil Progress* (What Research Says to the Teacher, no. 7). Washington, NEA, 1955. 32p.

One of a series designed to bring the results of research to the practicing teacher, this discusses the limitations that research has revealed about common techniques used for evaluating and reporting pupil progress.

1714   Smith, Fred M., and Adams, Sam. *Educational Measurement for the Classroom Teacher.* New York, Harper, 1966. 322p. biblio.

An introductory text that is correlated with Bloom's and Krathwohl's *Taxonomy of Educational Objectives,* Handbooks I and II (#2261 and #2271). Clearly written definitions of terms and descriptions of the usages of measurements, with excellent examples.

1715   Stanley, Julian C. *Measurement in Today's Schools,* 4th ed. Englewood Cliffs, N.J., Prentice-Hall, 1964. 414p. biblio.

A basic, comprehensive text in measurement and evaluation. Covers historical and theoretical material, fundamental principles, the construction and use of measuring instruments, analysis of results, grading, reporting, and promoting.

1716   Thomas, R. Murray. *Judging Student Progress.* New York, Longmans, 1954. 421p.

A thorough coverage of philosophies and theories, including practice as it is affected by varying approaches and policies. A practical guide to evaluating children's growth in the classroom. Illustrated with true incidents.

1717   Thorndike, Robert L., and Hagen, Elizabeth. *Measurement and Evaluation in Psychology and Education*, 2nd ed. New York, Wiley, 1961. 602p.

Designed to develop more restrained, discriminating, and insightful testers, this is concerned as much with what tests will not do as it is with what they will do. An excellent discussion also of the purposes and objectives of testing.

1718   Traxler, Arthur E. *The Nature and Use of Anecdotal Records,* 2nd ed. New York, Educational Records Bureau, 1939. 41p. biblio.

A discussion from the point of view of both administrator and teacher of the advantages and disadvantages of anecdotal records in providing data on pupil personality development. Samples are included.

1719   Wood, Dorothy A. *Test Construction: Development and Interpretation of Achievement Tests.* Columbus, Merrill, 1960. 134p. biblio.

For the classroom teacher. A useful how-to book for developing objective tests.

1720   Wrinkle, William L. *Improving Marking and Reporting Practices in the Elementary and Secondary Schools.* New York, Holt, 1947. 120p.

A comprehensive treatment based on ten years of experimentation. Systematic analysis of procedural steps intended to offer guidance in rethinking and reformulating present practices.

MEMORY

1721   Bartlett, Frederic C. *Remembering: a Study in Experimental and Social Psychology.* New York, Cambridge UP, 1932. 317p. biblio.

An important study of the processes of memory, based on the author's observations of social recall among Africans and experimental studies on perceiving, imaging, and remembering.

1722   Ebbinghaus, Hermann. *Memory: a Contribution to Experimental Psychology.* New York, Dover, 1964. 123p. biblio.

Translated from the original German publication of 1885, this remains a landmark in memory research. Based on the author's experiments with the use of nonsense syllables in testing memory.

1723 John, E. Roy. *Mechanisms of Memory*. New York, Academic, 1967. 425p.

Findings from various areas of brain research are integrated to provide an overview of present understanding of the mechanisms involved in storage and retrieval of information by the brain.

1724 Katona, George. *Organizing and Memorizing: Studies in the Psychology of Learning and Teaching*. New York, Hafner, 1967. 318p. biblio.

A republication of a 1940 book. Analyzes learning on a quantitative basis with regard to retention and application, employing gestalt methods and the technique of transfer as developed by American psychologists.

1725 Slamecka, Norman J., ed. *Human Learning and Memory: Selected Readings*. New York, Oxford UP, 1967. 543p.

A collection of 50 articles, not at all introductory, on human learning and psycholinguistics. Divided into ten sections, each representing an area currently under investigation.

1726 Underwood, Benton J., and Schulz, Rudolph W. *Meaningfulness and Verbal Learning*. Philadelphia, Lippincott, 1960. 430p. biblio.

A report of research dealing with meaningfulness of verbal materials and its influence on learning, especially in relation to rote memorization and association.

MENTAL RETARDATION
see also EXCEPTIONAL CHILDREN
MENTAL RETARDATION AND THE SCHOOLS
MENTALLY RETARDED ADULTS
SLOW LEARNING CHILDREN

1727 Begab, Michael J. *The Mentally Retarded Child: a Guide to Services of Social Agencies*. (U.S. Children's Bureau) Washington, GPO, 1963. 134p. biblio.

Stresses the social aspects of mental retardation and discusses definitions, causation, developmental factors, behavioral characteristics, family-related problems, and adjustability. An excellent introduction to this problem.

1728 Burt, Cyril. *The Backward Child*, 5th ed. London, U of London P, 1961. 704p. (Dist. by Verry, Mystic, Conn.)

Frequently revised in accordance with new findings, this is an excellent reference that describes, group by group, the principal forms of mental subnormality to be found among school children.

1729 Carter, Charles H., ed. *Medical Aspects of Mental Retardation*. Springfield, Ill., Thomas, 1964. 1062p.

Although written for the medical practitioner, this is an excellent reference for others concerned with retardation as it covers some of the rarer syndromes as well as the more common disorders. Consideration is also given to the use of drugs in therapy.

1730 Clausen, Johannes. *Ability Structure and Subgroups in Mental Retardation*. New York, Spartan, 1966. 208p. biblio.

An experimental research study that measured such psychological functions as sensory and motor tasks, reasoning, memory, and perceptual and integrative processes to differentiate the subgroups in mental retardation.

1731 Dybwad, Gunnar. *Challenges in Mental Retardation*. New York, Columbia UP, 1964. 287p. biblio.

A general discussion of the problems of mental retardation. Defines retardation, discusses the formative years of the retarded child, his relationship with and effect on his family, residential care for child and adult, and the retarded in society.

1732 Ellis, Norman R., ed. *Handbook of Mental Deficiency: Psychological Theory and Research*. New York, McGraw-Hill, 1963. 722p. biblio.

Twenty essays concerned with the status of behavioral research and theory in mental deficiency and the search for new and basic understandings of mental retardation. A systematic coverage including data on learning, perception, and motivation.

1733 _____, ed. *International Review of Research in Mental Retardation*. Vol. 1-   1966-   . New York, Academic.

An annual source of current information on research and theory development in the field of behavioral research pertaining to mental retardation.

1734   Heber, Rick, and others. *Bibliography of World Literature on Mental Retardation: January, 1940 to March, 1963.* (USOE) Washington, GPO, 1963. 564p.

Sponsored by the President's Panel on Mental Retardation, this is a comprehensive, systematic listing of major literature in the field. Arranged alphabetically by author, with a subject index, the titles are restricted to scientific and professional literature.

1735   Jordan, Thomas E. *The Mentally Retarded,* 2nd ed. Columbus, Merrill, 1966. 355p. biblio.

An analysis of the many forms of mental retardation and the problems it presents, based on empirical evidence. Includes data from the physical sciences and cites several hundred studies.

1736   _____, ed. *Perspectives in Mental Retardation.* Carbondale, Southern Illinois UP, 1966. 358p.

A compilation of readings and studies by European and American authorities that provide an overview of the field.

1737   Leland, Henry, and Smith, Daniel E. *Play Therapy with Mentally Subnormal Children.* New York, Grune and Stratton, 1965. 240p.

A discussion of play therapy procedures, with a sound theoretical basis, in which methods are varied in accordance with differences in subnormalities and intelligence.

1738   Masland, Richard L., and others. *Mental Subnormality: Biological, Psychological, and Cultural Factors.* New York, Basic, 1958. 442p. biblio.

A research study aimed at discovering the causes of mental subnormality, an affliction of nearly three and one-half per cent of the population. Focuses on the factors producing anatomical or chemical neurological abnormalities, thus preventing normal brain functioning, and on cultural and environmental factors which, through the establishment of unhealthy or inadequate patterns of intellectual response, prevent optimum functioning of normal nervous systems.

1739   Penrose, Lionel S. *The Biology of Mental Defect,* 2nd ed. New York, Grune and Stratton, 1963. 374p. biblio.

Discusses the medical and psychopathological conditions of mental deficiency chiefly within the framework of genetics.

1740 Philips, Irving, and Esser, Mary A., eds. *Prevention and Treatment of Mental Retardation*. New York, Basic, 1966. 463p. biblio.

Continuing research in all related fields has contributed to constant revision in theories, practices, and attitudes concerning the mentally retarded. An up-to-date review of research and thinking on the part of specialists in a wide variety of disciplines.

1741 Robinson, Halbert B., and Nancy M. *The Mentally Retarded Child: a Psychological Approach*. New York, McGraw-Hill, 1965. 639p. biblio.

A comprehensive review of retardation, incorporating a developmental theory of intelligence based on Piaget's work. A practical approach.

1742 Sarason, Seymour B. *Psychological Problems in Mental Deficiency*, 3rd ed. New York, Harper, 1959. 402p. biblio.

A review of the various types of mental deficiency and brain injury. Covers criteria, classification, diagnosis, and test interpretation, explores the psychological problems involved, and emphasizes the need for systematic research.

1743 Stevens, Harvey A., and Heber, Rick, eds. *Mental Retardation: a Review of Research*. Chicago, U of Chicago P, 1964. 502p. biblio.

Integrates the knowledge obtained from research in all the major disciplines.

History

1744 Kanner, Leo. *The History of the Care and Study of the Mentally Retarded*. Springfield, Ill., Thomas, 1964. 150p. biblio.

An account of the men in Europe, Canada, and this country who originated educational and institutional work with the feebleminded. Valuable listing of early periodicals on mental deficiency.

1745 Pritchard, David G. *Education and the Handicapped: 1760-1960*. London, Routledge, 1963. 250p. biblio.

An historical account that, in describing changes in approach over the years, demonstrates that the direction has been to draw the retarded into the social structure as much as possible.

MENTAL RETARDATION AND THE SCHOOLS
see also EXCEPTIONAL CHILDREN
MENTAL RETARDATION
SLOW LEARNING CHILDREN

1746 Baumgartner, Bernice B. *Helping the Trainable Mentally Retarded Child: a Handbook for Teachers, Parents, and Administration.* New York, TC, Columbia, 1960. 71p.

A guide for helping the retarded develop their capacities. Covers communication, classroom procedures, and evaluation. Advice for teachers and administrators.

1747 Cain, Leo F., and Levine, Samuel. *Effects of Community and Institutional School Programs on Trainable Mentally Retarded Children.* Washington, Council for Exceptional Children, 1963. 56p. biblio.

An assessment of the effect of special education classes on the development of the trainable mentally retarded child. Questions the hypothesis that the home environment is more conducive to the development of social competence than is the institutional environment.

1748 Carlson, Bernice W. *Play Activities for the Retarded Child.* New York, Abingdon, 1961. 224p.

Details programs suggested for use with retarded children.

1749 Charney, Leon, and LaCrosse, Edward. *The Teacher of the Mentally Retarded.* New York, Day, 1965. 192p. biblio.

Although basically a stirring appeal to recruit more teachers, this is full of information about the education of the mentally retarded.

1750 Clarke, Ann M., and Alan B., eds. *Mental Deficiency: the Changing Outlook,* 2nd ed. New York, Free Press, 1965. 596p. biblio.

Summarizes the literature on the psychological and social aspects of mental deficiency, shows the intimate and reciprocal relationship between theory and practice in the education of this group, and discusses the amelioration of learning difficulties and social problems.

1751 Cleugh, Mary F., ed. *Teaching the Slow Learner in the Special School.* London, Methuen, 1961. 338p. biblio.

Eighteen essays that consider the personality and the special needs of the educable slow learner as well as how training in special schools can best fit these children to take their place in the world.

1752 Connor, Frances P., and Talbot, Mabel E. *An Experimental Curriculum for Young Mentally Retarded Children.* New York, TC, Columbia, 1964. 312p.

Presents a program tested by five years of classroom experience, which was revised and improved in process. Outlines the progression of experiences that foster the greatest improvement in social and emotional adjustment, language development, motor and manipulative skills, and learning in general.

1753 Donahue, George T., and Nichtern, Sol. *Teaching the Troubled Child.* New York, Free Press, 1965. 202p.

An argument against institutionalization of the mentally retarded, except in extreme cases, and an argument for alternative programs that recognize the needs of both child and family. Describes the Elmont program, which is a fusion of community responsibility, the specialist team approach, and the one-to-one relationship.

1754 Erdman, Robert L. *Educable Mentally Retarded Children in Elementary Schools: Administration of Special Education in Small School Systems.* Washington, Council for Exceptional Children, 1961. 60p. biblio.

A guide for schools in rural areas and small communities that, increasingly, are establishing special classes, especially at the elementary school level.

1755 Gaitskell, Charles D., and Margaret R. *Art Education for Slow Learners.* Peoria, Ill., Bennett, 1953. 46p.

Based on a three-year study of nearly 600 mentally retarded children. Includes suggestions to aid teachers in using art as an educational medium for slow learners.

1756 Gallagher, James J. *Tutoring of Brain-Injured, Mentally Retarded Children: an Experimental Study.* Springfield, Ill., Thomas, 1960. 194p. biblio.

A report of an experiment dealing with the effects of individual tutoring on the intellectual development of mentally retarded children in an institution. Describes the children who showed improvement, the limits of their improvement, and the types of instructional methods and environmental factors most conducive to improvement.

1757   Ginglend, David R., and Stiles, Winifred E., arr. *Music Activities for Retarded Children*. Nashville, Abingdon, 1965. 140p.

A unique collection of specially edited and arranged words and musical scores for use with retarded children.

1758   Hutt, Max L., and Gibby, Robert G. *The Mentally Retarded Child: Development, Education, and Treatment*, 2nd ed. Boston, Allyn and Bacon, 1965. 441p. biblio.

An attempt to close the gap between the marked improvement in our knowledge and understanding of the retarded child and the dissemination of this knowledge and implementation of appropriate home and school programs. A thoughtful consideration of needs, development, useful programs, patterns of adjustment, and the retarded child's effect upon family and community.

1759   Ingram, Christine P. *Education of the Slow Learning Child*, 3rd ed. New York, Ronald, 1960. 390p. biblio.

A practical reference for the classroom teacher who must attempt to provide optimal learning situations for the slow learning child in the regular classroom. Examines the needs and potentialities of the mentally retarded and slow learning child and suggests methods and techniques for developing special education programs.

1760   Kirk, Samuel A. *Early Education of the Mentally Retarded: an Experimental Study*. Urbana, U of Illinois P, 1958. 216p. biblio.

A determination of the effect of preschool training on the development of mentally retarded children, with descriptions of experimental cases, and a study and evaluation of hereditary and environmental influences.

1761   ———, and Johnson, G. Orville. *Educating the Retarded Child*. Boston, Houghton Mifflin, 1951. 434p. biblio.

No longer the function of home or institution, the education of the retarded child has been accepted as the responsibility of the schools, usually as adapted instruction in special classes. This book presents teaching procedures and develops programs of rehabilitation and instruction.

1762   Kolstoe, Oliver P., and Frey, Roger M. *A High School Work-Study Program for Mentally Subnormal Students*. Carbondale, Southern Illinois UP, 1965. 179p.

A well-conceived and well-developed program that helps fill the gap between the rapidly growing number of programs and the demand for trained personnel to staff them.

1763 Molloy, Julia S. *Teaching the Retarded Child to Talk: a Guide for Parents and Teachers.* New York, Day, 1961. 125p.

An analysis of speech, the failure of some children to learn to talk, how children learn to talk, and how a retarded child learns about sounds and words. Provides clear, specific instruction in teaching procedures.

1764 Perry, Natalie. *Teaching the Mentally Retarded Child.* New York, Columbia UP, 1960. 282p. biblio.

Philosophy, methods, and curriculum are discussed, with suggestions for organizing and administering a program for the moderately and severely retarded child.

1765 Rothstein, Jerome H., ed. *Mental Retardation: Readings and Resources.* New York, Holt, 1961. 628p. biblio.

A multidisciplinary approach to mental retardation, covering diagnosis, learning theory, speech development, counseling, school programs, and research.

MENTALLY RETARDED ADULTS
see also VOCATIONAL REHABILITATION

1766 Avedon, Elliott M., and Arje, Frances B. *Socio-Recreative Programming for the Retarded: a Handbook for Sponsoring Groups.* New York, TC, Columbia, 1964. 84p. biblio.

New approaches and methods aimed at bringing retarded persons out of social isolation through recreation services.

1767 DiMichael, Salvatore G., ed. *New Vocational Pathways for the Mentally Retarded.* Washington, American Personnel and Guidance Association, 1966. 52p.

The papers of a symposium. Discuss predictive studies of vocational adjustment, vocational preparation in school, work-study programs, longitudinal follow-up studies, and key political and cultural factors affecting services in Europe and the United States.

1768 ———, ed. *Vocational Rehabilitation of the Mentally Retarded* (Office of Vocational Rehabilitation Service Series no. 113). Washington, GPO, 1950. 184p. biblio.

A description of three recent programs that are examples

of developing modes of practice, with consideration of counseling, education, place in the home and community, and employment.

1769 Gunzberg, Herbert C. *Social Rehabilitation of the Subnormal.* Baltimore, Williams and Wilkins, 1960. 263p. biblio.
Concerned with practical aspects of the social and vocational adjustment of the subnormal adult in the community following institutionalization for treatment and training.

1770 O'Connor, N., and Tizard, J. *The Social Problem of Mental Deficiency.* New York, Pergamon, 1956. 182p. biblio.
Summarizes the work of the Medical Research Council's Social Psychiatry Research Unit. Discusses the prevalence of mental deficiency, services for those who are retarded, psychometric theories of stability, neurotic tendencies among defectives, and the prediction of occupational success.

MIDDLE SCHOOLS
see also JUNIOR HIGH SCHOOLS

1771 Eichhorn, Donald H. *The Middle School.* New York, CARE, 1966. 116p. biblio.
A comprehensive description and analysis of the middle school, based on a new concept of school organization and a careful integration of age and growth needs with educational factors.

1772 Popper, Samuel H. *The American Middle School.* Boston, Ginn, 1967. 378p.
A plea for the junior high school or middle school as an institution with its own identity, purpose, and program.

MINORITY PROBLEMS
see also ATTITUDES AND PREJUDICE
INTEGRATION AND SEGREGATION

1773 Barron, Milton L., ed. *Minorities in a Changing World.* New York, Knopf, 1967. 481p. biblio.
Contains articles published since 1959 covering ethnic problems and relations in this country and abroad. Each section has a brief, pertinent introduction and a list of readings. An excellent collection.

1774 Bennett, Lerone, Jr. *Confrontation: Black and White.* Chicago, Johnson, 1965. 321p. biblio.

A descriptive analysis of the Negro revolt in America, its origins, history, and implications for the future. Offers numerous insights concerning the race problem.

1775 Clark, Kenneth. *Dark Ghetto: the Dilemmas of Social Power.* New York, Harper, 1965. 251p.

A classic quality pervades this definition of the mutuality of the black and white struggle for humanness in America.

1776 Davis, Allison, and Dollard, John. *Children of Bondage: the Personality Development of Negro Youth in the Urban South.* Washington, ACE, 1940. 299p.

Explores the personality development of Negro youth in Natchez and New Orleans by means of interviews and intensive study. An important document combining sociology, psychology, and psychiatry.

1777 Fuchs, Estelle. *Pickets at the Gates.* New York, Free Press, 1966. 205p. biblio.

The challenge of civil rights in urban schools is examined through two case studies of New York City boycotting. Although perhaps attempting too much generalization, it is nevertheless interesting and offers insights.

1778 Ginzberg, Eli, and others. *The Middle-Class Negro in the White Man's World.* New York, Columbia UP, 1967. 182p.

An analysis of case studies of Negro students that reveals that family background, not race, is the major determinant in advancement.

1779 ———, and others. *The Negro Potential.* New York, Columbia UP, 1956. 244p. biblio.

A factual, impartial report of research that analyzes the situation of the Negro in relation to his talents and discusses the interacting functions of education, environment, and segregation.

1780 Kvaraceus, William C., and others. *Negro Self-Concept: Implications for School and Citizenship.* New York, McGraw-Hill, 1965. 186p.

The papers and discussions of a 1963 conference on the relation of education to self-concept in Negro children and youth. The conclusions were that the environmental press of the American color caste system tends to develop conceptions of self that result in defeated behavior and that the schools, which tend to serve as part of this defeating process, can instead serve to strengthen self-concept.

MONTESSORI METHOD

1781 Montessori, Maria. *The Montessori Method: Scientific Pedagogy as Applied to Child Education in the Children's Houses.* New York, Schocken, 1965. 386p.

Translated from the Italian and a reissue of a 1912 book. Presents the author's ideas and their practical application to the education of young children.

1782 Standing, E. Mortimer. *The Montessori Revolution in Education.* New York, Schocken, 1966. 206p. biblio.

Current interest in Montessori accounts for the reissue of this book, originally published in 1962 as *The Montessori Method: a Revolution in Education.* Always controversial, Montessori's ideas are considered by some to be relevant to teaching the disadvantaged. This is a good review by an enthusiast.

MOTIVATION AND ACHIEVEMENT
see also MEASUREMENT AND EVALUATION IN EDUCATION
SLOW LEARNING CHILDREN
TESTS AND TESTING

1783 Cofer, Charles N., and Appley, M. H. *Motivation: Theory and Research.* New York, Wiley, 1964. 958p. biblio.

An examination of the main forms motivation concepts have assumed in the major theoretical systems current in psychology today.

1784 *Current Theory and Research on Motivation: Nebraska Symposium on Motivation.* Vol. I-   1953-   . Lincoln, U of Nebraska P.

An annual collection of papers. An excellent resource.

1785 Fine, Benjamin. *Underachievers: How They Can Be Helped.* New York, Dutton, 1967. 253p. biblio.

An examination of the factors that lead to underachievement and a description of what parents, teachers, and the community can do to help. The disadvantaged child is included as an underachiever, and the whole is illustrated with vivid case histories.

1786 Heckhausen, Heinz. *The Anatomy of Achievement Motivation.* New York, Academic, 1967. 215p.

Reviews empirical studies and international research on achievement motivation within a unifying theoretical framework. Discusses such topics as content analysis, evaluative dispositions, dimensions of experience, and conflict.

1787 McClelland, David C., and others. *The Achievement Motive.* New York, Appleton, 1953. 384p. biblio.

A summary of research conducted at Wesleyan University between 1947 and 1952. Covers the measurement of achievement, constructs a theory of motivation, and offers much data on the achievement motive and related variables.

1788 Maslow, Abraham H. *Motivation and Personality.* New York, Harper, 1954. 411p. biblio.

One of the leaders in the field of growth psychology analyzes the hierarchy of human needs that climaxes in self-actualization.

1789 Raph, Jane B., and others. *Bright Underachievers: Studies of Scholastic Underachievement among Intellectually Superior High School Students.* New York, TC, Columbia, 1966. 289p.

Based on the Talented Youth Project of the Horace Mann-Lincoln Institute of School Experimentation, which studied student self-perception in relation to school performance.

1790 Walsh, Ann M. *Self-Concepts of Boys with Learning Difficulties.* New York, TC, Columbia, 1956. 79p. biblio.

A contribution to the complex problem of underachievement that, by probing children's perceptions of family members and relationships as revealed through play with dolls and stimulated by incomplete stories, attempts to secure information that is more reliable than verbal tests.

MUSIC AND MUSIC EDUCATION

1791 Farnsworth, Paul R. *The Social Psychology of Music.* New York, Dryden, 1958. 304p. biblio.

A consideration of the psychological approach to music,

the social psychology of musical scales, the interval, and the language aspects of music. An attempt to present a coherent picture of the relation between music and psychology as well as the inherent problems and their most plausible solutions.

1792   Horner, V. *Music Education: the Background of Research and Opinion.* Victoria, Australian Council for Educational Research, 1966. 226p. biblio. (Dist. by Verry, Mystic, Conn.)

A survey of research literature, most of it from the United States, covering the nature of musical abilities, general learning problems, curriculum and curriculum planning, equipment and facilities, and measurement and prognosis. The most complete and up-to-date book available.

1793   Jones, Archie N., ed. *Music Education in Action: Basic Principles and Practical Methods.* Boston, Allyn and Bacon, 1960. 523p.

A search for valid solutions to problems in music education. Offers procedures and principles that have already been tested by practice.

1794   Kaplan, Max. *Foundations and Frontiers of Music Education.* New York, Holt, 1966. 261p. biblio.

Perceptive analyses of the arts in the social order, the aesthetic strengths and potentials of music, needed research, and recommendations of ways and means for enriched teaching of music. Clear, scholarly, and well-documented.

1795   Larson, William S., comp. *Bibliography of Research Studies in Music Education, 1932-1948* and *Bibliography of Research Studies in Music Education, 1949–1956,* 2 vols. (MENC) Washington, NEA, 1949 and 1957.

An inventory of completed research studies arranged alphabetically by state and university. Topical index.

1796   Laufer, R., ed. *Music in Education.* Paris, UNESCO, 1955. 355p.

The final report of a 1953 International Conference on the Role and Place of Music in the Education of Youth and Adults. Discusses the philosophy of music education, music education in the curriculum and in society, methods of teaching, teacher training, and the contribution of the professional musician to music education.

1797   Leonhard, Charles, and House, Robert W. *Foundations and Principles of Music Education.* New York, McGraw-Hill, 1959. 375p.

A comprehensive text that examines the historical, philosophical, and psychological foundations and develops principles for all aspects of the music program, including methods, administration, supervision, and evaluation.

1798   Machlis, Joseph. *The Enjoyment of Music: an Introduction to Perceptive Listening,* rev. ed. New York, Norton, 1963. 701p.

A good representative work in the field of music appreciation. A fine guide for the teacher wishing to introduce students to perceptive listening.

1799   Morgan, Hazel N., ed. *Music Education Source Book.* (MENC) Washington, NEA, 1947. 256p. biblio.

1800   ————, ed. *Music in American Education: Music Education Source Book Number Two.* (MENC) Washington, NEA, 1955. 365p. biblio.

1801   ————, ed. *Perspectives in Music Education: Music Education Source Book Number Three.* (MENC) Washington, NEA, 1966. 576p. biblio.

Successors of the MENC yearbooks, which ceased publication in 1940, these volumes provide a comprehensive survey of the entire field of music education and include such corollary subjects as music libraries and music in industry and hospitals.

1802   Snyder, Keith D. *School Music Administration and Supervision,* 2nd ed. Boston, Allyn and Bacon, 1965. 332p. biblio.

A practical guide for the music educator and school administrator. Contains many practical suggestions based on the author's teaching experience.

1803   Sunderman, Lloyd F. *School Music Teaching: Its Theory and Practice.* New York, Scarecrow, 1965. 219p.

An overview of public school music teaching and the problems encountered by the teacher at all grade levels.

1804   Weyland, Rudolph H. *A Guide to Effective Music Supervision.* Dubuque, Iowa, Brown, 1960. 339p.

A very detailed and concise handbook giving information relating to such aspects of supervision as scheduling, curriculum, materials, and the like.

Elementary Schools

1805 Elliott, Raymond. *Learning and Teaching Music: Skills, Methods, and Materials for the Elementary School Teacher,* 2nd ed. Columbus, Merrill, 1966. 390p. biblio.

A good standard work offering a variety of material including good lists of books, records, film, and other aids. Activities are treated individually and in progression through the grades, and concepts are approached through musical experience.

1806 Ellison, Alfred. *Music with Children.* New York, McGraw-Hill, 1959. 294p.

A developmental approach to the teaching of music in the classroom, primarily intended for the classroom teacher without a formal musical background. Provides specific ways in which children can be helped to experience music so that they love rather than reject it. Helpful to music teachers working with classroom teachers.

1807 Ernst, Karl D., and Gary, Charles L., eds. *Music in General Education.* (MENC) Washington, NEA, 1965. 224p. biblio.

An examination of the place of music in the education of all children in elementary and secondary schools.

1808 Flagg, Marion E. *Musical Learning: a Guide to Child Growth.* Evanston, Ill., Summy Birchard, 1949. 195p.

An examination of the curriculum, physical readiness, and the aural and written language of music directed to the mastery of tonal-rhythmical relations that make up the infinite range of musical meaning.

1809 Garretson, Robert L. *Music in Childhood Education.* New York, Appleton, 1966. 270p. biblio.

A consideration of the basic premises underlying instructional programs in music as they relate to the development of the child, the teacher-student relationship, and the learning situation. Covers effective ways and means of teaching music and offers specific suggestions for procedures.

1810 Hermann, Edward J. *Supervising Music in the Elementary School.* Englewood Cliffs, N.J., Prentice-Hall, 1965. 288p.

Stresses the cooperative approach, which involves the music specialist, the elementary teacher, and the elementary principal, and outlines the responsibilities of the specialist in developing this approach.

1811   Hood, Marguerite, and Schultz, Ernest J. *Learning Music Through Rhythm*. Boston, Ginn, 1949. 180p.

A practical rather than creative approach with simple piano accompaniments and suggestions for using rhythm and movement as a foundation for learning music.

1812   Humphreys, Louise, and Ross, Jerrold. *Interpreting Music Through Movement*. Englewood Cliffs, N.J., Prentice-Hall, 1964. 149p. biblio.

Based on the premise that effective listening is dependent upon an active and intimate identification with music, this book discusses the ways and means whereby the classroom teacher may achieve this goal.

1813   Hurd, Lyman C., and Savage, Edith J. *First Experiences in Music*. Belmont, Cal., Wadsworth, 1966. 202p. biblio.

Introductory, with brief coverage of learning music fundamentals, the background of musical knowledge, and teaching music to children.

1814   Kaplan, Max, and Steiner, Frances J. *Musicianship for the Classroom Teacher*. Chicago, Rand McNally, 1966. 147p.

A well-organized text covering methods and materials, with a sound discussion of basic music theory offered in some depth.

1815   Monsour, Sally, and others. *Rhythm in Music and Dance for Children*. Belmont, Cal., Wadsworth, 1966. 99p. biblio.

Emphasizes the creative approach and offers helpful ideas for both the classroom teacher and the specialists. Excellent list of recorded music.

1816   Myers, Louise K. *Teaching Children Music in the Elementary School*, 3rd ed. Englewood Cliffs, N.J., Prentice-Hall, 1961. 368p. biblio.

A teaching plan for the classroom teacher based on developing children's natural ability for making music and their natural interest in music.

1817   Nordholm, Harriet. *Singing in the Elementary Schools*. Englewood Cliffs, N.J., Prentice-Hall, 1966. 94p.

Deals with song as the foundation and keystone of the school music program. Includes advice on song selection and offers examples, techniques, and suggestions.

1818   Nye, Robert E., and Vernice T. *Music in the Elementary School: an Activities Approach to Music Methods and Materials,* 2nd ed. Englewood Cliffs, N.J., Prentice-Hall, 1964. 405p. biblio.

A highly recommended book that is complete, accurate, and up-to-date.

1819   Runkle, Aleta, and Eriksen, Mary L. *Music for Today's Boys and Girls: Sequential Learning through the Grades.* Boston, Allyn and Bacon, 1966. 280p. biblio.

A good readable text for elementary school music methodology.

1820   Sheehy, Emma D. *Children Discover Music and Dance: a Guide for Parents and Teachers.* New York, Holt, 1959. 282p.

Extends children's musical experiences beyond singing and the learning of musical notation to the exploration and discovery of sound and space. Natural rhythm, movement, and music are released, developed, and experienced creatively in the classroom setting. Classroom examples are cited.

1821   Slind, Lloyd H., and Davis, D. Evan. *Bringing Music to Children: Music Methods for the Elementary School Teacher.* New York, Harper, 1964. 369p.

A practical guide to developing skills in listening, singing, playing instruments, and physical movement. Presents fundamentals and understandings in a developmental sequence.

1822   Wisler, Gene C. *Music Fundamentals for the Classroom Teacher.* Boston, Allyn and Bacon, 1961. 250p.

Basic information for the non-musician. Mostly theory but includes a glossary, some songs, and lists of recordings.

Secondary Schools

1823   Cooper, Irvin, and Kuersteiner, Karl O. *Teaching Junior High School Music: General Music and the Vocal Program.* Boston, Allyn and Bacon, 1965. 440p.

An excellent treatise by two widely known educators.

1824   Richardson, Allen L., and English, Mary. *Living with Music,* 2 vols. New York, Witmark, 1956-1958.

A functional and creative approach to general music in the junior high school.

1825   Singleton, Ira C. *Music in Secondary Schools*. Boston, Allyn and Bacon, 1963. 404p. biblio.

A substantial coverage of a variety of music activities whose usefulness has been demonstrated by its favor among secondary school music teachers.

History

1826   Birge, Edward B. *History of Public School Music in the United States*. Washington, NEA, 1966. 296p. biblio.

A reprint of a 1937 book. Traces one hundred years of music education in American schools, starting with "singing schools" in 1838. Based on primary sources, which are liberally quoted, this is an absorbing story of the "first expressive subject" in the curriculum.

MUSIC EDUCATION—INSTRUMENTAL MUSIC

1827   Castellini, John. *Rudiments of Music: a New Approach with Application to the Keyboard*. New York, Norton, 1962. 239p.

An approach to music fundamentals through the use of the keyboard, which is helpful for adults wishing to learn basic skills and theory. Special feature is discussion of historical background.

1828   Duvall, W. Clyde. *The High School Band Director's Handbook*. Englewood Cliffs, N.J., Prentice-Hall, 1960. 209p.

Contains excellent information about areas of instrumental music teaching not covered elsewhere, such as improving sight reading, a point system for grading organizations, and band tours.

1829   Holz, Emil A., and Jacobi, Roger E. *Teaching Band Instruments to Beginners*. Englewood Cliffs, N.J., Prentice-Hall, 1966. 118p.

A practical manual for the beginning teacher.

1830   House, Robert W. *Instrumental Music for Today's Schools*. Englewood Cliffs, N.J., Prentice-Hall, 1965. 282p. biblio.

The most comprehensive and concise treatment of the subject to date. Author presents many excellent examples from his own teaching experience.

1831 Mandell, Muriel, and Wood, Robert E. *Make Your Own Musical Instruments*. New York, Sterling, 1959. 126p.

A handy, useful guide to making simple musical instruments.

1832 Payson, Al, and McKenzie, Jack. *The Music Educator's Guide to Percussion*. Rockville Centre, N.Y., Belwin, 1966. 128p. biblio.

An excellent text for percussion teachers. Contains useful information such as the care and repair of instruments and a bibliography of teaching materials.

NONGRADED SCHOOLS see **GROUPING IN SCHOOLS**

NURSERY SCHOOLS see **PRESCHOOL EDUCATION**

NURSING EDUCATION

1833 Anderson, Bernice E. *Nursing Education in Community Colleges: a 4-State, 5-Year Experience in the Development of Associate Degree Programs*. Philadelphia, Lippincott, 1966. 319p. biblio.

An enlightening report of programs in California, Florida, New York, and Texas, describing trials, errors, and triumphs and providing guidelines for organizing and developing nursing education programs in junior colleges.

1834 Fuerst, Elinor V., and Wolff, LuVerne. *Teaching Fundamentals of Nursing: Method, Content, and Evaluation*, 4th ed. Philadelphia, Lippincott, 1963. 159p.

Based on changing concepts in the teaching of nursing and the formulation of a sound philosophy. Offers course suggestions.

1835 Gallagher, Anna H. *Educational Administration in Nursing*. New York, Macmillan, 1965. 221p.

A practical discussion of such areas as effective utilization of student personnel services, recruitment of faculty, improvement of instruction, curriculum development, budget planning, research, and cooperation with other departments.

1836 Griffin, Gerald J., and others. *Clinical Nursing Instruction by Television.* New York, TC, Columbia, 1965. 79p. biblio.

A report of a two-year experiment using closed circuit television. Explores the questions of whether a larger number of nurses could be taught in a clinical setting through the use of television than with conventional methods and whether students could be taught as effectively.

1837 Guinee, Kathleen K. *The Aims and Methods of Nursing Education.* New York, Macmillan, 1966. 261p. biblio.

An up-to-date approach outlining and discussing the psychological processes of learning and the methodology of effective teaching.

1838 Heidgerken, Loretta E. *Teaching and Learning in Schools of Nursing*, 3rd ed. Philadelphia, Lippincott, 1965. 685p.

A scholarly and comprehensive reference work covering fundamentals, with emphasis on learning. Discusses the learning environment, teacher-learner relationships, curriculum, educational media, and evaluation.

1839 Henderson, Virginia. *The Nature of Nursing: a Definition and Its Implications for Practice, Research and Education.* New York, Macmillan, 1966. 84p.

A definition of the nursing function and area of expertise and authority, depicting the changing extent of the nurse's involvement. A challenging philosophy stressing the need for liberalizing nursing education.

1840 Lambertsen, Eleanor C. *Education for Nursing Leadership.* Philadelphia, Lippincott, 1958. 197p. biblio.

An outgrowth of experiment and study at Teachers College, Columbia, conducted from 1949-1956. Identifies the principles of professional nursing education and the learning experiences based on those principles.

1841 MacDonald, Gwendolyn. *Development of Standards and Accreditation in Collegiate Nursing Education.* Philadelphia, Lippincott, 1965. 184p. biblio.

A survey of the literature and an examination of the significant factors and forces influencing the evolution of educational standards and accreditation programs.

1842   Montag, Mildred L. *Community College Education for Nursing: an Experiment in Technical Education for Nursing.* New York, McGraw-Hill, 1959. 457p. biblio.

A report of a Teachers College, Columbia, project that describes the development of a junior and community college nursing education program. Contains an evaluation of project graduates and implications for the profession and for nursing education.

1843   _____. *The Education of Nursing Technicians.* New York, Putnam, 1951. 146p. biblio.

A serious effort, based on a study, to assess critically the present nursing education system and to analyze the implications of vocational and technical education in nursing training. Proposes improvements by utilizing some of the tested principles of technical education.

1844   Pillepich, Mary K. *Development of General Education in Collegiate Nursing Programs: Role of the Administrator.* New York, TC, Columbia, 1962. 86p. biblio.

A provocative study questioning existing curricula and goals in professional nursing education, based on the belief that a liberal education is primary and that occupational preparation is secondary.

1845   Rines, Alice R. *Evaluating Student Progress in Learning the Practice of Nursing.* New York, TC, Columbia, 1963. 76p. biblio.

The principles of learning and evaluation applied to nursing performance, plus a discussion of the need for a planned program of evaluation.

1846   Rogers, Martha E. *The Educational Revolution in Nursing.* New York, Macmillan, 1961. 65p. biblio.

An attempt to clarify some of the major misconceptions existing in the field. Explores the development of theoretical concepts in nursing, implementation, and research.

1847   _____. *Reveille in Nursing.* Philadelphia, Davis, 1964. 97p. biblio.

A significant book developing a rationale for formulating and implementing a professional curriculum in nursing. Proposes a five-year curriculum with less emphasis on training and more on liberal arts.

1848   Schmahl, Jane A. *Experiment in Change: an Interdisciplinary Approach to the Integration of Psychiatric Content in Baccalaureate Nursing Education.* New York, Macmillan, 1966. 460p. biblio.

Describes a five-year project at Skidmore College and, in a readable fashion, discusses the theories on which the project was based.

1849   Smeltzer, C. H. *Psychological Evaluations in Nursing Education.* New York, Macmillan, 1965. 192p.

A practical application of psychological principles to nursing education, providing suggestions for successful programs. A broad survey that can serve as a vehicle for provoking discussion on such topics as the selection of students, the attitudes of applicants, the psychological aspects of the teaching process, and counseling and guidance.

NUTRITION EDUCATION
see also **HEALTH EDUCATION**
HOME ECONOMICS

1850   Godshall, Frances R. *Nutrition in the Elementary School.* New York, Harper, 1958. 112p. biblio.

Basic principles for guiding the learning experiences of children. Suggestions for the classroom teacher for integrating the study of food and nutrition with the regular elementary school program.

1851   Lockhart, Helen S., and Whitehead, F. E., eds. *Nutrition Education in Elementary and Secondary Schools.* New York, The Nutrition Foundation, 1952. 43p. biblio.

A monograph describing studies in the field of nutrition conducted by the Harvard School of Public Health from 1943 to 1951 in Newton, Mass., Rutherford County, Tenn., and Ascension Parish, La.

1852   Pattison, Mattie, and others. *Teaching Nutrition,* 2nd ed. Ames, Iowa State UP, 1966. 345p. biblio.

A pragmatic approach aimed at simplifying technical material and motivating people to study their present food habits and change them as needed. A handbook for teachers and public health workers.

1853   Ritchie, Jean A. *Teaching Better Nutrition: a Study of Approaches and Techniques* (Food and Agricultural Organization of the United Nations Studies, no. 6). Washington, 1950. 148p. biblio.

A comparative study dealing with existing food patterns and diets in relation to economic and social background in a number of countries. Describes nutrition education programs in highly and less developed areas of the world.

ORGANIZATIONAL THEORY AND MANAGEMENT

1854   Archibald, Russell D., and Villoria, Richard L. *Network-based Management Systems (PERT/CPM)*. New York, Wiley, 1967. 508p.

A guide to network-based, management information and control systems: what they are, how they work, what they cost, and how they are put into practice.

1855   Argyris, Chris. *Personality and Organization: the Conflict Between System and the Individual*. New York, Harper, 1957. 291p.

Develops the thesis that formal administrative structure tends to make the employee feel dependent, passive, and submissive.

1856   Barnard, Chester I. *The Functions of the Executive*. Cambridge, Harvard UP, 1938. 334p.

A seminal work and a classic in the field of organizational theory.

1857   Blau, Peter M. *Bureaucracy in Modern Society: Studies in Sociology*. New York, Random, 1956. 127p. biblio.

A discussion of Max Weber's theory of bureaucracy and its modern adaptation.

1858   ————, and Scott, Richard W. *Formal Organizations: a Comparative Approach*. San Francisco, Chandler, 1962. 312p. biblio.

A broad treatment of organizational theory.

1859   Cooper, William W., and others, eds. *New Perspectives in Organizational Research*. New York, Wiley, 1964. 606p. biblio.

An interdisciplinary, theory-based resource containing numerous models of administrative and behavioral processes.

Of value in sharpening the educational administrator's perception of his role.

1860 Drucker, Peter F. *The Effective Executive.* New York, Harper, 1967. 178p.

The latest of Drucker's significant analyses of the nature of management.

1861 ―――. *The Practice of Management.* New York, Harper, 1954. 404p.

A study of managerial talent and how it operates.

1862 Etzioni, Amitai. *A Comparative Analysis of Complex Organizations: on Power, Involvement and Their Correlates.* New York, Free Press, 1961. 366p. biblio.

A discussion of the compliance theory of organization and a study of special aspects of the culture patterning of groups.

1863 Gouldner, Alvin W. *Patterns of Industrial Bureaucracy: a Case Study of Modern Factory Administration,* rev. ed. New York, Free Press, 1964. 282p. biblio.

A case study leading to a conceptualization of mock rules, representative rules, and punishment-centered rules.

1864 Gross, Bertram M. *The Managing of Organizations: the Administrative Struggle,* 2 vols. New York, Free Press, 1964.

A comprehensive review and synthesis of organizational theory.

1865 Gulick, Luther H., and others, eds. *Papers on the Science of Administration.* New York, Institute of Public Administration, Columbia, 1937. 195p.

A classic in the field of organizational theory. Essays by men scientifically interested in the phenomenon of administration, published "in the hope of constructing a valid and accepted theory of administration."

1866 Katz, Daniel, and Kahn, Robert L. *The Social Psychology of Organizations.* New York, Wiley, 1966. 498p. biblio.

The authors present an open-system theory, which they believe to be a more dynamic and adequate framework than classical-organization theory for the study of large scale organizations. Based on a program of research in human relations in organization begun in 1947 at the University of Michigan.

1867   Likert, Rensis. *The Human Organization: Its Management and Value.* New York, McGraw-Hill, 1967. 258p. biblio.
        Brings up to date and more thoroughly develops the theory first presented in *New Patterns of Management.*

1868   ———. *New Patterns of Management.* New York, McGraw-Hill, 1961. 279p. biblio.
        Based upon the major findings, since 1947, of the research program of the University of Michigan's Institute for Social Research. Stresses the importance of the social dimension of organization.

1869   March, James G., ed. *Handbook of Organizations.* Chicago, Rand McNally, 1965. 1247p. biblio.
        Contains 28 chapters giving an encyclopedic treatment of formal organizations and organizational behavior.

1870   ———, and Simon, Herbert A. *Organizations.* New York, Wiley, 1958. 262p. biblio.
        Historical review and analysis of current organizational theory.

1871   Presthus, Robert. *The Organizational Society: an Analysis and a Theory.* New York, Knopf, 1962. 323p. biblio.
        Analyzes patterns of accommodation to bureaucracy: the upward mobile, the indifferent, and the ambivalent.

1872   Roethlisberger, Fritz J. *Management and Morale.* Cambridge, Harvard UP, 1941. 194p.
        A volume that grew out of studies done in the late 1920's and early 1930's at a Western Electric Company plant and covering industrial efficiency and employment management.

1873   Simon, Herbert A. *Administrative Behavior: a Study of Decision-Making Processes in Administrative Organization,* 2nd ed. New York, Macmillan, 1957. 259p.
        A primary analysis of administrative decision-making as the basic theory of organization.

1874   Strauss, George, and Sayles, Leonard. *Personnel: the Human Problems of Management.* Englewood Cliffs, N.J., Prentice-Hall, 1960. 750p. biblio.
        Primarily a text on business personnel management, this book also provides insights into the problems of assessing the school administrator's functions.

OUTDOOR EDUCATION see **CAMPING AND OUTDOOR EDUCATION**
RECREATION AND LEISURE

PERCEPTION

1875   Allport, Floyd H. *Theories of Perception and the Concept of Structure: a Review and Critical Analysis with an Introduction to a Dynamic-Structural Theory of Behavior.* New York, Wiley, 1955. 709p. biblio.

An exposition and critical analysis of the major theories of perception by a well known social psychologist. Examines their achievements, their limitations, and their relationship to the author's theory of the structuring of events.

1876   Hall, Edward T. *The Hidden Dimension.* New York, Doubleday, 1966. 201p. biblio.

Concerned with space perception and space and time. Presents an analysis of "proxemics," the cultural dimension of territoriality.

1877   Solley, Gardner M., and Murphy, Charles M. *Development of the Perceptual World.* New York, Basic, 1960. 353p. biblio.

An advanced theoretical-experimental treatise on the role of learning in perception, discussing theoretical arguments on perceptual learning and analyzing the components of the perceptual act and the alteration of the components through learning.

1878   Soltis, Jonas F. *Seeing, Knowing, and Believing: a Study of the Language of Visual Perception.* Reading, Mass., Addison Wesley, 1966. 156p.

A philosophical approach to clarifying the language of perception. Analyzes what our eyes see or do not see and the complexities caused by the fact that knowledge and belief influence, and are influenced by, what we see.

1879   Taylor, James G. *The Behavioral Basis of Perception.* New Haven, Yale UP, 1962. 379p. biblio.

Develops a theory of perception as a complex interaction between behavior and sensory inputs. Based on three experiments involving the visual perception of the material environment.

PERSONALITY THEORY

see also BEHAVIOR

1880   Allport, Gordon W. *Becoming: Basic Considerations for a Psychology of Personality.* New Haven, Yale UP, 1955. 106p. biblio.

Three essays arguing for conceptual open-mindedness and for a reasoned eclecticism in the study of personality, which lay the groundwork for an adequate psychology of personality and deal with Lockean and Liebnitzian tradition, the importance of early affiliation, the dilemma of uniqueness, tribalism, and individuation.

1881   ———. *Personality and Social Encounter: Selected Essays.* Boston, Beacon, 1960. 386p. biblio.

A collection of the author's most important essays, which offers a naturalistic but open-ended approach to personality and the individual in the group. Discusses other, divergent viewpoints as well as expressing the author's concern with topical problems in social psychology.

1882   Bonner, Hubert. *Psychology of Personality.* New York, Ronald, 1961. 534p. biblio.

Describes personality from the holistic, field-psychological and perceptual point of view and challenges the mechanistic view of human behavior while considering its achievements.

1883   Cattell, Raymond B. *Description and Measurement of Personality.* New York, World, 1946. 602p. biblio.

Using a cross-sectional approach in describing and measuring personality, this research report coordinates existing knowledge and suggests problems and methods for future research.

1884   Eysenck, Hans J. *The Scientific Study of Personality.* New York, Macmillan, 1952. 320p. biblio.

An attempt to discover and define the dimensions of personality. Covers the normal and abnormal personality and discusses the applications of dimensional analysis.

1885   Janis, Irving L., and Hovland, Carl I., eds. *Personality and Persuasibility.* New Haven, Yale UP, 1959. 333p. biblio.

A series of interrelated investigations, by several authors, on the personality attributes of persons who are moderately persuasible in contrast to those who are resistant and those who are indiscriminately gullible. Analysis of emotional factors, personal adjustment, sex, and intelligence differences.

1886   Jung, Carl G. *Psychological Types: or the Psychology of Individuation.* New York, Pantheon, 1959. 654p.

A classic, translated from the 1921 German edition. The fruit of two decades of study in the domain of practical psychology, which discusses introversion and extroversion as basic personality types.

1887   Kelly, George A. *The Psychology of Personality Constructs,* 2 vols. New York, Norton, 1955.

Volume I is *Theory of Personality;* Volume II, *Clinical Diagnosis and Psychotherapy.* An original philosophy and theory—constructive alternativism—that are based on the proposition that the individual's view of the world is central to his personality, with the implications of this theory to the field of clinical practice.

1888   Kluckhohn, Clyde, and others, eds. *Personality in Nature, Society, and Culture,* 2nd ed. New York, Knopf, 1953. 701p. biblio.

An important collection of research articles on the relation of the individual to his society, with emphasis on personality formation.

1889   Lecky, Prescott. *Self-Consistency: a Theory of Personality.* (Edited by F. C. Thorne.) Hamden, Conn., Shoe String, 1951. 275p.

Describes Lecky's theory of self-consistency, based on the unity of the personality, and offers an evaluation by Thorne.

1890   Lewin, Kurt. *A Dynamic Theory of Personality.* New York, McGraw-Hill, 1935. 286p.

Selected papers by the eminent German proponent of Gestalt psychology, describing experimental studies in the psychology of the person and the environment.

1891   Lindzey, Gardner, and Hall, Calvin S., eds. *Theories of Personality: Primary Sources and Research.* New York, Wiley, 1965. 543p. biblio.

Compact yet comprehensive summaries of the major contemporary theories of personality. A detailed overview.

1892   Linton, Ralph. *The Cultural Background of Personality*. New York, Appleton, 1945. 157p.

An outgrowth of five lectures on the interrelations of culture, society, and the individual, with emphasis on the role of culture in personality formation.

1893   McClelland, David C. *Personality*. New York, Holt, 1951. 654p. biblio.

An important, theoretically oriented text that discusses measuring theories and abstractions, the study of personality, and personality variables.

1894   McKinney, Fred. *Psychology of Personal Adjustment: Students' Introduction to Mental Hygiene*, 3rd ed. New York, Wiley, 1960. 490p. biblio.

Almost a how-to book, enabling the individual to attain greater self-insight and thus improve his ability to meet realistic goals. Discusses motivation, habits and attitudes, self-understanding, vocational choice, and the nature and goals of adjustment.

1895   Murphy, Gardner. *Personality: a Biosocial Approach to Origins and Structure*. New York, Harper, 1947. 999p. biblio.

A highly technical evaluation of data on the growth of personality and an exploration into new areas of the study of personality development.

1896   Shaffer, Laurance F., and Shoben, Edward J., Jr. *The Psychology of Adjustment: a Dynamic and Experimental Approach to Personality and Mental Hygiene*, 2nd ed. Boston, Houghton Mifflin, 1956. 672p.

A systematic examination, based on the concepts of biology, of man's favorable and unfavorable adjustments to his environment. Discusses in detail varieties of adjustive behavior, personality, and techniques of mental hygiene.

1897   Sheldon, William H., and Stevens, S. S. *Varieties of Temperament: a Psychology of Constitutional Differences*. New York, Harper, 1942. 520p.

An interpretation of the relationship between temperament and physique, based on the development of a rating system that was tested in 200 cases.

1898   Stagner, Ross. *Psychology of Personality*, 3rd ed. New York, McGraw-Hill, 1961. 586p. biblio.

An easily read review of facts and theories that focuses

on normal personality. Attempts to develop a coherent, systematic viewpoint and stresses the interrelationships between problems of individual personality and problems of the social order.

1899   Symonds, Percival M. *The Dynamics of Human Adjustment.* New York, Appleton, 1946. 666p. biblio.

A theory of dynamic psychology, based on clinical studies and published case histories. Concerned with the ways an individual satisfies his inner drives in relation to the physical and social world in which he lives.

1900   White, Robert W. *Lives in Progess: a Study of the Natural Growth of Personality,* 2nd ed. New York, Holt, 1966. 422p. biblio.

Case studies furnish the foundation for this scientific study of personality.

1901   Wylie, Ruth C. *The Self Concept: a Critical Survey of Pertinent Research Literature.* Lincoln, Nebraska UP, 1961. 390p. biblio.

A critical review of recent research literature, with some attention devoted to investigations of non-phenomenological constructs but with major emphasis on studies of conscious self-concepts or phenomenal self.

1902   Young, Kimball. *Personality and Problems of Adjustment,* 2nd ed. New York, Appleton, 1952. 716p. biblio.

Describes, analyzes, and interprets the development and functioning of the personality against a background of physiological, societal, and cultural factors.

PHYSICAL EDUCATION AND ATHLETICS

1903   Barrow, Harold M., and McGee, Rosemary. *A Practical Approach to Measurement in Physical Education.* Philadelphia, Lea and Febiger, 1964. 560p. biblio.

Directed chiefly at elementary and secondary school programs, this useful book is a practical guide to effective testing and measuring.

1904   Bucher, Charles A. *Administration of School and College Health and Physical Education Programs,* 4th ed. St. Louis, Mosby, 1967. 671p. biblio.

An up-to-date, scientifically and philosophically sound as

well as readable revision of a long established textbook. Content relates administration to philosophy. Includes implications for programs and presents broad aspects and specific problems.

1905 ———, and Dupee, Ralph K., Jr. *Athletics in Schools and Colleges*. New York, CARE, 1965. 115p. biblio.

A comprehensive reference covering the full range of athletics, including units of competition, award systems, tournaments, and eligibility. Insurance, safety, subsidization, and finance are discussed as are intramurals, extramurals, and varsities.

1906 ———. *Foundations of Physical Education*, 4th ed. St. Louis, Mosby, 1964. 578p. biblio.

A major revision of a standard book. Covers the field of physical education and the allied areas of health education, recreation, camping, and other forms of outdoor education. New material on team teaching, programed instruction, and ability grouping.

1907 Clarke, Henry H. *Application of Measurement to Health and Physical Education*, 4th ed. Englewood Cliffs, N.J., Prentice-Hall, 1967. 487p. biblio.

Shows how the measurement of ability can be an effective administrative device in the development of health and physical education programs from elementary school through college.

1908 Cowell, Charles C., and France, Wellman L. *Philosophy and Principles of Physical Education*. Englewood Cliffs, N.J., Prentice-Hall, 1963. 236p.

Identifies principles of physical education as philosophy, science, and art.

1909 Davis, Elwood C. *The Philosophic Process in Physical Education*. Philadelphia, Lea and Febiger, 1961. 301p.

Discusses the philosophy of physical education as a heritage, as action, and as a quest.

1910 ———, and Wallis, Earl. *Toward Better Teaching in Physical Education*. Englewood Cliffs, N.J., Prentice-Hall, 1961. 488p.

A comprehensive coverage of principles of effective teaching and of learning in physical education.

1911 Fleishman, Edwin A. *The Structure and Measurement of Physical Fitness*. Englewood Cliffs, N.J., Prentice-Hall, 1964. 207p. biblio.

Provides detailed test procedures, methods for proper test interpretations, background support data, and a recommended evaluation program. A companion volume, *Examiner's Manual for the Basic Fitness Tests*, is also available.

1912 Forsythe, Charles E. *The Athletic Director's Handbook*. Englewood Cliffs, N.J., Prentice-Hall, 1956. 403p. biblio.

Outlines the duties and responsibilities of directors of athletic programs and how they can be most effectively carried out.

1913 Halsey, Elizabeth. *Inquiry and Invention in Physical Education*. Philadelphia, Lea and Febiger, 1964. 119p. biblio.

Physical education programs at the various school levels designed to free children and youth for inquiry and invention as well as solving problems.

1914 Havel, Richard C., and Seymour, E. W. *Administration of Health, Physical Education, and Recreation for Schools*. New York, Ronald, 1961. 440p.

A useful handbook discussing specific administrative practices and procedures.

1915 Howard, Glenn W., and Masonbrink, Edward. *Administration of Physical Education*. New York, Harper, 1963. 464p.

Outlines and discusses administrative practices in physical education programs.

1916 Hughes, William L., and others. *Administration of Physical Education for Schools and Colleges*, 2nd ed. New York, Ronald, 1962. 456p.

A thorough discussion of desirable practices and policies.

1917 Irwin, Leslie W. *The Curriculum in Health and Physical Education*, 3rd ed. Dubuque, Iowa, Brown, 1961. 383p.

A comprehensive review of the selection and conduct of activities at each grade level, elementary through college.

1918 Kozman, Hilda C., and others. *Methods in Physical Education*, 4th ed. Dubuque, Iowa, Brown, 1967. 334p. biblio.

Introduces the teaching of physical education through an understanding of growth, movement concepts, learning theory, and the school environment.

1919   Mosston, Muska. *Teaching Physical Education: from Command to Discovery.* Columbus, Merrill, 1966. 238p. biblio.
Combines learning principles with an emphasis on self-discovery and creativity as an approach to the teaching of physical education.

1920   Nixon, John E., and Jewett, Ann E. *Physical Education Curriculum.* New York, Ronald, 1964. 290p. biblio.
Principles of curriculum development in physical education presented with analysis of different patterns for organizing curriculum content.

1921   Oberteuffer, Delbert, and Ulrich, Celeste. *Physical Education,* 3rd ed. New York, Harper, 1962. 466p.
An intensive coverage of principles and practice.

1922   Rathbone, Josephine L., and Hunt, Valerie V. *Corrective Physical Education,* 7th ed. Philadelphia, Saunders, 1965. 267p. biblio.
Sees the physical educator's role as that of helping all people achieve a high level of body build and motor accomplishment. Deals with anatomy, the mechanics of joint action, development, a neuromuscular basis for reconditioning, etc.

1923   Scott, Harry A., and Westkamper, R. *From Program to Facilities in Physical Education.* New York, Harper, 1958. 483p.
Describes essential indoor and outdoor facilities for physical education programs and their relationship.

1924   Souder, Marjorie A., and Hill, P. W. *Basic Movement: Foundations of Physical Education.* New York, Ronald, 1963. 157p.
Emphasizes basic movement by providing a development sequence of activities fundamental to the more complex and coordinated activities of sports, games, and dance.

1925   Thorndike, Augustus. *Athletic Injuries,* 5th ed. Philadelphia, 1962. 259p. biblio.
Considerations of simple and complex injuries are coupled with advice on how they can be reduced to minimal proportions through adequate medical supervision, proper conditioning, and competent coaching.

1926 Voltmer, Edward F., and Esslinger, Arthur A. *The Organization and Administration of Physical Education,* 4th ed. New York, Appleton, 1967. 570p. biblio.

An examination of physical education at all educational levels in which the goal is seen to be education rather than health or exercise per se.

1927 Williams, Jesse F. *The Principles of Physical Education,* 8th ed. Philadelphia, Saunders, 1964. 524p. biblio.

A revision of a much-used standard book. Emphasizes the scientific basis of the principles of physical education.

1928 Zeigler, Earle F. *Administration of Physical Education and Athletics: the Case Method Approach.* Englewood Cliffs, N.J., Prentice-Hall, 1959. 248p.

Several chapters introducing students to the case method of learning about human relationships and administration are followed by a collection of cases in the administration of physical education and athletics.

1929 ———. *Philosophical Foundations for Physical, Health, and Recreation Education.* Englewood Cliffs, N.J., Prentice-Hall, 1964. 356p. biblio.

Designed to increase understanding of the philosophical foundations underlying education in this field in the Western world.

Elementary Schools

1930 Anderson, Marian H., and others. *Play with a Purpose: Elementary School Physical Education.* New York, Harper, 1966. 549p. biblio.

Divided into three parts: activities (movement, ball, and dance skills), planning (especially facilities and equipment), and special play programs and audiovisual aids. Not notably innovative or profound but of considerable significance in the discussion of movement, which stresses success for each individual in relation to enduring habits.

1931 Andrews, Gladys, and others. *Physical Education for Today's Boys and Girls.* Boston, Allyn and Bacon, 1960. 431p.

Bases physical education for ages 5 to 12 on the needs and interests of children.

1932   Bucher, Charles A., and Reade, Evelyn M. *Physical Education and Health in the Elementary School*. New York, Macmillan, 1964. 578p. biblio.

Explains the requirements for a successful elementary school program and covers methods of teaching both physical education and health. (First published in 1958 under a slightly different title.)

1933   Fait, Hollis. *Physical Education for the Elementary School Child*. Philadelphia, Saunders, 1964. 390p. biblio.

A how-to book for planning and organizing programs at each grade level.

1934   Humphrey, James H. *Child Learning Through Elementary School Physical Education*. Dubuque, Iowa, Brown, 1966. 256p. biblio.

Relates physical education to the total purposes of the elementary school and explains the effect of the physical education experience on learning in other curriculum areas.

1935   Miller, Arthur G., and Whitcomb, V. *Physical Education in the Elementary School Curriculum*, 2nd ed. Englewood Cliffs, N.J., Prentice-Hall, 1963. 331p.

Discusses the integration of the physical education program with the entire school curriculum and presents specific elementary school activities.

1936   Vannier, Maryhelen, and Foster, Mildred. *Teaching Physical Education in Elementary Schools*, 3rd ed. Philadelphia, Saunders, 1963. 429p.

Describes how children learn and teaching techniques.

Secondary Schools

1937   Bookwalter, Karl W. *Physical Education in the Secondary Schools*. New York, CARE, 1963. 118p. biblio.

A lucid and well-reasoned statement of the nature and goals of physical education and its role in the total educational experience. Includes practical advice on methods of teaching and of measurement and evaluation.

1938   Bucher, Charles A., and others. *Methods and Materials for Secondary Physical Education*, 2nd ed. St. Louis, Mosby, 1961. 387p.

Emphasis is on the most effective teaching at the secondary level and includes teaching techniques, methods, and problems.

1939   Cowell, Charles C., and Schwehn, Hilda. *Modern Principles and Methods in Secondary School Physical Education,* 2nd ed. Boston, Allyn and Bacon, 1964. 418p. biblio.

Analysis of adolescent learning patterns as a basis for promoting all-around development. Applies team teaching and dual progress plan to physical education.

1940   Vannier, Maryhelen, and Fait, Hollis F. *Teaching Physical Education in Secondary Schools,* 2nd ed. Philadelphia, Saunders, 1964. 489p. biblio.

Discusses planning the program, class procedures, and teaching methods.

History

1941   Hackensmith, Charles W. *History of Physical Education.* New York, Harper, 1966. 566p. biblio.

A well-written and interesting description of physical education from very early times to the present.

1942   Van Dalen, Deobald B., and others. *A World History of Physical Education: Cultural, Philosophical, Comparative.* Englewood Cliffs, N.J., Prentice-Hall, 1952. 640p. biblio.

The most extensive history available, covering all aspects and most parts of the world.

PHYSICAL EDUCATION—ADAPTED

1943   Clarke, Henry H., and David. *Development and Adapted Physical Education.* Englewood Cliffs, N.J., Prentice-Hall, 1963. 364p.

Modern concepts of physical medicine and rehabilitation applied to exercise for chronic or functional handicaps.

1944   Daniels, Arthur S., and Davies, Evelyn A. *Adapted Physical Education,* 2nd ed. New York, Harper, 1965. 547p. biblio.

Information on various kinds of disabilities with techniques for adapting physical education to the needs of the handicapped.

1945   Fait, Hollis F. *Special Physical Education: Adaptive, Corrective, Developmental,* 2nd ed. Philadelphia, Saunders, 1966. 368p.

Presents major classes of physical and mental disabilities and describes methods for treating handicapped children and adults.

1946   Kelly, Ellen D. *Adapted and Corrective Physical Education,* 4th ed. New York, Ronald, 1965.

Theory, methods, and techniques for improving the physical condition and physical skills of the handicapped.

1947   Mathews, Donald K., and others. *The Science of Physical Education for Handicapped Children.* New York, Harper, 1962. 317p.

Discussion of the principles involved in the construction of exercise programs for handicapped children.

1948   Mueller, Grover W., and Christaldi, Josephine. *A Practical Program of Remedial Physical Education.* Philadelphia, Lea and Febiger, 1966. 278p. biblio.

Examines the objectives of remedial physical education. Emphasis is on postural deviations, their evaluation, and correction through physical activity.

1949   Rosen, Elizabeth. *Dance in Psychotherapy.* New York, TC, Columbia, 1957. 178p. biblio.

The use of dance in treating psychiatric patients.

PHYSIOLOGY FOR PHYSICAL EDUCATORS

1950   Broer, Marion. *The Efficiency of Human Movement,* 2nd ed. Philadelphia, Saunders, 1966. 351p. biblio.

The application of basic mechanical principles to an analysis of human movements.

1951   Clarke, Henry H. *Muscular Strength and Endurance in Man.* Englewood Cliffs, N.J., Prentice-Hall, 1966. 211p. biblio.

A report of studies based on experiments conducted by the author or under his direction over a period of 20 years.

1952   Cratty, Bryant J. *Movement Behavior and Motor Learning.* Philadelphia, Lea and Febiger, 1964. 332p. biblio.

Provides physical educators and others concerned with motor activity a clear understanding of human movement and skill learning.

1953   Crouch, James E. *Functional Human Anatomy*. Philadelphia, Lea and Febiger, 1965. 662p. biblio.

A descriptive anatomy, examining the interrelationships of the structures and functions of the body, its organs, and its systems.

1954   De Vries, Herbert A. *Physiology of Physical Education and Athletics*. Dubuque, Iowa, Brown, 1967. 440p.

A selective review of basic physiology in relation to practice in physical education and to problems of athletic coaches.

1955   Johnson, Warren R., ed. *Science and Medicine of Exercise and Sports*. New York, Harper, 1960. 740p. biblio.

The first book of its kind. A symposium to which some 42 researchers—noted authorities in physiology, physical education, psychology, and medicine—have contributed chapters.

1956   Karpovich, Peter V. *Physiology of Muscular Activity*, 6th ed. Philadelphia, Saunders, 1965. 305p. biblio.

Focuses on the importance of the physiology of exercise as the scientific basis of physical education.

1957   Morehouse, Laurence E., and Miller, Augustus T., Jr. *The Physiology of Exercise*, 4th ed. St. Louis, Mosby, 1963. 323p. biblio.

An analysis of the physical potentials of the human body and of the manner in which they meet the exacting requirements of exercise. Covers the nature of neuro-muscular activity, circulatory and respiratory adjustments during exercise, metabolic and environmental aspects of exercise, fatigue and training, and fitness and health.

1958   Scott, Myrtle G. *Analysis of Human Motion*, 2nd ed. New York, Appleton, 1963. 443p. biblio.

Integrates and applies principles of anatomy, physiology, and mechanics to physical education activities.

1959   Wells, Katharine F. *Kinesiology: the Scientific Basis of Human Motion*. Philadelphia, Saunders, 1966. 554p. biblio.

Places emphasis on the most recent information on proprioceptors and their contributions to skillful, well-coordinated movement and on correct form in learning basic sport skills.

PLAY AND GAMES

see also **GAMES FOR CLASSROOM USE**
PHYSICAL EDUCATION
RECREATION

1960   Aaron, David, and Winawer, Bonnie P. *Child's Play: a Creative Approach to Providing Play Spaces for Today's Children.* New York, Harper, 1965. 160p.

A sculptor of imaginative types of playground equipment makes a sympathetic and perceptive analysis of the importance of play to a child. Many photographs.

1961   Bancroft, Jessie H. *Games,* rev. ed. New York, Macmillan, 1937. 685p.

A pioneer text for player and teacher. Includes chapters on organized athletics, active, quiet, and social games, singing games, and games for one or two people. Includes songs with music and an alphabetical list of games.

1962   Caillois, Roger. *Man, Play and Games.* New York, Free Press, 1961. 208p.

A systematized analysis of the games of various cultures. Finds that there are four forms of play that are universal and necessary to human development.

1963   Hartley, Ruth E., and others. *Understanding Children's Play.* New York, Columbia UP, 1952. 372p. biblio.

A study of the place of play in fostering healthy personality development in young children with a detailed examination of various kinds of play in school: dramatic play, the block corner, water play, the use of clay and graphic materials, finger painting, music, and movement.

1964   Huizinga, Johan. *Homo Ludens: a Study of the Play-Element in Culture.* Boston, Beacon, 1955. 220p.

A sociological study.

1965   Rapoport, Anatol. *Fights, Games, and Debates.* Ann Arbor, U of Michigan P, 1960. 400p. biblio.

A lucid and illuminating exploration of the many kinds of human conflict. Examines such topics as the role of ethics, game theory, and the logic of strategy.

1966   Sapora, Allen V., and Mitchell, E. D. *The Theory of Play and Recreation,* 3rd ed. New York, Ronald, 1961. 558p.

An examination of the role of play in different cultures.

Describes the concept of play and recreation today in relation to the organization and development of facilities and programs.

POETRY IN THE CLASSROOM

1967 Arnstein, Flora J. *Adventure into Poetry.* Stanford, Cal., Stanford UP, 1951. 217p.

A fascinating account of poetry sessions conducted with elementary school children, with numerous examples of children's poetry and their reactions to published poetry.

1968 ———. *Poetry in the Elementary Classroom.* New York, Appleton, 1962. 124p.

An instrument of great value for teachers eager to enrich their own content resources as well as their skills in conveying to children the "use value" of poetry in their lives. For use with individuals and large or small groups.

1969 Blackburn, Thomas, ed. *Presenting Poetry: a Handbook for English Teachers.* New York, Barnes and Noble, 1966. 221p.

A collection of articles by British poets and teachers. A wide divergence of opinion provides stimulating insight into ideas, techniques, and theories. Coverage includes the psychology of poetry, the therapeutic value of reading and writing poetry, and arguments for teaching contemporary poetry. Examples and lists of materials.

1970 Ciardi, John. *How Does a Poem Mean?* Boston, Houghton Mifflin, 1959. 395p.

A useful examination of the nature of poetry by a practicing poet who is also a teacher and an outspoken journalist. For teachers and students. (Originally Part 3 of an anthology, *Introduction to Literature.*)

1971 Mearns, Hughes. *Creative Youth: How a School Environment Set Free the Creative Spirit.* New York, Doubleday, 1925. 234p.

A classic that includes abundant examples of children's work. Discussion of the examples by the author, who was also the teacher responsible for the creative writing.

1972 Pettit, Dorothy, ed. *Poetry in the Classroom.* Champaign, Ill., NCTE, 1967. 78p.

A collection of articles, 1963-1966, from the *English*

Journal. A variety of inspiring approaches, offering many fresh insights. Of practical use in the classroom.

1973 Walter, Nina W. *Let Them Write Poetry.* New York, Holt, 1967. 179p. biblio.

Develops the thesis that the appreciation of poetry can best be taught by encouraging children to write poetry. A stimulating guide for teachers of all levels of schooling, offering suggestions for differentiating between creative and imitative work, presentations that evoke poetic responses, and developing standards of evaluation.

PRESCHOOL EDUCATION

1974 Hammond, Sarah, and others. *Good Schools for Young Children: a Guide for Working with Three, Four, and Five Year Old Children.* New York, Macmillan, 1963. 397p.

Examines the reasons for schooling for young children and, using the findings of research in biology, sociology, and psychology, discusses the planning and organizing of programs for preschool children.

1975 Headley, Neith E. *The Kindergarten: Its Place in Education.* New York, CARE, 1965. 110p. biblio.

Describes a program that experience has proved successful in adapting itself to the needs of growing children and to new sources of knowledge. Innovations are appraised in a balanced fashion, excluding both panic and unthinking enthusiasm.

1976 Hechinger, Fred M., ed. *Pre-School Education Today.* New York, Doubleday, 1966. 150p. biblio.

A knowledgeable and seasoned editor offers new approaches to teaching three, four, and five year olds. A stimulating, often challenging and controversial, sometimes unsupported, effort to bring a new perspective to work with young children.

1977 Leavitt, Jerome E., ed. *Nursery-Kindergarten Education.* New York, McGraw-Hill, 1958. 365p.

A comprehensive discussion of principles and philosophy. Explores curriculum and methods and offers suggestions for working with the two to six year-old child.

1978 Pines, Maya. *Revolution in Learning: the Years from Birth to Six.* New York, Harper, 1967. 244p.

A plea for more attention to the intellectual capacities of young children. Describes recent work by psychologists and educators who have been experimenting with fresh approaches and materials in an attempt to stimulate "early learning" among both advantaged and disadvantaged.

1979 Read, Katherine H. *The Nursery School,* 2nd ed. Philadelphia, Saunders, 1955. 297p.

A basic and near-classic text that discusses the nursery school, its purpose, the experiences needed by and valuable to the three and four year olds that extend beyond the home and neighborhood.

1980 Robison, Helen F., and Spodek, Bernard. *New Directions in the Kindergarten.* New York, TC, Columbia, 1965. 214p. biblio.

New concepts and new insights make this significant.

1981 Todd, Vivian E., and Heffernan, Helen. *The Years before School: Guiding Preschool Children.* New York, Macmillan, 1966. 658p. biblio.

A guide to effective ways of working with three, four, and five year olds, who are eager learners. Generously supplied with material illustrating the wide range of behavior of, preschool children, their actions, and reactions.

PRIVATE SCHOOLS
see also CHURCH-SPONSORED SCHOOLS

1982 Beach, Fred F., and Will, Robert F. *The State and Nonpublic Schools, with Particular Reference to the Responsibility of State Departments of Education* (USOE, Miscellaneous, no. 28). Washington, GPO, 1958. 152p.

Describes the legal framework under which the nonpublic schools are enabled to enjoy desirable freedom of operation and are encouraged to provide educational programs in the public interest.

1983 Blum, Virgil C. *Freedom of Choice in Education.* New York, Macmillan, 1958. 230p.

Emphasizes the importance of parental freedom in setting

up schools for their children. Advocates a "tax credit" plan to deal with some of the complexities of this problem.

1984 *The Handbook of Private Schools: an Annual Descriptive Survey of Independent Education.* Boston, Sargent.

The 48th edition of this indispensable annual listed in 1967 about 1,000 boarding and day schools in the United States. Includes summer academic programs and summer camps.

1985 Johnson, William, ed. *A Handbook for Independent School Operation.* Princeton, N.J., Van Nostrand, 1961. 296p.

A how-to book designed to meet the "increasing demand for non-public education." Covers all areas: organization, administration, curriculum, faculty, students, business management, public relations, finances, religion, extra-curricular activities, and boarding.

1986 *Private Independent Schools: the American Private Schools for Boys and Girls.* Wallingford, Conn., Bunting.

The 20th edition of this annual, 1967, lists 1,000 elementary and secondary schools, day and boarding, military and church affiliated. Includes some schools in other countries, despite subtitle's restriction.

1987 Springer, E. Laurence. *Independent School Administration.* New York, Harper, 1967. 156p.

A manual for the management of private day and boarding schools, based on many years of personal experience as well as on data compiled from studies of 16 independent schools.

1988 Tucker, Gilbert M. *The Private School.* New York, Vantage, 1965. 127p.

An opponent of federal aid to or intervention in education discusses the private school as the ideal, with some consideration of the problems as well as the advantages.

History

1989 Sizer, Theodore R., ed. *The Age of the Academies.* New York, TC, Columbia, 1964. 201p.

A study of the uniqueness and significance of the academy movement in this country, its independence of and relation to the development of public education, and its decline in the post-Civil War period as the result of its being a rural institution in an era of increasing urbanization. Includes a selection of pertinent writings ranging from Milton in 1644 to an NEA report of 1885.

PROGRAMED INSTRUCTION
see also TEACHING MACHINES

1990 Deterline, William A. *An Introduction to Programed Instruction.* Englewood Cliffs, N.J., Prentice-Hall, 1962. 131p.

Discusses learning theory related to programing, historical development, and methods of programing. Reports some experimental research.

1991 Garner, W. Lee. *Programed Instruction.* New York, CARE, 1966. 118p. biblio.

A thorough treatment of present trends and issues in teaching technology. Covers the theoretical base, applications, training the programer, and designing and developing programs in relation to computer-based instructional systems.

1992 Green, Edward J. *The Learning Process and Programmed Instruction.* New York, Holt, 1962. 233p.

Detailed discussion of learning principles and programing techniques. Topics on learning consist of assumptions, definitions, basic conditioning processes, motivation, and complex processes. Topics on programing are the concept of programed instruction, teaching machines, techniques of programing, evaluation, and problems.

1993 Lange, Phil C., ed. *Programed Instruction* (NSSE 66th Yearbook, Part II). Chicago, U of Chicago P, 1967. 334p. biblio.

A critical examination of programed teaching, its current development and potential. Discusses theory and the scientific and innovative strategies usable to improve student learning behavior. A scholarly approach stressing the need for system, specificity, and predictability in instruction as the range of individual differences in student populations increase.

1994 Lysaught, Jerome P. *Programed Learning: Evolving Principles and Industrial Applications.* Ann Arbor, Mich., Foundation for Research on Human Behavior, 1961. 179p.

Excellent account of the importance of understanding the relationship of principles to application and use of new media.

1995   ———, and Williams, Clarence M. *Guide to Programmed Instruction*. New York, Wiley, 1963. 180p.

A helpful text for those contemplating the production or use of programed materials. Clear outlines and diagrams to help in planning format and content.

1996   Mager, Robert F. *Preparing Objectives for Programed Instruction*. San Francisco, Fearon, 1961. 62p.

A programed text on preparing educational objectives. Useful in teaching more precise statement of objectives. Topics include the qualities of meaningful objectives, terminal behavior, and criterion characteristics.

1997   Margulies, Stuart, and Eigen, Lewis D., eds. *Applied Programed Instruction*. New York, Wiley, 1962. 387p.

Articles covering the economics of programing, the teaching machine or programed book, the uses of programing, the training of programers, and the feasibility of training through programed instruction versus conventional techniques. Includes samples of programs.

1998   Markle, Susan M., and others. *A Programed Primer on Programing*, 2 vols. New York, Center for Programed Instruction, 1961.

Programs the principles of programed instruction in volume 1 and the rules of practical application in volume 2.

1999   Ofiesch, Gabriel D., and Meierhenry, Wesley C., eds. *Trends in Programmed Instruction*. Washington, NEA, 1964. 289p.

Papers from the first annual convention in 1963 of the National Society for Programmed Instruction. Deals with the role of the teacher, experimentation, and the programing process and its application to industry, government, defense, and health.

2000   Schramm, Wilbur. *Programed Instruction: Today and Tomorrow*. New York, FAE, 1962. 75p.

Result of a study of the development of the teaching machine and programed learning. Suggestions on how a desirable rate and pattern of development might be encouraged.

2001   Smith, Wendell I., and Moore, J. Williams, eds. *Programmed Learning: Theory and Research*. Princeton, N.J., Van Nostrand, 1962. 240p.

Selected readings grouped according to the psychological theory that relates to programed learning and methods of programing and to the research concerned with methods of programing.

PROTESTANT EDUCATION
see also RELIGIOUS EDUCATION

2002   Boehlke, Robert R. *Theories of Learning in Christian Education.* Philadelphia, Westminster, 1962. 221p.

An examination of Christian education and learning. Includes a theoretical model, based upon an interdisciplinary theological and psychological approach.

2003   Bower, William C. *Christ and Christian Education.* New York, Abingdon, 1943. 128p.

An essay tracing the educational work of the church from its beginnings in the ministry of Jesus. Discusses a functional concept of Christian education, the Bible in Christian education, and the relationship between religious and public education.

2004   Chamberlin, John G. *Freedom and Faith: New Approaches to Christian Education.* Philadelphia, Westminster, 1965. 156p. biblio.

A re-examination of current approaches to Christian education and the presentation of an approach in which the context of church education is the whole experience of man in a worldwide pluralistic culture and which enables each individual to exercise his responsibilities.

2005   Cully, Iris V. *The Dynamics of Christian Education.* Philadelphia, Westminster, 1958. 205p. biblio.

Aims to clarify the Christian faith in terms that can be relevant to growing people. The life-centered methods of participation, recognition, and communication are designated as existential.

2006   Cully, Kendig B. *The Search for a Christian Education Since 1940.* Philadelphia, Westminster, 1965. 205p. biblio.

Discusses the need for studying Christian education in the light of historical dimensions and reviews and summarizes leading theories that have appeared since 1940.

2007 ———, ed. *The Westminster Dictionary of Christian Education.* Philadelphia, Westminster Press, 1965. 812p. biblio.

Hundreds of leaders from all over the world have contributed articles on almost every aspect of Christian education, covering teaching at various age levels, church denominations, ideas, movements, and personalities. A valuable reference work.

2008 Elliott, Harrison S. *Can Religious Education Be Christian?* New York, Macmillan, 1940. 338p. biblio.

A spirited defense of progressive, culture-oriented religious education during a period of theological transition.

2009 Fahs, Sophia B. *Today's Children and Yesterday's Heritage.* Boston, Beacon, 1952. 224p.

A philosophy of religious education based on the findings of psychology, anthropology, sociology, and education. Proposes changes in methods and context of teaching growing out of a liberal theological perspective and experiences with children and teachers.

2010 Hunter, David. *Christian Education as Engagement.* New York, Seabury, 1963. 128p. biblio.

Presents the theological and educational foundations of the Episcopal curriculum and develops some of the implications encountered when "engagement" rather than "detachment" is made the goal of Christian nurture.

2011 LeBar, Lois. *Education That Is Christian.* Westwood, N.J., Revell, 1958. 252p. biblio.

A theory, which has gained considerable respect in conservative circles, designed to help teachers discover a distinctive Christian system of Christian education based upon Scriptural conclusions. The various aspects of Christian education are examined in the light of insights gleaned from the Bible.

2012 Little, Lawrence C. *Foundations for a Philosophy of Christian Education.* Nashville, Tenn., Abingdon, 1962. 240p. biblio.

An exploration of the psychological, cultural, theological, and religious foundations on which an adequate philosophy of Christian education may be constructed. The discussion of the main developments in personality theory and their relation to Christian education form a significant contribution to the field.

2013   Miller, Randolph C. *Education for Christian Living*. Englewood Cliffs, N.J., Prentice-Hall, 1956. 418p.

An examination of the entire field of Christian education based on the premise that Christian theology is the cornerstone on which Christian education must be built. Theology is the means by which theories, objectives, and methods are determined and evaluated.

2014   Stinnette, Charles R., Jr. *Learning in Theological Perspective*. New York, Association, 1965. 96p. biblio.

Discusses the Biblical concept of transfiguration as the central idea of learning the Christian faith and examines the dynamics and social matrix of learning.

2015   Taylor, Marvin J., ed. *Introduction to Christian Education*. Nashville, Tenn., Abingdon, 1966. 412p. biblio.

A comprehensive survey of the field of Christian education, with articles by 32 religious educators. Includes developments in the field since the previous survey in 1960 by the same editor. Useful as a text or reference volume, especially as it includes a listing of agencies and organizations.

2016   Van Dusen, Henry P. *God in Education: a Tract for the Times*. New York, Scribner, 1951. 128p. biblio.

The author raises what he considers to be the basic and final issue of education and religion—the issue of ultimate truth. Deals with the question, "What, if any, is the meaning for educational theory and practice of the recognition of God?"

2017   Wyckoff, D. Campbell. *The Task of Christian Education*. Philadelphia, Westminster, 1955. 172p.

A theoretical framework for Christian education, developed systematically to include objectives, principles, personality development, curriculum, methods, and evaluation.

PROTESTANT EDUCATION—ADMINISTRATION AND TEACHING

2018   Anderson, Phoebe M. *Religious Living with Nursery Children: Children in Church and Home*. Boston, Pilgrim, 1956. 179p.

Focuses on teaching young children in the religious fellowship, with emphasis on the personal relationships of "living" situations.

2019 Baxter, Edna M. *Learning to Worship.* Valley Forge, Pa., Judson, 1965.

A manual for training children and youth for worship, with deep insights into their growth and potential.

2020 Bergevin, Paul E., and McKinley, John. *Design for Adult Education in the Church.* New York, Seabury, 1958. 320p.

A description of the Indiana Plan for Adult Religious Education developed through research in 14 local churches, from which are derived some principles and a method of developing a program based upon the principles.

2021 Bogardus, La Donna. *Christian Education for Retarded Children and Youth.* Nashville, Tenn., Abingdon, 1963. 108p. biblio.

A background for understanding and teaching retarded children is followed by a practical guide to types of programs, teaching methods, and the selection and use of materials.

2022 Bower, Robert K. *Administering Christian Education: Principles of Administration for Ministers and Christian Leaders.* Grand Rapids, Mich., Eerdmans, 1964. 227p. biblio.

A comprehensive treatment of the important and recurring problems of organization and administration of a church school program, covering delegation of authority and control.

2023 Brown, Jeannette P. *The Storyteller in Religious Education.* Boston, Pilgrim, 1951. 165p. biblio.

A discussion of the place of storytelling in religious education with suggestions for selecting, analyzing, and telling stories. Includes 16 excellent stories.

2024 Butler, James D. *Religious Education: the Foundations and Practice of Nurture.* New York, Harper, 1962. 321p.

A comprehensive survey of the entire field of religious education, including history and philosophy, methods, curriculum, administration, leadership, and the agencies of religious education.

2025 Chaplin, Dora P. *Children and Religion,* rev. ed. New York, Scribner, 1961. 238p. biblio.

Recognizes the importance of the early years of childhood

in the formation of religious attitudes, habits, and ideas. Examines some approaches to teaching, such as through the Bible, through pictures, music, and poetry, and through books.

2026 ———. *The Privilege of Teaching*. New York, Morehouse Barlow, 1962.

Discusses the requirements of the religious teacher and the relationships of teacher, pupil, and home. Offers practical suggestions on the art of teaching.

2027 Chave, Ernest J. *Supervision of Religious Education*. Chicago, U of Chicago P, 1931. 352p.

A definitive work, unsurpassed for thoroughness, with many practical suggestions for conferences, teaching techniques, observation, and evaluation as well as supervision of worship and recreation.

2028 *The Church's Educational Ministry: a Curriculum Plan*. St. Louis, Bethany, 1965. 848p.

A comprehensive reference work of the Cooperative Curriculum Project of the National Council of Churches. Presents a total plan useful for various denominations and local parishes. Covers curriculum design, scope, objectives, context, learning tasks, and organization.

2029 Clemmons, Robert S. *Education for Churchmanship*. Nashville, Tenn., Abingdon, 1966. 205p. biblio.

An interdisciplinary approach deriving insights from history, theology, and the social sciences. Applies those insights to the training of adults for leadership and service in the church.

2030 Cully, Iris V. *Children in the Church*. Philadelphia, Westminster, 1960. 204p. biblio.

An approach to the Christian education of children that explores the needs of the child in relation to faith, the church, and the family and discusses how the child learns through participation.

2031 ———. *Imparting the Word: the Bible in Christian Education*. Philadelphia, Westminster, 1962. 174p. biblio.

Summarizes current findings and viewpoints in technical Biblical scholarship and relates them to curriculum and teaching in Christian education.

2032   Douty, Mary A. *How to Work with Church Groups*. Nashville, Tenn., Abingdon, 1957. 170p. biblio.

The principles of group work and of democratic group leadership applied to the practical questions of teaching and leading in the local church.

2033   Ernsberger, David. *Education for Renewal*. Philadelphia, Westminster, 1965. 174p. biblio.

A rethinking of church education emphasizing training of the laity for the ministry by means of "concern groups."

2034   Evans, David M. *Shaping the Church's Ministry with Youth*. Valley Forge, Pa., Judson, 1965. 127p. biblio.

An examination of the principles, possibilities, and problems involved in the "youth ministry" approach to working with young people.

2035   Fallaw, Wesner. *Church Education for Tomorrow*. Philadelphia, Westminster, 1960. 219p. biblio.

A plea for a transition from *Sunday* school education to week-long, from volunteer lay teachers to a teaching ministry. Provides an outline for a church curriculum and practical suggestions for local churches and seminaries.

2036   Foster, Virgil E. *How a Small Church Can Have Good Christian Education*. New York, Harper, 1956. 127p.

A practical book with many suggestions for administration and teaching.

2037   Goldman, Ronald. *Readiness for Religion: a Basis for Developmental Religious Education*. London, Routledge, 1965. 238p. biblio.

A developmental, research-based approach that deals with the psychological foundations of religious development and the effect of current educational theory and practice on religious education. Examines content and methods of teaching consistent with a developmental theory.

2038   ———. *Religious Thinking from Childhood to Adolescence*. New York, Humanities, 1964. 276p.

A description, based on research findings, of the capacities of children of various ages, abilities, and backgrounds to understand religious concepts such as God, Jesus, the Bible, prayer, and the Church.

2039   Harrell, John. *Teaching Is Communicating: an Audio-Visual Handbook for Church Use.* New York, Seabury, 1965. 142p. biblio.

Offers a wide variety of media and materials, with an emphasis on communication.

2040   Heim, Ralph D. *Leading a Sunday Church School.* Philadelphia, Fortress, 1950. 368p.

A definitive work on the administration of the Sunday Church School, with practical help on all aspects including buildings and finance as well as organization and program.

2041   Keiser, Armilda B. *Here's How and When.* New York, Friendship, 1952. 174p.

A practical and helpful presentation of creative activities organized around the aims of religious education: creating a friendly feeling, finding out about other peoples, having fun while learning, expressing feelings of friendship, and bringing the unit of study to a happy ending.

2042   Little, Lawrence C., ed. *Wider Horizons in Adult Christian Education.* Pittsburgh, U of Pittsburgh P, 1962. 338p. biblio.

A selection of the addresses and papers of the 1961 Workshop on the Curriculum of Christian Education for Adults. Covers trends, communication theory, methodology, curriculum, evaluation, and other pertinent areas.

2043   Little, Sara. *Learning Together in the Christian Fellowship.* Richmond, Va., Knox, 1956. 104p.

Devoted to learning within the redeeming fellowship. Discusses learning together, methods of study and participation, studying the Bible, and group study.

2044   ———. *The Role of the Bible in Contemporary Christian Education.* Richmond, Va., Knox, 1961. 190p.

Considers the historical and theological roles of the Bible in Christian education and surveys and analyzes the views of several Christian educators regarding the Bible in the teaching-learning process.

2045   Lobingier, Elizabeth M. *Activities in Child Education: for the Church School Teacher.* Boston, Pilgrim, 1950. 226p. biblio.

A useful guide to the theory of activities in religious education with detailed suggestions on the use of drawing, painting, clay modeling, and dramatization in the classroom.

2046 McManis, Lester W. *Handbook on Christian Education in the Inner City.* New York, Seabury, 1966. 96p. biblio.

A practical guide for work with all age groups in disadvantaged communities. Covers methods, activities, and resources. Many helpful suggestions.

2047 Morrison, Eleanor S., and Foster, Virgil E. *Creative Teaching in the Church.* Englewood Cliffs, N.J., Prentice-Hall, 1963. 244p.

A book of methods that discusses the foundation of methods, procedures for various age groups, and some general procedures for use as needed. Many techniques and activity ideas suggested.

2048 Myers, Alexander J. W. *Teaching Religion Creatively.* Westwood, N.J., Revell, 1932. 289p. biblio.

A classic work that presents the essential qualities of creative teaching in religion. Although the illustrations are dated, the ideas are fresh and relevant today.

2049 Reinhart, Bruce. *The Institutional Nature of Adult Christian Education.* Philadelphia, Westminster, 1962. 242p. biblio.

Based on a sociological study of the effect of the structure of religious institutions upon adult religious education. Examines the implications arising from these cultural and institutional pressures.

2050 Rice, Rebecca. *Creative Activities.* Boston, Pilgrim, 1947. 148p.

Instructions for many activities particularly useful in achieving religious goals and teaching procedures that lend color and interest to the class period.

2051 Smither, Ethel L. *Children and the Bible.* Nashville, Tenn., Abingdon, 1960. 183p. biblio.

Examines the role of the Bible in teaching children, methods of teaching the Bible, and the use of the Bible with various age groups.

2052 Stewart, Charles W. *Adolescent Religion: a Developmental Study of the Religion of Youth.* Nashville, Tenn., Abingdon, 1967. 318p. biblio.

A developmental study of the religion of normal young people, including six case studies interpreted against the background of the larger study.

2053   Tobey, Katherine L. *The Church Plans for Kindergarten Children.* Philadelphia, Westminster, 1959. 192p. biblio.

Suggestions for working with very young children in the church. Includes discussions of the characteristics of the four and five year old, techniques to use, and the practical aspects of planning and organizing the program.

2054   Vieth, Paul H. *The Church School: Administration and Supervision of Christian Education in the Local Church.* Philadelphia, Christian Education Press, 1957. 279p.

A comprehensive guide for all who are responsible for Christian education in the local church.

2055   _____. *Worship in Christian Education.* Philadelphia, United Church, 1965. 174p. biblio.

A guide to principles and practice in church school worship.

2056   Wright, Kathryn S. *Let the Children Paint: Art in Religious Education.* New York, Seabury, 1966. 168p. biblio.

A wealth of reference and resource material is included in this book of practical suggestions for class procedures for children aged 6 to 12. A plea for teachers to help pupils find joy and acceptance through painting.

2057   Wyckoff, D. Campbell. *How to Evaluate Your Christian Education Program.* Philadelphia, Westminster, 1962. 103p. biblio.

Developed at the request of the National Council of Churches and subsequently tested and revised. Evaluation in the total context of Christian education and a plan for local appraisal of programs. Includes the forms developed for use in the evaluative process.

2058   _____. *Theory and Design of Christian Education Curriculum.* Philadelphia, Westminster, 1961. 219p. biblio.

Based on the findings of a study committee of the National Council of Churches. Presents a theory on which a curriculum can be built by the various denominations and which can be used by college and seminary teachers.

2059   Yeaxlee, Basil. *Religion and the Growing Mind,* 3rd ed. New York, Seabury, 1952. 220p.

An application of the findings of psychology of religion to the questions of the maturing mind. Explores such subjects as truth and fantasy, adolescent adjustments, conversion, sex and religion, the criticism of youth, and questions about religion.

History

2060   Bower, William C. *The Curriculum of Religious Education.* New York, Scribner, 1925. 283p. biblio.

A book of historical significance. Examines several approaches to curriculum in religious education and presents a dynamic view in which experience is enriched and controlled.

2061   Bushnell, Horace. *Christian Nurture.* New Haven, Yale UP, 1948. 351p.

A religious and educational classic, first published in parts between 1846 and 1861, which aroused much opposition at the time. Findings in education and the social sciences have subsequently borne out Bushnell's insights.

2062   Coe, George A. *A Social Theory of Religious Education.* New York, Scribner, 1917. 361p.

A classic theory of religious education based on the concept that a social interpretation of Christianity requires social reconstruction in religious education.

2063   _____. *What Is Christian Education?* New York, Scribner, 1929. 300p.

A creative approach to religious education by an outstanding leader in the field. Based on the concept of the possible self-discovery and reconstruction of Christianity through the teaching process.

2064   Cully, Kendig B., ed. *Basic Writings in Christian Education.* Philadelphia, Westminster, 1960. 350p.

Excerpts of writings of church leaders from the early days of the Church into the 20th century. A reference work revealing a cumulative heritage of ideas on religious education.

2065   Kennedy, William B. *The Shaping of Protestant Education: an Interpretation of the Sunday School and the Development of Protestant Educational Strategy in the United States.* New York, Association, 1966. 93p. biblio.

A brief survey of the development of the Sunday school between 1789 and 1860 and its relationship to the public school and to the church.

2066 Lynn, Robert. *Protestant Strategies in Education.* (Edited by C. Ellis Nelson.) New York, Association, 1964. 96p.

An analysis of the history of American Protestant education. Rejects a theologically oriented church education and thrusts toward realistic communication with general education as well as development of a strategy for a pluralistic world.

PSYCHOLOGICAL THEORY
see also EDUCATIONAL PSYCHOLOGY
LEARNING THEORY

2067 *Annual Review of Psychology.* 1st-   1950-   . Stanford, Cal., Annual Reviews. biblio.

A survey of research in which each chapter of each volume covers an aspect of the field. Some topics discussed in rotation every several years. Includes some related fields, work by foreign scholars, and excellent references.

2068 Arieti, Silvano, ed. *American Handbook of Psychiatry,* 3 vols. New York, Basic, 1959-1965.

A comprehensive coverage, not always consistent and by dozens of authors, of the development, concepts, trends, techniques, problems, and prospects of psychiatry today. Includes all leading schools of thought and major approaches.

2069 Brunswik, Egon. *The Conceptual Framework of Psychology.* Chicago, U of Chicago P, 1952. 102p. biblio.

A lucid essay, by no means introductory, on modern psychological systems. Examines such issues as the need for methodological unity with the other sciences, misconceptions of exactitude, and the emergence of the objective approach.

2070 Bush, Robert R., and Mosteller, Frederick. *Stochastic Models for Learning.* New York, Wiley, 1955. 365p. biblio.

Written for the psychologist with a limited mathematical background. A thorough discussion of the application of a model to specific experimental problems in learning.

2071 Chaplin, James P., and Krawiec, T. S. *Systems and Theories of Psychology.* New York, Holt, 1960. 473p. biblio.

An introduction to systematic psychology emphasizing the evolution of contemporary theoretical concepts from their historical origins in philosophy and the natural sciences.

Presents a sampling of representative theoretical viewpoints in some depth.

2072   English, Horace B., and Ava C. *A Comprehensive Dictionary of Psychological and Psychoanalytical Terms: a Guide to Usage*. New York, McKay, 1958. 594p.

A useful reference (in crying need of updating) that includes, in alphabetical order, terms denoting mental and behavioral phenomena and the constructs and concepts used in ordering these phenomena. Over 11,000 entries.

2073   Goldenson, Robert M. *The Encyclopedia of Human Behavior: Psychology, Psychiatry, and Mental Health*. New York, Doubleday, 1968. 980p.

Over 1,000 scholarly articles with many bibliographic references, alphabetically arranged, covering all important terms, topics, and fields in normal and abnormal psychology. Includes case summaries. An authoritative reference work that has been much needed.

2074   *The Harvard List of Books in Psychology*, 3rd ed. Cambridge, Harvard UP, 1965. 111p.

Self-styled as idiosyncratic, this is a superb list of psychological books, chosen and pithily annotated by Harvard psychologists. The 704 titles are arranged under 23 subject divisions. Author index.

2075   Hilgard, Ernest R. *Introduction to Psychology*, 3rd ed. New York, Harcourt, 1962. 678p. biblio.

A standard, well-illustrated review of the old and new, based on the idea that psychological explanations usually take one or the other of two contrasting but not conflicting modes: the developmental and the interactive.

2076   Koch, Sigmund, ed. *Psychology: a Study of a Science*, 6 vols. New York, McGraw-Hill, 1959-1963.

An encyclopedia of psychology with contributions by well-known scholars. The several volumes are divided into two main subject divisions: Study I (volumes 1, 2, and 3) Conceptual and Systematic, and Study II (volumes 4, 5, and 6) Empirical Substructure and Relations with Other Sciences. A final volume containing the editor's conclusions and resumé is planned.

2077   Marx, Melvin H., and Hillix, William A. *Systems and Theories in Psychology*. New York, McGraw-Hill, 1963. 489p. biblio.
       An excellent and lucid coverage of the older systems of psychology and the newer theories. Appendix on Europe and the Far East.

2078   ———, ed. *Theories in Contemporary Psychology*. New York, Macmillan, 1963. 628p. biblio.
       A collection of papers, some reprints and others written for this book, concerned with theory construction and kinds of theories and such functions as learning and perception.

2079   Munn, Norman L. *Introduction to Psychology*. Boston, Houghton Mifflin, 1962. 588p. biblio.
       An exceptional book, a work of creative scholarship that is a clearly written, accurate survey of contemporary psychology. Offers insights into the nature of psychological processes and the application of psychological insights to the solution of personal and social problems.

History

2080   Dennis, Wayne, ed. *Readings in the History of Psychology*. New York, Appleton, 1948. 587p.
       A selection of 61 classics in the history of psychology, beginning with the 17th century (except for two by Aristotle) and going through into the 20th. Foreign contributions are perhaps neglected, but otherwise a good collection.

2081   Miller, George A. *Psychology: the Science of Mental Life*. New York, Harper, 1962. 388p. biblio.
       A non-technical attempt to explain the science of psychology and how it grew. A selective sampling covering past and present as well as several different areas of the field.

PSYCHOPATHOLOGY
see also EMOTIONALLY DISTURBED CHILDREN

2082   Cameron, Norman A., and Ann M. *Behavior Pathology*. Boston, Houghton Mifflin, 1951. 645p. biblio.
       A comprehensive examination of pathological behavior. Discusses behavior organization and utilizes the principle

of continuity, i.e., that abnormal behavior is related to and derived from normal behavior and that therapy is dependent upon this relationship.

2083   Coleman, James C. *Abnormal Psychology and Modern Life*, 3rd ed. Chicago, Scott Foresman, 1964. 694p. biblio.

An analysis of psychological abnormalities in relation to the settings in which they develop, with emphasis on methods of prevention as well as cure.

2084   *Diagnostic and Statistical Manual of Mental Disorders.* Washington, American Psychiatric Association, 1952. 130p.

An effort at uniformity in the field. Presents a nomenclature relating to the classification of disturbances of mental functioning and discusses the recording of psychiatric conditions as well as statistical reporting and classification of mental disorders.

2085   Dorcus, Roy M., and Shaffer, G. Wilson. *Textbook of Abnormal Psychology*, 4th ed. Baltimore, Williams and Wilkins, 1950. 717p. biblio.

A research-based description of abnormalities of the sensory and motor systems, disorders of central functions, and other abnormalities as they are manifest in the total personality. Some coverage of psychotherapy.

2086   Erikson, Erik H. *Insight and Responsibility: Lectures on the Ethical Implications of Psychoanalytic Insight.* New York, Norton, 1964. 256p. biblio.

A distinguished analyst offers some illuminating comments on the nature of clinical evidence, identity and uprootedness today, human strength and the cycle of generations, psychological reality and historical actuality, and the Golden Rule in the light of new insight.

2087   Eysenck, Hans J., ed. *Handbook of Abnormal Psychology: an Experimental Approach.* New York, Basic, 1961. 816p. biblio.

A conception of abnormality as the defective functioning of certain psychological systems. Covers the description and measurement, the causes and determinants, and the experimental study and modification of abnormal behavior. A major source book of experimental research data on behavior disorders.

2088   Fenichel, Otto. *Psychoanalytic Theory of Neurosis.* New York, Norton, 1945. 703p. biblio.

A systematic and comprehensive summary of psychoanalytic doctrines with emphasis on the theory of neurosis as it relates to psychoanalysis.

2089   Horney, Karen. *The Neurotic Personality in Our Time.* New York, Norton, 1937. 299p.

An influential interpretation of neurosis deviated from that of Freud, as it considers that cultural as well as sexual factors must be considered.

2090   Hunt, Joseph McV., ed. *Personality and the Behavior Disorders: a Handbook Based on Experimental and Clinical Research,* 2 vols. New York, Ronald, 1944. biblio.

A comprehensive, interdisciplinary survey of personality and behavior disorders. Covers theory, investigative fact, and clinical practice.

2091   Kisker, George W. *The Disorganized Personality.* New York, McGraw-Hill, 1964. 631p. biblio.

Profusely illustrated with case histories, this is a clinically oriented survey of abnormal psychology. Includes relevant data from biochemistry, social psychiatry, and experimental psychopathology.

2092   May, Rollo. *The Meaning of Anxiety.* New York, Ronald, 1950. 376p. biblio.

A non-technical review of various theories of anxiety. Attempts to discern their common elements and to formulate concepts for further inquiry. Conclusions supported by investigations of anxiety situations and case studies.

2093   Munroe, Ruth L. *Schools of Psychoanalytic Thought: an Exposition, Critique, and Attempt at Integration.* New York, Holt, 1955. 670p. biblio.

A lengthy, semi-technical, but clearly written survey of the diverse and often conflicting approaches of the various schools, with a valiant attempt at integrating the diversity into a coherent unity.

2094   O'Kelly, Lawrence P., and Muckler, F. *Introduction to Psychopathology,* 2nd ed. Englewood Cliffs, N.J., Prentice-Hall, 1955. 736p. biblio.

Clinical examples and case studies illustrate this discussion of disordered personalities. Defines psychopathology and normal and abnormal behavior and considers the problems and causes of disordered behavior.

2095 White, Robert W. *The Abnormal Personality*, 3rd ed. New York, Ronald, 1964. 619p. biblio.

An introductory text with emphasis on the pertinence to all students of human nature of the study of abnormal psychology. Provides an historical review of the study of abnormal psychology, examples of disordered personalities, and a description of various neurotic, psychotic, and psychosomatic disabilities.

PUBLIC RELATIONS see SCHOOL-COMMUNITY RELATIONS

READING INSTRUCTION
see also CHILDREN'S LITERATURE
LANGUAGE ARTS

2096 Anderson, Irving H., and Dearborn, Walter F. *The Psychology of Teaching Reading*. New York, Ronald, 1952. 382p. biblio.

Still an excellent survey, emphasizing the psychological foundations of method in teaching reading. Reviews the psychological evidence that provides the basis of method and illustrates principles with case material and references to classroom performance.

2097 Austin, Mary C., and others. *The First R: the Harvard Report on Reading in Elementary Schools*. New York, Macmillan, 1963. 263p. biblio.

The so-called Harvard-Carnegie Report, based on the findings of a study of elementary school reading programs across the country. Develops some 45 general recommendations intended to provide the spark for creative action in the schools.

2098 Barbe, Walter B., ed. *Teaching Reading: Selected Materials*. New York, Oxford UP, 1965. 444p. biblio.

An excellent collection of articles on all phases of reading: research, methods, philosophy. Covers all levels, K-12.

2099 Betts, Emmett A. *Foundations of Reading Instruction, with Emphasis on Differentiated Guidance*. New York, American, 1957. 757p.

A classic in the field offering a thorough and detailed examination of methods of teaching reading.

2100 Bond, Guy L., and Wagner, Eva B. *Teaching the Child to Read,* 4th ed. New York, Macmillan, 1966. 404p. biblio.

A solid and conservative approach that does not include some of the more recent research but is a useful basic book. Much illustrative material and attention to classroom diagnostics.

2101 Chall, Jeanne. *Learning to Read: the Great Debate.* New York, McGraw-Hill, 1967. 372p. biblio.

The results of a three-year Carnegie Corporation-sponsored study based on an analysis of research, hundreds of classroom visits, and searching examination of textbooks. The author presents evidence that the most successful teaching method—phonics—is the least used, blames researchers, publishers, school administrators, and teachers, and presents some challenging recommendations for reform.

2102 Cleary, Florence D. *Blueprints for Better Reading: School Programs for Promoting Skill and Interest in Reading.* New York, Wilson, 1957. 216p.

An "idea" book for teachers and librarians. Outlines the role of the librarian in the reading program and offers suggestions for evaluation and selection of instructional materials.

2103 Conference and Course on Reading. *Report.* 1st-   1945- Pittsburgh, Reading Laboratory, U of Pittsburgh.

A variety of papers presented at the conference. Published annually, each volume has a specific focus. Some recent titles are: *Individualizing Instruction in Reading* (1964), *Reading and the Related Arts* (1965).

2104 Conference on Reading, University of Chicago. *Proceedings.* vol. 1-   1917- . (Supplementary Educational Monographs.) Chicago, U of Chicago P.

A venerable and eminent series that is a compilation of annual conference papers, in recent years under the editorship of H. Alan Robinson. An invaluable resource. Recent titles: *Recent Developments in Reading* (1965) and *Reading: Seventy-Five Years of Progress* (1966). (For some years this was a series of monographs on a variety of educational subjects. In 1939, one of them was the first Conference on Reading. In recent years the Conference proceedings has been the only monograph.)

2105 Cutts, Warren G. *Modern Reading Instruction*. New York, CARE, 1964. 118p. biblio.

A thorough coverage of recent research into the mechanics of reading is combined with the practical aspects of reading instruction and the administration of the reading program.

2106 Dawson, Mildred A., and Bamman, Henry A. *Fundamentals of Basic Reading Instruction*, 2nd ed. New York, McKay, 1963. 325p. biblio.

A specific and practical coverage of modern philosophy and practice in the teaching of reading.

2107 De Boer, John J., and Dallmann, Martha. *The Teaching of Reading*, rev. ed. New York, Holt, 1964. 422p.

A careful analysis of the basic requirements for developing reading skills in the elementary school, with a discussion of appropriate activities.

2108 Dechant, E. V. *Improving the Teaching of Reading*. Englewood Cliffs, N.J., Prentice-Hall, 1964. 568p. biblio.

A valuable reference with detailed sections on phonetic analysis and phonic skills, developing a meaningful vocabulary, and advancing comprehension skills. Includes materials for teaching.

2109 Delacato, Carl H. *Neurological Organization and Reading*. Springfield, Ill., Thomas, 1966. 180p. biblio.

An intensive and enlightening examination of the physiological aspects of reading and learning to read.

2110 Durkin, Dolores. *Children Who Read Early*. New York, TC, Columbia, 1966. 192p.

A report of two studies and their implications. Several thousand children in different schools were tested at the first-grade level and then retested over a period of years. Interview data and the test data reveal important differences in the preschool lives of the early readers and other children.

2111 Fay, Leo, and others. *Improving Reading in the Elementary Social Studies*. Washington, NCSS, 1961. 72p. biblio.

Provides the elementary teacher with practical assistance. Organized around a series of questions such as how to evaluate reading growth and how to cope with individual differences in ability. Valuable for its recognition of reading as a skill to be used throughout the curriculum, not just as a process learned in isolation.

2112   Fry, Edward B. *Teaching Faster Reading: a Manual.* New York, Cambridge UP, 1963. 142p.

Discusses reading improvement patterns experienced by students in classes as well as how the teacher can assist students with reading flexibility and vocabulary development.

2113   Gans, Roma. *Common Sense in Teaching Reading: a Practical Guide.* Indianapolis, Bobbs Merrill, 1963. 414p. biblio.

A general and comprehensive book primarily devoted to beginning and developmental reading but covering also the influence of the home, high school reading, remedial practices, and teaching children for whom English is a second language.

2114   Gray, Lillian. *Teaching Children to Read,* 3rd ed. New York, Ronald, 1963. 446p.

An introductory guide with specific suggestions for the preparation of lesson plans, the use of basal readers, and remedial instruction in the classroom.

2115   Gray, William S. *On Their Own in Reading: How to Give Children Independence in Analyzing New Words,* rev. ed. Chicago, Scott Foresman, 1960. 248p.

A classic for teachers seeking an authoritative rationale and exposition of word recognition teaching techniques.

2116   ———. *The Teaching of Reading and Writing: an International Survey.* Paris, UNESCO, 1956. 286p. biblio.

Focused on the problems of the world's underdeveloped areas, this examines the role of reading and writing in fundamental education, the nature of the reading process in various languages, the efficacy of currently employed methods, and the findings of research and experience.

2117   Harris, Albert J. *Effective Teaching of Reading.* New York, McKay, 1962. 387p. biblio.

An up-to-date, concise explanation of the elementary school (K-8) reading program, with illustrative material and sample plans with provisions for individual and group instructions.

2118 ———. *Readings on Reading Instruction.* New York, McKay, 1963. 466p.

Nearly 100 articles, written over a 20-year period, organized into more than a dozen categories. Not easy but very useful.

2119 Heilman, Arthur W. *Principles and Practices of Teaching Reading.* Columbus, Merrill, 1961. 405p.

Principles and useful suggestions are included in this practical guide for the classroom teacher.

2120 Hester, Kathleen B. *Teaching Every Child to Read,* 2nd ed. New York, Harper, 1964. 384p. biblio.

A discussion of reading as a process of thinking and a description of the development of reading skills, with numerous suggestions for the practitioner.

2121 International Reading Association. *Conference Proceedings.* Vol. 1-   1956-   . Newark, Del.

An annual publication that, although uneven in quality and therefore usefulness, is generally helpful. Each volume has a distinctive title: *Reading and Inquiry* (1965), and *Vistas in Reading* (1966).

2122 Lee, Dorris M., and Allen, Roach V. *Learning to Read Through Experience,* 2nd ed. New York, Appleton, 1963. 146p. biblio.

Reading is viewed as only one of several skills that can be developed on an integrated basis, incorporating the experience of the child in the process.

2123 McKee, Paul G., and Durr, William K. *Reading: a Program of Instruction for the Elementary School.* Boston, Houghton Mifflin, 1966. 498p. biblio.

A detailed description and explanation of a carefully built program of instruction including some excellent ideas gleaned from the authors' many years of experience.

2124 McKim, Margaret G., and Caskey, Helen. *Guiding Growth in Reading in the Modern Elementary School,* 2nd ed. New York, Macmillan, 1963. 454p. biblio.

A practical book of assistance in day-to-day teaching.

2125   Newton, John R. *Reading in Your School.* New York, Mc-
Graw-Hill, 1960. 297p.
Emphasizes that reading and reading instruction are the
responsibility of all teachers in all subjects and offers
specifics.

2126   Reeves, Ruth. *The Teaching of Reading in Our Schools.*
New York, Macmillan, 1966. 120p. biblio.
An introductory overview on reading readiness, the first
steps in reading, essential reading skills, the reading of
literature, and general reading programs.

2127   Robinson, H. Alan, and Rauch, Sidney J. *Guiding the Reading Program.* Chicago, SRA, 1965. 120p. biblio.
For the reading consultant rather than the classroom
teacher. Concerned with developing an overall, district-wide
program.

2128   Russell, David H. *Children Learn to Read,* 2nd ed. Boston,
Ginn, 1961. 612p.
Recognizing reading as a universal skill, the author,
knowledgeable in recent research in the field, discusses a
sequential program of reading development.

2129   Smith, Henry P., and Dechant, E. V. *Psychology in Teaching
Reading.* Englewood Cliffs, N.J., Prentice-Hall, 1961. 470p.
biblio.
An examination of the psychological foundations of the
reading process, the learning process, basic reading skills,
diagnosis and remediation, and reading in the content areas.

2130   Smith, Nila B. *Reading Instruction for Today's Children.*
Englewood Cliffs, N.J., Prentice-Hall, 1963. 594p. biblio.
An excellent exposition of current reading theory based
on both child development and reading research. Reading is
viewed as interrelated with the other language arts. Emphasizes skill development and offers practical suggestions for
use in the elementary grades.

2131   Spache, George D. *Reading in the Elementary School.* Boston, Allyn and Bacon, 1964. 356p.
An analysis of current theories of reading instruction leading to the development of a rational approach.

2132   Strang, Ruth M., and others. *The Improvement of Reading*, 4th ed. New York, McGraw-Hill, 1967. 564p. biblio.

A developmental approach to reading instruction. Includes methods of evaluation, many practical suggestions, and a helpful listing of reading skills in sequential order. This book has had a justifiably long life.

2133   Tinker, Miles A. *Bases for Effective Reading*. Minneapolis, U of Minnesota P, 1965. 322p. biblio.

Not entirely comprehensive but an authoritative and well-documented resource. Covers most major aspects of reading instruction and includes the teaching of adults as well as children.

2134   Umans, Shelley. *Designs for Reading Programs*. New York, TC, Columbia, 1964. 76p. biblio.

An examination of the reasons for setting up a school-wide reading program with practical suggestions for its organization, administration, and evaluation.

2135   _____. *New Trends in Reading Instruction*. New York, TC, Columbia, 1963. 145p.

A description of some of the newer approaches to reading instruction, especially those of supervisory concern: grouping, the use of programed materials, team teaching, in-service education, and evaluation.

2136   Witty, Paul A. *Reading in Modern Education*. Boston, Heath, 1949. 319p. biblio.

Although now somewhat outdated, this is still a useful book. The approach is developmental.

Secondary Schools

2137   Bamman, Henry A., and others. *Reading Instruction in the Secondary School*. New York, McKay, 1961. 266p.

Discusses teaching reading in the major content areas and includes suggestions for the improvement of reading skills as well as a section on remedial programs and lists of materials for teachers and students.

2138   Bullock, Harrison. *Helping the Non-Reading Pupil in the Secondary School*. New York, TC, Columbia, 1956. 180p.

Case materials and suggestions to help teachers understand the non-reading pupil and to work more effectively with him.

2139   Dawson, Mildred A., ed. *Developing High School Reading Programs.* Newark, Del., International Reading Association, 1967. 180p. biblio.
A well-selected collection of reprints from the Association's publications.

2140   Elkins, Deborah, and others. *Reading Improvement in the Junior High School.* New York, TC, Columbia, 1963. 76p.
A report of some imaginative and effective steps taken by three teachers to help groups of junior high school students who were seriously below grade in reading.

2141   Hafner, Lawrence E., ed. *Improving Reading in Secondary Schools: Selected Readings.* New York, Macmillan, 1967. 445p. biblio.
Well-chosen, realistic articles covering every major aspect of the reading program with practical orientation to the complex problems of teaching reading. An excellent handbook.

2142   Karlin, Robert. *Teaching Reading in the High School.* Indianapolis, Bobbs Merrill, 1964. 301p.
A thorough discussion of the nature of reading, problems in reading, and evaluation of reading skills. Attention is given to word recognition, comprehension, study skills, speed, and reading in the content fields.

2143   Marksheffel, Ned D. *Better Reading in the Secondary School: Principles and Practices for Teachers.* New York, Ronald, 1966. 272p. biblio.
A comprehensive handbook for helping students whose reading is below grade, with some aspects applicable to all students, such as teaching technical vocabularies in the various content areas and developing critical reading ability.

2144   Weiss, Morton J., ed. *Reading in Secondary Schools.* New York, Odyssey, 1961. 463p.
A collection of readings organized around a number of areas. Generally useful in spite of some unevenness in the quality of the selections.

Colleges and Universities

2145   Brown, James I. *Explorations with College Reading*. Boston, Heath, 1959. 248p.

Provides models of good writing and a selection of writing useful in effective reading.

2146   Robinson, Francis P. *Effective Reading*. New York, Harper, 1962. 94p.

Sections from the author's more detailed *Effective Study* (#428) explain his "SQ3R" method of reading (survey, question, read, recite, review) and its application.

Adults

2147   Otto, Wayne, and Ford, David H. *Teaching Adults to Read*. Boston, Houghton Mifflin, 1967. 176p.

A guidebook for adult literacy instructors. Presents a general survey and specific discussion of problems. Offers a variety of ideas, materials, and methods as well as a description of scope and sequence of program.

2148   Smith, Edwin H., and Marie P. *Teaching Reading to Adults*. Washington, National Association of Public School Adult Educators, 1962. 71p. biblio.

Recognizes that the adult student is quite different from the school child. Lists a number of activities to enrich vocabulary and encourage critical reading.

History

2149   Mathews, Mitford M. *Teaching to Read, Historically Considered*. Chicago, U of Chicago P, 1966. 218p. biblio.

A well-written, historical account including England and Germany as well as the United States. Traces the changing and often conflicting methods that have been and still are used. A lucid discussion favoring a linguistic approach, based on synthesis rather than analysis.

2150   Smith, Nila B. *American Reading Instruction: Its Development and Its Significance in Gaining a Perspective on Current Practices in Reading*. Newark, Del., International Reading Association, 1965. 449p. biblio.

An insightful treatise on the history of reading instruction in this country, which, with its analysis of successive movements, provides perspective on current practices. Emphasis on 20th century developments.

READING INSTRUCTION—INDIVIDUALIZED APPROACH

2151   Barbe, Walter B. *Educator's Guide to Personalized Reading Instruction.* Englewood Cliffs, N.J., Prentice-Hall, 1961. 241p.

A comprehensive description of an individualized reading program. Provides useful sections on selecting reading material for children and determining reading levels. Includes skills checklist.

2152   Carter, Homer L., and McGinnis, Dorothy J. *Teaching Individuals to Read.* Boston, Heath, 1962. 229p.

Case studies are used as a demonstration of methods for use in the elementary school.

2153   Veatch, Jeannette. *Individualizing Your Reading Program: Self-Selection in Action.* New York, Putnam, 1959. 242p.

Descriptions of programs and methods and persuasive arguments by a well-known exponent.

2154   ————, and Acinapuro, Philip J. *Reading in the Elementary School.* New York, Ronald, 1966. 535p. biblio.

A pioneer and enthusiastic advocate of individualized reading presents theory and detailed descriptions of techniques for use in handling every aspect of the reading process.

READING INSTRUCTION—LINGUISTICS AND PHONICS

2155   Bloomfield, Leonard, and Barnhart, Clarence L. *Let's Read: a Linguistic Approach.* Detroit, Wayne State UP, 1961. 465p.

A theory of teaching reading based on the correlation of a sound image with its corresponding visual or spelled image, a pedagogical approach derived from scientific information not previously applied to the teaching of reading.

2156   Durkin, Dolores. *Phonics and the Teaching of Reading,* rev. ed. New York, TC, Columbia, 1965. 112p.

Examples of classroom procedures are included in this discussion of phonics, phonic principles, and linguistic approaches to reading.

2157   Fries, Charles C. *Linguistics and Reading.* New York, Holt, 1963. 265p. biblio.

Concerned primarily with teaching reading to English-speaking children but provides insights into teaching reading to learners of English as a second language. Deals with basic relevant concepts, history of language study and the teaching of reading, and the nature of the reading process, spelling, methods, and materials.

2158   Heilman, Arthur W. *Phonics in Proper Perspective.* Columbus, Merrill, 1964. 103p. biblio.

A succinct and well-organized discussion of the relation of phonics to reading instruction, including purpose and limitations.

2159   Lefevre, Carl A. *Linguistics and the Teaching of Reading.* New York, McGraw-Hill, 1964. 252p. biblio.

An excellent discussion of the relationship of linguistics

READING PROBLEMS

2160   Bond, Guy L., and Tinker, Miles A. *Reading Difficulties: Their Diagnosis and Correction,* 2nd ed. New York, Appleton, 1967. 564p. biblio.

Designed to give the teacher specific help in the diagnosis and correction of minor reading difficulties in the formative stages before they have accumulated and become a major disability.

2161   De Hirsch, Katrina, and others. *Predicting Reading Failure: a Preliminary Study of Reading, Writing, and Spelling Disabilities in Preschool Children.* New York, Harper, 1966. 144p. biblio.

A highly recommended, useful text. Its Predictive Index, currently being validated, will hopefully become a standard tool.

2162   Delacato, Carl H. *The Treatment and Prevention of Reading Problems: the Neuro-Psychological Approach.* Springfield, Ill., Thomas, 1959. 122p. biblio.

A psychological, research-based approach, which examines the nature of the retarded reader and such contributing factors as sleep and brain injuries. Considers evaluation, treatment, and prevention. Illustrated with case histories.

2163   Fernald, Grace M. *Remedial Techniques in Basic School Subjects.* New York, McGraw-Hill, 1943. 349p. biblio.

A classic work on methods of teaching remedial reading, spelling, and mathematics. Includes kinesthetic and other techniques proven effective in clinical work.

2164   Flower, Richard M., and others, eds. *Reading Disorders: a Multidisciplinary Symposium.* Philadelphia, Davis, 1965. 156p.

      The report of a University of California symposium in which medical specialists and educators explore the identification, diagnosis, evaluation, and treatment of neurological, visual, speech, and auditory problems and their effect on reading disorders.

2165   Gates, Arthur I. *The Improvement of Reading,* 3rd ed. New York, Macmillan, 1947. 657p. biblio.

      A hardy and enduring perennial by a pioneer in the field of reading tests. Presents a diagnostic and remedial program.

2166   Harris, Albert J. *How to Increase Reading Ability: a Guide to Developmental and Remedial Methods,* 4th ed. New York, McKay, 1961. 624p.

      Inclusive treatment of the psychology and pedagogy of reading instruction from the developmental point of view. Covers causes of reading difficulties, evaluation by informal techniques and standardized tests, and reasonable expectations for slow learners. Lists of tests, trade books, plus case studies and a chart summary of word study skills.

2167   Kirk, Samuel A. *Teaching Reading to Slow-Learning Children.* Boston, Houghton Mifflin, 1940. 225p. biblio.

      A discussion of the problems involved in teaching the slow-learning child. Presents techniques for helping him acquire skills for developing maximum reading ability.

2168   Money, John, ed. *The Disabled Reader: Education of the Dyslexic Child.* Baltimore, John Hopkins UP, 1966. 421p. biblio.

      A collection of papers on the origins and many aspects of reading disability and on the teaching methods that may be used. Provides specific techniques and suggestions for the diagnosis and treatment of dyslexia.

2169   Monroe, Marion. *Children Who Cannot Read: the Analysis of Reading Disabilities and the Use of Diagnostic Tests in the Instruction of Retarded Readers.* Chicago, U of Chicago P, 1932. 205p. biblio.

      A classic that has not been superseded. Its thorough coverage includes case studies, methods, and results.

2170 Pollack, M. F., and Piekarz, Josephine A. *Reading Problems and Problem Readers.* New York, McKay, 1963. 242p.

Not designed to give specific directions for the diagnosis and correction of reading problems but rather to develop insights and understandings into the difficulties that besiege the retarded reader.

2171 Roswell, Florence, and Natchez, Gladys. *Reading Disability: Diagnosis and Treatment.* New York, Basic, 1964. 248p. biblio.

An optimistic, practical approach for teachers. Includes illustrative case histories and excellent lists of supplementary readings.

2172 Strang, Ruth M. *Diagnostic Teaching of Reading.* New York, McGraw-Hill, 1964. 314p. biblio.

A useful discussion of reading instruction, especially on a remedial basis. Recommends a program of continuous diagnosis and emphasizes individualized instruction.

2173 Webster, James. *Practical Reading: Some New Remedial Techniques.* New York, Humanities, 1965. 158p. biblio.

Sound theory and practical advice are presented in a deceptively brief, lightly written, and extremely valuable book.

READING READINESS

2174 Frostig, Marianne, and Horne, David. *The Frostig Program for the Development of Visual Perception.* Chicago, Follett, 1964. 168p. biblio.

A guide for developing fundamental visual perception skills, which serves as a diagnostic aid in detecting incipient problems. Covers spatial relationships, perceptual constancy, visual-motor coordination, and figure-ground perception. For use with reading readiness groups and in special classes.

2175 Hymes, James L., Jr. *Before the Child Reads.* New York, Harper, 1958. 96p.

Defines readiness as a stage of development unique to each child and points out that readiness cannot be developed but rather can be capitalized upon by the knowledgeable and perceptive adult.

2176   Monroe, Marion, and Rogers, Bernice. *Foundations for Reading: Informal Prereading Procedures.* Chicago, Scott Foresman, 1964. 208p. biblio.

An excellent reading readiness guide that relates child development to school experiences. A revised version of Dr. Monroe's *Growing into Reading.*

RECREATION AND LEISURE
see also CAMPING AND OUTDOOR EDUCATION

2177   Anderson, Jackson. *Industrial Recreation.* New York, McGraw-Hill, 1955. 304p.

A study of the many aspects of recreation in industry, including both philosophy and management.

2178   Brightbill, Charles K. *Educating for Leisure-Centered Living.* Harrisburg, Pa., Stackpole, 1966. 232p. biblio.

A philosophical analysis of the need to educate for leisure and for effective living. Considers the role of government and school in the more purposeful use of leisure.

2179   Butler, George D. *Introduction to Community Recreation,* 4th ed. New York, McGraw-Hill, 1967. 612p. biblio.

A comprehensive view of the field with a sound theoretical approach. In its succeeding editions it has remained the definitive work, basing its coverage of history, facilities, types of recreation, and so forth on the principle of equal opportunity and on individual satisfaction as the testing criterion.

2180   Carlson, Reynold E., and others. *Recreation in American Life.* Belmont, Cal., Wadsworth, 1963. 530p.

Explores the values in recreation as an important component of living today and tomorrow.

2181   Danford, Howard G. *Creative Leadership in Recreation.* Boston, Allyn and Bacon, 1964. 398p. biblio.

A discussion of recreation in contemporary American life, basic concepts of leadership, and the application of these to a variety of recreational programs.

2182   De Grazia, Sebastian. *Of Time, Work, and Leisure.* New York, Doubleday, 1962. 559p.

A detailed analysis of leisure today. Controversial in many of its concepts.

2183 Doell, Charles E. *Elements of Park and Recreation Administration.* Minneapolis, Burgess, 1963. 340p.

Includes a study of the development of parks and their uses for recreation purposes.

2184 Gabrielson, M. Alexander, and Caswell, M. Miles, eds. *Sports and Recreational Facilities for School and Community.* Englewood Cliffs, N.J., Prentice-Hall, 1958. 370p.

A practical discussion of programs, equipment, and the development and construction of buildings and outdoor areas based on school and community interrelationships and needs.

2185 Hjelte, George, and Shivers, Jay S. *Public Administration of Park and Recreation Services.* New York, Macmillan, 1963. 357p.

A comprehensive outline of administrative practices for recreation services.

2186 Kaplan, Max. *Leisure in America: a Social Inquiry.* New York, Wiley, 1960. 350p. biblio.

A sociological study of leisure.

2187 Kerr, Walter. *The Decline of Pleasure.* New York, Simon and Schuster, 1962. 319p.

A study of the values in pleasurable experience.

2188 Kraus, Richard G. *Recreation and the Schools: Guides to Effective Practices in Leisure Education and Community Sponsorship.* New York, Macmillan, 1964. 308p. biblio.

Examines thoroughly and critically the history and current rationale for leisure education. Covers the problems of leisure and recreation in modern society, the process of leisure education, and the role of the public school in providing or assisting in community recreation sponsorship. An unbiased handling of a sometimes controversial subject.

2189 ———. *Recreation Today: Program Planning and Leadership.* New York, Appleton, 1966. 451p. biblio.

A textbook covering recreation leadership principles and methodology, program planning, and methods of organizing a recreation service.

2190 Meyer, Harold D., and Brightbill, Charles K. *Community Recreation: a Guide to Its Organization,* 3rd ed. Englewood Cliffs, N.J., Prentice-Hall, 1964. 461p. biblio.

A standard and extremely useful work. An overall review of methods of organizing recreation programs.

2191   Nash, Jay Bryan. *Philosophy of Recreation and Leisure.* Dubuque, Iowa, Brown, 1960. 222p.

A truly philosophic approach to the fundamentals of recreation and leisure.

2192   ————, ed. *Recreation: Pertinent Readings: Guide Posts to the Future.* Dubuque, Iowa, Brown, 1965. 265p. biblio.

A stimulating collection of concepts and theories.

2193   Outdoor Recreation Resources Review Commission. *Outdoor Recreation for America: a Report to the President and Congress.* Washington, GPO, 1962. 245p. biblio.

A summary of the Commission's 27 individual reports (also published and available from the GPO), based on the data and recommendations in those reports. Covers economics, needs, guidelines, organization, federal policies and programs, state and private roles, current use, present resources and facilities, and so on. An exhaustive survey that is also a commentary on American recreational habits.

2194   *Recreation in the Age of Automation* (Annals, vol. 313). Philadelphia, American Academy of Political and Social Science, 1957. 208p. biblio.

Outstanding authors contributed to this important collection of concepts relating to recreation today.

2195   Romney, G. Ott. *Off the Job Living: a Modern Concept of Recreation and Its Place in the Postwar World.* New York, Barnes, 1945. 232p.

A pioneering study of leisure in relation to total living.

2196   Shivers, Jay S. *Leadership in Recreational Service.* New York, Macmillan, 1963. 510p.

A comprehensive text covering principles, processes, and methods.

RECREATION FOR THE HANDICAPPED

2197   Case, Maurice. *Recreation for Blind Adults.* Springfield, Ill., Thomas, 1966. 208p. biblio.

A manual for operating recreation programs in centers for blind adults, providing information on the organization, development, and conduct of the programs.

2198   Chapman, Frederick M. *Recreation Activities for the Handicapped.* New York, Ronald, 1960. 309p.

A program book including recreation for a variety of disabilities.

2199   Davis, John E. *Clinical Applications of Recreational Therapy.* Springfield, Ill., Thomas, 1952. 118p.

Discusses recreational experiences as an adjunctive therapy.

2200   Hawley, Esther. *Recreation Is Fun: a Handbook on Hospital Recreation and Entertainment.* New York, The American Theater Wing, 1949. 115p.

A review of the principles of hospital recreation and entertainment. Stresses the need for active participation on the part of patients and the necessity of studying individual needs. Describes programs and games.

2201   Hunt, Valerie V. *Recreation for the Handicapped.* Englewood Cliffs, N.J., Prentice-Hall, 1955. 340p.

Describes the characteristics of people with differing disabilities and types of activities that may be adapted to their needs.

2202   Kaplan, Jerome. *A Social Program for Older People.* Minneapolis, U of Minnesota P, 1953. 158p. biblio.

An examination of the needs of older people and a discussion of the importance of socialization for them.

2203   Lucas, Carol. *Recreational Activity Development for the Aging in Homes, Hospitals and Nursing Homes.* Springfield, Ill., Thomas, 1962. 59p. biblio.

Fills a need effectively. Describes a variety of programs in an area that has received little attention.

2204   Pomeroy, Janet. *Recreation for the Physically Handicapped.* New York, Macmillan, 1964. 382p. biblio.

How to initiate and conduct programs of recreation for the disabled.

2205   Rathbone, Josephine L., and Lucas, Carol. *Recreation in Total Rehabilitation.* Springfield, Ill., Thomas, 1959. 389p. biblio.

Discusses the part played by and the use of recreation in the total treatment program.

2206   *Recreation and Psychiatry.* Washington, National Recreation and Park Association, 1960. 36p.

A philosophic discussion of the role of recreation in the treatment of psychiatric patients.

2207   Rich, Mildred K. *Handcrafts for the Homebound Handicapped.* Springfield, Ill., Thomas, 1960. 104p. biblio.

A guide for homebound pupils, their teachers, and parents.

2208   Williams, Arthur M. *Recreation in the Senior Years.* New York, Association Press, 1962. 252p. biblio.

Deals with program, leadership, organization, and activities in the area of recreation for older people, with a description of the broad range of community resources available.

History

2209   Dulles, Foster R. *America Learns to Play: a History of Popular Recreation, 1607-1940.* New York, Appleton, 1940. 441p. biblio.

A classic historical analysis of popular recreation. Sees our recreational patterns as affected by the continuing influence of inherent puritanism and the complexities of the machine age.

2210   Rainwater, Clarence E. *The Play Movement in the United States: a Study of Community Recreation.* Chicago, U of Chicago P, 1922. 371p. biblio.

A pioneering study and history that remains unique in its contribution to the understanding of the development of recreation as a philosophic concept.

REFERENCE AND GENERAL INFORMATION

2211   *America's Education Press: 29th Yearbook, 1967.* Syracuse, N.Y., Syracuse UP. 192p.

An irregularly published yearbook, which first appeared in 1925, this lists Canadian as well as United States journals. Within the main headings of national, regional, and local associations, the publications are arranged by subject. Includes title and editor indexes.

2212   *Education Directory.* (USOE) Washington, GPO.

An annual publication in four parts: Part 1, *State Governments,* provides the names of state education officials. Part 2,

Public School Systems, lists, by state, all systems, the name of the superintendent, number of pupils, and inclusive grades of each system. Part 3, *Higher Education,* lists, by state, institutions of higher education. Part 4, *Education Associations,* is an alphabetical listing of national organizations and includes the name of the chief officer and titles of publications. Local associations are listed by state.

2213   *Education Index.* Vol. 1-   1929-   . New York, Wilson.

A monthly subject listing, with trimonthly and annual cumulations, to articles in nearly 200 journals, mostly in the field of education. Indexing prior to 1929 was in *Readers' Guide to Periodical Literature,* and until a few years ago *Education Index* resembled it closely as it included author listings. Indispensable if not entirely adequate or satisfactory.

2214   *Encyclopedia of Educational Research,* 3rd ed. New York, Macmillan, 1960. 1564p. biblio.

Happily the fourth edition of this invaluable work is in preparation and presumably it will continue to provide discussions by experts of persistent problems and basic issues in the field of education. The individual articles are scholarly, well-researched, and well-documented. The older volumes are still useful on an historical basis and for subjects no longer included in the newer editions.

2215   Good, Carter V., ed. *Dictionary of Education,* 2nd ed. New York, McGraw-Hill, 1959. 676p.

Definitions of approximately 25,000 terms used in education. Now no longer entirely up-to-date or inclusive but useful as far as it goes.

2216   *International Encyclopedia of the Social Sciences,* 17 vols. New York, Macmillan, 1968.

Complements, without supplanting, the *Encyclopedia of the Social Sciences* (Macmillan, 1930-1935, 15 vols.). A monumental work, which has been more than a decade in the making, composed of scholarly, signed articles covering fairly large subjects within the various disciplines, each with an extensive bibliography. Numerous biographies of persons now dead who have made significant contributions. As this is not a revision but a new work, the original encyclopedia remains a valuable source of information.

2217   NEA. Research Division. *Research Reports.* Washington.

A series of pamphlets, mostly containing statistical information for practical use by school administrators, on such subjects as salaries, other benefits such as insurance programs and leaves of absence, school laws, and so on. Many are revised annually; some are monographs reporting surveys such as *What Teachers Think: 1960-1965,* a report of teacher opinion about school practices. There are about 15 each year, and the information is difficult to obtain elsewhere.

2218   *Standard Education Almanac: 1968.* Los Angeles, Academic Media. 416p.

A new publication, hopefully to be updated frequently as it is a single source of information and statistics covering the field of education comprehensively. Under such divisions as elementary, secondary, and higher education, the federal government, and related statistics, it brings together data otherwise difficult to find.

2219   *The Teachers' Library: How to Organize It and What to Include.* Washington, NEA, 1966. 204p.

A cooperative project of the NEA and ALA, with the help of other professional organizations, this is an annotated subject listing of books relating to instruction, professional standards and preparation, films and filmstrips, and professional journals. Basically a purchase guide with, quite naturally, some bias toward NEA publications, the selections are graded 1, 2, and 3 to indicate the committee's opinion as to whether the titles are essential, very valuable, or merely important.

2220   *What Research Says to the Teacher.* Washington, NEA.

A series of 30-page booklets, now numbering in the 30's, each by a well-known authority in a particular area, which translate research findings into classroom terms. Occasionally revised, each has a selected bibliography. The subjects include such topics as classroom misbehavior, creativity, listening, physical education, and testing.

2221   White, Carl M., and others. *Sources of Information in the Social Sciences: a Guide to the Literature.* Totowa, N.J., Bedminster, 1964. 498p.

Intended for librarians and library students, this is an excellent guide to the social sciences as well as to the literature. The several disciplines, including education, are covered in separate sections, each of which contains annotated lists of references and bibliographies, lists of journals and organizations, and an essay by a specialist explaining the history and methodology of the field.

REHABILITATION
see also VOCATIONAL REHABILITATION

2222   Allan, W. Scott. *Rehabilitation: a Community Challenge.* New York, Wiley, 1958. 247p.

An intensive discussion of ways of planning rehabilitation services for the physically handicapped in communities throughout the country. A broad approach to the several aspects of rehabilitation stressing key facts and general principles.

2223   Barker, Roger G., and others. *Adjustment to Physical Handicaps and Illness: a Survey of the Social Psychology of Physique and Disability* (Bulletin no. 55, rev.). New York, Social Science Research Council, 1953. 456p. biblio.

Discusses the fundamental unity of the somatopsychological problem manifested in the various disabilities.

2224   Garrett, James F., ed. *Psychological Aspects of Physical Disability* (U.S. Vocational Rehabilitation Service Bulletin no. 210). Washington, GPO, 1952. 195p.

Provides guidance for the rehabilitation counselor in planning better programs and points out the need for awareness of the psychological adjustment mechanisms of the physically disabled.

2225   _____, and Levine, Edna S., eds. *Psychological Practices with the Physically Disabled.* New York, Columbia UP, 1962. 463p. biblio.

A scientific study, based on the person-environment constellation, of the role of personal adjustment in the total life situation of the physically disabled.

2226   Hamilton, Kenneth W. *Counseling the Handicapped in the Rehabilitation Process.* New York, Ronald, 1950. 296p. biblio.

A useful handbook that establishes the practicality of the rehabilitation process and its goal of "realization of the greatest competitive capacity, independence, usefulness, and satisfaction of which the impaired person may become capable."

2227   Jacobs, Abraham, and others, eds. *Counseling in the Reha-bilitation Process.* New York, TC, Columbia, 1961. 128p. biblio.

A training institute presentation of critical issues in reha-bilitation counseling techniques, staff relationships, current lit-erature, and research. An orientation in a theoretical frame-work from which practices and concepts may be drawn.

2228   Kessler, Henry H., ed. *The Principles and Practices of Re-habilitation.* Philadelphia, Lea and Febiger, 1950. 448p. biblio.

Articles by medical specialists provide comprehensive cov-erage of the problems of physical rehabilitation.

2229   _____. *Rehabilitation of the Physically Handicapped,* 2nd ed. New York, Columbia UP, 1953. 275p.

A classic presentation by an author of vast experience of his views on the problems of the physically handicapped.

2230   Lawton, Edith B. *Activities of Daily Living for Physical Rehabilitation.* New York, McGraw-Hill, 1963. 301p. biblio.

A discussion based on a functional concept of disability. Provides a basis for standardization of teaching and testing, hopefully leading to more uniform procedures.

2231   Myers, Julian S., ed. *An Orientation to Chronic Disease and Disability.* New York, Macmillan, 1965. 486p. biblio.

Provides a background of information on chronic respira-tory, cardiac, orthopedic, glandular, and other diseases for non-medical people, such as counselors and teachers, who may work with afflicted persons.

2232   O'Morrow, Gerald S., ed. *The Administration of Activity Therapy Service.* Springfield, Ill., Thomas, 1966. 419p. biblio.

The application of management principles to certain modal-ities and agencies in physical therapy.

2233   Patterson, Charles H., ed. *Readings in Rehabilitation Coun-seling.* Champaign, Ill., Stipes, 1960. 342p. biblio.

A collection of noteworthy articles concerned with general principles and practices applicable to all disabilities. Pre-sents stimulating ideas and viewpoints.

2234   Pattison, Harry A., ed. *The Handicapped and Their Rehabil-itation.* Springfield, Ill., Thomas, 1957. 944p.

Contributions from diverse fields provide information about

disabilities and the requisite training and responsibilities of the team of various specialists involved in rehabilitation. Emphasis on cooperation for the team and individualization for the patient.

2235   Ratchick, Irving, and Koenig, Frances G. *Guidance and the Physically Handicapped Child.* Chicago, SRA, 1963. 64p. biblio.

A brief review covering planning, the role of parents and teachers, the enrichment of educational programs, vocational planning, and community resources.

2236   Redkey, Henry. *Rehabilitation Centers Today* (US Vocational Rehabilitation Administration, Service Bulletin no. 490). Washington, GPO, 1959. 231p.

A report, unfortunately no longer up-to-date, on the operations of 77 centers in this country and Canada.

2237   Rusk, Howard A., and others. *Living with a Disability.* New York, McGraw-Hill, 1953. 207p.

A description of the coordinated approach of the Self-Help Device Research Project in disseminating information about self-help devices and gadgets helpful to the disabled in the performance of daily activities.

2238   ———, and Taylor, Eugene J. *New Hope for the Handicapped.* New York, Harper, 1949. 231p.

The story of the remarkable advances made in the rehabilitation of the military presented as a challenge to communities to help all the disabled, civilian as well as military.

2239   ———, and others. *Rehabilitation Medicine: a Textbook on Physical Medicine and Rehabilitation,* 2nd ed. St. Louis, Mosby, 1964. 668p. biblio.

A useful reference and basic text that is a collaboration by medical specialists representing every discipline involved in the field of rehabilitation.

2240   Wright, Beatrice A. *Physical Disability: a Psychological Approach.* New York, Harper, 1960. 408p. biblio.

Integrates the entire problem of physical disability into the context of persisting psychological issues. An organized conception of the somatopsychology of physique emerges that contributes to making rehabilitation psychology an applied science rather than a welfare specialty based on art and experience.

RELIGIOUS EDUCATION
see also CATHOLIC EDUCATION
JEWISH EDUCATION
PROTESTANT EDUCATION

2241   Lotz, Philip H., ed. *Orientation in Religious Education.* New York, Abingdon, 1950. 618p.

Articles on education in the various faiths and covers many areas of concern to religious education today.

2242   Taylor, Marvin J. *Religious and Moral Education.* New York, CARE, 1965. 118p. biblio.

Covers the legal bases of religion in the public schools as well as Protestant, Jewish, and Roman Catholic philosophies and practices of education. Discusses other agencies for religious and moral education.

2243   ————, ed. *Religious Education: a Comprehensive Survey.* Nashville, Tenn., Abingdon, 1960. 446p. biblio.

A collection of articles by 37 specialists that, considering its scope, has remarkable unity and coherence. Covers principles, programs, methods, materials, administration, agencies and organizations, with a cross section of opinion, in Catholic education, Jewish, and many of the Protestant denominations. This survey is done periodically, the last having been in 1950.

History

2244   Poehler, William A. *Religious Education Through the Ages.* Minneapolis, Masters Church and School Supply, 1966. 394p. biblio.

A courageous attempt at total coverage: the history of religious education in various parts of the world from preliterate cultures to modern societies. Major emphasis on Christian education and the benefits of missionary schools in Africa.

RELIGIOUS EDUCATION IN THE PUBLIC SCHOOLS
see also CHURCH AND STATE
LAWS AND LEGISLATION

2245   Beggs, David W., and McQuigg, R. Bruce, eds. *America's Schools and Churches: Partners in Conflict.* Bloomington, Indiana UP, 1966. 241p. biblio.

A selection of differing viewpoints by scholars, educators, and religious men on the issue of religion's place in elementary and secondary schools.

2246 Bower, William C. *Church and State in Education.* Chicago, U of Chicago P, 1944. 103p. biblio.

An argument for the teaching of religion in the public schools, based on the thesis that the public school can teach the content of religion and offer children religious values more effectively than can the home, any special agency, or the church.

2247 Brown, Nicholas C., ed. *The Study of Religion in the Public Schools: an Appraisal.* Washington, ACE, 1958. 229p.

A report of the 1957 Conference on Religion and Public Education. Reviews and appraises prevailing attitudes and existing practices in such areas as religious matter in the teaching of history and public authority in relation to religious education. Includes recommendations.

2248 Dunn, William K. *What Happened to Religious Education? The Decline of Religious Teaching in the Public Elementary School.* Baltimore, Johns Hopkins UP, 1958. 346p. biblio.

A condensation and partly rewritten version of the author's doctoral dissertation.

2249 Freund, Paul A., and Ulich, Robert. *Religion and the Public Schools.* Cambridge, Harvard UP, 1965. 54p.

Freund discusses "The Legal Issue." Clear and precise explanations of the doors that have been closed to religion and those that remain open clarify many of the cloudy issues. Ulich's "The Educational Issue" is a beautifully written summary of the arguments for and against the inclusion of religion in the public schools. (The Burton and the Inglis Lectures.)

2250 *The Function of the Public Schools in Dealing with Religion.* Washington, ACE, 1953. 145p. biblio.

The report of the Committee on Religion and Education, this focuses on public elementary and secondary schools and on teacher education. Offers a frame of reference within which tax-supported educational institutions can operate with respect to religion.

2251   Gaebelein, Frank E., ed. *Christian Education in a Democracy.* New York, Oxford UP, 1951. 305p. biblio.

With an emphasis upon the centrality of evangelical doctrines for an adequate Christian education, this criticizes attempts to introduce religion into the public schools and affirms the belief that the public schools can only be religiously neutral.

2252   Gordis, Robert, and others. *Religion and the Schools.* New York, Fund for the Republic, 1959. 96p.

A collection of controversial articles on a controversial subject.

2253   Hay, Clyde L. *The Blind Spot in American Public Education.* New York, Macmillan, 1950. 110p.

Charts a trend in educational opinion and policy that supports the introduction of studies in religion into public schools, a trend the author approves.

2254   Johnson, Frederick E., ed. *American Education and Religion: the Problem of Religion in the Schools.* New York, Harper, 1952. 211p.

A series of addresses, published originally by the Institute for Religious and Social Studies, Jewish Theological Seminary of America, present Jewish, Catholic, and various Protestant denominational points of view. The opinions are divergent and conflicting.

2255   Moehlman, Conrad H. *School and Church: the American Way; an Historical Approach to the Problems of Religious Instruction in Public Education.* New York, Harper, 1944. 178p. biblio.

A defense of public education. Contains criticism on historical grounds of the vigorous propaganda for the return of the formal teaching of religion to the public schools.

2256   Nielsen, Niels C., Jr. *God in Education: a New Opportunity for American Schools.* New York, Sheed and Ward, 1966. 245p.

Arguing that religion has a place in public education, as a teaching *about* religion rather than *for* religion, the author raises important issues about the future relationship between religion and secular public education.

2257   Sizer, Theodore R., ed. *Religion and Public Education.* Boston, Houghton Mifflin, 1967. 361p. biblio.

A comprehensive scholarly examination of the problem of whether religion should be studied in the schools and, if so, what the content of such courses should be and how they should be taught. Based on a 1966 conference, the papers discuss the question from the educational, religious, and legal points of view.

2258   Walter, Erich A. *Religion and the State University.* Ann Arbor, U of Michigan P, 1958. 321p. biblio.

An attempt to describe and define the place of religion in higher education.

RESEARCH METHODS
see also COMPUTERS IN EDUCATION
STATISTICAL METHODS

2259   Barzun, Jacques, and Graff, Henry F. *The Modern Researcher.* New York, Harcourt, 1957. 386p. biblio.

A standard source on historical research methods.

2260   Best, John W. *Research in Education.* Englewood Cliffs, N.J., Prentice-Hall, 1959. 320p.

Still useful for basic techniques and approaches but sadly out-of-date as far as references are concerned.

2261   Bloom, Benjamin S., and others. *The Taxonomy of Educational Objectives: Classification of Educational Goals: Handbook I: The Cognitive Domain.* New York, McKay, 1956. 207p.

See Krathwohl, David R., *Handbook II*, #2271.

2262   Burke, Arvid J., and Mary A. *Documentation in Education,* 5th ed. New York, TC, Columbia, 1967. 413p.

A complete revision of the classic *How to Locate Educational Information and Data,* which provides guidance for sophisticated documentary and bibliographic work in the field of education. Because of its emphasis on the correct use of library resources and its clarity in describing the use of standard reference tools and government documents, this is actually useful in other fields. Those in education are fortunate to have such an excellent aid to doing research.

2263 Cattell, Raymond B., ed. *Handbook of Multivariate Experimental Psychology*. Chicago, Rand McNally, 1967. 959p. biblio.

A comprehensive survey of the use of multivariate methods in psychological research. Includes some settled issues and some new ideas as well as a critical examination of some abstract models. A readable presentation, primarily for the researcher, of which nearly half is devoted to the application of research in specific areas.

2264 Cook, Desmond L. *Program Evaluation and Review Technique: Applications in Education* (USOE Cooperative Research Monograph no. 17). Washington, GPO, 1966. 100p.

Examines the newly developing area of management of research through network systems. The only monograph on the subject written in terms of educational research.

2265 Cooley, William W., and Lohnes, Paul K. *Multivariate Procedures for the Behavioral Sciences*. New York, Wiley, 1962. 211p.

A highly technical work that presents some of the more useful multivariate techniques and how to compute and report them. Ample discussion of computer programing with the mathematics of particular procedures and computed examples to illustrate analyses.

2266 Culbertson, Jack A., and Hencley, Stephen P., eds. *Educational Research: New Perspectives*. Danville, Ill., Interstate, 1963. 374p. biblio.

A compilation of selected papers presented at three 1961 conferences concerned with the improvement of research in educational administration.

2267 Doby, John T., ed. *An Introduction to Social Research,* 2nd ed. New York, Appleton, 1967. 381p. biblio.

A discussion of the logic and philosophy of science, methods and techniques of research, and research administration, based on the premise that researchers in the social sciences must acquire formal skills and fundamental knowledge of methodology.

2268 Evarts, Harry F. *Introduction to PERT*. Boston, Allyn and Bacon, 1964. 112p. biblio.

Although directed to business and economics and not

stated in an educational research framework, this is useful for its description of the PERT network for those concerned with educational research management.

2269 Green, Bert F. *Digital Computers in Research: an Introduction for Behavioral and Social Scientists.* New York, McGraw-Hill, 1963. 333p. biblio.

A good introduction to computer programing. Covers such topics as digital codes, the structure of computer words, numerical and non-numerical applications, and the logical foundations of computers, with particular attention to research problems of the behavioral sciences.

2270 Kerlinger, Fred N. *Foundations of Behavioral Research: Educational and Psychological Inquiry.* New York, Holt, 1964. 739p. biblio.

A comprehensive text on research methods, research design, and techniques of data collection and interpretation. An excellent presentation for those in education and in psychology.

2271 Krathwohl, David R., and others. *The Taxonomy of Educational Objectives: Classification of Educational Goals: Handbook II: The Affective Domain.* New York, McKay, 1964. 196p. biblio.

With Handbook I (see #2261) these two volumes have been unanimously discussed as "classic" and "landmarks." They attempt to bring order to our basic conceptions and word uses and provide a terminology, with highly specific definitions, that is coming to be used as standard in research and theory development.

2272 Lindzey, Gardner. *Projective Techniques and Cross-Cultural Research.* New York, Appleton, 1961. 339p. biblio.

Intended primarily for the researcher, this defines the projective technique and discusses its varieties, theoretical foundations, and the hazards of the interpretive process.

2273 Phi Delta Kappa. *Symposium on Educational Research.* 1st- 1959- . Chicago, Rand McNally.

An annual series of which each volume covers a particular aspect of research. Recent titles: *Education and the Structure of Knowledge* (5th), *The Training and Nurture of Educational Researchers* (6th), and *Improving Experimental Design and Statistical Analysis* (7th).

2274 Riley, Matilda W., ed. *Sociological Research: a Case Approach*, 2 vols. New York, Harcourt, 1963. biblio.

A highly competent presentation of various research designs, many appropriate for educational research.

2275 Rogers, Everett M. *Diffusion of Innovations*. New York, Free Press, 1962. 367p. biblio.

A basic source for research in educational change processes.

2276 Selltiz, Claire, and others. *Research Methods in Social Relations*, rev. ed. New York, Holt, 1959. 622p. biblio.

Published for the Society for the Psychological Study of Social Issues. Deals with the basic steps of scientific inquiry into social relations and specific methodological problems. Illustrative material included.

2277 Stone, Philip J. *The General Inquirer: a Computer Approach to Content Analysis*. Cambridge, MIT Press, 1966. 651p. biblio.

A reference work on content analysis, presented in the context of past research. Discusses the application of methods in a variety of social science areas.

2278 Van Dalen, Deobald B. *Understanding Educational Research: an Introduction*, rev. ed. New York, McGraw-Hill, 1962. 525p. biblio.

Standard research methodology for graduate students, in an extensively revised edition, with two additional chapters by William J. Meyer.

2279 Young, Michael. *Innovation and Research in Education*. New York, Humanities, 1965. 184p. biblio.

Valuable to the American researcher in the field of education, although the perspective is British. Covers every facet of research, whether university or foundation sponsored, and emphasizes the non-traditional and innovative.

RHETORIC AND PERSUASION

2280 Aristotle. *The Rhetoric of Aristotle: an Expanded Translation with Supplementary Examples for Students of Composition and Public Speaking*. (Edited by Lane Cooper) New York, Appleton, 1932. 259p. biblio.

This first complete treatment of Aristotle's *Rhetoric* is still invaluable in persuasion and communications studies.

2281 Brembeck, Winston L., and Howell, William S. *Persuasion: a Means of Social Control.* Englewood Cliffs, N.J., Prentice-Hall, 1952. 488p.

A thorough discussion of the principles and practices of persuasion for the teacher of written or oral communication.

2282 Burke, Kenneth. *A Rhetoric of Motives.* Englewood Cliffs, N.J., Prentice-Hall, 1950. 340p.

Stimulating analysis and philosophic discussion of the rhetoric of persuasion.

2283 Corbett, Edward P. *Classical Rhetoric for the Modern Student.* New York, Oxford UP, 1965. 584p. biblio.

A good presentation of the principles of rhetoric for present-day speaking.

2284 Crocker, Lionel, and Hildebrandt, Herbert W. *Public Speaking for College Students,* 4th ed. New York, American, 1965. 511p.

A succinct statement of the concepts and principles of the technique of public speaking. A practical rather than philosophical approach.

2285 ———, and Cormack, Paul A., eds. *Readings in Rhetoric.* Springfield, Ill., Thomas, 1965. 599p. biblio.

An anthology of readings covering all aspects of rhetoric.

2286 Freeley, Austin J. *Argumentation and Debate: Rational Decision Making,* 2nd ed. Belmont, Cal., Wadsworth, 1966. 454p.

Although designed for the undergraduate course in argumentation, this is useful in any broad liberal arts course.

2287 Kruger, Arthur N. *A Classified Bibliography of Argumentation and Debate.* New York, Scarecrow, 1964. 400p.

The first comprehensive bibliography on this subject. A convenient reference for debaters as well as for those doing research.

2288 Nichols, Marie Hochmuth. *Rhetoric and Criticism.* Baton Rouge, Louisiana State UP, 1963. 151p.

Rhetorical criticism as distinguished from literary criticism is explored in depth. Complex philosophical problems relating to the nature of rhetoric are clarified, and some important contemporary rhetorical writers are discussed.

2289 Oliver, Robert T. *The Psychology of Persuasive Speech*, 2nd ed. New York, McKay, 1957. 466p.

An interesting and useful study of persuasion for the more advanced students of public address.

2290 Richards, I. A. *Interpretation in Teaching*. London, Routledge and Kegan, 1938. 420p.

A discussion of language and meaning that views rhetoric, grammar, and logic as interdependent and analyzes both the theory and method of teaching them.

2291 Speech Association of America. *A History and Criticism of American Public Address*, 3 vols. (vols. 1 and 2 edited by W. N. Brigouce; vol. 3 edited by Marie K. Hochmuth.) New York, McGraw-Hill, 1943-55.

An examination of the men and women who, by oral discourse, have helped shape American ideals and policy. An important reference work.

RURAL EDUCATION

2292 Archer, Clifford P. *Elementary Education in Rural Areas*. New York, Ronald, 1958. 448p.

A broad general approach that specifically identifies the unique aspects of rural education and gives guidelines for evaluation and improvement.

2293 Beverly, Archie S. *Growing Years: the Development of the Whitmell Farm-Life School*. New York, Vantage, 1955. 196p.

Describes how this consolidated public school in the open country, developing from a two-room schoolhouse, became the dynamic center of a forward-looking rural community.

2294 Butterworth, Julian E., and others. *The Modern Rural School*. New York, McGraw-Hill, 1952. 494p. biblio.

A detailed and stimulating examination of rural education, the characteristics and content of good community education programs, and the ways and means by which such programs might be developed.

2295 Cooper, Shirley, and Fitzwater, Charles O. *County School Administration*. New York, Harper, 1954. 566p.

An informative consideration of the functions of the rural

county superintendent with special emphasis on his role as educational leader.

2296 English, Mildred E. *College in the Country: a Program of Education for Adults.* Athens, U of Georgia P, 1959. 120p.

A description of a ten-year program sponsored by West Georgia College that, through 31 centers within a single geographical area, aimed to help the local residents help themselves move toward improved living and a fuller life as a result of their own efforts and planning.

2297 Greene, Shirley E. *The Education of Migrant Children.* Washington, Dept. of Rural Education, NEA, 1954. 179p.

A report of a study by the National Council of Agricultural Life and Labor of the educational opportunities and experiences of the children of agricultural migrants in Florida, Virginia, Texas, and Illinois, in which needs were identified on which to base a program of action. Sadly, little has been done since to implement the recommendations.

2298 Henry, Nelson B., ed. *Education in Rural Communities* (NSSE 51st Yearbook, Part II). Chicago, U of Chicago P, 1952. 359p.

If the current trend to the cities continues, there may in time no longer be a need to be concerned about rural education. However, at this date, people still attend schools outside of urban and suburban areas, and it appears to be a neglected educational sector. This book identifies the patterns of education oriented to rural life and describes promising programs, problems, and trends. No longer current but not yet replaced.

2299 Kretilow, Burton W., and others. *Leadership for Action in Rural Communities.* Danville, Ill., Interstate, 1960. 346p.

An analysis of the factors of inheritance, social relations, and environment that interact in the experience of individuals in the rural community. Details suggestions for the improvement of rural life through improved leadership.

2300 ———. *Rural Education: Community Backgrounds.* New York, Harper, 1954. 411p.

Deals with the educational and vocational needs of the rural population and discusses the role of the rural school in relation to the needs and position of the community as well as other sources of needed facilities.

2301   Loomis, Charles P. *Rural Social Systems and Adult Education.* East Lansing, Michigan State College P, 1953. 392p.

A report of a study sponsored by the FAE and the Association of Land Grant Colleges and Universities. Describes systems of communication that provide information and attitudes governing action. Covers adult education as carried on in families, informal groups, schools, churches, libraries, colleges and universities, farm organizations, political parties, the agricultural extension service, service organizations, and governmental agencies.

2302   Stevens, Glenn Z. *Agricultural Education.* New York, CARE, 1967. 115p. biblio.

A discussion of the scope and organization of vocational-technical education in agriculture, with chapters on objectives, curriculum, teaching high school students, and the education of adults. Includes instructional resources and administration and supervision.

2303   Swanson, Gordon I., ed. *Vocational Education for Rural America.* Washington, Dept. of Rural Education, NEA, 1959. 354p. biblio.

A collection of useful facts and helpful ideas for the non-urban and often neglected teaching situation.

SAFETY AND SAFETY EDUCATION

2304   Brody, Leon. *Basic Aspects and Applications of the Psychology of Safety.* New York, Center for Safety Education, New York University, reprinted 1966. 21p. biblio.

A brief summary of factors affecting accidents and safe behavior with emphasis on the need for a broad program of safety education at all levels of schooling.

2305   _____. *Human Factors Research in Occupational Accident Prevention: Its Status and Needs.* New York, Center for Safety Education, New York University, 1962. 44p. biblio.

Sponsored by the American Society of Safety Engineers. A selective annotated bibliography on workers and their environment, accident investigation, and safety programing, which points up the need for more research and lists numerous sources of additional information.

2306 Chapanis, Alphonse. *Research Techniques in Human Engineering*. Baltimore, Johns Hopkins UP, 1959. 316p. biblio.

Describes various methods of collecting trustworthy data on men, machines, and the relationships between them. Discusses some principles and guidelines for dependable studies on people, with examples of both good and poor scientific investigations of human factors.

2307 Cutter, Walter A. *Organization and Functions of the Safety Department: Responsibility, Authority, Training of Personnel*. New York, American Management Association, 1951. 31p.

A study of managerial safety practices.

2308 Haddon, William, and others. *Accident Research: Methods and Approaches*. New York, Harper, 1964. 752p.

A compilation of accident studies with critical comments.

2309 Jacobs, Herbert H., and others. *Behavioral Approaches to Accident Research*. New York, Association for the Aid of Crippled Children, 1961. 178p.

Behavioral scientists and researchers consider safety.

2310 Robb, Dean A., and Philo, Harry M. *Lawyers Desk Reference: a Source Guide to Safety Information, What to Find, How to Find It, 1966-67*. Rochester, N.Y., Lawyers Cooperative, 1966. 835p.

This is the latest edition of an invaluable resource whose subtitle is more accurate than its title. Of great value to those working, studying, teaching, and doing research in the field. Up-to-date information on all aspects of safety, with lists of books, periodicals, standards and codes, films, and organizations.

2311 Schulzinger, Morris S. *The Accident Syndrome: the Genesis of Accidental Injury, a Clinical Approach*. Springfield, Ill., Thomas, 1956. 234p. biblio.

A clinical study of 35,000 consecutive accidental injuries.

2312 Stack, Herbert J., and Elkow, J. Duke. *Education for Safe Living*, 4th ed. Englewood Cliffs, N.J., Prentice-Hall, 1966. 374p. biblio.

An introduction to the entire field of safety and safety education.

2313   _____, ed. *Safety for Greater Adventures: the Contributions of Albert Wurts Whitney.* New York, Center for Safety Education, New York University, 1953. 98p. biblio.

A brief biography of a leader in the safety movement, which includes excerpts from his writings on the philosophy and principles of safety and his ideas on safety education.

2314   Strasser, Marland K., and others. *Fundamentals of Safety Education.* New York, Macmillan, 1964. 453p. biblio.

A text for safety educators.

2315   Stratemeyer, Clara G. *Accident Research for Better Safety Teaching.* Washington, NEA, 1964. 32p. biblio.

A brief and thorough review of research.

2316   Tarrants, William E. *A Selected Bibliography of Reference Materials in Safety Engineering and Related Fields.* Chicago, American Society of Safety Engineers, 1967. 152p.

A directory, for teachers and students, of printed material on safety subjects drawn from managerial, scientific, social, and educational literature. More than 2,000 references to books and articles in 36 subject classifications.

2317   *Two Reviews of Accident Research.* New York, Association for the Aid of Crippled Children, 1960. 74p. biblio.

Each review offers a critical survey of information available: "Current Research in Childhood Accidents" by Edward A. Suchman and Alfred L. Scherzer, and "Youth and the Automobile" by Ross A. McFarland and Roland C. Moore.

SCHOOL BOARDS
see also GOVERNMENT AND EDUCATION
LAWS AND LEGISLATION

2318   Goldhammer, Keith. *The School Board.* New York, CARE, 1964. 114p. biblio.

A review of research on school boards and an attempt to apply social theory to this important branch of government.

2319   Hamilton, Robert R., and Reutter, E. Edmund, Jr. *Legal Aspects of School Board Operations.* New York, Columbia UP, 1958. 199p.

Emphasizes the rights, privileges, and duties of the board and board members. Includes excerpts from important cases.

2320 *School Board-Superintendent Relationships* (AASA 34th Yearbook). Washington, NEA, 1956. 502p.

Major aspects of the board-administrator relationships are covered, with perhaps some bias toward the superintendent. Provides an opportunity to see a growth in thinking over the decade.

2321 Tuttle, Edward M. *School Board Leadership in America.* Danville, Ill., Interstate, 1963. 320p.

A traditional how-to approach, offering advice to the school board member: what he should believe and how he should think in order to be a "good" member. Prescription and proscription.

SCHOOL-COMMUNITY RELATIONSHIPS

2322 Campbell, Roald R., and Ramsmeyer, John A. *The Dynamics of School-Community Relationships.* Boston, Allyn and Bacon, 1955. 205p.

A description of the roles of the citizen and the educator and basic principles for working together.

2323 Cremin, Lawrence A., and Borrowman, Merle L. *Public Schools in Our Democracy.* New York, Macmillan, 1956. 226p. biblio.

A plea for greater citizen and community involvement in public education. Gives a brief historical review, offers case studies of students, teachers, and citizens in a hypothetical community, and suggests principles and methods for citizen participation in the resolution of educational problems.

2324 Fine, Benjamin. *Educational Publicity,* rev. ed. New York, Harper, 1951. 561p. biblio.

Since public support of education is to some extent dependent upon public understanding of issues and problems, educators and editors have an important responsibility. A discussion and how-to book by an experienced journalist.

2325 Graham, Grace. *The Public School in the American Community.* New York, Harper, 1963. 556p.

One of the less mundane texts on school-community relations. Introduces some theoretical aspects such as power and participation, mass society, and social relations. Unavoidable were the usual topics such as democracy, the teacher and the community, and even the NEA code of ethics.

2326 Hymes, James L., Jr. *Effective Home-School Relations*. Englewood Cliffs, N.J., Prentice-Hall, 1953. 264p.

A reminder of the philosophy that has dominated the public schools until recently and perhaps still does in some places. Topics covered are group meetings, newsletters, PTA, and teacher attitude. Practical public relations but no reference to broader implications.

2327 Jones, James J. *School Public Relations*. New York, CARE, 1966. 116p. biblio.

A handbook for school officials on the fundamentals of a public relations program. Discusses the conduct of the program, materials needed, responsibilities of all school people, top to bottom, and techniques of evaluation.

2328 McCloskey, Gordon. *Education and Public Understanding*, 2nd ed. New York, Harper, 1967. 622p.

A standard treatment of the subject of school-community relations that does include, however, some theoretical material on communication and leadership as well as some methodological material on citizen participation and the use of mass media.

2329 Olsen, Edward G., ed. *The School and Community Reader*. New York, Macmillan, 1963. 523p.

A compilation of numerous essays about the place and function of education as related to society. An overview of current thinking that, however, lacks a systematic analysis of the problem.

2330 *Public Relations for America's Schools* (AASA 28th Yearbook). Washington, NEA, 1950. 327p.

Not exciting reading, but a solid, practical coverage as contemporary as most community relations books just off the press. One can learn what to do and where and when to do it, but not why.

2331 Stearns, Harry L. *Community Relations and the Public Schools*. Englewood Cliffs, N.J., Prentice-Hall, 1955. 363p.

Emphasizes the importance of a two-way communication system between citizens of the community and educators.

2332 Sumption, Merle R., and Engstrom, Yvonne. *School-Community Relations: a New Approach.* New York, McGraw-Hill, 1966. 238p. biblio.

Direct, practical, and readable approach with several outstanding chapters, such as that which applies power concepts to school-community cooperation and those dealing with the communication process.

SCHOOL BUSINESS AND FINANCE see ECONOMICS OF EDUCATION

SCHOOL PERSONNEL ADMINISTRATION

2333 Fawcett, Claude W. *School Personnel Administration.* New York, Macmillan, 1964. 160p. biblio.

A handbook on employee practices. Includes evaluation, wage and salary policies, terminations, transfers, promotions, work loads, and the like. Proposes a departure from the endorsement system common in public schools.

2334 Gibson, Robert O., and Hunt, Herold C. *The School Personnel Administrator.* Boston, Houghton Mifflin, 1965. 493p. biblio.

A basic text in which administration is viewed as a social process involving four dimensions: proposing, maintaining, allocating, and evaluating.

2335 Griffiths, Daniel E. *Human Relations in School Administration.* New York, Appleton, 1956. 458p.

An early application of organizational theory to educational administration. Chapters on basic concepts of human relations and problem areas of school administration, plus 30 cases.

2336 Gross, Neal, and Herriott, Robert E. *Staff Leadership in Public Schools: a Sociological Inquiry.* New York, Wiley, 1965. 247p. biblio.

Provocative concepts in an examination of the relationship between the leadership efforts of building principal and staff morale, performance, and student achievement. Attempts to understand the influence of personal background and experience and the relationship with higher administration upon principals' leadership.

2337   Hughes, James M. *Human Relations in Educational Organization: a Basic Text in Personnel Administration.* New York, Harper, 1957. 425p.

A broad view and general guide for the improvement of personal relationships between administration and instructional staffs.

2338   Keppel, Francis. *Personnel Policies for Public Education.* Pittsburgh, U of Pittsburgh P, 1961. 50p.

Emphasizes the need for qualified men and women to carry out improved school programs. Examines present personnel policies and offers plans for the future.

2339   Kindred, Leslie W., and Woodward, Prince B. *Staff Welfare Practices in the Public Schools.* New York, CARE, 1963. 117p. biblio.

Based on an analysis of practices in many schools, this gives attention to all aspects of staff welfare and fringe benefits, with emphasis on their influence on and relation to efficiency and effectiveness of instruction.

2340   Koopman, George R., and others. *Democracy in School Administration.* New York, Appleton, 1943. 360p. biblio.

An examination of carefully selected reports to make clear the still valid principles that must be followed to achieve a democratic school administration.

2341   Lutz, Frank W., and others. *Grievances and Their Resolution: Problems in School Personnel Administration.* Danville, Ill., Interstate, 1967. 108p. biblio.

Resulting from a conference on teacher-administrator-school board relationships, this book includes a discussion of the social context of conflict and a simulated case study of a grievance.

2342   ———, and Azzarelli, Joseph J. *The Struggle for Power in Education.* New York, CARE, 1966. 120p.

Economic, historical, sociological, political, organizational, and operational analyses of the problem of teacher power in education.

2343   McKenna, Bernard H. *Staffing the Schools.* New York, TC, Columbia, 1965. 120p. biblio.

Summarizes the various aspects of the interrelation between

staff policies and school quality. Size and kind of staff, principles of selection and deployment, qualifications, and manpower trends as they affect planning are discussed on the basis of research.

2344 Moore, Harold E. *Administration of Public School Personnel.* New York, CARE, 1966. 115p. biblio.
Provides added knowledge and a comprehensive overview of both traditional and current topics. Includes recruitment, selection, placement, promotion, remuneration, and motivation of staff members.

2345 Van Zwoll, James A. *School Personnel Administration.* New York, Appleton, 1964. 470p. biblio.
The author views school personnel administration from the vantage point of general personnel administration and brings into focus the practices and findings of private industry and public administration.

SCHOOL PSYCHOLOGY

2346 Eiserer, Paul E. *The School Psychologist.* New York, CARE, 1963. 114p. biblio.
A broad conception of the school psychologist's potential contribution to the total educational program and to the improvement of educational services.

2347 Gottsegen, Monroe B., and Gloria B., eds. *Professional School Psychology,* 2 vols. New York, Grune and Stratton, 1960 and 1963. biblio.
A comprehensive coverage by experts in psychiatry, clinical psychology, sociology, and education of the psychologist in relation to the school. Discusses psychological skills and techniques, the problems of the exceptional child, varieties of role activities, and administrative and organizational aspects.

2348 Gray, Susan W. *The Psychologist in the Schools.* New York, Holt, 1963. 406p. biblio.
An examination of the role of the psychologist in the school in relation to current and future developments in psychology and to the emerging needs of the schools and the society. Illustrative case examples.

2349 Magary, James F., ed. *School Psychological Services: in Theory and Practice.* Englewood Cliffs, N.J., Prentice-Hall, 1967. 736p. biblio.

A detailed examination of the diagnostic, consultative, and research skills required by the school psychologist. A collection of articles written by specialists.

2350 Rosenbaum, Dorothy S., and Toepfer, Conrad F., Jr. *Curriculum Planning and School Psychology: the Coordinated Approach.* Buffalo, N.Y., Hertillon, 1966. 146p. biblio.

A realistic book, based on a plan used in Newfane, N.Y. Describes how the curriculum specialist and the school psychologist (viewed as an educational specialist rather than a clinical psychologist) can work together with the individual pupil to provide the best learning situation.

SCIENCE TEACHING
see also MATHEMATICS AND SCIENCE TEACHING

2351 Allen, Hugh, Jr. *Attitudes of Certain High School Seniors Toward Science and Scientific Careers.* New York, TC, Columbia, 1959. 53p.

_____. *The High School Seniors: Two Years Later.* New York, TC, Columbia, 1961. 58p.

The first monograph reports a 1957 study of some 3,000 New Jersey high school students. It revealed both a positive attitude and the need for better science teaching at all grade levels—instruction that would emphasize principles and the relation of science to society. The second monograph is a follow-up stressing college study of science and recruitment of science careerists.

2352 Cole, Charles C., Jr. *Encouraging Scientific Talent: a Study of America's Able Students Who Are Lost to College, and of Ways of Attracting Them to College.* New York, CEEB, 1956. 259p. biblio.

A pre-Sputnik study to determine the nature of scientific ability, its supply and demand, and the factors encouraging or discouraging the production of scientists. Detailed consideration of the means of attracting more capable persons to college and to science careers.

412 • SCIENCE TEACHING — 2353

2353   Conant, James B. *Science and Common Sense*. New Haven, Yale UP, 1951. 371p. biblio.

A discussion of science, scientific methods and concepts, reasoning, and experimentation. Of interest to the general reader and, in part, of especial interest to the science teacher.

2354   Henry, Nelson B., ed. *Rethinking Science Education* (NSSE 59th Yearbook, Part I). Chicago, U of Chicago P, 1960. 344p.

————. *Science Education in American Schools* (NSSE 46th Yearbook, Part I). Chicago, U of Chicago P, 1947. 306p.

With the 1932 Yearbook edited by Guy Whipple (#2412), these yearbooks cover the state of science education from K-12 over a period of 28 years and give a picture of changes in curriculum and practice.

2355   Hurd, Paul DeH., ed. *Theory into Action in Science Curriculum Development*. Washington, NSTA, 1964. 48p. biblio.

The report of the Association's Curriculum Committee, which is a ringing call for revision of instruction in science from K-12. Presents a reasonable and possible theory concerning selection of science concepts and experiences for children.

2356   Johnson, Lloyd K., and others. *Research in the Teaching of Science* (USOE Bulletin no. 10). Washington, GPO, 1965. 149p.

An analysis, with selected abstracts, covering the years 1959-1961, and studies completed, 1959-1963. Continues a series of reports on earlier years: *Analysis of Research in the Teaching of Science*, by Ellsworth S. Obourn (July, 1955-July, 1956, USOE Bulletin no. 7, 1958; July, 1956-July, 1957, USOE Bulletin no. 2, 1960, and July, 1957-July, 1959, USOE Bulletin no. 3, 1962).

2357   Marshall, J. Stanley, and Burkman, Ernest. *Current Trends in Science Education*. New York, CARE, 1966. 115p. biblio.

A rich source of ideas and practical suggestions, a timely statement on the necessity of curriculum revisions, and a description of the changes that have taken place in all the science courses of study.

2358   Mills, Lester C., and Dean, Peter M. *Problem-Solving Methods in Science Teaching*. New York, TC, Columbia, 1960. 88p.

Chapters on earth sciences, biological sciences, and physical sciences are presented in terms of problem situations, with suggestions for use.

2359   Nedelsky, Leo. *Science Teaching and Testing*. New York, Harcourt, 1965. 368p. biblio.

Highly unusual, as it is a methods book written by a physicist, this is a rigorous, original approach with an emphasis on testing and test validity.

2360   *The New School Science: a Report to Administrators on Regional Orientation Conferences in Science*. Washington, AAAS, 1963. 92p.

An excellent summary of the new science curricula, consisting of the material presented at nine regional conferences held in 1962 across the country plus excerpts from the keynote speeches of the scientists present at the meetings, which give an indication of the thinking of today's scientists about science education.

2361   Richardson, John S., ed. *School Facilities for Science Teaching*. Washington, NSTA, 1954. 266p. biblio.

A comprehensive and authoritative study of facilities, concerned with room arrangements, furniture, equipment, and supplies.

2362   Roucek, Joseph S., ed. *The Challenge of Science Education*. New York, Philosophical Library, 1959. 491p. biblio.

A view of science education at all levels as a means of stimulating greater interest. Some discussion of mathematics and the social sciences included.

2363   Schwab, Joseph J., and Brandwein, Paul F. *The Teaching of Science*. Cambridge, Harvard UP, 1962. 144p. biblio.

The 1961 Inglis and Burton Lectures, in which Schwab's "The Teaching of Science as Enquiry" explains that science teaching should be "fluid enquiry" based on "stable enquiry": investigation of established principles. Brandwein's "Elements in a Strategy for Teaching Science in the Elementary School" sees science instruction as building toward an understanding of conceptual schemes, a point of view currently receiving much attention.

2364   *Theory into Action in Science Curriculum Development*. (NSTA) Washington, NEA, 1964. 48p. biblio.

Three articles that establish criteria for sound curriculum

development and for assessing the need and direction in curriculum reform and curriculum building in all fields of science at all educational levels.

Elementary Schools

2365 Blough, Glenn O., and Schwartz, Julius. *Elementary School Science and How to Teach It,* 3rd ed. New York, Dryden, 1964. 655p.

A revision of an excellent standard work reflecting both the current changes in course content and the newer, more effective methods of teaching.

2366 Bryan, Bernice, and others. *Young Children and Science.* Washington, ACEI, 1964. 56p. biblio.

A careful analysis of the potentialities of children aged four to eight for instruction in science. Many practical suggestions included.

2367 Burnett, Raymond Will. *Teaching Science in the Elementary School.* New York, Holt, 1953. 542p. biblio.

A still-valid exploration of the nature of science, its potential meaning to the child, and its place in the elementary school program. Description of curriculum and activities.

2368 Craig, Gerald S. *Science for the Elementary School Teacher,* 5th ed. Waltham, Mass., Blaisdell, 1966. 962p. biblio.

A complete revision of the first source book for teachers of science in the elementary school. Contains a wealth of information for teachers, numerous experiences for children, and a consistently forward-looking point of view.

2369 Dunfee, Maxine. *Elementary School Science: a Guide to Current Research.* (ASCD) Washington, NEA, 1967. 77p. biblio.

A review of research findings, opinion, and practice.

2370 ———, and Greenlee, Julian. *Elementary School Science: Research, Theory, and Practice.* Washington, NEA, 1957. 67p. biblio.

Supplies answers, based on research studies, to specific questions asked by classroom teachers. Although no longer entirely up to date, the format renders it of continuing use.

2371 Erickson, Jay W. *The Earth in Space: a Source Book for Elementary School Teachers.* New York, TC, 1965. 274p.

First in a series designed to provide an articulated program of science instruction, this covers content in a readable style and suggests teaching methods, materials, and learner activities.

2372 Freeman, Kenneth, and others. *Helping Children Understand Science.* New York, Holt, 1954. 314p. biblio.

A how-to book for elementary school science teachers.

2373 Gega, Peter C. *Science in Elementary Education.* New York, Wiley, 1966. 451p.

A useful source book for classroom teachers. Several excellent chapters on teaching the processes of science to young children are followed by units of study.

2374 Greenlee, Julian. *Teaching Science to Children.* Dubuque, Iowa, Brown, 1955. 185p. biblio.

A source book for classroom teachers of young children. Describes experiments in the nature of substances (water, metal, etc.), mechanics (movement, friction), heat, rocks and soils, sound, light, electricity, and magnetism.

2375 Hone, Elizabeth B., and others. *Teaching Elementary Science: a Source Book.* New York, Harcourt, 1962. 552p. biblio.

Techniques, demonstrations, projects, field trips, and suggestions for the elementary science teacher reflect the scope of the scientist: observation, thought, imagination, clarification of problems, invention of hypotheses and theories, discussion, and reporting of phenomena.

2376 Hopman, Anne, ed. *Helping Children Learn Science.* (NSTA) Washington, NEA, 1966. 192p.

A carefully selected compilation of articles that have appeared in *Science and Children* over a period of three years, grouped according to content. Covers goals, background information for teachers, experiences for children, evaluation of instruction, and information about funded projects.

2377 Hubler, Clark. *Working with Children in Science.* Boston, Houghton Mifflin, 1957. 425p. biblio.

A source book for elementary and junior high school teachers containing numerous practical suggestions on developing a science program, conducting experiments, improvising equipment, and classroom procedures.

2378   Jacobson, Willard J., and Tannenbaum, Harold E. *Modern Elementary School Science: a Recommended Sequence.* New York, TC, Columbia, 1961. 194p.

Focused on a two-pronged program: a flexible dimension based on children's own questions and experiences and a planned dimension based on six major phases of science. Includes a discussion of goals, administration, equipment, and evaluation.

2379   Navarra, John G., and Zafforoni, Joseph. *Science Today for the Elementary School Teacher.* Evanston, Ill., Row Peterson, 1960. 470p.

A broad and intensive overview of the contribution of science to children's education. Applies the methodology of science education to the content of scientific knowledge.

2380   Piltz, Albert. *Science Equipment and Materials: for Elementary Schools: Suggestions for Supervisors, Administrators, and Teachers* (USOE Bulletin no. 28). Washington, GPO, 1961. 66p.

Offers general guidelines concerning the relationship of equipment to the various elements of the instructional program.

2381   Rasmussen, Margaret, ed. *Science for the Eights to Twelves.* Washington, ACEI, 1964. 55p.

A report of committee discussions covering science in the upper elementary grades, purposes, curriculum and evaluation. Many practical suggestions included.

2382   *Science for Today's Children* (Dept. of Elementary Principals 32nd Yearbook). Washington, NEA, 1953. 311p. biblio.

It seems hardly possible that only 15 years have passed since science in the elementary school curriculum was called "a relatively new subject." With that thought as a base, this yearbook sampled experience and practice in order to describe what to teach and how to teach it.

2383   Tannenbaum, Harold E., and Stillman, Nathan. *Science Education for Elementary School Teachers,* 2nd ed. Boston, Allyn and Bacon, 1960. 339p.

Coordinates child development and the teaching of science,

discusses the goals of the elementary science program, and outlines the means for reaching those goals.

2384 Vessel, Matthew F. *Elementary School Science Teaching.* New York, CARE, 1963. 119p. biblio.

An assessment of current changes in the content and methodology in elementary school science and a recommendation for further change based on empirical data drawn from the nature of science and the nature of learning.

2385 Wensberg, Katherine. *Experiences with Living Things: an Introduction to Ecology for Five- to Eight-Year-Olds.* Boston, Beacon, 1966. 143p.

An appealing, well-written, and well-organized book based on 15 experiences involving reasonably common items of nature: sand and grass, birds, animals, and insects. Natural study is tied to other experiences involving pictures, songs, art, dramatics, dancing, and books.

Secondary Schools

2386 Alexander, Uhlman S., ed. *Supervision for Quality Education in Science* (USOE Bulletin no. 3). Washington, GPO, 1963. 172p.

The report of a 1962 conference of state science supervisors. Consists of 10 papers covering the broad implications of science education in secondary schools, science in the curriculum, and supervision for the improvement of science instruction. Offers some guidelines.

2387 Brandwein, Paul F., and others. *Teaching High School Science: a Book of Methods.* New York, Harcourt, 1958. 568p. biblio.

A foundation for the development of individual patterns in science teaching, which is "not prescriptive but illustrative." An excellent source of ideas intended to help the teacher be imaginative and inventive.

2388 Burnett, Raymond Will. *Teaching Science in the Secondary School.* New York, Holt, 1957. 382p. biblio.

An analysis of the basic problems that must be solved for science teaching to become effective, with a review of the status of science teaching.

2389 Fischler, Abraham S. *Modern Junior High School Science: a Recommended Sequence of Courses.* New York, TC, Columbia, 1961. 127p.

A sequence constructed around three themes: the environment and human needs, the use and control of energy, and frontiers in science, outlined as four units per year for a three-year period.

2390 Ford, Renee G., and Cullmann, Ralph E. *Dimensions, Units, and Numbers in the Teaching of Physical Sciences.* New York, TC, Columbia, 1959. 49p.

Examines the relationship between skills in mathematics and learning in the physical sciences and discusses methods of analysis and certain number concepts to show how they can facilitate learning.

2391 Fowler, H. Seymour. *Secondary School Science Teaching Practices.* New York, CARE, 1966. 113p. biblio.

An appraisal of instructional practices such as lectures, demonstrations, experiments, and field trips. Identifies those approaches and techniques that make for superior teaching and solid learning.

2392 *Guidelines for Development of Programs in Science Instruction* (Publication no. 1093). Washington, National Academy of Sciences, National Research Council, 1963. 68p.

The report of a study that makes specific references to the teaching function of the laboratory in secondary school science programs.

2393 Joseph, Alexander, and others. *Teaching High School Science: a Sourcebook for the Physical Sciences.* New York, Harcourt, 1958. 674p. biblio.

A mine of information for the high school science teacher. Describes a multitude of class-tested demonstration and laboratory procedures, projects, and experiments.

2394 Lacey, Archie. *Guide to Science Teaching in Secondary Schools.* Belmont, Cal., Wadsworth, 1966. 143p. biblio.

Not a conventional methods textbook, but a collection of materials, resources, principles, and guidelines to assist teachers in providing meaningful experiences and to enhance scientific literacy.

2395 Morholt, Evelyn, and others. *A Sourcebook for the Biological Sciences,* 2nd ed. New York, Harcourt, 1966. 795p. biblio.

A vastly expanded revision incorporating Biological Science Curriculum Study material. An excellent basic text with broad and general coverage.

2396   Pierce, Edward F. *Modern High School Chemistry: a Recommended Course of Study.* New York, TC, Columbia, 1960. 109p.

Traces the development of chemistry as a modern science and presents selected concepts for unifying knowledge.

2397   *Planning for Excellence in High School Science.* (NSTA) Washington, NEA, 1961. 67p.

A report offering guidelines for reshaping science courses so they will yield an understanding of the scientific process and not be restricted, as in the past, to knowledge of the subject. Devoted also to studying ways for assuring proper personnel, facilities, and materials for use in future programs.

2398   Richardson, John S. *Science Teaching in Secondary Schools.* Englewood Cliffs, N.J., Prentice-Hall, 1957. 384p. biblio.

A comprehensive offering of methods and procedures in high school science teaching. Includes laboratory work, demonstrations, projects, field trips, etc. Based on the concept that science teaching must be concerned with the social and economic implications of science and technology, problems that transcend the transmittal of content.

2399   Schwab, Joseph J., ed. *Biology Teacher's Handbook.* New York, Wiley, 1963. 585p. biblio.

A product of the Biological Science Curriculum Study sponsored by the American Institute of Biological Sciences. Covers the BSCS approach, guidance in teaching biology as inquiry, basic knowledge in biology and related sciences, and teaching information and materials.

2400   Stone, Dorothy F. *Modern High School Biology: a Recommended Course of Study.* New York, TC, Columbia, 1959. 96p. biblio.

Recent theoretical and practical developments in the field are discussed in connection with detailed units of study.

2401   Thurber, Walter A., and Collette, Alfred T. *Teaching Science in Today's Secondary Schools,* 2nd ed. Boston, Allyn and Bacon, 1964. 703p. biblio.

Specific suggestions and practical help for the science

teacher. Covers the use of experiments and demonstrations, field trips, tests, unit planning, science clubs, science fairs, providing for the exceptional student, and science workbooks.

2402 Vitrogan, David. *Modern High School Physics: a Recommended Course of Study.* New York, TC, Columbia, 1959. 88p.

Incorporates materials resulting from recent advances, giving special attention to the comprehension of basic theories and principles. For classes in comprehensive senior high schools.

2403 Washton, Nathan S. *Teaching Science Creatively in the Secondary Schools.* Philadelphia, Saunders, 1967. 430p. biblio.

An expanded version of the author's *Science Teaching in the Secondary School,* which stresses creativity as an objective to be achieved through inquiry. Excellent coverage of the new approaches to science teaching (BSCS, PSSC, CBA, and Chem. Study) makes this an invaluable reference.

Colleges and Universities

2404 Cohen, I. Bernard, and Watson, Fletcher G., eds. *General Education in Science.* Cambridge, Harvard UP, 1952. 217p. biblio.

The papers of a 1950 workshop whose purpose was to study the means of insuring some degree of scientific literacy to the student whose college years are devoted to the study of non-scientific subjects.

2405 McGrath, Earl J., ed. *Science in General Education.* Dubuque, Iowa, Brown, 1948. 400p. biblio.

A formulation of some general philosophic principles about science courses for the student who does not intend to be a scientist. Based on a study of such courses in some representative institutions.

History

2406 Beauchamp, Wilbur L. *Instruction in Science* (USOE Bulletin no. 17, part 22). Washington, GPO, 1932. 63p. biblio.

One of the series of government-sponsored studies of education in the United States, which appeared in several dozen parts. The author's survey of school curricula and practices across the country revealed a dismaying lack of consistency in aims, content, and teaching procedures.

2407   Curtis, Francis D. *A Digest of Investigations in the Teaching of Science in the Elementary and Secondary Schools*, 3 vols. Philadelphia, Blakiston, 1926-1939.

A monumental work covering published research on science teaching from its beginnings in the early years of the 20th century to about 1937. Focuses on research emphasizing learning and curriculum. Touches on some work done at the college level.

2408   Hurd, Paul DeH. *Biological Education in American Secondary Schools: 1890-1960* (Biological Sciences Curriculum Study Bulletin no. 1). Washington, American Institute of Biological Sciences, 1961. 263p. biblio.

A thorough historical and critical study of the development of high school education in biology in the United States, limited to curriculum developments and investigations of classroom and laboratory learning.

2409   Huxley, Thomas H. *Science and Education: Essays.* New York, Appleton, 1899. 451p.

A collection of essays published a few years after the death of Darwin's strong-minded advocate, which reveal his antipathies to the prevailing curriculum and his conviction that intellectual discipline could be taught best through the teaching of physical science.

2410   Progressive Education Association. *Science in General Education: Suggestions for Science Teachers in the Secondary School and the Lower Division of the College: a Progress Report.* New York, Appleton, 1937. 397p.

A report growing out of a seminar that, in turn, was inspired by Beauchamp's 1932 report on the state of science teaching in the United States. An effort on the part of specialists in the natural sciences, teachers of natural science, and specialists in adolescent development to clarify purpose and practice in science teaching in relation to increasing knowledge of learning and individual needs. It is doubtful whether, three decades later, the central question posed (Is science teaching a mental discipline for the good of society or for the purpose of meeting everyday individual needs?) has yet been answered.

2411   Underhill, Orra E. *The Origin and Development of Elementary School Science*. Chicago, Scott Foresman, 1941. 347p. biblio.

An historical review from the late 18th century. Includes a description of objectives, methods, materials, and content.

2412   Whipple, Guy M., ed. *A Program for Teaching Science* (NSSE 31st Yearbook, Part I). Chicago, U of Chicago P, 1932. 364p.

The first in a series of three yearbooks devoted to science instruction (see also #2354).

SECONDARY EDUCATION
see also JUNIOR HIGH SCHOOLS

2413   Barker, Roger G., and Gump, Paul V. *Big School, Small School: High School Size and Student Behavior*. Stanford, Cal., Stanford UP, 1964. 250p. biblio.

The report of an investigation into the relationship between school enrollment, the number of divisions in the school organization, and student behavior, based on the hypothesis that differences in size affect the educational environment. The authors conclude that the smaller school provides a more favorable climate.

2414   Chase, Francis S., and Anderson, Harold E., eds. *The High School in a New Era*. Chicago, U of Chicago P, 1958. 465p. biblio.

Papers of a 1957 conference. Briefly reviews the contributions of the high school to American society, analyzes the new technological and social demands to which the secondary school must respond, and considers how it can best adapt itself to the new conditions.

2415   Conant, James B. *The American High School Today: a First Report to Interested Citizens*. New York, McGraw-Hill, 1959. 140p.

A critical and controversial examination of the organization and functioning of the American secondary school, considered both radical and conservative. Makes recommendations for modification and improvement.

2416   _____. *The Comprehensive High School: a Second Report to Interested Citizens*. New York, McGraw-Hill, 1967. 95p.

A follow-up to *The American High School Today: a First Report to Interested Citizens.* A summary of offerings in 2,000 medium-sized schools, and a study to determine, eight years after the first report, how many of its recommendations had been implemented. Concludes that the pace is slow but the trends encouraging.

2417 Douglass, Harl R. *Trends and Issues in Secondary Education.* New York, CARE, 1962. 109p. biblio.

An appraisal of the most significant changes now taking place in the secondary school, involving new concepts of learner growth, new and revised subject offerings, new media, flexibility in grouping and scheduling, team teaching, and buildings to accommodate these developments.

2418 French, Will, and others. *Behavioral Goals of General Education.* New York, Russell Sage Foundation, 1957. 247p. biblio.

A statement of a consensus of citizens and educators of what can be expected of high school graduates in the way of thinking, feeling, and acting, as a result of their high school education. In brief, a statement of the goals of high school education in terms of observable behavior.

2419 Johnson, Mauritz, Jr. *American Secondary Schools.* New York, Harcourt, 1965. 150p. biblio.

A well-written, up-to-date, concise description of the diversity in viewpoint and practice in United States high schools, spiced with historical background. An excellent introductory discussion.

2420 Keller, Franklin J. *The Comprehensive High School.* New York, Harper, 1955. 302p. biblio.

The report of a nationwide study of comprehensive high schools and other forms of educational organization. Advocates a fully comprehensive school combining the best features of the academic and vocational schools.

2421 _____. *The Double-Purpose High School: Closing the Gap Between Vocational and Academic Preparation.* New York, Harper, 1953. 207p.

Primarily addressed to those responsible for providing terminal, vocational training as well as college preparatory programs, this deals with a yet-to-be-resolved problem.

2422   National Study of Secondary Schools Evaluation. *Evaluative Criteria: 1960 Edition.* Washington, ACE, 1960. 376p.

A revision of an instrument in use for more than 20 years in discovering the characteristics of a good secondary school. Contains 13 general area and 19 subject field sections.

2423   Stiles, Lindley J., and others. *Secondary Education in the United States.* New York, Harcourt, 1962. 528p. biblio.

A comprehensive, descriptive review of the state of American secondary education in the early 1960's.

History

2424   Commission on the Reorganization of Secondary Education. *Reports.* (USOE) Washington, GPO, 1914-1921.

Sixteen committees, appointed by a joint commission sponsored by the USOE and the NEA, studied the needs of American youth and all aspects of the secondary school, including curriculum, physical plant, articulation with the elementary school, testing, vocational guidance, and moral values. Each committee's report was published as a USOE bulletin, and the final report may be found in the NEA *Proceedings* for 1921 (pages 163-167). The work of this commission was of enormous influence in changing the terminal school year from the 8th to the 12th and in developing the modern high school.

2425   *National Survey of Secondary Education* (USOE Bulletin no. 17), 28 vols. Washington, GPO, 1932.

A survey conducted by Leonard V. Koos of the University of Chicago. Like its predecessor some years before, it covered curriculum and organization but, in addition, studied such topics as the nature of the secondary school population, Negro education, the selection and appointment of teachers, provision for individual differences, and programs of research. The additional studies reflect changes in educational approach and what might be called greater pedagogical sophistication.

SEX EDUCATION

2426   Baruch, Dorothy. *New Ways in Sex Education: a Guide for Parents and Teachers.* New York, McGraw-Hill, 1959. 206p.

A simply written book addressed to parents and teachers, it remains one of the best to deal with the feelings and experiences involved in sex education. Offers facts and discusses various stages of growth from birth through adolescence.

2427 Farber, Seymour M., and Wilson, Roger H., eds. *Sex Education and the Teen-Ager: a Symposium.* Berkeley, Cal., Diablo, 1967. 151p. biblio.

Essays from three symposia at the University of California that discuss the need for providing the adolescent with an education in sex. Helpful to the school interested in introducing this subject into the curriculum.

2428 Hettlinger, Richard F. *Living with Sex: the Student's Dilemma.* New York, Seabury, 1966. 185p. biblio.

A candid and honest approach, neither popular nor academic, to the student's problem. Offers no answers but provides a relaxed, mature discussion.

2429 Johnson, Eric W. *Love and Sex in Plain Language,* rev. ed. Philadelphia, Lippincott, 1967. 70p.

For teachers as well as children, especially junior high school age youngsters. A thorough, factual, frank, and simple presentation. Of special value is the discussion of the varying rates of sexual development.

2430 Johnson, Warren R. *Human Sex and Sex Education: Perspectives and Problems.* Philadelphia, Lea and Febiger, 1963. 205p. biblio.

Well-written, non-technical discussion of perspectives and problems related to human sexuality. Discusses various theories of sex education.

2431 Kirkendall, Lester A. *Sex Education as Human Relations: a Guidebook on Content and Method for School Authorities and Teachers.* Sweet Springs, Mo., Inor Pub. Co., 1950. 351p. biblio.

Relates sex education to total personal and social adjustment and considers the subject from the early grades through college and as related to home, school, and community.

2432 Manley, Helen. *A Curriculum Guide in Sex Education.* St. Louis, State Publishing Co., 1964. 60p. biblio.

A guide to establishing objectives for a K-12 program in sex education. A helpful feature is questions that children ask at various stages of development from early childhood to late adolescence.

2433   *What Shall I Tell My Child? the Scandinavian Approach to Sex Education.* New York, Crown, 1966. 170p.

A source on accomplishments in Scandinavia in sex education and a useful guide in developing programs here. Includes a section on school instruction, and the appendix lists teaching materials.

2434   Wheelwright, J. B., and others, eds. *Sex and the College Student.* New York, Atheneum, 1965. 178p. biblio.

A report sponsored by the Group for the Advancement of Psychiatry. Suggests sound bases for guidelines that college administrators might find appropriate in setting policies for handling sexual issues on various types of residential campuses.

SLOW LEARNING CHILDREN
see also LEARNING DISABILITIES
MOTIVATION AND ACHIEVEMENT
MENTAL RETARDATION AND THE SCHOOLS

2435   Abraham, Willard. *The Slow Learner.* New York, CARE, 1964. 113p. biblio.

A challenge to teachers to identify the slow learner and to set about modifying his school experience to prevent or alleviate his lack of productiveness. Specific advice on how to identify the slow learner and how to use community resources and other available means of assistance.

2436   Cleugh, Mary F. *The Slow Learner: Some Educational Principles and Policies.* London, Methuen, 1957. 186p.

An examination of various ways of providing special educational treatment for the slow learner. Based on the philosophy of starting from the needs of each deviant child rather than from the lock-step system that rejects him.

2437   Featherstone, William B. *Teaching the Slow Learner,* rev. ed. New York, TC, Columbia, 1951. 128p.

A practical approach that, in this revision, includes the high school student and discusses firsthand experiences, more tangible goals, and concrete activities that will help meet the needs of the slow learner.

2438   Johnson, G. Orville. *Education for the Slow Learners*. Englewood Cliffs, N.J., Prentice-Hall, 1963. 330p. biblio.

A discussion aimed at better understanding of the slow learners and the total scope of educational problems they present in order to organize a systematic attack on these problems.

2439   Kephart, Newell C. *The Slow Learner in the Classroom*. Columbus, Merrill, 1960. 292p.

Proposes body development and perceptual training for children who appear to learn at a slower rate than average children. (See also #333.)

SOCIAL ANTHROPOLOGY
see also CHILD DEVELOPMENT

2440   Beals, Alan R., and others. *Culture in Process*. New York, Holt, 1967. 284p.

Draws on the disciplines of anthropology, psychology, and sociology in an investigation of the meaning, structure, and influence of culture from the primitive to the modern.

2441   Benedict, Ruth. *Patterns of Culture*. Boston, Houghton Mifflin, 1934. 272p. biblio.

A classic and influential study of three widely separated and disparate primitive groups in which the culture of each is viewed as a unique and integrated whole and psychological concepts are applied on a group basis.

2442   Doob, Leonard W. *Becoming More Civilized: a Psychological Exploration*. New Haven, Yale UP, 1960. 333p. biblio.

A psychological analysis, based on studies of primitive peoples, of acculturation and its effects on values, beliefs, intelligence, skills, and personality.

2443   Hall, Edward T. *The Silent Language*. New York, Doubleday, 1959. 240p.

An anthropological analysis of culture as communication and a study of non-verbal language and patterns of culture as they affect people in and out of their own culture.

2444   Ianni, Francis A. *Culture, System and Behavior: Behavioral Sciences and Education*. Chicago, SRA, 1967. 134p. biblio.

A delightful and distinguished discussion of human behavior and man's urge to know himself scientifically. Chapters on sociology, anthropology, and psychology emphasize the interaction of formal and informal education.

2445 Kardiner, Abram. *The Individual and His Society: the Psychodynamics of Primitive Social Organization.* New York, Columbia UP, 1939. 503p.

A synthesis of psychoanalysis and anthropology presenting concepts, principles, and theoretical questions based on studies of other cultures.

2446 Malinowski, Bronislaw. *A Scientific Theory of Culture and Other Essays.* Chapel Hill, U of North Carolina P, 1944. 228p.

A posthumous volume summarizing the author's functional theory of culture, which considers cultural phenomena as determined by basic needs and the possibilities of satisfying them.

2447 Mead, Margaret, ed. *Cultural Patterns and Technical Change.* Paris, UNESCO, 1953. 348p. biblio.

A manual intended to guide technical experts at work in underdeveloped countries through brief analyses of five cultures.

2448 Pelto, Perti J. *The Study of Anthropology.* Columbus, Merrill, 1965. 116p. biblio.

A brief overview of this discipline, which includes an excellent section on teaching anthropology.

SOCIAL PSYCHOLOGY
see also EDUCATIONAL PSYCHOLOGY
PSYCHOLOGICAL THEORY

2449 Allport, Floyd H. *Social Psychology.* Boston, Houghton Mifflin, 1924. 453p. biblio.

A pioneering attempt to integrate psychological and psychoanalytic findings into a coherent theory of social psychology. An important book of more than historical interest.

2450 Asch, Solomon E. *Social Psychology.* Englewood Cliffs, N.J., Prentice-Hall, 1952. 646p. biblio.

Well-written but difficult text, with an original approach. Concentrates on the aspects of behaviorism and psychoanalysis that have a direct impact on social psychology.

2451 Deutsch, Morton, and Krauss, R. M. *Theories in Social Psychology*. New York, Basic, 1965. 244p. biblio.

Presents the major ideas of social psychology in the context of the theoretical orientations from which they have emerged, such as Gestalt psychology, field theory, role theory, and psychoanalytic theory.

2452 Erikson, Erik H. *Childhood and Society*, rev. ed. New York, Norton, 1963. 445p. biblio.

Considered a classic in the study of the social significance of childhood.

2453 Heider, Fritz. *The Psychology of Interpersonal Relations*. New York, Wiley, 1958. 322p. biblio.

Focusing on the conscious level, this treats the phenomena of ordinary social interaction, covering thought, feeling, perception, expectation, and reaction as well as the theory of balance.

2454 Homans, George C. *Social Behavior: Its Elementary Forms*. New York, Harcourt, 1961. 404p. biblio.

Studies from the field of social psychology illustrate this presentation of the elements of social behavior (status, influence, satisfaction, justice, competition, and conformity). Explanation of behavior based on theories of economics and learning psychology.

2455 Krech, David, and others. *Individual in Society: a Textbook in Social Psychology*. New York, McGraw-Hill, 1962. 564p. biblio.

An excellent, comprehensive text that imaginatively develops a theory of interpersonal behavior, viewing the functioning of groups and organizations as larger aspects of individual functioning and interaction.

2456 Lindzey, Gardner, ed. *Handbook of Social Psychology*, 2 vols. Reading, Mass., Addison Wesley, 1954. biblio.

An authoritative, critical survey in which the first volume deals with theory and method and the second focuses on the substantive findings and applications of social psychology.

2457 Maccoby, Eleanor E., and others, eds. *Readings in Social Psychology*, 3rd ed. New York, Holt, 1958. 674p. biblio.

Research studies selected as illustrations of the influence of social conditions upon psychological processes. An important, useful rather than representative, collection. The revised edition does not replace the earlier two, as they contain valuable papers omitted from subsequent editions. Sponsored by the Society for the Psychological Study of Social Issues.

2458 McDougall, William. *An Introduction to Social Psychology.* New York, Barnes and Noble, 1950.

Originally published in 1908, this has only historic interest now. Its coverage of human instincts and emotions and the growth of self-consciousness provided the impetus for the establishment of social psychology as an independent discipline.

2459 Mead, George H. *Mind, Self and Society from the Standpoint of a Social Behaviorist.* Chicago, U of Chicago P, 1934. 400p. biblio.

Based on a student's 1927 notes and on Mead's unpublished manuscripts, this is a collection of essays by an influential social psychologist, who viewed the individual as derived from the social process.

2460 Rohrer, John H., and Sherif, Muzafer, eds. *Social Psychology at the Crossroads.* New York, Harper, 1951. 437p. biblio.

A collection of papers from a 1950 conference of scientists and social scientists who discuss some aspects of their various academic fields in relation to such aspects of social psychology as biological factors and human behavior, group structures and individual roles, and interaction in the cultural setting.

2461 Sherif, Muzafer, and Carolyn W. *An Outline of Social Psychology,* 2nd ed. New York, Harper, 1956. 792p. biblio. ·

An integrated, multidisciplinary survey of social psychology based on systematic observational and experimental studies of natural groups and their structure.

2462 _____. *The Psychology of Social Norms.* New York, Harper, 1936. 209p. biblio.

An influential Gestalt-oriented approach to the investigation of social norms. Examines such areas as stimulus situations, the individual in the group situation, and the normation of a norm in a group situation.

SOCIAL SCIENCES

2463 Broek, Jan O. M. *Geography: Its Scope and Spirit*. Columbus, Merrill, 1965. 114p.

As in the case with the other titles in this excellent series published by Merrill, a scholar discusses his field and includes a section of its teaching in the schools.

2464 Commager, Henry S., and others. *The Nature and Study of History*. Columbus, Merrill, 1965. 160p. biblio.

A gracefully written, lucid analysis of the field of history for the elementary and secondary school teacher, with a section on methods of teaching history.

2465 Gottschalk, Louis. *Understanding History: a Primer of Historical Method*. New York, Knopf, 1950. 290p.

A standard reference for historical research and of particular interest to the social studies teacher who is directing his students toward independent study of historical records.

2466 Muller, Herbert J. *The Uses of the Past: Profiles of Former Societies*. New York, Oxford UP, 1952. 394p. biblio.

A well-written survey arguing that there are no patterns to be observed in human history and that the chief lesson we learn from the past is from the achievements made possible by the rationalist human spirit.

2467 Sorauf, Francis J. *Political Science: an Informal Overview*. Columbus, Merrill, 1965. 115p. biblio.

A student of American politics describes political science and includes a section on its instruction.

SOCIAL STUDIES

2468 Carr, Edwin R. *The Social Studies*. New York, CARE, 1965. 115p. biblio.

Documents the changes now occurring in the social studies curriculum. An illuminating statement of the issues and new directions in which this discipline is going.

2469 Cox, C. Benjamin, and Massialas, Byron G., eds. *Social Studies in the United States: a Critical Appraisal*. New York, Harcourt, 1967. 355p. biblio.

Critical evaluation of current teaching in elementary and

secondary schools, organized by subject areas (history, geography, etc.) for the secondary level.

2470 Fenton, Edwin. *The New Social Studies*. New York, Holt, 1967. 160p.

Examines the aims and results of various social studies projects and emphasizes the inductive method of approach.

2471 Gibson, John S. *New Frontiers in the Social Studies*. Volume I: *Goals for Students, Means for Teachers*. Volume II: *Action and Analysis*. New York, Citation, 1967.

Volume I, a reorganized, updated, and expanded version of a 1965 monograph, surveys and examines the many research, development, and curriculum revision projects now underway across the country. In Volume II, articles and reports parallel the first volume and expand and supplement the views and innovative approaches discussed. The two volumes provide an invaluable, informative resource.

2472 *How To Do It Series* (NCSS nos. 1-19). Washington, NEA, 1958-65.

A useful series of brief, inexpensive pamphlets on using motion pictures, textbooks, local history, bulletin boards, newspapers, group discussion, recordings, oral reports, government publications, field trips, community resources, controversial issues, socio-drama, maps and globes, and the like.

2473 Johnson, Earl S. *Theory and Practice of the Social Studies*. New York, Macmillan, 1956. 476p. biblio.

Stresses the interdependence of theory and practice—in the author's words, "the science and the art of teaching the social studies."

2474 Massialas, Byron G., and Kazamias, Andreas M., eds. *Crucial Issues in the Teaching of Social Studies: a Book of Readings*. Englewood Cliffs, N.J., Prentice-Hall, 1964. 278p. biblio.

Articles on curriculum in elementary and secondary schools, methods of the social scientist, measurement and evaluation, and research findings.

2475 _____, and Cox, C. Benjamin. *Inquiry in Social Studies*. New York, McGraw-Hill, 1966. 353p. biblio.

An approach to the social studies based on inquiry and critical thinking, in which inquiry is seen as emphasis on ideas and hypotheses, on analytical rather than descriptive processes, and as the functional use of facts. Of value also for its teaching suggestions, which include questions and a reporting of actual classroom discussions.

2476 ———, and Smith, Frederick R., eds. *New Challenges in the Social Studies: Implications of Research for Teaching.* Belmont, Cal., Wadsworth, 1965. 261p. biblio.

A group of educators cover several major categories in the field of the social studies, summarizing and analyzing current research, translating the research into generalizations useful to teachers, and pointing out where further research is needed.

2477 Michaelis, John U., and Johnston, A. Montgomery, eds. *The Social Sciences: Foundations of the Social Studies.* Boston, Allyn and Bacon, 1965. 350p. biblio.

An introduction to the social science disciplines for the social studies teacher whose teaching, in accord with contemporary recommendations, is increasingly dependent upon a wide range of academic areas with which he may not be comfortably familiar. Chapters by specialists and a summary of current developments make this valuable.

2478 Morrissett, Irving, ed. *Concepts and Structure in the New Social Science Curricula.* New York, Holt, 1967. 184p.

A summary of the results of a conference sponsored by the Social Science Education Consortium. Explores and contrasts the conceptual approach of a number of social studies curriculum projects and aims at stimulating understanding and collaboration between educators and scientists.

2479 NCSS. *Yearbook.* 1st-   1930-   . Washington, NEA.

Consistently of high quality, these annuals are edited each year by leading persons in the field and are focused on particular aspects of the social studies. Recent titles have been: *Skill Development in Social Studies* (1963), *New Perspectives in World History* (1964), *Evaluation in Social Studies* (1965), and *Political Science in the Social Studies* (1966).

2480 Polner, Murray. *Enriching Social Studies.* Englewood Cliffs, N.J., Prentice-Hall, 1961. 64p.

Practical advice for the teacher, outlining methods and suggesting materials.

2481   Price, Roy A., ed. *Needed Research in the Teaching of the Social Studies.* (NCSS) Washington, NEA, 1964. 135p.

An excellent analysis of needed research, mostly at the secondary level but with suggestions for elementary schools. The report of a 1963 Syracuse University Conference.

2482   *The Social Studies and the Social Sciences.* New York, Harcourt, 1962. 303p.

A joint undertaking of the American Council of Learned Societies and the NCSS. Proposes the ideas and concepts that should be part of the social studies program.

2483   Sowards, G. Wesley, ed. *The Social Studies: Curriculum Proposals for the Future.* Chicago, Scott Foresman, 1963. 136p. biblio.

Papers of the 1963 Cubberly Conference at Stanford University. Discusses the present status of social studies instruction and its development in elementary and secondary schools. Emphasis on curriculum innovation in the proposals.

2484   Womack, James G. *Discovering the Structure of Social Studies.* New York, Benziger, 1966. 139p.

A theoretical and practical book that uses an interdisciplinary approach, attempts some generalizations regarding the purpose and curriculum of the social studies, and suggests a coordinated K-12 program, with sample units.

Elementary Schools

2485   Chase, W. Linwood. *A Guide for the Elementary Social Studies Teacher.* Boston, Allyn and Bacon, 1966. 234p.

Many practical suggestions and useful listings. A how-to resource for the classroom teacher.

2486   Clements, H. Millard, and others. *Social Study: Inquiry in Elementary Classrooms.* Columbus, Merrill, 1966. 402p. biblio.

A book for the mature and experienced reader that exemplifies the current tendency to view social *study* as a problem-solving approach rather than as a social *studies* catch-all for several related subjects. Analyzes the use of children's natural curiosity to teach modes of inquiry.

2487   Darrow, Helen F. *Social Studies for Understanding.* New York, TC, Columbia, 1964. 91p.

An amply illustrated description of how social studies can

be made useful and significant to young children. A unit studies approach drawing considerable content from the social sciences.

2488　Douglass, Malcolm P. *Social Studies: from Theory to Practice in Elementary Education.* Philadelphia, Lippincott, 1967. 576p.

Content based on the social science disciplines is skillfully integrated to methods of presenting social studies as stimulating learning experiences. Particular stress on the method of discovery, with detailed illustrative material, as well as a discussion of the use of language arts in the social studies.

2489　Dunfee, Maxine, and Sagl, Helen. *Social Studies Through Problem Solving: a Challenge to Elementary School Teachers.* New York, Holt, 1966. 386p.

A well-written, thorough approach that is a good analysis of current thinking and offers suggestions for helping children engage actively in problem solutions concerning their social environment.

2490　Hill, Wilhelmina. *Social Studies in the Elementary School Program* (USOE Bulletin, no. 5). Washington, GPO, 1960. 110p. biblio.

Reviews practices and trends and offers ideas for developing and improving social studies programs. Drawn from research literature as well as from descriptions and summaries of ongoing programs across the country.

2491　Jarolimek, John, and Walsh, Huber M., eds. *Readings for Social Studies in Elementary Education.* New York, Macmillan, 1965. 481p. biblio.

A well-organized compilation of writings by authorities in elementary curriculum and social studies.

2492　————. *Social Studies in Elementary Education,* 3rd ed. New York, Macmillan, 1967. 464p. biblio.

A good basic text, well revised. Gives excellent suggestions for classroom procedures as well as presenting a clear point of view.

2493　Joyce, Bruce R. *Strategies for Elementary Social Science Education.* Chicago, SRA, 1965. 302p. biblio.

A contemporary approach, as indicated by its title's emphasis on "social science" rather than social studies. Describes content, discusses methods, and lists sources of materials.

2494   Lee, John R., and McLendon, Jonathon C., eds. *Readings on Elementary Social Studies: Prologue to Change.* Boston, Allyn and Bacon, 1965. 447p. biblio.

An excellent collection of articles that examine some programs, discuss the various disciplines, and point out some trends in today's teaching.

2495   Michaelis, John U. *Social Studies for Children in a Democracy: Recent Trends and Developments,* 3rd ed. Englewood Cliffs, N.J., Prentice-Hall, 1963. 624p. biblio.

A comprehensive discussion that relates the teaching of social studies to child development and to youngsters' developing thinking processes. Practical coverage of such topics as organizing instruction, teaching current affairs, group work, and evaluation with suggested reading and materials for classroom use.

2496   Miel, Alice, and Brogan, Peggy. *More Than Social Studies: a View of Social Learning in the Elementary School.* Englewood Cliffs, N.J., Prentice-Hall, 1957. 452p.

An emphasis on the values to be learned from the problem-solving approach and democratic discipline, with a description of existing practices and suggested aids for the teacher.

2497   Preston, Ralph C. *Teaching Social Studies in the Elementary School,* rev. ed. New York, Holt, 1958. 382p.

A tried-and-true source book based on child development. Discusses social trends and research findings and gives specific advice on classroom practices and curriculum.

2498   Ragan, William B., and McAulay, John D. *Social Studies for Today's Children.* New York, Appleton, 1964. 409p. biblio.

A basic source book that discusses some of the more recent programs and emphases in this field.

2499   Shaftel, Fannie R., and George. *Role-Playing for Social Values: Decision-Making in the Social Studies.* Englewood Cliffs, N.J., Prentice-Hall, 1967. 431p. biblio.

A comprehensive study that, although directed to social studies teaching, presents methods and techniques applicable to other subjects and other fields. Describes role-playing procedures, analyzes children's personal and group needs, and examines in detail the process of decision-making.

2500   Tiegs, Ernest W. *Teaching the Social Studies: a Guide to Better Citizenship*. Boston, Ginn, 1959. 562p. biblio.

Sees the social studies as preparation for effective participation in the democratic community and describes an appropriate curriculum, unit plans, skill development, evaluation, and materials. Basically a problem-solving approach.

2501   Wesley, Edgar B., and Cartwright, William H. *Teaching Social Studies in Elementary Schools*, 3rd ed. Boston, Heath, 1968. 354p. biblio.

A good, reliable, standard text. Comprehensively covers theory, practice, and curriculum.

2502   Willcockson, Mary, ed. *Social Education of Young Children: Kindergarten-Primary Grades*, 2nd ed. (NCSS Curriculum Series no. 4). Washington, NEA, 1956. 156p. biblio.

Twenty-five essays concerned with curriculum improvement. Focuses on social growth and experiences. Includes chapters on the use of teaching aids and community resources.

Secondary Schools

2503   Bining, Arthur C., and David H. *Teaching the Social Studies in Secondary Schools*, 3rd ed. New York, McGraw-Hill, 1952. 350p.

A standard work, thorough and practical, with a conservative approach to methods.

2504   Fenton, Edwin. *Teaching the New Social Studies in Secondary Schools: an Inductive Approach*. New York, Holt, 1966. 526p. biblio.

Inquiry as the base of educational study in which the secondary school student places his reliance on the methods of the social scientist and learns from primary and secondary sources rather than from a textbook. Includes lesson plans.

2505   Fraser, Dorothy M., and West, Edith. *Social Studies in Secondary Schools*. New York, Ronald, 1961. 476p.

A sound, comprehensive coverage of curriculum planning, methods, and materials.

2506   Hunt, Erling, and others. *High School Social Studies: Perspectives*. Boston, Houghton Mifflin, 1962. 344p. biblio.

Deals with major themes for the social studies.

2507 Hunt, Maurice P., and Metcalf, Lawrence E. *Teaching High School Social Studies: Problems in Reflective Thinking and Social Understanding.* New York, Harper, 1955. 471p. biblio.

Social studies method is seen as reflective study of problems and the content as data that make understandable to high school students the major value conflicts of today.

2508 Jennings, Manson V. *The Development of the Modern Problems Course in the Senior High School.* New York, TC, Columbia, 1950. 180p. biblio.

An historical examination of the evolution of today's course in problems of democracy.

2509 Kenworthy, Leonard S. *Background Papers for Social Studies Teachers.* Belmont, Cal., Wadsworth, 1966. 248p. biblio.

A workbook for teachers with background sheets on all social studies courses in secondary schools and suggestions for lesson plans.

2510 _____. *Guide to Social Studies Teaching in Secondary Schools,* 2nd ed. Belmont, Cal., Wadsworth, 1966. 400p. biblio.

A comprehensive resource covering philosophy, curriculum, methods, and evaluation, with excellent lists of sources and materials.

2511 Lewenstein, Morris R. *Teaching Social Studies in Junior and Senior High Schools.* Chicago, Rand McNally, 1963. 556p. biblio.

A good, encyclopedic coverage of aims, methods, and material.

2512 McLendon, Jonathon C., ed. *Readings on Social Studies in Secondary Education.* New York, Macmillan, 1966. 414p. biblio.

A well-selected, well-organized collection of articles from education journals on methods of teaching social studies.

2513 _____. *Social Studies in Secondary Education.* New York, Macmillan, 1965. 556p. biblio.

Concerned with social studies as an integral part of the total curriculum. Describes curriculum methods. Helpful suggestions for materials to be used.

2514 Moffatt, Maurice P. *Social Studies Instruction,* 3rd ed. Englewood Cliffs, N.J., Prentice-Hall, 1963. 416p. biblio.

A discussion of a secondary school core program that covers planning units, methods, the various disciplines, materials, and evaluation.

2515 Oliver, Donald W., and Shaver, James P. *Teaching Public Issues in the High School*. Boston, Houghton Mifflin, 1966. 330p. biblio.

An argument for a "jurisprudential" approach in the teaching of social studies, based on the thesis that the analysis of the legal, ethical, historic, and factual issues of public policy is the most effective method of preparing citizens for active participation in a democracy. A technical, not easily read book offering a stimulating and thought-provoking approach.

2516 Quillen, Isaac J., and Hanna, Lavone A. *Education for Social Competence: the Social Studies in the Secondary School*, rev. ed. Chicago, Scott Foresman, 1961. 536p. biblio.

An approach emphasizing the goal of social studies instruction rather than content. Offers appropriate curriculum, methods, and materials.

2517 Selakovich, Daniel. *Problems in Secondary Social Studies*. Englewood Cliffs, N.J., Prentice-Hall, 1965. 292p. biblio.

A discussion of the teaching of high school social studies using the problems approach. Spells out curriculum, methodology, and the use of content from history, economics, sociology, geography, and political science.

2518 Wesley, Edgar B., and Wronski, Stanley P. *Teaching Social Studies in High Schools*, 5th ed. Boston, Heath, 1964. 628p. biblio.

A substantial perennial that provides a thorough coverage of curriculum, methods, and materials.

Colleges and Universities

2519 McGrath, Earl J., ed. *Social Science in General Education*. Dubuque, Iowa, Brown, 1948. 286p.

A survey of the purpose, content, and organization of social science courses at a number of colleges and universities. Describes some innovations designed for students whose primary interest is not in one of the social disciplines.

SOCIOLOGY
see also EDUCATIONAL SOCIOLOGY
SOCIAL ANTHROPOLOGY

2520 Bennis, Warren G., and others, eds. *The Planning of Change: Readings in the Applied Behavioral Sciences.* New York, Holt, 1961. 781p. biblio.

A reference work on planned change that bridges the gap between theory, research, and practice in this area.

2521 Biddle, Bruce J., and Thomas, Edwin J., eds. *Role Theory: Concepts and Research.* New York, Wiley, 1966. 453p.

Sociological essays on the roles assumed by individuals, groups, families, and professional field workers. A reasonably successful attempt to introduce a little understood and relatively new field of scholarly study.

2522 Bruyn, Severyn T. *The Human Perspective in Sociology: the Methodology of Participant Observation.* Englewood Cliffs, N.J., Prentice-Hall, 1966. 286p. biblio.

Exemplifies the "new sociology" in its approach. Discusses rhetorical devices, such as metaphors and analogies, as they bear upon sociological studies, while drawing from all the social sciences, including linguistics. An exploration of the similar characteristics of sociology and the social sciences in relation to the human perspective.

2523 Cooley, Charles H. *Social Organization: a Study of the Larger Mind.* New York, Schocken, 1962. 436p. biblio.

Originally published in 1909, this is a classic study of social organization that covers social classes, institutions, communication, public will, and the democratic mind.

2524 Fromm, Erich. *The Sane Society.* New York, Holt, 1955. 370p. biblio.

An analysis of 20th century democratic society pointing out that as increasing urbanization and bureaucracy lead to alienation, so alienation leads to increasing disinterest in the democratic process. This corrosion can be checked only by fundamental changes in all spheres: economic, socio-political, and cultural. A thoughtful essay with implications for understanding individual behavior as well as for the total process of education.

2525   Loomis, Charles P. *Social Systems: Essays on Their Persistence and Change.* New York, Van Nostrand, 1960. 350p.

The "processually articulated structural model" is presented and its elements discussed. The model is used to account for the behavior of social systems, one with another. Included are descriptions of specific categories of social systems.

2526   Merrill, Francis E. *Society and Culture: an Introduction to Sociology,* 3rd ed. Englewood Cliffs, N.J., Prentice-Hall, 1965. 618p. biblio.

Based upon the unifying theme of social interaction, this examines concepts of culture, social structure, social institutions, and social change. Includes results of studies in the field of sociology.

2527   Merton, Robert K. *Social Theory and Social Structure,* rev. ed. New York, Free Press, 1957. 645p.

A major work including such important concepts as latent social roles (local and cosmopolitan) and reference group theory.

2528   Riesman, David, and others. *The Lonely Crowd: a Study of the Changing American Character.* New Haven, Yale UP, 1950. 386p. biblio.

A now-classic study of the correlation of changes in population and technology with changes in social character in the United States. A provocative exploration combining several of the social sciences, chronologically describing and evaluating modes of conformity. The source of the telling descriptive phrases, "inner-directed" and "other-directed."

2529   Rose, Caroline B. *Sociology: the Study of Man in Society.* Columbus, Merrill, 1965. 117p. biblio.

An authoritative, lucid essay on the nature of the discipline. Offers suggestions for using content from sociology in the basic social studies program.

2530   Russell, Bertrand. *Authority and the Individual.* New York, Simon and Schuster, 1949. 79p.

A series of six lectures concerned with individual reaction to authority and the fundamental problem of how we can combine individual initiative with social cohesion.

SPEECH AND SPEECH EDUCATION

2531   Auer, J. Jeffery. *An Introduction to Research in Speech.*
        New York, Harper, 1959. 244p. biblio.
        A handbook of research methods, bibliographical resources,
        and professional writing for scholars, would-be scholars, and
        those interested in assessing research.

2532   Balcer, Charles L., and Seabury, Hugh F. *Teaching Speech
        in Today's Secondary Schools.* New York, Holt, 1965. 435p.
        biblio.
        Two experienced people in the field have written a prac-
        tical, well-documented reference with an emphasis on meth-
        ods, materials, and the "fundamentals" approach.

2533   Crandell, S. Judson, and others. *Speech: a Course in Funda-
        mentals.* Chicago, Scott Foresman, 1963. 547p. biblio.
        A discussion of speech as a humanistic study. An intro-
        ductory coverage of the practice of speech, discussion, listen-
        ing, and reading aloud.

2534   Fest, Thorrel B., and Cobin, Martin T. *Speech and Theater.*
        New York, CARE, 1965. 120p. biblio.
        Presents the thesis that socialization through speech should
        be of central concern to the educator. Noting the different
        types and functions of speech and the unique role of the
        theater as a setting for speech, shows the numerous ways in
        which vocal expression is used to control and change society.

2535   Golden, Ruth. *Improving Patterns of Language Usage.* De-
        troit, Wayne State UP, 1960. 196p. biblio.
        A study of non-standard language expressions and their
        prejudicial effect on the socio-economic level of the speaker.

2536   Gray, Giles W., and Wise, Claude M. *The Bases of Speech,*
        3rd ed. New York, Harper, 1959. 562p.
        An excellent introduction to the physiological, psycho-
        logical, phonetic, and linguistic approaches to speech.

2537   Huckleberry, Alan W., and Strother, Edward S. *Speech Edu-
        cation for the Elementary Teacher.* Boston, Allyn and Bacon,
        1966. 280p.
        The science and art of speech in relation to speech im-
        provement are discussed, with attention to the development
        of voice, vocabulary, the sounds of language, and normal
        and abnormal problems of speech. An additional bonus is

the book's coverage of reading in unison, solo reading, story-telling, and dramatics.

2538   Labov, William. *The Social Stratification of English in New York City.* Washington, CAL, 1966. 655p. biblio.

A linguistic analysis of social class usage and stylistic usage in the speech of New York City, of intrinsic interest and also because of the spread of Eastern speech patterns through the mass media.

2539   Lee, Charlotte I. *Oral Interpretation,* 3rd ed. Boston, Houghton Mifflin, 1965. 470p. biblio.

An excellent guide to the appreciation of literature as works of art that can be communicated through the voice and body. Discusses basic principles of oral interpretation and analyzes thought, structure, and various devices used by poets, dramatists, and prose writers.

2540   Malmstrom, Jean, and Ashley, Annabel. *Dialects—U.S.A.* Champaign, Ill., NCTE, 1963. 62p. biblio.

Written in response to the need for a serious and authentic treatment of regional variety in American English. Includes student exercises and tests for secondary school students.

2541   Mulgrave, Dorothy I. *Speech for the Classroom Teacher,* 3rd ed. Englewood Cliffs, N.J., Prentice-Hall, 1955. 470p. biblio.

A comprehensive treatment of speech that discusses the teacher's voice and speech as potent teaching tools, the ability to communicate, and student speech. Covers also oral interpretation, group discussion, and speech pathology.

2542   Ogilvie, Mardel. *Speech in the Elementary School.* New York, McGraw-Hill, 1954. 318p. biblio.

An excellent discussion of ways to promote effective communication in the elementary school classroom. Describes the speaking activities that are part of the language arts program and notes the role that the classroom teacher plays in improving children's speech.

2543   Reid, Loren. *Teaching Speech,* 3rd ed. Columbia, Mo., Artcraft, 1960. 424p.

A helpful text for student and teacher, with a focus on the individual pupil. Taken into account are varying abilities, interests, motivations, and attitudes.

2544 Robinson, Karl F., and Kerikas, E. J. *Teaching Speech: Methods and Materials.* New York, McKay, 1963. 535p.

Concerned with the fundamental considerations on which speech education is based and concentrates on teaching methods and materials. Includes some material on organization and judging of contests.

2545 Shuy, Roger W., ed. *Social Dialects and Language Learning.* Champaign, Ill., NCTE, 1965. 157p.

The proceedings of a 1964 conference concerned with relating the language problems of the underprivileged to the needs of today's school.

2546 Stewart, William A., ed. *Non-Standard Speech and the Teaching of English.* Washington, CAL, 1964. 32p.

Three papers dealing with both the linguistic and the pedagogical aspects of non-standard English.

History

2547 Wallace, Karl R., ed. *A History of Speech Education in America.* New York, Appleton, 1954. 687p. biblio.

American speech education from Colonial times to about 1925. All branches of communication are covered, except of course, radio and television.

SPEECH PATHOLOGY
see also DEAF
SPEECH THERAPY

2548 Barbara, Dominick A., ed. *New Directions in Stuttering.* Springfield, Ill., Thomas, 1965. 188p. biblio.

Deals with various aspects of stuttering, including recent research investigations of prominent workers in the field.

2549 Berry, Mildred, and Eisenson, Jon. *Speech Disorders: Principles and Practices of Therapy.* New York, Appleton, 1956. 573p.

An introduction to the field of speech pathology. Includes fundamental information on articulation, aphasia, stuttering, cleft palate, cerebral palsy, hearing loss, and voice disorders. A revision of an older book, *The Defective in Speech.*

2550 Darley, Frederic L. *Diagnosis and Appraisal of Communication Disorders.* Englewood Cliffs, N.J., Prentice-Hall, 1964. 152p. biblio.

Discusses the principles and methods of diagnosis of communication disorders, with major emphasis on appraisal, which is seen as preliminary to therapy, which in turn permits reappraisal.

2551 Delacato, Carl H. *The Diagnosis and Treatment of Speech and Reading Problems.* Springfield, Ill., Thomas, 1963. 188p.

An outline of the basic premises of the neuro-psychological approach to language and reading problems. Essentially an addendum to *The Treatment and Prevention of Reading Problems* (#2162).

2552 Eisenson, Jon. *Stuttering: a Symposium.* New York, Harper, 1958. 402p. biblio.

Deals with various theories of stuttering as conceptualized by prominent workers in the field. Consideration of stuttering as related to psychoneurosis, psychological behavior, organic predisposition, and learning theory.

2553 Johnson, Wendell, and others. *Diagnostic Methods in Speech Pathology.* New York, Harper, 1963. 347p. biblio.

A comprehensive coverage of all aspects of diagnosis in speech pathology, with consideration of principles and techniques of interviewing, speech, voice, language examination procedures, tests, clinical forms, norms, and suggestions for reporting case examinations.

2554 _____, and others. *The Onset of Stuttering: Research Findings and Implications.* Minneapolis, U of Minnesota P, 1959. 276p. biblio.

An analysis of the origins of stuttering, the correlation between speaking and listening (since the problem concerns both), and the differences between stutterers and nonstutterers. One conclusion: the listener does more than the speaker to set in motion the interactions that create the stuttering problem.

2555 Karlin, Isaac W., and others. *Development and Disorders of Speech in Childhood.* Springfield, Ill., Thomas, 1965. 311p. biblio.

A pediatric approach to the development of normal and abnormal speech, with consideration of organic and functional speech and language disorders and suggested therapy.

2556 Luchsinger, Richard, and Arnold, Godfrey E. *Voice-Speech Clinical Communicology: Its Physiology and Pathology.* Belmont, Cal., Wadsworth, 1965. 812p. biblio.

A comprehensive reference work, translated from the German, which is divided into two parts: the first examines voice in all its aspects, normal and abnormal, and the second details normal and abnormal speech and language development and patterns.

2557 McDonald, Eugene T. *Articulation Testing and Treatment: a Sensory Motor Approach.* Pittsburgh, Stanwix, 1964. 189p. biblio.

Concerned with the diagnosis and therapy of articulation disorders in children. Discusses "deep testing" for discovery of inconsistency of misarticulation, and develops a theory of articulation and an approach to therapy based on research.

2558 Morley, Muriel. *Cleft Palate and Speech,* 6th ed. Baltimore, Williams and Wilkins, 1966. 279p. biblio.

The problem of cleft palate and speech therapy for remediation of resultant speech and voice disorders.

2559 Robinson, Frank B. *Introduction to Stuttering.* Englewood Cliffs, N.J., Prentice-Hall, 1964. 137p. biblio.

A well-written, lucid discussion, illustrated with case histories of the etiology and therapy of stuttering. Stresses the dependence of therapy upon the patterns of stuttering behavior.

2560 Schuell, Hildred, and others. *Aphasia in Adults.* New York, Harper, 1964. 428p. biblio.

An examination of adult aphasia based on research findings and concepts developed by the authors. Discusses techniques of therapy based on various phases of linguistic impairments.

2561 Travis, Lee E., ed. *Handbook of Speech Pathology.* New York, Appleton, 1957. 1088p. biblio.

A reference with contributions by authorities in speech pathology and audiology. Describes the nature of the field, organic and non-organic deviations in speech and language, and the relation of psychotherapy to speech habilitation and rehabilitation.

2562 Van Riper, Charles. *Speech Correction: Principles and Methods,* 4th ed. Englewood Cliffs, N.J., Prentice-Hall, 1963. 528p. biblio.

An introductory text that includes fundamental information on stuttering, articulation, cleft palate, and other areas.

2563 _____, and Irwin, John. *Voice and Articulation*. Englewood Cliffs, N.J., Prentice-Hall, 1958. 566p. biblio.

An authoritative coverage of research and therapy in relation to voice and articulation disorders.

2564 West, Robert W., and others. *Rehabilitation of Speech*, 3rd ed. New York, Harper, 1957. 688p.

Comprehensive coverage of the field of speech pathology. Deals with the diagnosis and therapy of such problems as stuttering, cerebral palsy, cleft palate, voice disorders, and hearing loss.

2565 Westlake, Harold, and Rutherford, David R. *Cleft Palate*. Englewood Cliffs, N.J., Prentice-Hall, 1966. 137p. biblio.

An examination of the nature of the problem, its classification, severity, incidence, and causes. Includes discussion of personal adjustment, related hearing loss, speech problems, and rehabilitation.

SPEECH THERAPY
see also DEAF

2566 Agranowitz, Aleen, and McKeown, Milfred R. *Aphasia Handbook for Adults and Children*. Springfield, Ill., Thomas, 1963. 319p. biblio.

Provides an orientation to the field of speech therapy and describes techniques for retraining the cerebral palsied, the hard-of-hearing, the mentally retarded, and others with speech disabilities.

2567 Beasley, Jane. *Slow to Talk: a Guide for Teachers and Parents of Children with Delayed Language Development*. New York, TC, Columbia, 1956. 109p. biblio.

Rich in scientific content and wise in its practical recommendations and discussion of practical procedures, this demonstrates also that technical skill must be accompanied by an empathetic approach.

2568 Black, Martha E. *Speech Correction in the Schools.* Engle-
wood Cliffs, N.J., Prentice-Hall, 1964. 145p. biblio.
   A guide for the speech therapist working in the schools.
Emphasizes proper preparation for this task. A practical
handbook on organizing programs, activities, and practices.
Illustrated with cases.

2569 Eisenson, Jon, and Ogilvie, Mardel. *Speech Correction in
the Schools,* 2nd ed. New York, Macmillan, 1963. 399p.
biblio.
   An introduction to the problems and therapeutic needs of
school age children whose speech requires professional
remedial attention.

2570 Johnson, Wendell, and others. *Speech-Handicapped School
Children,* 3rd ed. New York, Harper, 1956. 464p. biblio.
   Concerns the child with speech defects as he must be
dealt with in the classroom rather than in the clinic and
considers the kinds of defects found among school children,
what the classroom teacher may do about them, and what
the classroom teacher should avoid doing.

2571 _____, ed. *Speech Problems of Children: a Guide to Care
and Correction.* New York, Grune and Stratton, 1950. 265p.
biblio.
   A guide to the treatment of the speech-handicapped child.
Covers functional disorders of articulation, speech retardation, cleft palate and cleft lip, cerebral palsy, voice disorder,
hesitant speech, impaired hearing, and the problems of those
for whom English is a second language.

2572 Kastein, Shulamith, and Trace, Barbara. *The Birth of Language: the Case History of a Non-Verbal Child.* Springfield,
Ill., Thomas, 1966. 182p.
   The longitudinal history of a language disordered child
written by her mother. Describes in detail an 11-year program of home training under the guidance of a speech pathol-
ogist, who provides an introduction and, in a concluding
chapter, relates this story to general principles of speech
education. An unusual and important contribution.

2573 Van Riper, Charles, and Gruber, Leslie. *A Casebook on
Stuttering.* New York, Harper, 1957. 149p. biblio.
   A guide to the examination, diagnosis, and therapy plan-

ning for the severe secondary stutterer. Covers interviewing techniques, attitudes toward stuttering, the stutterer's evaluation of his problem, and emotional factors involved in treatment.

SPELLING

2574 Fitzgerald, James A. *The Teaching of Spelling.* Milwaukee, Bruce, 1951. 233p. biblio.
A basic text covering methods, materials, techniques, and testing. Includes enrichment exercises and activities to encourage vocabulary growth.

2575 Hildreth, Gertrude H. *Teaching Spelling: a Guide to Basic Principles and Practices.* New York, Holt, 1955. 346p.
Approaches spelling as a vital tool for writing and an integral phase of the language arts. Covers the learning process in spelling and word usage as well as instructional techniques.

STATISTICAL METHODS
see also RESEARCH METHODS

2576 Fischer, Ronald A. *Statistical Methods for Research Workers,* 13th ed. New York, Hafner, 1958. 356p.
A classic that examines statistical methods and advanced statistical problems as well as presenting practical procedures based on mathematical theory.

2577 Garrett, Henry E. *Statistics in Psychology and Education,* 6th ed. New York, McKay, 1966. 491p. biblio.
The application of statistical methods to problems in psychology and education. Covers descriptive statistics, inference and prediction, correlation, and test construction.

2578 Harman, Harry H. *Modern Factor Analysis.* Chicago, U of Chicago P, 1960. 469p. biblio.
An excellent, rather technical coverage of the historical background and basic notions of factor analysis, the resolution of observed variables in terms of the factors, and the use of the computer.

2579   Meyer, Donald L. *Educational Statistics*. New York, CARE, 1967. 116p. biblio.

The basics of probability, frequency and probability distributions and summarization of these distributions, estimation and hypothesis testing for the simple cases, the elements of Bayesian inference, and a treatment of relationship and prediction. Illustrative examples are included in this succinctly comprehensive book.

2580   Mosteller, Frederick, and others. *Probability and Statistics*. Reading, Mass., Addison Wesley, 1961. 395p.

An introductory text for the beginner, based on elementary algebra and designed to be used with a minimum of guidance.

2581   Siegel, Sidney. *Nonparametric Statistics for the Behavioral Sciences*. New York, McGraw-Hill, 1956. 312p. biblio.

A thorough coverage of the nonparametric techniques of hypothesis testing uniquely suited to the data of the behavioral sciences, as well as the tests themselves, data, proof, computation, and some comparison of parametric with nonparametric tests.

2582   Winer, B. J. *Statistical Principles in Experimental Design*. New York, McGraw-Hill, 1962. 672p. biblio.

A reference source on statistical principles underlying experimental design, primarily for research in the behavioral sciences. Covers basic concepts in statistical inference, testing hypotheses for means and variances, and design and analysis of single-factor experiments.

STORYTELLING AND DRAMATICS
see also CHILDREN'S LITERATURE

2583   Chilver, Peter. *Staging a School Play*. New York, Harper, 1968. 160p.

A practical and useful book focusing on the educational purposes of school plays. Gives excellent advice on every aspect of play selection, production, and direction.

2584   Lease, Ruth, and Siks, Geraldine B. *Creative Dramatics in Home, School, and Community*. New York, Harper, 1952. 306p. biblio.

A practical handbook that defines creative dramatics, discusses its value to children, and offers suggestions for its use in the elementary school.

2585 Sawyer, Ruth. *The Way of the Storyteller*. New York, Viking, 1942. 318p.

The dos and don'ts of telling stories to children, emphasizing that it is an art requiring practice and rehearsal. A few selections included.

2586 Shedlock, Marie L. *The Art of Storytelling*, 3rd ed. New York, Dover, 1951. 290p.

Briefly surveys the history, development, and changes in the art of storytelling. Focuses on formal storytelling to audiences, with suggestions for the novice and for the experienced storyteller.

2587 Siks, Geraldine B. *Children's Literature for Dramatization*. New York, Harper, 1964. 331p. biblio.

An anthology of dramatic literature (stories and verse) for children from four to 14 years of age, selected for enjoyment and for creative dramatics. Arranged in accordance with dramatic complexity. Title, age-level, and subject indexes.

2588 Ward, Winifred. *Playmaking with Children from Kindergarten to High School*, 2nd ed. New York, Appleton, 1957. 341p. biblio.

A unique examination of the creative use of drama, movement, dance, and informal conversation to enable children to release their own imaginative forces and "compose" experiences they have never had or recreate those they have experienced. Careful consideration is given to the adult's role as guide, mediator, and catalyst.

STUDENT TEACHING

2589 Adams, Harold P., and Dickey, Frank G. *Basic Principles of Student Teaching*. New York, American, 1956. 372p. biblio.

Based on the concept that the preparation of teachers is truly a professional task, this is a straightforward presentation of principles, less idealistic than some, and genuinely useful.

2590 Andrews, Leonard O. *Student Teaching*. New York, CARE, 1964. 116p. biblio.

A critical appraisal of what student teaching is today and

a challenging picture of what it might and should be as the result of improved use of talent, resources, knowledge, and research.

2591 Association for Student Teaching. *Yearbook.* Vol. 1-   1921-
Cedar Falls, Iowa.

Each annual examines a particular aspect of student teaching. Some notable titles of especial interest are: *Evaluating Student Teaching* (1960), *Teacher Education and the Public Schools* (1961), and *The College Supervisor: Conflict and Challenge* (1964).

2592 Batchelder, Howard T., and others. *Student Teaching in Secondary Schools,* 4th ed. New York, McGraw-Hill, 1964. 340p. biblio.

A standard work and basic reference enabling the student teacher to integrate philosophy, psychology, curriculum, methods, and the needs of children into a single pattern of knowledge. Principal author of original edition was Raleigh Schorling.

2593 Curtis, Dwight K., and Andrews, Leonard O. *Guiding Your Student Teacher.* Englewood Cliffs, N.J., Prentice-Hall, 1954. 384p.

A useful handbook for supervisors of student teachers.

2594 Lindsey, Margaret, and Gruhn, William T. *Student Teaching in the Elementary School.* New York, Ronald Press, 1957. 214p. biblio.

A superior text for the student teacher. Deals with the common problems he faces, considers the teacher's responsibilities to the school, to the community, and to himself for continuous improvement, and helps to integrate formal educational theory into practice.

2595 Steeves, Frank L. *Issues in Student Teaching: a Casebook with Related Problems in Teacher Education.* New York, Odyssey, 1963. 324p. biblio.

Designed for supervising teachers, this describes the case study as a method of teaching and learning. Suggests group procedures for student teaching and for supervision and covers basic concepts and patterns, relationships during student teaching, administrative and supervisory problems, placement, and follow-up.

2596   Woodruff, Asahel D. *Student Teaching Today: a Survey of Selected Aspects of Student Teaching.* Washington, American Association of Colleges for Teacher Education, 1960. 50p. biblio.

A review of current literature and of present and past practices. Includes a proposal for a state-wide student teaching program and other suggestions for improving the quality of present programs.

SUPERVISION IN EDUCATION

2597   Adams, Harold P., and Dickey, Frank G. *Basic Principles of Supervision.* New York, American, 1953. 320p.

Based upon the concept that there are certain skills and competencies necessary for supervisors to be effective in improving instruction. Examples given to illustrate principles.

2598   Douglass, Harl R., and others. *Democratic Supervision in Secondary Schools,* 2nd ed. Boston, Houghton Mifflin, 1961. 354p. biblio.

A basic text on the philosophy of supervision, techniques, the application of techniques, and appraising the supervisory program.

2599   Lucio, William H., and McNeil, John D. *Supervision: a Synthesis of Thought and Action.* New York, McGraw-Hill, 1962. 282p. biblio.

An introduction to instructional supervision containing a theoretical perspective of supervisory processes and requisite skills.

2600   McKean, Robert, and Mills, H. H. *The Supervisor.* New York, CARE, 1964. 118p. biblio.

A thorough examination of all aspects of supervision and the responsibilities of the supervisor. Well-written, readable, and reflects current thinking and research.

2601   Wiles, Kimball. *Supervision for Better Schools: the Role of the Official Leader in Program Development,* 3rd ed. Englewood Cliffs, N.J., Prentice-Hall, 1967. 343p. biblio.

Supervision is seen as the release of the creative talents

of teachers, children, and the community. Defines and discusses supervision as skill in leadership, human relations, group process, evaluation, and personnel administration.

2602   Williamson, Margaret. *Supervision: New Patterns and Processes.* New York, Association, 1961. 176p. biblio.

The practice of supervision in relation to group methods in service agencies, dealing with objectives and functions, supervision as an educational process, the supervisory relationship, recruitment and selection of personnel, and interviewing.

TEACHER EDUCATION

2603   Axelrod, Joseph, ed. *Graduate Study for Future College Teachers.* Washington, ACE, 1959. 114p.

The complete report of the Conference on College Teacher Preparation Programs. Includes discussion of program planning at the graduate level.

2604   Barker, H. Kenneth, ed. *AACTE Handbook of International Education Programs.* Washington, American Association of Colleges for Teacher Education, 1963. 72p.

Created to guide college and university administrators, especially those in the field of teacher education, through the bewildering number of international programs in existence.

2605   Beggs, Walter K. *The Education of Teachers.* New York, CARE, 1965. 116p. biblio.

Concerned with the classroom teacher at elementary and secondary levels. Summarizes current programs and proposes that teacher education be based on the impact of the learning process on the student and on the kind of person who is needed as a teacher.

2606   Broudy, Harry S. *The Scholars and the Public School.* Columbus, College of Education, Ohio State University, 1964. 71p.

Two lectures delivered in 1963. They discuss education as a field of study and the problems and dimensions of professional study. Mr. Broudy says, "At stake is the control of the schools and the crucial battle is for control of the training of teachers, administrators, and other school personnel."

2607   Conant, James B. *The Education of American Teachers.* New York, McGraw-Hill, 1963. 275p. biblio.

A provocative study of teacher education. Like other Conant reports, it disappointed some by being too conservative and infuriated others by being too rash. Includes 28 recommendations for the improvement of teacher education programs, which stress the need for more experimentation and less restrictive certification requirements. The New York State Education Department has issued an interim report (1967) on a Five College Project for Innovation in Teacher Education, a three-year joint venture designed to give a practical test to Conant's thesis.

2608 Elam, Stanley M., ed. *Improving Teacher Education in the United States*. Bloomington, Ind., Phi Delta Kappa, 1967. 214p. biblio.

The report of a 1965 symposium jointly sponsored by Phi Delta Kappa and Stanford University. Assesses teacher preparation today and makes specific recommendations.

2609 *The Graduate Study of Education: Report of the Harvard Committee*. Cambridge, Harvard UP, 1965. 65p.

Although focused entirely on the particular school in the particular university, this study of the best use of resources to improve the quality of teacher education has implications for all teacher training institutions.

2610 Grommon, Alfred H., ed. *The Education of Teachers of English for American Schools and Colleges* (NCTE Curriculum series, vol. V). New York, Appleton, 1963. 604p. biblio.

Discusses current and recommended preparation of elementary, secondary, and college teachers as well as the continuing education of elementary and secondary teachers.

2611 Henry, Nelson B., ed. *Graduate Study in Education* (NSSE 50th Yearbook, Part I). Chicago, U of Chicago P, 1951. 369p.

Theory, practice, and the status of the organization and administration of graduate programs in teacher education.

2612 Hodenfield, G. K., and Stinnett, Timothy M. *The Education of Teachers: Conflict and Consensus*. Englewood Cliffs, N.J., Prentice-Hall, 1961. 177p.

A summary of the conflicts between warring elements in the field of education: the liberal arts college vs. the teachers college, the private vs. the public institution, and the academic professors vs. the teacher training professors.

2613 Holbrook, David. *The Exploring Word: Creative Disciplines in the Education of Teachers of English.* New York, Cambridge UP, 1967. 283p. biblio.

Although geared to the British system, this has some valid criticisms and creative suggestions.

2614 Houston, W. Robert, ed. *Improving Mathematics Education for Elementary School Teachers.* East Lansing, College of Education, Michigan State University, 1967. 105p.

The report of a 1967 conference on improving the education of teachers of mathematics. Focuses on the instructional aspects of presenting the content of the newer programs: a blend of current knowledge of psychology, mathematics, and educational methods.

2615 Koerner, James D. *The Miseducation of American Teachers.* Boston, Houghton Mifflin, 1963. 360p. biblio.

A lively attack on teacher training institutions. Views the inferior intellectual quality of education faculty as the fundamental problem and calls for overhauling the curriculum, upgrading admission standards and requirements, and better instruction.

2616 Lindsey, Margaret, ed. *New Horizons for the Teaching Profession.* (National Commission on Teacher Education and Professional Standards) Washington, NEA, 1961. 243p.

The report of a committee that makes recommendations for the improvement of teacher education in the areas of professional standards, teacher education, accreditation, certification, and admission standards. Develops definitive statements that can be used as guidelines for action programs working toward the professionalization of teaching.

2617 Masoner, Paul H. *A Design for Teacher Education.* Pittsburgh, U of Pittsburgh P, 1964. 42p.

A lecture outlining a Utopian dream. A rigorously selected, highly qualified and motivated student body spends five years in fertile learning situations wherein liberal and professional studies are integrated, as are theory and practice, and the culminating experience is a true internship.

2618 Mayor, John R., and Swartz, Willis G. *Accreditation in Teacher Education: Its Influence on Higher Education.* Washington, ACE, 1965. 311p. biblio.

The report of a study on an aspect of higher education

that has been notable for a lack of consensus among educators and non-educators. Discusses types of accreditation and their effects, and makes recommendations.

2619 Moffitt, John C. *In-Service Education for Teachers.* New York, CARE, 1963. 114p. biblio.

A challenging exploration of the problems involved in promoting professional growth. Discusses the organization of in-service programs, the role of the teacher and administrator, the use of action research, and the evaluation of results.

2620 Paton, James M. *Current Thinking on Teacher Education.* Toronto, Gage, 1966. 56p. biblio.

A small book that has been highly praised for its straightforward approach to some controversial issues. An interpretation and discussion of the proceedings of a 1966 seminar of the Canadian Teachers' Federation.

2621 Richey, Robert W. *Planning for Teaching: an Introduction to Teaching,* 4th ed. New York, McGraw-Hill, 1968. 672p.

A good overview of recent changes, developments, and trends. Discusses problems, principles, facts, and attitudes in planning teaching careers.

2622 Rugg, Harold O. *The Teacher of Teachers: Frontiers of Theory and Practice in Teacher Education.* New York, Harper, 1952. 308p. biblio.

A lecture whose thesis is that Creative Man, long viewed only with condescending tolerance in our practical, industrialized Western culture, must be the one to run our schools and teach our prospective teachers if our schools are to fulfill their purpose.

2623 Sarason, Seymour B., and others. *The Preparation of Teachers: an Unstudied Problem in Education.* New York, Wiley, 1962. 124p. biblio.

The authors state that the content and procedures of elementary teacher education frequently have little relevance to the actual teaching task. They go on to more specific diagnoses and hypotheses for improvement and point out the need for empirical reference and a clear definition of criteria.

2624 Smith, Elmer R., ed. *Teacher Education: a Reappraisal.* New York, Harper, 1962. 213p.

A report of a conference sponsored by the FAE. Primarily concerned with the professional aspects of a teacher's education. Attempts to discover what, if anything, a teacher must know beyond the subject he teaches, how best this knowledge may be acquired, and how one can tell when a teacher possesses it.

2625   Stabler, Ernest, ed. *The Education of the Secondary School Teacher.* Middletown, Conn., Wesleyan UP, 1962. 239p. biblio.

Ten essays discuss the nature and extent of the training needed by those who would be teachers and the ever-present controversy over the relative importance of a broad and liberal education, scholarship in at least one academic discipline, and professional training.

2626   Stiles, Lindley J., and others. *Teacher Education in the United States.* New York, Ronald, 1960. 512p. biblio.

A concise and yet comprehensive overview of the dimensions and pertinent developments in teacher education. Provides a background of information for the study and redesign of teacher education programs.

History

2627   Bates, Samuel P. *Method of Teachers' Institutes and the Theory of Education.* New York, Barnes and Burr, 1862. 75p.

Written as a practical guide for the organization and operation of teacher training institutes, this is a solemn treatise on the indoctrination of proper attitudes and behavior. Offers a delightful yardstick for measuring subsequent changes.

2628   Borrowman, Merle L. *The Liberal and Technical in Teacher Education: a Historical Survey of American Thought.* New York, TC, Columbia, 1956. 247p. biblio.

Focused on the need for and search for balance between the two essential educational functions: the necessity of training individuals to perform special technical tasks and the equal need to provide educated individuals who are not simply vocational technicians.

2629   _____, ed. *Teacher Education in America: a Documentary History.* New York, TC, Columbia, 1965. 261p. biblio.

An historical account of the pendulum swings in teacher preparation from emphasis on liberal courses to professional courses and back again. Illustrated with original documents.

2630   Monroe, Walter S. *Teaching-Learning Theory and Teacher Education: 1890-1950.* Urbana, U of Illinois P, 1952. 426p. biblio.

A comprehensive account illuminating present thinking and the problems and issues faced by teacher educators today.

TEACHERS
see also FACULTY IN COLLEGES AND UNIVERSITIES
TEACHING AS A PROFESSION

2631   Amidon, Edmund J., and Flanders, Ned A. *The Role of the Teacher in the Classroom: a Manual for Understanding and Improving Teachers' Classroom Behavior.* Minneapolis, Paul S. Amidon and Associates, 1963. 69p. biblio.

A description of some conditions and tools necessary for understanding and improving teacher behavior in the classroom. Based on the assumption that, especially through a program of in-service training, a teacher can be helped to define his own concept of desirable teacher behavior and to subsequently modify his behavior accordingly.

2632   Bellack, Arno A., and others. *The Language of the Classroom.* New York, TC, Columbia, 1967. 274p. biblio.

The report of a research project to determine the function of verbal exchange in teaching, based on categories and analysis techniques developed for this study. The conclusions are perhaps best summarized by the title of the concluding chapter, "Rules of the Language Game of Teaching."

2633   Biddle, Bruce J., and Ellena, William J. *Contemporary Research on Teacher Effectiveness.* New York, Holt, 1964. 352p. biblio.

A compilation of nine research reports regarding the relation between teacher characteristics and other variables, including effectiveness. A review of the state of knowledge in this often-spoken-of but little examined area.

2634   Jersild, Arthur T. *When Teachers Face Themselves.* New York, TC, Columbia, 1955. 169p.

Based in part on a study of more than 1,000 teachers and students of education and in part on philosophical and psychological theory, this is concerned with the satisfactions and disappointments that pervade the teacher's life and work.

2635 Nordstrom, Carl, and others. *Society's Children: a Study of Ressentiment in the Secondary School.* New York, Random, 1967. 224p.

An analysis of nine different types of high schools in which largely unconscious resentment on the part of teachers and administrators was found to affect the development of the social and intellectual values of students. Methodology and tests used explained in appendices.

2636 Rosenthal, Robert, and Jacobson, Lenore. *Pygmalion in the Classroom.* New York, Holt, 1968. 256p.

Presents a thesis, based on experiments conducted in South San Francisco and other school districts, that the teacher's subtly transmitted faith in the student's ability to succeed is a determining factor in the student's actual performance. The authors conclude that "it is the teacher to whom we should direct more of our research attention."

2637 Ryans, David G. *Characteristics of Teachers: Their Description, Comparison, and Appraisal: a Research Study.* Washington, ACE, 1960. 416p. biblio.

Stressing the fact that the qualities of good teachers are variants dependent upon numerous external factors, the study nevertheless succeeds in identifying certain types of teacher traits that significantly relate to teacher success. Includes inventories for experimental use in appraising these traits.

2638 Ziegler, Harmon. *The Political World of the High School Teacher.* Eugene, Center for the Advanced Study of Educational Administration, U of Oregon, 1966. 160p. biblio.

Deals with teachers as individuals reacting to their jobs and environments, as participants in an interest group, as expressers of political values in class, and as reactors to community sanctions.

TEACHING AIDS
see also AUDIOVISUAL AIDS
PROGRAMED INSTRUCTION
TEACHING MACHINES
TELEVISION IN EDUCATION
TEXTBOOKS

2639 Allison, Mary L., comp. *New Educational Materials: Pre-Kindergarten Through Grade 12.* New York, Citation, 1967. 256p.

A compilation of reviews and evaluations appearing in *Scholastic Teacher* during 1966-67. Prepared by educators, the references cover every variety of teaching aid. Includes articles on the use of materials, books for teachers, and a list of sources.

2640 Bottrel, Harold R. *Teaching Tools.* Pittsburgh, Pa., Boxwood, 1957. 139p.

A unique contribution to encourage the intelligent use of community resources in teaching.

2641 *Educational Media Index,* 14 vols. New York, McGraw-Hill, 1964.

An indexed inventory of all types of instructional materials, except those that are printed, divided into subjects by volumes, which are available separately. For all the justified criticism directed against this set (difficult to use, full of errors and omissions), it remains the most complete guide available. Annual supplements have been promised but have not appeared.

2642 *Educators Guides.* Randolph, Wisc., Educators Progress Service.

Guides to sponsored materials that may be used by teachers as classroom instructional materials. In most cases, the school need pay only mailing costs. Annual revisions. Titles include: *Educators Guide to Free Films, Educators Guide to Social Studies Materials, Educators Guide to Free Science Materials, Educators Guide to Guidance Materials, Educators Guide to Free Tapes, Scripts and Transcriptions, Educators Guide to Free Filmstrips,* and *Elementary Teachers Guide to Free Curriculum Materials.*

2643 *Innovations for Time to Teach.* Washington, NEA, 1966. 147p. biblio.

Series of 26 articles indicating potentials of various instructional media and techniques for more effective teaching methods.

2644 Minor, Ed. *Simplified Techniques for Preparing Visual Instructional Materials.* New York, McGraw-Hill, 1963. 123p. biblio.

Uncomplicated, easy approaches to the preparation of visual instructional materials are emphasized, using the contemporary materials, equipment, and techniques the author has found to be sound and most practical.

2645 Nelson, Leslie W. *Instructional Aids*. Dubuque, Iowa, Brown, 1958. 259p.

Hundreds of ideas for instructional materials that can be made easily by the teacher and the student. Contains suggestions for practically every area of the curriculum, using simple, inexpensive, and easily available materials.

2646 Shores, Louis. *Instructional Materials: an Introduction for Teachers*. New York, Ronald, 1960. 408p.

Orients the teacher in the use and administration of all teaching materials: those that are printed, those that are pictorial, and those known as audiovisual.

2647 Thomas, R. Murray, and Swartout, Sherwin G. *Integrated Teaching Materials: How to Choose, Create and Use Them*, rev. ed. New York, McKay, 1963. 559p.

Guidance and assistance for the classroom teacher. A variety of specific examples is given.

2648 Williams, Catharine M. *Learning from Pictures*. Washington, NEA, 1963. 163p.

A well-illustrated guide and source book on choosing and using pictures in the classroom.

History

2649 Anderson, Charnel. *Technology in American Education, 1650-1900* (USOE Bulletin no. 19). Washington, GPO, 1962. 53p.

An outline reviewing the history of school architecture, furnishings, writing equipments, blackboards and slates, maps, globes, textbooks, and other classroom materials. Based on primary sources.

TEACHING AND TEACHING METHODS

2650 Bingham, Alma. *Improving Children's Facility in Problem Solving*. New York, TC, Columbia, 1963. 85p.

A practical guide to inquiry-focused teaching. Gives examples and analyses of teachers' and children's developing competence in problem-solving, techniques, and procedures.

2651 Burton, William H. *The Guidance of Learning Activities: a Summary of the Principles of Teaching Based on the Growth of the Learner*, 3rd ed. New York, Appleton, 1962. 581p.

An examination of the principles of learning, the learner and the teacher, and the organization of the setting for learning, plus a discussion of techniques common to traditional and modern methods.

2652 Frymier, Jack R. *The Nature of Educational Method.* Columbus, Merrill, 1965. 338p. biblio.

Written from the point of view of educational psychology and sociology, this focuses on the teacher as "the most important instructional device in the classroom." The teacher's ideas and personality are perceived by children and, in turn, adopted by them. He must provide the classroom environment that links children's inner energies to meaningful learning experiences. Offers a critical analysis of contemporary practices.

2653 Gage, Nathaniel L., ed. *Handbook of Research on Teaching.* Chicago, Rand McNally, 1965. 1218p.

Sponsored by the American Educational Research Association. Improves the conceptual and methodological equipment used in research on teaching, with creative examination of past research and an imaginative appropriation of what related disciplines have to offer. An important book.

2654 Hudgins, Bryce B. *Problem Solving in the Classroom.* New York, Macmillan, 1966. 96p.

A research-based discussion of problem-solving as an educational goal, not a teaching method but "a disposition toward inquiry" and the development of new ideas based on older ones.

2655 Jeffries, Derwin J. *Lesson Planning and Lesson Teaching.* Titusville, N.J., Home and School Press, 1966. 581p.

"An accumulation of experiences and interpretations dug out of years of daily lessons one chunk at a time." A well-organized handbook on basic teaching competencies, which is practice rather than theory.

2656 Kuethe, James L. *The Teaching-Learning Process.* Chicago, Scott Foresman, 1967. 160p.

The dynamics of learning are covered with particular emphasis on the classroom learning process. Covers also the psychological nature of teaching, stressing interpersonal relationships and the relationship between teaching and learning.

2657 McDonald, James B., ed. *Theories of Instruction.* (ASCD) Washington, NEA, 1965. 95p.

A collection of eight articles independently model the instructional process.

2658 Massialas, Byron G., and Zevin, Jack. *Creative Encounters in the Classroom: Teaching and Learning through Discovery.* New York, Wiley, 1967. 269p. biblio.

The result of a three-year study, the book identifies ways in which teachers may organize the curriculum and instructional procedures to enhance learning. Based on actual cases that have tested, in the classroom, some of the ideas of Piaget, Bruner, Conant, and others.

2659 Miel, Alice, ed. *Creativity in Teaching: Invitations and Instances.* Belmont, Cal., Wadsworth, 1961. 300p. biblio.

Creativity is seen as a way of responding that is available to all humans, enabling them to cope with increasingly complex problems and conditions and, in particular, as a way of lifting teaching from the humdrum and transforming it into an exciting and satisfying venture.

2660 Moustakas, Clark E. *The Authentic Teacher: Sensitivity and Awareness in the Classroom.* Cambridge, Mass., Doyle, 1966. 265p. biblio.

A retitled revision of a 1956 book that is a compelling plea for creative personal interaction as the basis for a richer, expanding relationship between teacher and child, freeing the child for new experiences and greater fulfillment of his potential.

2661 Pitcher, Evelyn G., and others. *Helping Young Children Learn.* Columbus, Merrill, 1966. 110p.

Not concerned with the total curriculum but rather with some areas: art, music, literature, and science. Emphasis on the materials that promote learning.

2662 Raths, Louis E., and others. *Teaching for Thinking: Theory and Application.* Columbus, Merrill, 1967. 348p. biblio.

A lucid analysis for the classroom teacher of the various operations involved in the process of thinking, drawn from the work of such men as Whitehead and Bruner.

2663   Rose, Homer C. *The Instructor and His Job,* 2nd ed. Chicago, American Technical Society, 1966. 345p. biblio.
        A description of basic teaching techniques used in schools, industries, government, and the military services.

2664   Sanders, Norris M. *Classroom Questions: What Kinds?* New York, Harper, 1965. 176p.
        An exploratory use of *Taxonomy of Educational Objectives* (#2271) in the classroom. A sequential and cumulative system for categorizing questions, which is relevant to several curriculum areas.

2665   Smith, Bunnie O., and others. *A Study of the Logic of Teaching.* Urbana, Bureau of Educational Research, U of Illinois, 1962. 231p. biblio.
        A logical analysis of classroom discourse that studies the forms verbal behavior takes as the teacher shapes the subject matter in the course of instruction. An attempt to develop ways of dividing verbal teaching behavior into pedagogically significant units and to analyze the units in logically meaningful ways.

2666   Smith, Eugene R. *Some Challenges to Teachers: a Book of Thoughts for Teachers Entrusted with Guidance and Training of Youth and for Those Preparing to Teach.* New York, Exposition, 1963. 191p.
        A collection of suggestions designed to stimulate a fuller conception of the possibilities inherent in teaching.

2667   Smith, James A. *Setting Conditions for Creative Teaching in the Elementary School.* Boston, Allyn and Bacon, 1966. 207p. biblio.
        Devoted to releasing the creative potential, this presents an up-to-date analysis of the creative process based on recent research, followed by an exciting as well as practical description of ways to develop creativity.

2668   Woodruff, Asahel D. *Basic Concepts of Teaching.* San Francisco, Chandler, 1961. 238p. biblio.
        Drawing on concepts from philosophy and psychology, this discusses formal education, its purposes, the learning experience, the processes involved, and the planning necessary as well as adjustment, motivation, and readiness. A practical rather than a theoretical book.

Elementary Schools

2669 Ashton-Warner, Sylvia. *Teacher.* New York, Simon and Schuster, 1963. 224p.

A semi-fictionalized account of the author's experience as a teacher of Maori children in New Zealand. A delightful, acute, and sensitive tale of creative teaching.

2670 Burrows, Alvina T. *Teaching Children in the Middle Grades.* Boston, Heath, 1952. 280p.

Somewhat in advance of its time when first published and quite pertinent in its contribution to the solution of many of today's problems. Emphasizes the need to understand the wide variety of children's differences and offers sound points of view in many different content areas.

2671 Crow, Lester D., and others, eds. *Teaching in the Elementary School.* New York, McKay, 1961. 571p.

A selection of articles containing helpful suggestions on all phases of learning in the elementary school.

2672 Cullum, Albert. *Push Back the Desks.* New York, Citation, 1967. 223p.

An elementary school teacher draws on 20 years of experience in a lively description of a variety of innovative, creative, and imaginative classroom "happenings."

2673 Hanna, Lavone A., and others. *Unit Teaching in the Elementary School: Social Studies and Related Sciences,* rev. ed. New York, Holt, 1963. 595p.

Defines the unit method and describes how to develop it. Deals with general concepts and aspects of total classroom operation as well as the teaching of social studies.

2674 *Helping Teachers Understand Children.* Washington, ACE, 1945. 468p.

A study of the behavior of several dozen children, with an analysis of the forces influencing their actions in various situations. Describes how individual teachers gradually increased their understanding of the causes underlying pupil conduct and their skill in identifying behavioral causes.

2675 Mehl, Marie, and others. *Teaching in Elementary School,* 3rd ed. New York, Ronald, 1965. 560p. biblio.

Bases of instruction, the teacher in action, curriculum materials, and the teacher as a person, are the four parts of this comprehensive treatment of fundamental elementary school teaching theory and practice. To be used as a companion to books on teaching specific subjects.

2676 Rasmussen, Margaret, ed. *Readings from Childhood Education.* Washington, ACEI, 1966. 414p.

An anthology of articles from ACEI's journal, *Childhood Education.* A delectable feast with many, well-worth-digesting courses.

2677 Shulman, Lee S., and Keislar, Evan R., eds. *Learning by Discovery: a Critical Appraisal.* Chicago, Rand McNally, 1966. 224p. biblio.

The proceedings of a conference sponsored by Stanford University and the Social Science Research Council. A multidisciplinary examination, wide-ranging and provocative, of the potential applications of knowledge and methodology from the different fields to promote learning by discovery.

2678 Warner, Ruby H. *Elementary School Teaching Practices.* New York, CARE, 1962. 120p. biblio.

A brief historical review that provides a perspective from which to observe current trends. Advocates a balance between the needs of the individual and the needs of society and practices to heighten the child's sense of personal worth while also teaching him responsible citizenship.

Secondary Schools

2679 Blount, Nathan S., and Klausmeier, Herbert J. *Teaching in the Secondary School,* 3rd ed. New York, Harper, 1968. 582p.

An attractive, comprehensive book that gives a coherent focus to the philosophic and social ends of education. Presents with vigor and clarity the most significant developments of the last decade in research and practice.

2680 Callahan, Sterling G. *Successful Teaching in Secondary Schools: a Guide for Student and In-Service Teachers.* Chicago, Scott Foresman, 1966. 566p. biblio.

Effective teaching must be equated with goal achievement, and goals can be reached most effectively only when instruction moves forward under scientific direction. Offers plans and procedures in accordance with the best instructional criteria.

2681 Lee, Florence H., ed. *Principles and Practices of Teaching in Secondary Schools: a Book of Readings.* New York, McKay, 1965. 523p.

An easily read, up-to-date collection of articles, mostly from periodicals. Provides an excellent background for the prospective secondary school teacher and has a particularly good section on teaching techniques.

2682 Nordberg, H. Orville, and others. *Secondary School Teaching.* New York, Macmillan, 1962. 401p. biblio.

Compulsory attendance laws and the original sins of adolescents combine to create the instructional problems peculiar to the secondary school. Three college professors offer some interesting solutions for the secondary school teacher.

2683 Oliva, Peter F., and Scrafford, Ralph A. *Teaching in a Modern Secondary School.* Columbus, Merrill, 1965. 293p. biblio.

A well-written, scholarly discussion of the role of today's high school teacher. Covers traditional responsibilities and gives ample coverage to such topics as the impact of automation on the classroom, team membership, counseling, television, and programed instruction.

2684 Steeves, Frank L. *Fundamentals of Teaching in Secondary Schools.* New York, Odyssey, 1962. 458p. biblio.

An outline of the essential characteristics of a systematic practice of successful teaching, stressing principles rather than formulas.

2685 Walton, John. *Toward Better Teaching in the Secondary School.* Boston, Allyn and Bacon, 1966. 338p. biblio.

A sound, conservative, and comprehensive discussion of all aspects of high school teaching. Covers the conditions and responsibilities of teaching, testing, and classroom management and develops a synthesized teaching theory.

Colleges and Universities

2686 Brown, James W., and Thornton, James W., Jr. *College Teaching: Perspectives and Guidelines.* New York, McGraw-Hill, 1963. 260p.

Examines the need for good teaching practices and suggests teaching internships, graduate seminars, and in-service training for first-year teachers.

2687   Buxton, Claude E. *College Teaching: a Psychologist's View.* New York, Harcourt, 1956. 404p.

Although slanted toward teaching psychology, this is more generally applicable and includes a discussion of attitudes, techniques, goals, the role of the faculty, student characteristics, and practical ideas for improving college teaching.

2688   Estrin, Herman A., and Goode, Delmar M., eds. *College and University Teaching.* Dubuque, Iowa, Brown, 1964. 628p. biblio.

A selection of articles from the journal *Improving College and University Teaching*, which, with its comprehensive coverage of undergraduate teaching, is intended to be a reference and seminar text.

2689   Evans, Richard I., and Leppman, Peter K. *Resistance to Innovation in Higher Education: a Social Psychological Exploration Focused on Television and the Establishment.* San Francisco, Jossey Bass, 1967. 224p.

A study in considerable depth of teachers and teaching and of the nature and diffusion of innovation, which for the purposes of this study was confined to the use of television. The initial study at the University of Houston was expanded to include nine others, in part to verify the original findings and in part to determine the relevance of the findings to other campuses.

2690   Highet, Gilbert. *The Art of Teaching.* New York, Knopf, 1950. 291p. biblio.

A great teacher examines teaching as an art, a science, and a way of life.

2691   Johnson, Byron L., ed. *New Directions for Instruction in the Junior Colleges.* Los Angeles, School of Education, U of California, 1965. 132p.

The report of a conference in 1964 at which people from 15 states described a variety of practices and new developments in junior college teaching. Extensive discussion of the use of programed instruction and television.

2692   Lee, Calvin B., ed. *Improving College Teaching.* Washington, ACE, 1967. 407p.

Essays addressed primarily to the academic administrator

pleading for re-examination and improvement of instructional programs, curriculum reform, innovations in teaching, and evaluation.

TEACHING AS A PROFESSION
see also FACULTY IN COLLEGES AND UNIVERSITIES

2693   Burrup, Percy E. *The Teacher and the Public School System,* 2nd ed. New York, Harper, 1967. 466p. biblio.

An interesting, informative, and challenging book. Discusses the organization, operation, and offerings of educational institutions, the nature of teachers and teaching, and teaching as a profession.

2694   Hontz, Glenn. *Finding the Right Teaching Position.* Columbus, Merrill, 1965. 78p. biblio.

A short and helpful guide with basic information about the procedures and techniques to be used by those wanting to teach. Includes details on certification, salary, and locating vacancies.

2695   Kearney, Nolan C. *A Teacher's Professional Guide.* Englewood Cliffs, N.J., Prentice-Hall, 1958. 358p.

Offers assistance to teachers wishing to improve their professional status. Although no longer up-to-date, no substitute has appeared to give advice to a group that, as a group, is singularly diffident about such matters.

2696   Lieberman, Myron. *Education as a Profession.* Englewood Cliffs, N.J., Prentice-Hall, 1956. 540p. biblio.

A rigorous analysis of the problems of professionalizing education. Sets forth the criteria of a profession and examines the status of education in relation to these criteria.

2697   *Manual on Certification Requirements for School Personnel in the United States.* Washington, NEA, 1967. 256p.

A triennial publication that covers such topics as certification practices and trends among the states, a state by state listing of requirements, and data on securing a teaching job in the United States and abroad.

2698   Stinnett, Timothy M. *The Profession of Teaching.* New York, CARE, 1962. 118p. biblio.

A description of teaching that includes such topics as

teachers' professional and legal status, their social and economic status, professional organization, teacher education and characteristics, some history, and some trends.

2699 _____, and Huggett, Albert J. *Professional Problems of Teachers*, 2nd ed. New York, Macmillan, 1963. 516p. biblio.

Provides basic information on a cluster of problems with which teachers must deal daily as practitioners and as effective members of their professional organizations. Contributes to the growth of teaching as a profession by developing competence in the individual to function as a professional as well as a teacher.

2700 _____, and Haskew, Laurence D. *Teaching in American Schools: a Handbook for the Future Teacher*. New York, Harcourt, 1962. 184p. biblio.

Offers perspectives on the origin, development, and purposes of public education and on the desirability of becoming part of that system. Chapters on teaching as a profession and a career and on the organization of the school system.

2701 Vollmer, Howard M., and Mills, Donald L., eds. *Professionalization*. Englewood Cliffs, N.J., Prentice-Hall, 1966. 365p.

Fifty-seven readings on the characteristics, circumstances, and consequences of the attempt to turn an occupation into a profession. As there are those who believe that some current activities on the part of teachers to improve their lot resemble union strategies, this is of particular interest to members of the teaching profession.

2702 Woellner, Elizabeth H., and Wood, M. Aurilla. *Requirements for Certification for Elementary Schools, Secondary Schools, and Junior Colleges*. 1st- 1935- . Chicago, U of Chicago P.

An annual publication (32nd ed., 1967-68, 214p.), containing summaries of initial requirements for teachers, counselors, librarians, and administrators. Arranged by state.

History

2703 Elsbree, Willard S. *The American Teacher: Evolution of a Profession in a Democracy*. New York, American, 1939. 566p. biblio.

In contrast to most histories of education, which discuss the development of education in terms of legislation, organization, administration, and curriculum, this book stresses the role of the public school teacher in America during the last 300 years.

TEACHING MACHINES
see also AUDIOVISUAL INSTRUCTION
COMPUTERS IN EDUCATION
PROGRAMED INSTRUCTION
TEACHING AIDS

2704   Cram, David. *Explaining Teaching Machines and Programming*. San Francisco, Fearon, 1961. 86p.
A description of teaching machine devices, including the relationship between the machine and its program and the rationale between linear and branching programing.

2705   Fine, Benjamin. *Teaching Machines*. New York, Sterling, 1962. 176p.
Explanation and evaluation, containing many photographs and drawings and a table of contents uniquely arranged in the format of a teaching-machine text.

2706   Finn, James D., and Perrin, Donald G. *Teaching Machines and Programed Learning, 1962: a Survey of the Industry.* (USOE) Washington, GPO, 1962. 85p. biblio.
A directory of machines, with illustrations of programs, manufacturers, and publishers.

2707   Fry, Edward B. *Teaching Machines and Programmed Learning: an Introduction to Autoinstruction.* New York, McGraw-Hill, 1962. 244p.
Explains the various types of teaching machines and describes how to write and use programs. Includes samples of various sorts of programing with comments from leaders in the field.

2708   Galanter, Eugene, ed. *Automatic Teaching: the State of the Art.* New York, Wiley, 1959. 198p. biblio.
Based on the Symposium on Teaching Machines, 1958. Programing, analysis, machine design, experimental results, and criticism covered in what is a valuable introduction to the concept of machine teaching.

2709   Glaser, Robert, ed. *Teaching Machines and Programmed Learning, II: Date and Directions.* Washington, NEA, 1965. 831p. biblio.

A sequel to Lumsdaine (#2711) and devoted to educational technology rather than to teaching machines, this supplements and updates Volume I, summarizing the state of the art and practice. Provides a deeper understanding of how people learn and how the findings of a huge amount of research in this area are fitting together to set new directions for education.

2710   Lumsdaine, Arthur A. *New Teaching Aids for the American Classroom.* (USOE) Washington, GPO, 1960. 173p.

The papers of a 1959 symposium. Appraises newer developments, for example, teaching machines and programed instruction.

2711   ———, and Glaser, Robert, eds. *Teaching Machines and Programmed Learning: a Source Book.* Washington, NEA, 1960. 736p. biblio.

A collection of papers on self-instructional devices. An historical review as well as a description of the present. Appendices abstract research reports and other papers and consolidate the bibliography cited in the text with that of the abstracts. (See #2709 for sequel.)

TEAM TEACHING
see also GROUPING IN EDUCATION

2712   Bair, Medill, and Woodward, Richard G. *Team Teaching in Action.* Boston, Houghton Mifflin, 1964. 229p. biblio.

A practical treatment of the subject that includes numerous examples of practices drawn from programs across the country. Detailed descriptions and illustrations of the kinds of spaces and equipment required for effective team teaching programs.

2713   Beggs, David W., ed. *Team Teaching: Bold New Venture.* Bloomington, Indiana UP, 1966. 192p. biblio.

One of a new series designed to be informative about new developments in education. A dozen articles covering all levels of schooling and viewing team teaching from several aspects. List of team teaching schools appended.

2714   Peterson, Carl H. *Effective Team Teaching: the Easton Area High School Program.* West Nyack, N.Y., Parker, 1966. 216p. (Dist. by Prentice-Hall.)

A full description of the introduction of team teaching into the Easton Area High School in Pennsylvania in 1958, the growth and development of the program, and its present greatly expanded operation in a new building designed around the concept of team teaching. In depth coverage with an empirical approach.

TELEVISION IN EDUCATION
see also AUDIOVISUAL AIDS

2715   Adams, John C., and others, eds. *College Teaching by Television.* Washington, ACE, 1958. 234p.

Report of a conference that describes campus activity in this area and gives accounts of actual teaching by means of television. Good resource.

2716   Boutwell, William D., ed. *Using Mass Media in the Schools.* New York, Appleton, 1962. 292p. biblio.

An attempt to answer questions regarding the proper attitude toward mass media, the nature of modern media, and what teachers are doing to help students learn to discriminate, evaluate, and live with mass media.

2717   Brown, James W., and Norberg, Kenneth D. *Administering Educational Media.* New York, McGraw-Hill, 1965. 357p. biblio.

Both a theoretical and a practical guide for media programs at the several administrative levels. Case studies cited to clarify general principles.

2718   Campion, Lee E., and Kelley, Clarice Y. *Studies in the Growth of Instructional Technology, II: a Directory of Closed-Circuit Television Installations in American Education with a Pattern of Growth.* Washington, NEA, 1963. 141p.

A companion volume to Finn (#2706), this reviews the uses of television systems and finds that so far television has not yet altered our conventional instructional methodology, the systems are often designed to use television minimally, and uses beyond direct instruction need further study.

2719　Cassirer, Henry R. *Television Teaching Today*. Paris, UNESCO, 1960. 267p. biblio.

The use of television for teaching purposes by educational institutions in the United States and various other countries. General principles are developed as a guide to future action.

2720　Costello, Lawrence, and Gordon, George N. *Teaching with Television*. New York, Hastings, 1961. 192p.

How to produce and use instructional programs, for all school levels, and for both closed and open circuit TV.

2721　de Bernardis, Amo, and others. *Planning Schools for New Media*. Portland, Ore., Portland State College, 1961. 72p. biblio.

A reference guide providing essential information needed for planning schools to utilize modern teaching technology.

2722　*Design for ETV: Planning for Schools with Television*. New York, EFL, 1960. 96p.

A well-illustrated report of an industrial design study concerned with the environment in which television may be most effectively used.

2723　Diamond, Robert M. *A Guide to Instructional Television*. New York, McGraw-Hill, 1964. 304p. biblio.

A guide for those interested in the applications and uses of television within a single school or school system.

2724　*Educational Television: the Next Ten Years*. Stanford, Cal., Institute for Communication Research, Stanford U, 1962. 375p. biblio.

A report and summary of major studies on problems and potentials. Forecasts and theorizes on the uses, impact, and meaning of educational television.

2725　Erickson, Clifford G., and Chausow, Hymen M. *Chicago's TV College*. Chicago, Chicago City Junior College, 1960. 98p.

A final report of a successful three-year experiment sponsored by the Chicago Board of Education. Starting in 1956, a complete junior college curriculum, offering courses for credit, was presented on open circuit television.

2726　Gordon, George N. *Educational Television*. New York, CARE, 1965. 113p. biblio.

Examines the elements necessary for an objective appreciation of the advantages and disadvantages of this educational medium. Discusses history, financing, the effectiveness of ETV.

2727 Green, Alan C., ed. *Educational Facilities with the New Media.* Washington, NEA, 1966. 230p.

Report of an architectural research study divided into three parts: guide for policy-makers—boards, administrators, planning committees, and institutional planners; guide for the design professions; technical guide intended for those concerned with design details and equipment.

2728 Hazard, Patrick D., ed. *TV as Art: Some Essays in Criticism.* Champaign, Ill., NCTE, 1967. 221p.

Invites teachers to consider TV's best. Articles discuss specific types of programs and ponder the effect on children of so-called juvenile programs. Basically optimistic.

2729 Levenson, William B., and Stasheff, Edward A. *Teaching through Radio and Television,* rev. ed. New York, Holt, 1952. 560p. biblio.

A plea for the improvement of school broadcasting and more effective use of educational programs. The pitfalls and limitations, as well as potentialities, of radio and television are discussed.

2730 Lewis, Philip. *Educational Television Guidebook.* New York, McGraw-Hill, 1961. 238p.

Useful guide for those faced with the prospect of purchasing and using television systems in schools.

2731 Murphy, Judith, and Gross, Ronald. *Learning by Television.* New York, FAE, 1966. 95p.

A report examining television's role in instruction. Concludes that it is still a marginal enterprise, an educational tool whose effectiveness has been proved but whose ultimate contribution to improved teaching and learning remains to be determined.

2732 *New Teaching Aids for the American Classroom.* Stanford, Cal., Institute for Communication Research, Stanford U, 1960. 173p.

Eleven papers presented at a symposium on the state of research in instructional television and tutorial machines.

2733 Siepmann, Charles A. *TV and Our School Crisis*. New York, Dodd, Mead, 1958. 198p.

Presents a good philosophic basis for understanding the use of television as a medium for instruction. Excellent material dealing with the inherent characteristics of TV.

2734 Trow, William C. *Teachers and Technology: New Designs for Learning*. New York, Appleton, 1963. 198p. biblio.

Considers the need for instructional media and the possibilities of grouping the various media into a commonsense pattern of instruction, which would be workable and do a better educational job.

TESTS AND TESTING
see also MEASUREMENT AND EVALUATION IN EDUCATION

2735 Anderson, Harold H., and Gladys L., eds. *An Introduction to Projective Techniques and Other Devices for Understanding the Dynamics of Human Behavior*. Englewood Cliffs, N.J., Prentice-Hall, 1951. 720p.

A collection of articles providing a survey of the field. Includes discussions of the Rorschach test, various tests of personality mechanisms, the use of intelligence tests in personality appraisal, and projective techniques in therapy.

2736 Buros, Oscar K., ed. *Mental Measurements Yearbook*. Highland Park, N.J., Gryphon. 1st- 1938- .

The latest of these mis-named yearbooks, the 6th, appeared in 1965. A monumental and unique undertaking that is *the* reference work on published tests of all kinds. A subject listing, with authoritative reviews of each test plus a bibliography of references for each. The succeeding volumes include new tests and revisions of older ones, so that they do not supersede previous volumes. Buros' *Tests in Print* (1961) can be used as an index to the first five yearbooks.

2737 Cronbach, Lee J. *Essentials of Psychological Testing*, 2nd ed. New York, Harper, 1960. 650p. biblio.

An introductory text presenting the principles of testing. Discusses the various kinds of tests available from the point of view of their specific use, their limitations, and their potentials.

2738   Goldman, Leo. *Using Tests for Counseling.* New York, Appleton, 1961. 434p. biblio.

A discussion of the principles of testing. Emphasizes the selection of the appropriate test and competency in the interpretation of test results.

2739   Goodenough, Florence L. *Measurement of Intelligence by Drawings.* Chicago, World, 1926. 176p. biblio.

A classic effort to measure intelligence by non-verbal means, which develops a method of scoring based on drawings of the human figure by elementary school children.

2740   _____. *Mental Testing: Its History, Principles, and Applications.* New York, Holt, 1949. 609p. biblio.

A survey of intelligence testing that examines the potentials and limitations of testing and considers the implicit and explicit assumptions underlying the construction, administration, and interpretation of tests.

2741   Guilford, Joy P. *Psychometric Methods*, 2nd ed. New York, McGraw-Hill, 1954. 597p. biblio.

An examination of psychophysical and psychological measurement, concepts, and methods in relation to their statistical basis and the logic of measurement.

2742   Gulliksen, Harold. *Theory of Mental Tests.* New York, Wiley, 1950. 486p. biblio.

Designed for those with some mathematical knowledge, this comprehensively covers the numerous aspects of test theory and presents them in historical perspective.

2743   Harris, Chester W., ed. *Problems in Measuring Change.* Madison, U of Wisconsin P, 1963. 259p. biblio.

The proceedings of a conference sponsored by the Committee on Personality Development in Youth of the Social Science Research Council. Twelve essays dealing with various aspects of the problems involved in measuring psychological change.

2744   Horrocks, John E. *Assessment of Behavior: the Methodology and Content of Psychological Measurement.* Columbus, Merrill, 1964. 736p. biblio.

An excellent discussion of measurement as an essential tool of psychology. Covers background and applications.

2745 Invitational Conference on Testing Problems. *Proceedings.* 1st- 1948- . Princeton, N.J., Educational Testing Service.

An annual collection of papers and reports. Each volume focuses on a relevant topic in the field of testing.

2746 Magnusson, David. *Test Theory,* 2nd rev. ed. Reading, Mass., Addison Wesley, 1967. 270p. biblio.

Translated from the Swedish. A theoretical, statistical, and stimulating presentation of test theory, which is also well-organized and well-written. Emphasis on test construction diagnosis, counseling, selection, and classification.

2747 Rabin, Albert I., and Haworth, Mary R., eds. *Projective Techniques with Children.* New York, Grune and Stratton, 1960. 392p. biblio.

Assumes a knowledge of basic principles and provides a comprehensive review of projective tests and testing for the clinician and researcher.

2748 Rapaport, David. *Diagnostic Psychological Testing: the Theory, Statistical Evaluation, and Diagnostic Application of a Battery of Tests,* 2 vols. Chicago, Yearbook, 1945-46.

An exhaustive and systematic exploration of the diagnostic potential of the simultaneous use of seven psychological tests.

2749 Schafer, Roy. *Psychoanalytic Interpretation in Rorschach Testing: Theory and Application.* New York, Grune and Stratton, 1954. 446p. biblio.

Concerned with the need for a broad treatment of the contributions that psychoanalysis has made and can make to test theory and interpretation, with particular reference to the Rorschach test.

2750 Spearman, Charles E. *The Abilities of Man: Their Nature and Measurement.* New York, Macmillan, 1927. 415p.

A classic, now of historical interest, which applies cognitive laws to individual differences in ability and examines the factors involved in their measurement.

2751 Terman, Lewis M., and Merrill, Maud A. *Measuring Intelligence: a Guide to the Administration of the New Revised Stanford-Binet Tests of Intelligence.* Boston, Houghton Mifflin, 1937. 461p.

In addition to describing the tests and the procedures for

using them, this describes the significant importance for public education of the careful measurement of children's intelligence. An unarguable thesis, but the testing tool appears less definitive today.

2752 Thurstone, Louis L. *The Measurement of Values.* Chicago, U of Chicago P, 1959. 322p.

An important collection of papers dealing with psychology as a quantitative, rational science, which applies mathematics to problems in psychological measurement.

2753 ———. *Primary Mental Abilities.* Chicago, U of Chicago P, 1938. 121p.

A report of the first major application of the theory of factor analysis. Describes each of the 56 psychological tests used in the investigation.

2754 Tomkins, Silvan S. *The Thematic Appercertion Test: the Theory and Technique of Interpretation.* New York, Grune and Stratton, 1947. 297p. biblio.

An examination of the usefulness and limitations of this test as a diagnostic instrument in clinical practice.

2755 Tyler, Leona E. *The Psychology of Human Differences,* 3rd ed. New York, Appleton, 1965. 573p. biblio.

A comprehensive examination of the major dimensions of individual differences as attributable to birth, to environment, to individual development, and to such factors as age and sex. An interpretation on the basis of these variables of the meaning of testing for group planning and individual placement.

2756 Vernon, Philip E. *The Structure of Human Abilities.* New York, Wiley, 1950. 160p. biblio.

Drawing on both British and American research, this deals with the results of factor analysis in educational and other branches of applied psychology.

2757 Wechsler, David. *The Measurement of Adult Intelligence,* 4th ed. Baltimore, Williams and Wilkins, 1958. 297p. biblio.

Centers on the theory, findings, and applications of the author's Adult Intelligence Scales (WAIS). This revision discusses age changes in intelligence, sex differences, brain damage, and the use of tests in counseling.

TEXTBOOKS

2758 Black, Hillel. *The American Schoolbook.* New York, Morrow, 1967. 193p.

A discussion of American textbooks. Provides an historical survey and argues that they have an enormous influence on the development of youthful values. Describes the factors that influence both the content and adoption of texts by schools.

2759 Redding, M. Frank. *Revolution in the Textbook Publishing Industry.* Washington, NEA, 1963. 32p.

An excellent statement of the situation that exists in the textbook industry as a result of the technological revolution in the field of education.

History

2760 Elson, Ruth M. *Guardians of Tradition: American Schoolbooks of the Nineteenth Century.* Lincoln, U of Nebraska P, 1964. 424p. biblio.

The intellectual history of the average American citizen of the last century, based on the interpretation of his textbooks. A compendium of the approved ideas of the time offering an excellent index to the concepts considered "proper" for the 19th century American.

2761 Nietz, John A. *The Evolution of American Secondary School Textbooks.* Rutland, Vt., Tuttle, 1966. 265p.

A thorough study, based on careful research, of the books used in Latin and grammar schools from Colonial days until 1900. Of interest to the student of changes in curriculums insofar as the books reflect what was taught and how it was taught.

UNDERDEVELOPED COUNTRIES
see also EDUCATION IN FOREIGN COUNTRIES

2762 Anderson, C. Arnold, and Bowman, Mary J., eds. *Education and Economic Development.* Chicago, Aldine, 1965. 436p. biblio.

Outgrowth of a conference whose purpose was to stimulate interchange between the various branches of the social sciences in an effort to define the role of education in the early stages of economic development.

2763 Becker, Gary S. *Human Capital: a Theoretical and Empirical Analysis, with Special Reference to Education.* New York, Columbia UP, 1964. 187p. biblio.

Illustrates how society can make investments in the productive capacity of men. People are wealth and capital assets, and education is a major source of investment in this human capital. Man is a resource increasing in economic value as a result of acquiring skills and knowledge.

2764 Butts, R. Freeman. *American Education in International Development.* New York, Harper, 1963. biblio.

Emphasis on how best to formulate a policy that will enable the developing countries to achieve economic growth, self-government, and the new perspective required in today's international community of nations.

2765 Coleman, James S., ed. *Education and Political Development.* Princeton, N.J., Princeton UP, 1965. 620p. biblio.

Papers presented at a 1962 seminar that analyze the use of education for political ends, especially in the developing countries.

2766 Gardner, John W. *AID and the Universities.* New York, Education and World Affairs, 1964. 57p. biblio.

In a day when university interests are far-flung, this report, based on seven months of intensive fact-finding, examines the relationship between the Agency for International Development and the universities. Problems are studied in an attempt to work out practical improvements in future joint undertakings.

2767 Hansom, John W., and Brembeck, Cole S., eds. *Education and the Development of Nations.* New York, Holt, 1966. 529p. biblio.

Deals with the capacity of education to assist in the development of nations and to bring about desirable social change.

2768 Harbison, Frederick, and Myers, Charles A. *Education, Manpower, and Economic Growth: Strategies of Human Resource Development.* New York, McGraw-Hill, 1964. 229p. biblio.

An analysis of economic, political, and social development from the perspective of the education, training, and energizing of human resources. Emphasis on policy and strategy rather than estimates of returns on human investment. A generalized concept and a blueprint for action.

2769   Humphrey, Richard A., ed. *Universities and Development Assistance Abroad.* Washington, ACE, 1967. 196p.

Eight essays by men experienced in many phases of overseas developmental activities. Evaluates the complex collaboration between government and the universities. Concerned with the problems of rationale and the lessons to be learned from experience.

2770   Piper, Don C., and Cole, Taylor, eds. *Post-Primary Education and Political and Economic Development.* Durham, N.C., Duke UP, 1964. 238p.

Primary attention is given to the newest nations in this collection of papers, originally read at a Duke University seminar, which dealt with the impact of education on development.

2771   Sicault, George, ed. *The Needs of Children: a Survey of the Needs of Children in the Developing Countries.* New York, Free Press, 1963. 175p. biblio.

A condensed version of the principal reports submitted to a 1961 UNICEF executive board session. Covers needs in the areas of health, nutrition, education, social welfare, and vocational preparation.

2772   Staley, Eugene. *The Future of Underdeveloped Countries: Political Implications of Economic Development,* 2nd ed. New York, Harper, 1961. 483p. biblio.

Arguing that economic growth alone is not a sufficient condition to ensure well-being in Asia, Africa, and Latin America, the author examines different types of development and builds a case for a world community approach. Emphasis on the thesis that "bettering the system of public education is one of the most important levers of economic, social, and political advance."

2773   United Nations Children's Fund. *Children of the Developing Countries.* Cleveland, World, 1963. 130p. biblio.

A report describing the needs of children in the developing countries, some of the policy questions involved in meeting these needs, the principal measures being taken, and the assistance being provided by the world community.

URBAN PROBLEMS AND EDUCATION

see also DISADVANTAGED

DISADVANTAGED—GHETTO SCHOOLS

MINORITY PROBLEMS

2774   Carlson, William S. *The Municipal University.* New York, CARE, 1962. 104p. biblio.

A not altogether optimistic view of the fate of the municipal university, which is heavily obligated to a local community that is less than eager to support it. As it becomes more dependent upon support outside the local area, it tends to lose its unique identity.

2775   Cox, Harvey. *The Secular City: Secularization and Urbanization in Theological Perspective,* rev. ed. New York, Macmillan, 1966. 244p. biblio.

A theological approach viewing urbanization and secularization as epochal opportunities to be embraced rather than sinister curses to be escaped.

2776   Dobbins, Charles G., ed. *The University, the City, and Urban Renewal.* Washington, ACE, 1964. 58p. biblio.

A conference report stressing the importance of sound leadership in coping with urban renewal problems and campus programs on a mutual basis.

2777   Goldstein, Bernard, and others. *Low Income Youth in Urban Areas: a Critical Review of the Literature.* New York, Holt, 1967. 288p. biblio.

A synthesis of recent research on the behavior and attitudes of low income youth with emphasis on basic social institutions—family, school, and church. The bibliography is annotated and extensive.

2778   Harrington, Michael. *The Other America.* New York, Macmillan, 1962. 191p.

Required reading for those seeking greater understanding of the problems faced by the underprivileged and by those hoping to help them. The book, more than any other, focused the country's attention on the plight of millions of people, white and black, rural and urban, who exist in poverty amid general affluence.

2779   Havighurst, Robert J. *Education in Metropolitan Areas.* Boston, Allyn and Bacon, 1966. 260p. biblio.

Defining "metropolitanism" as a set of contemporary social

events and as a set of goals or tasks, the author discusses the role of the schools in achieving these goals for improving society. Suggests ways of improving the schools through metropolitan area cooperation.

2780 Klotsche, J. Martin. *The Urban University: and the Future of Our Cities.* New York, Harper, 1966. 149p.

A thoughtful, stimulating challenge to urban universities, which enroll nearly half our students, to serve urban life and needs more fully. A pioneering study proposing a symbiotic relationship in which the knowledge of the scholar is applied to the practical problems of the city.

2781 Lonsdale, Richard C. *The School's Role in Metropolitan Area Development.* Syracuse, N.Y., Syracuse UP, 1960. 68p. biblio.

A pertinent discussion of the complex social, economic, and political problems of the metropolitan areas. Views the public schools as having a role in their solution by providing leadership and research and working with other agencies.

2782 Sexton, Patricia C. *Spanish Harlem: an Anatomy of Poverty.* New York, Harper, 1965. 208p. biblio.

A detailed portrait of the East Harlem (New York City) slum. Attempts to identify problems and solutions. An exploratory description whose theme is social change and searches for preventives, not placebos.

VALUES

2783 Brown, Kenneth I. *Not Minds Alone: Frontiers of Christian Education.* New York, Harper, 1954. 206p.

A plea for a deeper appreciation of the place of ethical and religious values in the classroom.

2784 Raths, Louis E., and others. *Values and Teaching: Working with Values in the Classroom.* Columbus, Merrill, 1966. 274p. biblio.

A provocative, pioneering approach to values theory. Scraps all traditional methods and describes both a value clarifying process and instructional strategies for implementation. Stresses the concept of free choice, students' actual, not self-imaged behavior, and the process used to acquire values.

VOCATIONAL EDUCATION
see also INDUSTRIAL ARTS EDUCATION
MANPOWER NEEDS AND EDUCATION

2785   Barlow, Melvin L. *Principles of Trade and Industrial Education.* Austin, U of Texas P, 1963. 150p.

Includes an historical account and reviews the philosophical basis of industrial education.

2786   ———, ed. *Vocational Education* (NSSE 64th Yearbook, Part I). Chicago, U of Chicago P, 1965. 301p.

A contribution to clearer thinking about vocational education in the context of contemporary American life. Each of the 13 chapters is devoted to a different phase of vocational education, and information given on the Vocational Education Act of 1963. (See also #2796 and #2807.)

2787   Burt, Samuel M. *Industry and Vocational-Technical Education: a Study of Education-Advisory Committees.* New York, McGraw-Hill, 1967. 520p. biblio.

The report of a 16-month study in depth sponsored by the FAE. With detailed case studies, examines techniques used by educators to involve employers in various facets of occupational education.

2788   Byram, Harold M., and Wenrich, Ralph C. *Vocational Education and Practical Arts in the Community School.* New York, Macmillan, 1956. 512p.

Emphasizes the role of the community in introducing and maintaining vocational programs in its schools. Coverage of federal and state laws that promote and assist these programs.

2789   Clark, Harold F., and Sloan, Harold S. *Classrooms in the Factories: an Account of Educational Activities Conducted by American Industry.* Rutherford, N.J., Institute of Research, Fairleigh Dickinson U, 1958. 139p. biblio.

Describes the courses offered within 300 or so of the largest American industrial corporations and the means used in judging the achievement of those participating. Course offerings were primarily technical and business, but about one-sixth of the corporations also sponsored courses in general education.

2790   ———, and ———. *Classrooms on Main Street: an Account of Specialty Schools in the United States That Train for*

Work and Leisure. New York, TC, Columbia, 1966. 162p. biblio.

Depicts an area that is meeting urgent educational demands not supplied by conventional institutions—those non-collegiate and non-elementary or secondary schools that are concerned with preparing students for particular business or industrial employment.

2791   De Carlo, Charles R. *Education in Business and Industry.* New York, CARE, 1966. 117p. biblio.

A discussion of the role of business and industry in meeting present educational demands. Traces historical backgrounds from the days of the guilds and points out resemblances with the past. Highlights new developments and trends.

2792   *Educationally Deficient Adults: Their Education and Training Needs.* (USOE) Washington, GPO, 1965. 60p.

The report of a survey that furnishes guidelines for a plan to meet the needs of educationally deficient adults and the materials that might be used in providing vocational training for jobs.

2793   *Education for a Changing World of Work.* (USOE) Washington, GPO, 1963. 296p. biblio.

A comprehensive review of the entire field of vocational education, including historical development and current programs. Points up the needs of the culturally disadvantaged, the school dropout and the functionally illiterate. The report of a panel chaired by Benjamin C. Willis.

2794   Graney, Maurice R. *The Technical Institute.* New York, CARE, 1964. 111p. biblio.

A study of the technical institute in American higher education and its role in providing trained manpower.

2795   Henniger, G. Ross. *The Technical Institute in America.* New York, McGraw-Hill, 1959. 276p.

This study of the three decades following 1929, sponsored by the American Society for Engineering Education, supplements the Society's original review, published in 1929.

2796   Henry, Nelson B., ed. *Vocational Education* (NSSE 42nd Yearbook, Part I). Chicago, U of Chicago P, 1943. 494p.

Covers legislative commitments affecting vocational education, vocational education through non-school governmental agencies, and vocational programs in different educational institutions. (See also #2786 and #2808.)

2797 Keller, Franklin J. *Principles of Vocational Education: the Primacy of the Person.* Boston, Heath, 1948. 402p.

Philosophical principles underlying vocational education and a discussion of the aims and objectives of the ideal program.

2798 Olson, Delmar W. *Industrial Arts and Technology.* Englewood Cliffs, N.J., Prentice-Hall, 1963. 277p.

An attempt to place today's industrial arts within the context of today's technology.

2799 Patterson, William F. *Educating for Industry: Policies and Procedures of a National Apprenticeship System.* Englewood Cliffs, N.J., Prentice-Hall, 1946. 229p. biblio.

A survey of the apprenticeship system in the United States, including the role of the federal government in introducing the national apprenticeship system.

2800 Roberts, Roy W. *Vocational and Practical Arts Education: History, Development, and Principles,* 2nd ed. New York, Harper, 1965. 596p. biblio.

A practical review of the latest information available at the date of publication, including federal legislation and current needs as shown by statistics. Bibliography excellent.

2801 Selvidge, Robert W., and Fryklund, Verne C. *Principles of Trade and Industrial Teaching.* Peoria, Ill., Manual Arts, 1946. 419p. biblio.

A clear presentation of professional requirements, subject matter selection and organization, and practical methods of instruction.

2802 Silvius, George H., and Bohn, Ralph C. *Organizing Course Materials for Industrial Education.* Bloomington, Ind., McKnight, 1961. 459p. biblio.

A guide in the preparation of curricula, courses of study, and other instructional materials.

2803 ———, and Curry, Estell H. *Teaching Multiple Activities in Industrial Education.* Bloomington, Ind., McKnight, 1956. 484p. biblio.

Handbook on the management and organization of general shops.

2804 Smith, Leo F., and Lypsett, Lawrence. *The Technical Institute*. New York, McGraw-Hill, 1956. 319p.

A handbook covering the purposes of the technical institute. Also a source of information about the various types of institutes and their curricula.

2805 Swanson, J. Chester, comp. *Development of Federal Legislation for Vocational Education,* 2nd ed. Chicago, American Technical Society, 1966. 120p.

Originally published in the 1940's by Layton Hawkins, this has twice been updated with additional chapters. This edition includes information on the Vocational Education Act of 1963.

2806 Thomas, Lawrence G. *The Occupational Structure and Education.* Englewood Cliffs, N.J., Prentice-Hall, 1956. 502p.

A study of the relationship of American vocational training and the occupational structure in our economy. The structure is discussed in terms of income, prestige, job satisfactions, qualifications demanded by employers, and the contribution of vocational schools.

2807 Warren, Hugh A. *Vocational and Technical Education: a Comparative Study of Present Practice and Future Trends in Ten Countries.* Paris, UNESCO, 1967. 222p. biblio.

An illuminating study that discusses problems and ways of facing them.

2808 Whipple, Guy M., ed. *Vocational Guidance and Vocational Education for the Industries* (NSSE 23rd Yearbook, Part II). Bloomington, Ind., Public School Publ., 1924. 435p.

Covers guidance problems in large cities, guidance activities in small cities, day and evening industrial courses in smaller cities, and training foremen and other leaders in industry. Of primary interest as an historical record. (See also #2786 and #2796.)

History

2809 Anderson, Lewis F. *History of Manual and Industrial School Education.* New York, Appleton, 1926. 251p.

A general survey of the development of manual and industrial education in Europe and the United States, showing the influence of European movements in America.

2810 Bawden, William T. *Leaders in Industrial Education*. Milwaukee, Bruce, 1950. 196p. biblio.

Each chapter is devoted to the work of a leader in the field: such men as Woodward, Russell, Bonser, Griffith, Runkle, Harvey, Stout, Roberts, and Struck.

2811 Bennett, Charles A. *History of Manual and Industrial Education*, 2 vols. Peoria, Ill., Bennett, 1937. biblio.

A definitive work dealing with the technology and methods of industrial education from ancient times. Volume 2 covers innovations in vocational and industrial education in Europe and the United States and ends with the passage of the Smith-Hughes Act in 1917.

2812 Mays, Arthur D. *Principles and Practices of Vocational Education*. New York, McGraw-Hill, 1948. 303p. biblio.

A revision of an earlier work, useful for its coverage of the history of vocational training in this country.

2813 Weinryb, Bernard D. *Jewish Vocational Education: History and Appraisal of Training in Europe*. New York, Jewish Teachers Seminary and Peoples UP, 1948. 189p.

An historical survey to 1939 covering Germany and Eastern Europe. An interesting sidelight on the history of vocational education, not only because it details those occupations that were open to Jews but also because much of the training and retraining was sponsored by voluntary Jewish organizations in other countries.

VOCATIONAL GUIDANCE
see also MANPOWER NEEDS AND EDUCATION
VOCATIONAL REHABILITATION

2814 Barry, Ruth E., and Wolf, Beverly. *An Epitaph for Vocational Guidance: Myths, Actualities, Implications*. New York, TC, Columbia, 1962. 241p.

Questions old theories and methodologies and seeks new ones. Myths, actualities, and implications of current vocational practices are analyzed.

2815 Bell, Howard M. *Matching Youth and Jobs: a Study of Occupational Adjustment*. Washington, ACE, 1940. 277p.

Valuable as an early examination of a now commonly accepted premise—the community's responsibility for the proper training, guidance, and placement of beginning workers.

Discusses the research-based development of a program and describes a 1938-39 project.

2816   Berdie, Ralph F., and Hood, Albert B. *Decisions for Tomorrow: Plans of High School Seniors for after Graduation.* Minneapolis, U of Minnesota P, 1965. 195p. biblio.

Using the same questionnaire, Berdie and Hood repeated a study made in 1950 to compare conditions and note changes. Readable as well as scholarly.

2817   Blum, Milton L., and Balinsky, Benjamin. *Counseling and Psychology: Vocational Psychology and Its Relation to Educational and Personal Counseling.* Englewood Cliffs, N.J., Prentice-Hall, 1951. 586p. biblio.

The contributions of psychology to vocational counseling with a discussion and evaluation of various kinds of interviewing, tests, counseling approaches, and the concept of interest.

2818   Borow, Henry, ed. *Man in a World at Work.* Boston, Houghton Mifflin, 1964. 606p. biblio.

Represents the best professional thinking on the nature of vocational guidance, the meaning of the human work experience, the relationship of the individual to the labor force, and research and practice in vocational guidance.

2819   Dolan, Eleanor F., and others. *Counseling Techniques for Mature Women.* Washington, Educational Foundation for the American Association of University Women, 1966. 448p.

The adult woman's history, psychology, education, and place in society are covered, in addition to counseling techniques and the economic aspects of counseling adult women.

2820   Forrester, Gertrude, ed. *Occupational Literature: an Annotated Bibliography,* rev. ed. New York, Wilson, 1964. 675p.

Approximately 6,000 selected references, including books and pamphlets, charts, and graphic aids, which are sources of information about occupations. For young people looking for help in making plans and for their elders who wish to select materials to assist them.

2821   Ginzberg, Eli, and others. *Occupational Choice: an Approach to a General Theory.* New York, Columbia UP, 1951. 271p. biblio.

Based on 91 interviews with students from the sixth grade

to graduate school, this provides information on the process involved in making a choice and on the vocational subjects to be taught.

2822   Hopke, William E., ed. *The Encyclopedia of Careers and Vocational Guidance.* Volume I, *Planning Your Career.* 752p. Volume II, *Careers and Occupations.* 784p. New York, Doubleday, 1967. biblio.

Articles on career planning, major industries or areas of work, and specific occupations, describing each fully. Fuller coverage than the *Occupational Outlook Handbook* but duplicates much material.

2823   Hoppock, Robert. *Occupational Information: Where to Get It and How to Use It in Counseling and Teaching,* 3rd ed. New York, McGraw-Hill, 1967. 598p. biblio.

A textbook for use in the education of counselors, teachers, psychologists, rehabilitation counselors, and all others in fields dealing with occupational counseling.

2824   Katz, Martin. *Decisions and Values: a Rationale for Secondary School Guidance.* New York, CEEB, 1963. 67p. biblio.

A succinct and useful discussion of the theory of occupational choice and guidance. Offers a rationale for the nature of guidance intervention.

2825   *Occupational Outlook Handbook: Employment Information on Occupations for Use in Guidance, 1966-67* (U.S. Bureau of Labor Statistics, Dept. of Labor Bulletin no. 1450). Washington, GPO, 1966. 858p.

A biennial publication giving career information on a large proportion of professional, technical, managerial, sales, clerical, and service occupations in this country, including new jobs developing as a direct result of automation. Detailed descriptions of occupations, requirements and training needed, trends, average earnings, and sources of further information such as associations and unions.

2826   Peters, Herman J., and Hanson, James C. *Vocational Guidand and Career Development.* New York, Macmillan, 1966. 466p. biblio.

A selection of readings stressing materials helpful to school and college counselors and student teachers who will be counselors. Also emphasizes vocational guidance for normal, average students. Contributions by authorities in field.

2827 Roe, Anne. *The Psychology of Occupations.* New York, Wiley, 1956. 340p.

In a search for a general pattern and for basic principles, this structures the broad field of the relations between occupation and the other aspects of life.

2828 Slocum, Walter L. *Occupational Careers: a Sociological Perspective.* Chicago, Aldine, 1966. 272p.

A summary of sociological theory and research in relation to the meaning of work, technology and change, aspirations, status, mobility, and the professions.

2829 Strong, Edward K., Jr. *Vocational Interests of Men and Women.* Stanford, Cal., Stanford UP, 1943. 746p.

An early work in this field that, accepting the thesis that interests play an important role in the direction of life, is based on research toward the use of interests as a means of solving practical problems.

2830 Super, Donald E., and Crites, John O. *Appraising Vocational Fitness by Means of Psychological Tests,* 2nd ed. New York, Harper, 1962. 688p. biblio.

Discussion of tests, selection criteria, and relevant research.

2831 ———, and others. *Career Development: Self-Concept Theory: Essays in Vocational Development.* New York, CEEB, 1963. 95p. biblio.

Five essays that attempt to develop, in detail, current thinking on some important aspects of vocational development. Focuses on various aspects of self-concept theory and its relationship to vocational development.

2832 ———. *The Dynamics of Vocational Adjustment.* New York, Harper, 1942. 286p. biblio.

A basic work on vocational guidance, dealing with the principles of vocational adjustment, the needs to be met, the social setting, the psychological and economic factors affecting vocational adjustment as well as counseling and methods of making vocational choices.

2833 ———. *The Psychology of Careers: an Introduction to Vocational Development.* New York, Harper, 1957. 362p. biblio.

Incorporates the results of significant research and theory development by psychologists, sociologists, and economists.

Deals with the nature of work, the cycle of working life, the dynamics of vocational development, and implications and applications.

2834 ———, and others. *The Vocational Maturity of Ninth-Grade Boys.* New York, TC, Columbia, 1960. 212p. biblio.

Contributes to the construction of a theory of vocational development by means of analyzing the vocational maturity of ninth-grade boys. The findings help clarify the nature of the educational problems associated with making prevocational and vocational decisions.

2835 Tiedeman, David, and others. *Career Development: Choice and Adjustment, Differentiation and Integration in Earlier Development.* New York, CEEB, 1963. 108p. biblio.

Deals with the experience of career development and introduces technical terminology in analyzing the situation. Offers a more formal explication of primary mechanisms and processes involved in fashioning a vocational identity. Includes summary of research.

History

2836 Bloomfield, Meyer. *The Vocational Guidance of Youth.* Boston, Houghton Mifflin, 1911. 123p. biblio.

A pioneering work in the field that discusses the need, then largely unmet, for guidance and counseling in order to avoid "vocational chaos" and some of its consequences.

2837 Brewer, John M. *A History of Vocational Guidance: Origins and Early Development.* New York, Harper, 1942. 344p. biblio.

Chiefly concerned with early developments but includes recent events when they seem to indicate important trends or raise vital issues.

2838 ———. *The Vocational Guidance Movement: Its Problems and Possibilities.* New York, Macmillan, 1918. 333p. biblio.

A comprehensive and thoughtful consideration of the problems inherent in the then new field of vocational guidance. Discusses vocational guidance through educational guidance, vocational counseling, the young worker, and problems of employment.

2839 Kitson, Harry D. *The Psychology of Vocational Adjustment.* Philadelphia, Lippincott, 1925. 273p. biblio.

An early and important work dealing with the psychological problems involved in choosing a vocation and becoming proficient therein. Explores scientific methods and solutions.

VOCATIONAL REHABILITATION
see also MENTALLY RETARDED ADULTS

2840 Bridges, Clark D. *Job Placement of the Physically Handicapped.* New York, McGraw-Hill, 1946. 329p. biblio.

Primarily addressed to those responsible for the effective employment of handicapped workers. Serves as a practical guide in the rehabilitation and employment of the disabled, a vast source of valuable manpower. Some of the factual information is now outdated, but the principles are still valid and useful.

2841 Conley, Ronald W. *The Economics of Vocational Rehabilitation.* Baltimore, Johns Hopkins UP, 1965. 177p.

An examination of the economic benefits to society of the rehabilitation of the physically and mentally disabled, with an evaluation of disability and its cost as well as of current rehabilitative programs in the United States. A valuable book with a refreshing approach.

2842 Lofquist, Lloyd H. *Vocational Counseling with the Physically Handicapped.* New York, Appleton, 1957. 384p.

Deals systematically with the subject. A valuable reference for counselors and psychologists.

2843 Neuschutz, Louise M. *Vocational Rehabilitation for the Physically Handicapped.* Springfield, Ill., Thomas, 1959. 136p. biblio.

Discusses the problems of occupations for the handicapped, presenting information for employers and others concerned with vocational placement of the disabled.

2844 *Sheltered Workshops: a Handbook,* 2nd ed. Washington, National Association of Sheltered Workshops and Homebound Programs, 1966. 83p.

Provides objective standards for the development and continuance of services. Covers such practical topics as planning, organization, physical plant, establishing a market, determining products, job placement, and the like.

History

2845 Obermann, Carl E. *A History of Vocational Rehabilitation in America.* Minneapolis, Denison, 1965. 389p.
Wonderfully comprehensive from past to present.

VOLUNTEERS IN EDUCATION

2846 Ball, Edith L. *Developing Volunteers for Service in Recreation Programs.* Washington, National Recreation and Park Association, 1958. 58p.
Methods of recruiting, training, and using volunteers.

2847 Janowitz, Gayle. *Helping Hands: Volunteer Work in Education.* Chicago, U of Chicago P, 1966. 125p. biblio.
A book for both volunteers and administrators, this is full of useful information on organization, supervision, and methods used in after school centers for academically retarded children.

2848 Sleisenger, Lenore. *Guidebook for the Volunteer Reading Teacher.* New York, TC, Columbia, 1965. 51p.
Although intended for the nonprofessional, there are many suggestions experienced teachers will find helpful. Focused on the needs of the disadvantaged child and the necessity of relating reading experiences to his life experiences. Includes excellent, selected list of books of high interest, low reading level.

WRITING AND COMPOSITION

2849 Applegate, Mauree. *Helping Children Write: a Thinking Together about Children's Creative Writing.* Evanston, Ill., Row Peterson, 1954. 173p. biblio.
Discusses the many forms of children's written and creative expression—stories, poems, letters, plays, and memoranda. Contains practical suggestions and novel ideas for releasing children to express themselves, their thoughts, and feelings.

2850 Braddock, Richard, and others. *Research in Written Composition.* Champaign, Ill., NCTE, 1963. 142p.
A summary of a two-year study of research. Reviews the current state of knowledge, classic investigations, and future needs.

2851   Burrows, Alvina T., and others. *Children's Writing: Research in Composition and Related Skills.* Champaign, Ill., NCTE, 1961. 73p.

A useful effort to bring the fruits of research to the teacher wanting to improve the teaching of composition, grammar, spelling, and handwriting.

2852   _____, and others. *They All Want to Write,* 3rd ed. New York, Holt, 1964. 281p. biblio.

The real needs of children are discussed in relation to writing as communication. Rich with anecdotal material showing the development of children's practical and personal writing abilities.

2853   Corbin, Richard. *The Teaching of Writing in Our Schools.* New York, Macmillan, 1966. 118p.

Written for parents and the beginning student, this discusses the nature of the act of writing, teaching methods, and suggestions for helping children at home.

2854   Hook, Julius N. *Guide to Good Writing: Grammar, Style, Usage.* New York, Ronald, 1962. 575p.

Approximately 1,650 entries, arranged alphabetically, cover every aspect of the mechanics and art of good writing.

2855   Jewett, Arno, and Bish, Charles E., eds. *Improving English Composition.* Washington, NEA, 1965. 116p. biblio.

A collection of narrative reports of projects developed in nine experimental centers across the country. Some subjects covered are diversified programs for meeting pupil differences, using linguistics, and working with theme readers. A practical and helpful book.

2856   Pease, Don. *Creative Writing in the Elementary School: Psychology and Technique.* New York, Exposition, 1964. 180p.

"The teacher's role in developing creativity is characterized by helping children to fully utilize what they already are . . .and by helping rather than telling or letting." Many suggestions, examples, and examples of growth.

2857   Strunk, William, Jr. *The Elements of Style.* New York, Macmillan, 1959. 71p. biblio.

A monument to purity and simplicity, this small book has had its devoted advocates for many years. Herewith republished with revisions by E. B. White.

Index

Numbers refer to entries, not to pages.

DATE DUE

HETERICK MEMORIAL LIBRARY
016.37 M34n   onuu
Marks, Barbara S./The New York Universit

3 5111 00102 9978